Object-Oriented Jav

CU00797541

Third Edition

Learn everything you need to know about object-oriented
JavaScript (OOJS)

Ved Antani
Stoyan Stefanov

BIRMINGHAM - MUMBAI

Object-Oriented JavaScript

Third Edition

First published: July 2008

Second edition: July 2013

Third edition: January 2017

Production reference: 1050117

Published by Packt Publishing Ltd.
Livery Place
35 Livery Street
Birmingham
B3 2PB, UK.
ISBN 978-1-78588-056-8

www.packtpub.com

Credits

Authors

Ved Antani

Stoyan Stefanov

Reviewer

Mohamed Sanaulla

Commissioning Editor

Wilson Dsouza

Acquisition Editor

Denim Pinto

Content Development Editor

Arun Nadar

Technical Editor

Abhishek Sharma

Copy Editor

Zainab Bootwala

Project Coordinator

Ritika Manoj

Proofreader

Safis Editing

Indexer

Rekha Nair

Graphics

Jason Monteiro

Production Coordinator

Arvindkumar Gupta

About the Authors

Ved Antani has been building scalable server and mobile platforms using JavaScript, Go, and Java since 2005. He is an associate vice president at Myntra and has previously worked at Electronic Arts and Oracle. He is an avid reader and author on several subjects. He has studied computer science and currently lives in Bangalore, India. Ved is passionate about classical music and loves to spend time with his son.

Writing this book required a significant investment of my time, and I would like to thank my parents and family for their support and encouragement during those long days and weekends when I was practically invisible.

Stoyan Stefanov is a Facebook engineer, author, and speaker. He talks regularly about web development topics at conferences, and his blog, `www.phpied.com`. He also runs a number of other sites, including `JSPatterns.com` - a site dedicated to exploring JavaScript patterns. Previously at Yahoo!, Stoyan was the architect of YSlow 2.0 and creator of the image optimization tool, Smush.it.

A "citizen of the world", Stoyan was born and raised in Bulgaria, but is also a Canadian citizen, currently residing in Los Angeles, California. In his offline moments, he enjoys playing the guitar, taking flying lessons, and spending time at the Santa Monica beaches with his family.

I'd like to dedicate this book to my wife, Eva, and my daughters, Zlatina and Nathalie. Thank you for your patience, support, and encouragement.

About the Reviewer

Mohamed Sanaulla is a software developer with more than 7 years of experience in developing enterprise applications and Java-based back-end solutions for e-commerce applications.

His interests include Enterprise software development, refactoring and redesigning applications, designing and implementing RESTful web services, troubleshooting Java applications for performance issues, and TDD.

He has strong expertise in Java-based application development, ADF (JSF-based JavaEE web framework), SQL, PL/SQL, JUnit, designing RESTful services, Spring, Struts, Elasticsearch, and MongoDB. He is also a Sun Certified Java Programmer for the Java 6 platform. He is a moderator for `JavaRanch.com`. He likes to share findings on his blog (`http://sanaulla.info`).

www.PacktPub.com

For support files and downloads related to your book, please visit www.PacktPub.com.

Did you know that Packt offers eBook versions of every book published, with PDF and ePub files available? You can upgrade to the eBook version at www.PacktPub.com and as a print book customer, you are entitled to a discount on the eBook copy. Get in touch with us at service@packtpub.com for more details.

At www.PacktPub.com, you can also read a collection of free technical articles, sign up for a range of free newsletters and receive exclusive discounts and offers on Packt books and eBooks.

https://www.packtpub.com/mapt

Get the most in-demand software skills with Mapt. Mapt gives you full access to all Packt books and video courses, as well as industry-leading tools to help you plan your personal development and advance your career.

Why subscribe?

- Fully searchable across every book published by Packt
- Copy and paste, print, and bookmark content
- On demand and accessible via a web browser

Customer Feedback

Thank you for purchasing this Packt book. We take our commitment to improving our content and products to meet your needs seriously--that's why your feedback is so valuable. Whatever your feelings about your purchase, please consider leaving a review on this book's Amazon page. Not only will this help us, more importantly it will also help others in the community to make an informed decision about the resources that they invest in to learn. You can also review for us on a regular basis by joining our reviewers' club. **If you're interested in joining, or would like to learn more about the benefits we offer, please contact us**: customerreviews@packtpub.com.

Table of Contents

[iv]

Preface

JavaScript has emerged as one of the most robust and versatile programming language around. Modern JavaScript embraces a vast array of time-tested and cutting edge features. Several of these features are slowly giving shape to the next generation of web and server platforms. ES6 introduces very important language constructs, such as promises, classes, arrow functions, and several, much anticipated features. This book takes a detailed look at the language constructs and their practical uses. This book doesn't assume any prior knowledge of JavaScript and works from the ground up to give you a thorough understanding of the language. People who know the language will still find it useful and informative. For people who already know JavaScript and are familiar with ES5 syntax, this book will be a very useful primer for ES6 features.

What this book covers

Chapter 1, *Object-Oriented JavaScript*, talks briefly about the history, present, and future of JavaScript, and then moves on to explore the basics of object-oriented programming (OOP) in general. You will then learn how to set up your training environment (Firebug) in order to dive into the language on your own, using the book examples as a base.

Chapter 2, *Primitive Data Types, Arrays, Loops, and Conditions*, discusses the language basics--variables, data types, primitive data types, arrays, loops, and conditionals.

Chapter 3, *Functions*, covers functions that JavaScript uses, and here you will learn to master them all. You will also learn about the scope of variables and JavaScript's built-in functions. An interesting, but often misunderstood, feature of the language--closures--is demystified at the end of the chapter.

Chapter 4, *Objects*, talks about objects, how to work with properties and methods, and the various ways to create your objects. This chapter also talks about built-in objects such as Array, Function, Boolean, Number, and String.

Chapter 5, *ES6 Iterators and Generators*, introduces the most anticipated features of ES6, Iterators and Generators. With this knowledge, you will proceed to take a detailed look at the enhanced collections constructs.

Chapter 6, *Prototype,* is dedicated to the all-important concept of prototypes in JavaScript. It also explains how the prototype chain works, hasOwnProperty(), and some gotchas of prototypes.

Chapter 7, *Inheritance,* discusses how inheritance works. This chapter also talks about a method to create subclasses like other classic languages.

Chapter 8, *Classes and Modules,* shows that ES6 introduces important syntactical features that makes it easier to write classical object-oriented programming constructs. ES6 class syntax wraps the slightly complex syntax of ES5. ES6 also has full language support for modules. This chapter goes into the details of the classes and module constructs introduced in ES6.

Chapter 9, *Promises and Proxies,* explains that JavaScript has always been a language with strong support for asynchronous programming. Up until ES5, writing asynchronous programs meant you needed to rely on callbacks--sometimes resulting in callback hell. ES6 promises are a much-awaited feature introduced in the language. Promises provide a much cleaner way to write asynchronous programs in ES6. Proxies are used to define custom behavior to some of the fundamental operations. This chapter looks at practical uses of both promises and proxies in ES6.

Chapter 10, *The Browser Environment,* is dedicated to browsers. This chapter also covers BOM (Browser Object Model), DOM (W3C's Document Object Model), browser events, and AJAX.

Chapter 11, *Coding and Design Patterns,* dives into various unique JavaScript coding patterns, as well as several language-independent design patterns, translated to JavaScript from the Book of Four, the most influential work of software design patterns. This chapter also discusses JSON.

Chapter 12, *Testing and Debugging,* talks about how Modern JavaScript is equipped with tools that support Test Driven Development and Behavior Driven Development. Jasmine is one of the most popular tools available at the moment. This chapter discusses TDD and BDD using Jasmine as the framework.

Chapter 13, *Reactive Programming and React,* explains that with the advent of ES6, several radical ideas are taking shape. Reactive programming takes a very different approach to how we manage change of states using data flows. React, however, is a framework focusing on the View part of MVC. This chapter discusses these two ideas.

Appendix A, *Reserved Words,* lists the reserved words in JavaScript.

Appendix B, *Built-in Functions*, is a reference of built-in JavaScript functions together with sample uses.

Appendix C, *Built-in Objects*, is a reference that provides details and examples of the use of every method and property of every built-in object in JavaScript.

Appendix D, *Regular Expressions*, is a regular expressions pattern reference.

Appendix E, *Answers to Exercise Questions*, has solutions for all the exercises mentioned at the end of the chapters.

What you need for this book

You need a modern browser--Google Chrome or Firefox are recommended, and an optional Node.js setup. Most of the code in this book can be executed in `http://babeljs.io/repl/` or `http://jsbin.com/`. To edit JavaScript, you can use any text editor of your choice.

Who this book is for

This book is for anyone who is starting to learn JavaScript, or who knows JavaScript but isn't very good at the object-oriented part of it. This book can be a useful primer for ES6 if you are already familiar with the ES5 features of the language.

Conventions

In this book, you will find a number of text styles that distinguish between different kinds of information. Here are some examples of these styles and an explanation of their meaning.

Code words in text, database table names, folder names, filenames, file extensions, pathnames, dummy URLs, user input, and Twitter handles are shown as follows: "The `Triangle` constructor takes three point objects and assigns them to `this.points` (its own collection of points)."

A block of code is set as follows:

```
function sum(a, b) {
var c = a + b;
return c;
}
```

Any command-line input or output is written as follows:

```
mkdir babel_test
cd babel_test && npm init
npm install --save-dev babel-cli
```

New terms and **important words** are shown in bold. Words that you see on the screen, for example, in menus or dialog boxes, appear in the text like this: "In order to bring up the console in Chrome or Safari, right-click anywhere on a page and select **Inspect Element** . The additional window that shows up is the Web Inspector feature. Select the **Console** tab, and you're ready to go".

 Warnings or important notes appear in a box like this.

 Tips and tricks appear like this.

Reader feedback

Feedback from our readers is always welcome. Let us know what you think about this book-what you liked or disliked. Reader feedback is important for us as it helps us develop titles that you will really get the most out of.

To send us general feedback, simply e-mail feedback@packtpub.com, and mention the book's title in the subject of your message.

If there is a topic that you have expertise in and you are interested in either writing or contributing to a book, see our author guide at www.packtpub.com/authors.

Customer support

Now that you are the proud owner of a Packt book, we have a number of things to help you to get the most from your purchase.

Errata

Although we have taken every care to ensure the accuracy of our content, mistakes do happen. If you find a mistake in one of our books-maybe a mistake in the text or the code-we would be grateful if you could report this to us. By doing so, you can save other readers from frustration and help us improve subsequent versions of this book. If you find any errata, please report them by visiting http://www.packtpub.com/submit-errata, selecting your book, clicking on the **Errata Submission Form** link, and entering the details of your errata. Once your errata are verified, your submission will be accepted and the errata will be uploaded to our website or added to any list of existing errata under the Errata section of that title.

To view the previously submitted errata, go to https://www.packtpub.com/books/content/support and enter the name of the book in the search field. The required information will appear under the **Errata** section.

Piracy

Piracy of copyrighted material on the Internet is an ongoing problem across all media. At Packt, we take the protection of our copyright and licenses very seriously. If you come across any illegal copies of our works in any form on the Internet, please provide us with the location address or website name immediately so that we can pursue a remedy.

Please contact us at copyright@packtpub.com with a link to the suspected pirated material.

We appreciate your help in protecting our authors and our ability to bring you valuable content.

Questions

If you have a problem with any aspect of this book, you can contact us at questions@packtpub.com, and we will do our best to address the problem.

1
Object-Oriented JavaScript

Ever since the early days of the web, there has been a need for more dynamic and responsive interfaces. While it's OK to read static HTML pages of text, and even better when they are beautifully presented with the help of CSS, it's much more fun to engage with applications in our browsers, such as e-mail, calendars, banking, shopping, drawing, playing games, and text editing. All that is possible thanks to JavaScript, the programming language of the web. JavaScript started with simple one-liners embedded in HTML, but is now used in much more sophisticated ways. Developers leverage the object-oriented nature of the language to build scalable code architectures made up of reusable pieces.

If you look at the past and present buzzwords in web development, DHTML, Ajax, Web 2.0, HTML5, they all essentially mean HTML, CSS, and JavaScript–HTML for **content**, CSS for **presentation**, and JavaScript for **behavior**. In other words, JavaScript is the glue that makes everything work together so that we can build rich web applications.

However, that's not all; JavaScript can be used for more than just the web.

JavaScript programs run inside a host environment. The web browser is the most common environment, but it's not the only one. Using JavaScript, you can create all kinds of widgets, application extensions, and other pieces of software, as you'll see in a bit. Taking the time to learn JavaScript is a smart investment; you learn one language and can then write all kinds of different applications running on multiple platforms, including mobile and server-side applications. These days, it's safe to say that JavaScript is everywhere.

This book starts from zero, and does not assume any prior programming knowledge other than some basic understanding of HTML. Although there is one chapter dedicated to the web browser environment, the rest of the book is about JavaScript in general, so it's applicable to all environments.

Let's start with the following:

- A brief introduction to the story behind JavaScript
- The basic concepts you'll encounter in discussions on object-oriented programming

A bit of history

Initially, the web was not much more than just a number of scientific publications in the form of static HTML documents connected together with hyperlinks. Believe it or not, there was a time when there was no way to put an image in a page. However, that soon changed. As the web grew in popularity and size, the webmasters who were creating HTML pages felt they needed something more. They wanted to create richer user interactions, mainly driven by the desire to save server round trips for simple tasks such as form validation. Two options came up—Java applets and LiveScript, a language conceived by Brendan Eich at *Netscape* in 1995 and later included in the Netscape 2.0 browser under the name of JavaScript.

The applets didn't quite catch on, but JavaScript did. The ability to use short code snippets embedded in HTML documents and alter otherwise static elements of a web page was embraced by the webmaster community. Soon, the competing browser vendor, Microsoft, shipped **Internet Explorer** (**IE**) 3.0 with JScript, which was a reverse engineered version of JavaScript plus some IE-specific features. Eventually, there was an effort to standardize the various implementations of the language, and this is how ECMAScript was born. **European Computer Manufacturers Association** (**ECMA**) created the standard called ECMA-262, which describes the core parts of the JavaScript programming language without browser and web page-specific features.

You can think of JavaScript as a term that encompasses the following three pieces:

- **ECMAScript**: The core language—variables, functions, loops, and so on. This part is independent of the browser and this language can be used in many other environments.
- **Document Object Model** (**DOM**): This provides ways to work with HTML and XML documents. Initially, JavaScript provided limited access to what's scriptable on the page, mainly forms, links, and images. Later, it was expanded to make all elements scriptable. This led to the creation of the DOM standard by the **World Wide Web Consortium** (**W3C**) as a language-independent (no longer tied to JavaScript) way to manipulate structured documents.

- **Browser Object Model** (**BOM**): This is a set of objects related to the browser environment and was never part of any standard until HTML5 started standardizing some of the common objects that exist across browsers.

While there is one chapter in this book dedicated to the browser, the DOM, and the BOM, most of this book describes the core language and teaches you skills you can use in any environment where JavaScript programs run.

Browser wars and renaissance

For better or for worse, JavaScript's instant popularity happened during the period of the browser wars I (approximately 1996 to 2001). Those were the times during the initial Internet boom when the two major browser vendors, Netscape and Microsoft, were competing for market share. Both were constantly adding more bells and whistles to their browsers and their versions of JavaScript, DOM, and BOM, which naturally led to many inconsistencies. While adding more features, the browser vendors were falling behind on providing proper development and debugging tools and adequate documentation. Often, development was a pain; you would write a script while testing in one browser, and once you're done with development, you test in the other browser, only to find that your script simply fails for no apparent reason, and the best you can get is a cryptic error message, such as operation aborted.

Inconsistent implementations, missing documentation, and no appropriate tools painted JavaScript in such a light that many programmers simply refused to bother with it.

On the other hand, developers who did try to experiment with JavaScript got a little carried away, adding too many special effects to their pages without much regard of how usable the end results were. Developers were eager to make use of every new possibility the browsers provided, and ended up enhancing their web pages with things such as animations in the status bar, flashing colors, blinking texts, objects stalking your mouse cursor, and many other innovations that actually hurt the user experience. These various ways to abuse JavaScript are now mostly gone, but they were one of the reasons why the language had something of a bad reputation. Many serious programmers dismissed JavaScript as nothing but a toy for designers to play around with, and dismissed it as a language unsuitable for serious applications. The JavaScript backlash caused some web projects to completely ban any client-side programming and trust only their predictable and tightly controlled server. And really, why would you double the time to deliver a finished product and then spend additional time debugging problems with the different browsers?

Everything changed in the years following the end of the browser wars I. A number of events reshaped the web development landscape in a positive way. Some of them are given as follows:

- Microsoft won the war with the introduction of IE6, the best browser at the time, and for many years they stopped developing Internet Explorer. This allowed time for other browsers to catch up and even surpass IE's capabilities.
- The movement for web standards was embraced by developers and browser vendors alike. Naturally, developers didn't like having to code everything two (or more) times to account for browsers' differences; therefore, they liked the idea of having agreed-upon standards that everyone would follow.
- Developers and technologies matured and more people started caring about things such as usability, progressive enhancement techniques, and accessibility. Tools such as Firebug made developers much more productive and the development less of a pain.

In this healthier environment, developers started finding out new and better ways to use the instruments that were already available. After the public release of applications such as Gmail and Google Maps, which were rich on client-side programming, it became clear that JavaScript is a mature, unique in certain ways, and powerful prototypal object-oriented language. The best example of its rediscovery was the wide adoption of the functionality provided by the `XMLHttpRequest` object, which was once an IE-only innovation, but was then implemented by most other browsers. `XMLHttpRequest` object allows JavaScript to make HTTP requests and get fresh content from the server in order to update some parts of a page without a full page reload. Due to the wide use of the `XMLHttpRequest` object, a new breed of desktop-like web applications, dubbed Ajax applications, was born.

The present

An interesting thing about JavaScript is that it always runs inside a host environment. The web browser is just one of the available hosts. JavaScript can also run on the server, on the desktop, and on mobile devices. Today, you can use JavaScript to do all of the following:

- Create rich and powerful web applications (the kind of applications that run inside the web browser). Additions to HTML5, such as application cache, client-side storage, and databases, make browser programming more and more powerful for both online and offline applications. Powerful additions to Chrome WebKit also include support for service workers and browser push notifications.
- Write server-side code using `Node.js`, as well as code that can run using Rhino (a JavaScript engine written in Java).

- Make mobile applications; you can create apps for iPhone, Android, and other phones and tablets entirely in JavaScript using **PhoneGap** or **Titanium**. Additionally, apps for Firefox OS for mobile phones are entirely in JavaScript, HTML, and CSS. React Native from Facebook is an exciting new way to develop native iOS, Android, and Windows (experimental) applications using JavaScript.
- Create rich media applications, such as Flash or Flex, using ActionScript, which is based on ECMAScript.
- Write command-line tools and scripts that automate administrative tasks on your desktop using **Windows Scripting Host** (**WSH**) or WebKit's **JavaScriptCore**, which is available on all Macs.
- Write extensions and plugins for a plethora of desktop applications, such as Dreamweaver, Photoshop, and most other browsers.
- Create cross-operating system desktop applications using Mozilla's **XULRunner** and **Electron**. Electron is used to build some of the most popular apps on the desktop, such as Slack, Atom, and Visual Studio Code.
- **Emscripten**, on the other hand, allows code written in C/C++ to be compiled into an `asm.js` format, which can then be run inside a browser.
- Testing frameworks like **PhantomJS** are programmed using JavaScript.
- This is by no means an exhaustive list. JavaScript started inside web pages, but today it's safe to say it is practically everywhere. In addition, browser vendors now use speed as a competitive advantage and are racing to create the fastest JavaScript engines, which is great for both users and developers, and opens doors for even more powerful uses of JavaScript in new areas such as image, audio and video processing, and games development.

The future

We can only speculate what the future will be, but it's quite certain that it will include JavaScript. For quite some time, JavaScript may have been underestimated and underused (or maybe overused in the wrong ways), but every day, we witness new applications of the language in much more interesting and creative ways. It all started with simple one-liners, often embedded in HTML tag attributes, such as `onclick`. Nowadays, developers ship sophisticated, well-designed and architected, and extensible applications and libraries, often supporting multiple platforms with a single codebase. JavaScript is indeed taken seriously, and developers are starting to rediscover and enjoy its unique features more and more.

Once listed in the nice-to-have sections of job postings, today, knowledge of JavaScript is often a deciding factor when it comes to hiring web developers. Common job interview questions you can hear today include–Is JavaScript an object-oriented language? Good. Now, how do you implement inheritance in JavaScript? After reading this book, you'll be prepared to ace your JavaScript job interview and even impress your interviewers with some bits that, maybe, they didn't know.

ECMAScript 5

The last most important milestone in ECMAScript revisions was **ECMAScript 5 (ES5)**, officially accepted in December 2009. ECMAScript 5 standard is implemented and supported on all major browsers and server-side technologies.

ES5 was a major revision because apart from several important syntactic changes and additions to the standard libraries, ES5 also introduced several new constructs in the language.

For instance, ES5 introduced some new objects and properties, and also the so-called **strict** mode. Strict mode is a subset of the language that excludes deprecated features. The strict mode is opt-in and not required, meaning that if you want your code to run in the strict mode, you will declare your intention using (once per function, or once for the whole program) the following string:

```
"use strict";
```

This is just a JavaScript string, and it's ok to have strings floating around unassigned to any variable. As a result, older browsers that don't speak ES5 will simply ignore it, so this strict mode is backwards compatible and won't break older browsers.

For backwards compatibility, all the examples in this book work in ES3, but at the same time, all the code in the book is written so that it will run without warnings in ES5's strict mode. Additionally, any ES5-specific parts will be clearly marked. Appendix C, *Built-in Objects*, lists the new additions to ES5 in detail.

Strict mode in ES6

While strict mode is optional in ES5, all ES6 modules and classes are strict by default. As you will see soon, most of the code we write in ES6 resides in a module; hence, strict mode is enforced by default. However, it is important to understand that all other constructs do not have implicit strict mode enforced. There were efforts to make newer constructs, such as arrow and generator functions, to also enforce strict mode, but it was later decided that doing so would result in very fragmented language rules and code.

ECMAScript 6

ECMAScript 6 revision took a long time to finish and was finally accepted on June 17, 2015. ES6 features are slowly becoming part of major browsers and server technologies. It is possible to use transpilers to compile ES6 to ES5 and use the code on environments that do not yet support ES6 completely (we will discuss transpilers in detail later).

ES6 substantially upgrades JavaScript as a language and brings in very exciting syntactical changes and language constructs. Broadly, there are two kinds of fundamental changes in this revision of ECMAScript, which are as follows:

- Improved syntax for existing features and editions to the standard library; for example, classes and promises
- New language features; for example, generators

ES6 allows you to think differently about your code. New syntax changes can let you write code that is cleaner, easier to maintain, and does not require special tricks. The language itself now supports several constructs that required third-party modules earlier. Language changes introduced in ES6 need a serious rethink in the way we have been coding in JavaScript.

A note on the nomenclature–ECMAScript 6, ES6, and ECMAScript 2015 are the same, but used interchangeably.

Browser support for ES6

The majority of the browsers and server frameworks are on their way towards implementing ES6 features. You can check out the what is supported and what is not by clicking `http://kangax.github.io/compat-table/es6/`.

Though ES6 is not fully supported on all browsers and server frameworks, we can start using almost all features of ES6 with the help of **transpilers**. Transpilers are source-to-source compilers. ES6 transpilers allow you to write code in ES6 syntax and compile/transform them into equivalent ES5 syntax, which can then be run on browsers that do not support the entire range of ES6 features.

The defacto ES6 transpiler at the moment is Babel. In this book, we will use Babel and write and test our examples.

Babel

Babel supports almost all ES6 features out of the box or with custom plugins. Babel can be used from a wide range of build systems, frameworks, and languages to template engines, and has a good command line and **read-eval-print loop** (**REPL**) built in.

To get a good idea about how Babel transpiles ES6 code to its ES5 equivalent form, head over to Babel REPL (`http://babeljs.io/repl/`).

Babel REPL allows you to quickly test small snippets of ES6. When you open Babel REPL in the browser, you will see some ES6 code defaulted there. On the left pane, remove the code and type in the following text:

```
var name = "John", mood = "happy";
console.log(`Hey ${name}, are you feeling ${mood} today?`)
```

When you type this and tab out of the left pane, you will see REPL transpiling this ES6 code into something like the following code:

```
"use strict";
var name = "John",
  mood = "happy";
console.log("Hey " + name + ",
  are you feeling " + mood + " today?");
```

This is the ES5 equivalent of the code we wrote earlier in the left pane. You can see that the resulting code in the right pane is a familiar ES5. As we said, Babel REPL is a good place to try and experiment with various ES6 constructs. However, we need babel to automatically transpile your ES6 code into ES5, and for that, you can include Babel into your existing build systems or frameworks.

Let's begin by installing Babel as a command-line tool. For this, we will assume that you are familiar with node and **Node Package Manager** (**npm**). Installing Babel using npm is easy. Let's first create a directory where we will have Babel installed as a module and rest of the source code. On my Mac, the following commands will create a directory called babel_test, initialize the project using npm init, and install Babel command line using npm:

```
mkdir babel_test
cd babel_test && npm init
npm install --save-dev babel-cli
```

If you are familiar with npm, you may get tempted to install Babel globally. However, installing Babel as a global module is not generally a good idea. Once you have installed Babel in your project, your package.json file will look something like the following block of code:

```
{
  "name": "babel_test",
  "version": "1.0.0",
  "description": "",
  "main": "index.js",
  "scripts": {
    "test": "echo "Error: no test specified" && exit 1"
  },
  "author": "",
  "license": "ISC",
  "devDependencies": {
    "babel-cli": "^6.10.1"
  }
}
```

You can see a development dependency created for Babel for version > 6.10.1. You can use Babel to transpile your code by either invoking it from the command line or as part of the build step. For any non-trivial work, you will need the later approach. To invoke Babel as part of the project build step, you can add a `build` step invoking Babel inside your script tag to your `package.json` file, for example:

```
"scripts": {
  "build": "babel src -d lib"
},
```

When you do npm build, Babel will be invoked on your `src` directory and the transpiled code will be placed inside `lib` directory. Alternatively, you can run Babel manually also by writing the following command:

```
$ ./node_modules/.bin/babel src -d lib
```

We will talk about various Babel options and plugins later in the book. This section will equip you to start exploring ES6.

Object-oriented programming

Before diving into JavaScript, let's take a moment to review what people mean when they say object-oriented, and what the main features of this programming style are. Here's a list of concepts that are most often used when talking about **object-oriented programming** (**OOP**):

- Object, method, and property
- Class
- Encapsulation
- Aggregation
- Reusability/inheritance
- Polymorphism

Let's take a closer look into each one of these concepts. If you're new to the object-oriented programming lingo, these concepts might sound too theoretical, and you might have trouble grasping or remembering them from one reading. Don't worry, it does take a few tries, and the subject can be a little dry at a conceptual level. However, we'll look at plenty of code examples further on in the book, and you'll see that things are much simpler in practice.

Objects

As the name object-oriented suggests, objects are important. An object is a representation of a thing (someone or something), and this representation is expressed with the help of a programming language. The thing can be anything, a real-life object, or a more convoluted concept. Taking a common object, a cat, for example, you can see that it has certain characteristics–color, name, weight, and so on and can perform some actions–meow, sleep, hide, escape, and so on. The characteristics of the object are called properties in OOP-speak, and the actions are called methods.

The analogy with the spoken language are as follows:

- Objects are most often named using nouns, such as book, person, and so on
- Methods are verbs, for example, read, run, and so on
- Values of the properties are adjectives

Take the sentence "The black cat sleeps on the mat" as an example. "The cat" (a noun) is the object, "black" (adjective) is the value of the color property, and "sleep" (a verb) is an action or a method in OOP. For the sake of the analogy, we can go a step further and say that "on the mat" specifies something about the action "sleep", so it's acting as a parameter passed to the `sleep` method.

Classes

In real life, similar objects can be grouped based on some criteria. A hummingbird and an eagle are both birds, so they can be classified as belonging to some made-up `Birds` class. In OOP, a class is a blueprint or a recipe for an object. Another name for object is instance, so we can say that the eagle is one concrete instance of the general `Birds` class. You can create different objects using the same class because a class is just a template, while the objects are concrete instances based on the template.

There's a difference between JavaScript and the classic OO languages such as C++ and Java. You should be aware right from the start that in JavaScript, there are no classes; everything is based on objects. JavaScript has the notion of prototypes, which are also objects (we'll discuss them later in detail). In a classic OO language, you'd say something like–create a new object for me called `Bob`, which is of class `Person`. In a prototypal OO language, you'd say–I'm going to take this object called Bob's dad that I have lying around (on the couch in front of the TV?) and reuse it as a prototype for a new object that I'll call `Bob`.

Encapsulation

Encapsulation is another OOP related concept, which illustrates the fact that an object contains (encapsulates) the following:

- Data (stored in properties)
- The means to do something with the data (using methods)

One other term that goes together with encapsulation is information hiding. This is a rather broad term and can mean different things, but let's see what people usually mean when they use it in the context of OOP.

Imagine an object, say, an MP3 player. You, as the user of the object, are given some interface to work with, such as buttons, display, and so on. You use the interface in order to get the object to do something useful for you, like play a song. How exactly the device is working on the inside, you don't know, and, most often, don't care. In other words, the implementation of the interface is hidden from you. The same thing happens in OOP when your code uses an object by calling its methods. It doesn't matter if you coded the object yourself or it came from some third-party library; your code doesn't need to know how the methods work internally. In compiled languages, you can't actually read the code that makes an object work. In JavaScript, because it's an interpreted language, you can see the source code, but the concept is still the same–you work with the object's interface without worrying about its implementation.

Another aspect of information hiding is the visibility of methods and properties. In some languages, objects can have `public`, `private`, and `protected` methods and properties. This categorization defines the level of access the users of the object have. For example, only the methods of the same object have access to the `private` methods, while anyone has access to the `public` ones. In JavaScript, all methods and properties are `public`, but we'll see that there are ways to protect the data inside an object and achieve privacy.

Aggregation

Combining several objects into a new one is known as aggregation or composition. It's a powerful way to separate a problem into smaller and more manageable parts (divide and conquer). When a problem scope is so complex that it's impossible to think about it at a detailed level in its entirety, you can separate the problem into several smaller areas, and possibly then separate each of these into even smaller chunks. This allows you to think about the problem on several levels of abstraction.

Take, for example, a personal computer. It's a complex object. You cannot think about all the things that need to happen when you start your computer. But, you can abstract the problem saying that you need to initialize all the separate objects that your `Computer` object consists of the `Monitor` object, the `Mouse` object, the `Keyboard` object, and so on. Then, you can dive deeper into each of the subobjects. This way, you're composing complex objects by assembling reusable parts.

To use another analogy, a `Book` object can contain (aggregate) one or more `Author` objects, a `Publisher` object, several `Chapter` objects, a `TOC` (table of contents), and so on.

Inheritance

Inheritance is an elegant way to reuse existing code. For example, you can have a generic object, `Person`, which has properties such as `name` and `date_of_birth`, and which also implements the `walk`, `talk`, `sleep`, and `eat` functionality. Then, you figure out that you need another object called `Programmer`. You can reimplement all the methods and properties that a `Person` object has, but it will be smarter to just say that the `Programmer` object inherits a `Person` object, and save yourself some work. The `Programmer` object only needs to implement more specific functionality, such as the `writeCode` method, while reusing all of the `Person` object's functionality.

In classical OOP, classes inherit from other classes, but in JavaScript, as there are no classes, objects inherit from other objects.

When an object inherits from another object, it usually adds new methods to the inherited ones, thus extending the old object. Often, the following phrases can be used interchangeably–B inherits from A and B extends A. Also, the object that inherits can pick one or more methods and redefine them, customizing them for its own needs. This way, the interface stays the same and the method name is the same, but when called on the new object, the method behaves differently. This way of redefining how an inherited method works is known as **overriding**.

Polymorphism

In the preceding example, a `Programmer` object inherited all of the methods of the parent `Person` object. This means that both objects provide a `talk` method, among others. Now imagine that somewhere in your code, there's a variable called `Bob`, and it just so happens that you don't know if `Bob` is a `Person` object or a `Programmer` object. You can still call the `talk` method on the `Bob` object and the code will work. This ability to call the same method on different objects, and have each of them respond in their own way, is called polymorphism.

OOP summary

Here's a quick table summarizing the concepts discussed so far:

Feature	Illustrates concept
Bob is a man (an object).	Objects
Bob's date of birth is June 1, 1980, gender – male, and hair – black.	Properties
Bob can eat, sleep, drink, dream, talk, and calculate his own age.	Methods
Bob is an instance of the `Programmer` class.	Class (in classical OOP)
Bob is based on another object called `Programmer`.	Prototype (in prototypal OOP)
Bob holds data, such as `birth_date`, and methods that work with the data, such as `calculateAge()`.	Encapsulation
You don't need to know how the calculation method works internally. The object might have some private data, such as the number of days in February in a leap year. You don't know, nor do you want to know.	Information hiding

Bob is part of a `WebDevTeam` object together with Jill, a `Designer` object, and Jack, a `ProjectManager` object.	Aggregation and composition
`Designer`, `ProjectManager`, and `Programmer` are all based on and extend a `Person` object.	Inheritance
You can call the methods `Bob.talk()`, `Jill.talk()`, and `Jack.talk()`, and they'll all work fine, albeit producing different results. Bob will probably talk more about performance, Jill about beauty, and Jack about deadlines. Each object inherited the method talk from Person and customized it.	Polymorphism and method overriding

Setting up your training environment

This book takes a do-it-yourself approach when it comes to writing code, because I firmly believe that the best way to really learn a programming language is by writing code. There are no cut-and-paste-ready code downloads that you simply put in your pages. On the contrary, you're expected to type in code, see how it works, and then tweak it and play around with it. When trying out the code examples, you're encouraged to enter the code into a JavaScript console. Let's see how you go about doing this.

As a developer, you most likely already have a number of web browsers installed on your system, such as Firefox, Safari, Chrome, or Internet Explorer. All modern browsers have a JavaScript console feature that you'll use throughout the book to help you learn and experiment with the language. More specifically, this book uses WebKit's console, which is available in Safari and Chrome, but the examples should work in any other console.

WebKit's web inspector

This example shows how you can use the console to type in some code that swaps the logo on the google.com home page with an image of your choice. As you can see, you can test your JavaScript code live on any page:

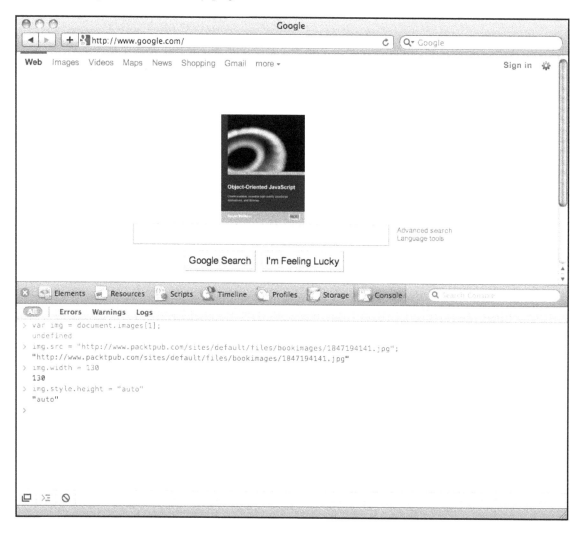

In order to bring up the console in Chrome or Safari, right click anywhere on a page and select **Inspect Element**. The additional window that shows up is the Web Inspector feature. Select the **Console** tab, and you're ready to go.

You type code directly into the console, and when you press *Enter*, your code is executed. The return value of the code is printed in the console. The code is executed in the context of the currently loaded page, so, for example, if you type `location.href`, it will return the URL of the current page.

The console also has an autocomplete feature. It works in a similar way to the normal command-line prompt in your operating system or autocomplete feature of the full-fledged IDEs. If, for example, you type `docu` and hit the *Tab* or right arrow key, `docu` will be autocompleted to document. Then, if you type . (the dot operator), you can iterate through all the available properties and methods you can call on the `document` object.

By using the up and down arrow keys, you can go through the list of already executed commands and bring them back in the console.

The console gives you only one line to type in, but you can execute several JavaScript statements by separating them with semicolons. If you need more lines, you can press *Shift + Enter* to go to a new line without executing the result just yet.

JavaScriptCore on a Mac

On a Mac, you don't actually need a browser; you can explore JavaScript directly from your command line **Terminal** application.

If you've never used **Terminal**, you can simply search for it in **Spotlight search**. Once you've launched it, type the following command:

```
alias jsc='/System/Library/Frameworks/JavaScriptCore.framework/
    Versions/Current/Resources/jsc'
```

This command makes an alias to the little `jsc` application that stands for JavaScriptCore and is part of the WebKit engine. JavaScriptCore is shipped together with Mac operating systems.

You can add the `alias` line shown previously to your `~/.profile` file so that `jsc` is always there when you need it.

Now, in order to start the interactive shell, you will simply type `jsc` from any directory. Then, you can type JavaScript expressions, and when you hit Enter, you'll see the result of the expression. Take a look at the following screenshot:

```
● ○ ○                    Terminal — jsc — 80×24
Last login: Tue May 31 01:07:35 on ttys002
stoyanstefanov:~ stoyanstefanov$ jsc
> 1+1
2
> var a = "hello";
undefined
> a
hello
> var b = "console";
undefined
> b
console
> a + " " + b
hello console
>
```

More consoles

All modern browsers have consoles built in. You have seen the Chrome/Safari console previously. In any Firefox version, you can install the Firebug extension, which comes with a console. Additionally, in newer Firefox releases, there's a console built in and accessible via the **Tools** | **Web Developer** | **Web Console** menu.

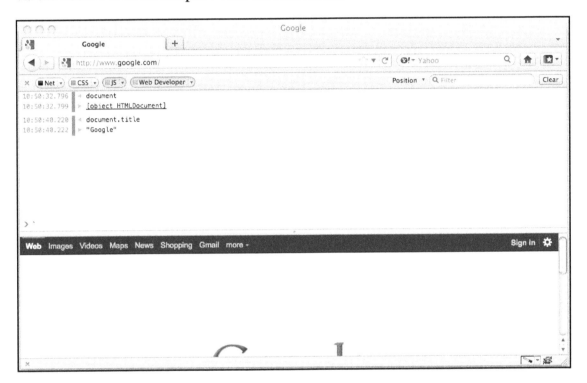

Internet Explorer, since version 8, has an F12 Developer Tools feature, which has a console in its **Script** tab.

It's also a good idea to familiarize yourself with Node.js, and you can start by trying out its console. Install Node.js from http://nodejs.org and try the console in your command prompt (terminal):

```
stoyanstefmbp15:~ stoyanstefanov$ node
> var a = 1; var b = 2;
undefined
> a + b;
3
>
(^C again to quit)
>
stoyanstefmbp15:~ stoyanstefanov$ cat test.js
var a = 101;
var b = 202;

console.log(a + b);
stoyanstefmbp15:~ stoyanstefanov$ node test.js
303
stoyanstefmbp15:~ stoyanstefanov$
```

As you can see, you can use the Node.js console to try out quick examples. But, you can also write longer shell scripts (test.js in the screenshot) and run them with the scriptname.js node.

Node REPL is a powerful development tool. When you type 'node' on the command line, the REPL invokes. You can try out JavaScript on this REPL:

```
node
> console.log("Hellow World");
Hellow World
undefined
> a=10, b=10;
10
> console.log(a*b);
100
undefined
```

Summary

In this chapter, you learned about how JavaScript was born, and where it is today. You were also introduced to object-oriented programming concepts and have seen how JavaScript is not a class-based OO language, but a prototype-based one. Finally, you learned how to use your training environment–the JavaScript console. Now, you're ready to dive into JavaScript and learn how to use its powerful OO features. However, let's start from the beginning.

The next chapter will guide you through the data types in JavaScript (there are just a few), conditions, loops, and arrays. If you think you know these topics, feel free to skip the next chapter, but not before you make sure you can complete the few short exercises at the end of the chapter.

2

Primitive Data Types, Arrays, Loops, and Conditions

Before diving into the object-oriented features of JavaScript, let's first take a look at some of the basics. This chapter walks you through the following topics:

- The primitive data types in JavaScript, such as strings and numbers
- Arrays
- Common operators, such as +, -, `delete`, and `typeof`
- Flow control statements, such as loops and `if...else` conditions

Variables

Variables are used to store data; they are placeholders for concrete values. When writing programs, it's convenient to use variables instead of the actual data as it's much easier to write `pi` instead of `3.141592653589793`; especially when it happens several times inside your program. The data stored in a variable can be changed after it initially assigned, hence the name **variable**. You can also use variables to store data that is unknown to you while you write the code, such as the result of a later operation.

Using a variable requires the following two steps. You will need to:

- Declare the variable
- Initialize it, that is, give it a value

To declare a variable, you will use the `var` statement like the following piece of code:

```
var a;
var thisIsAVariable;
var _and_this_too;
var mix12three;
```

For the names of the variables, you can use any combination of letters, numbers, the underscore character, and the dollar sign. However, you can't start with a number, which means that the following declaration of code is invalid:

```
var 2three4five;
```

To initialize a variable means to give it a value for the first (initial) time. The following are the two ways to do so:

- Declare the variable first, then initialize it
- Declare and initialize it with a single statement

An example of the latter is as follows:

```
var a = 1;
```

Now the variable named `a` contains the value `1`.

You can declare, and optionally initialize, several variables with a single `var` statement; just separate the declarations with a comma, as shown in the following line of code:

```
var v1, v2, v3 = 'hello', v4 = 4, v5;
```

For readability, this is often written using one variable per line, as follows:

```
var v1,
    v2,
    v3 = 'hello',
    v4 = 4,
    v5;
```

The $ character in variable names

You may see the dollar sign character (`$`) used in variable names, as in `$myvar` or less commonly `my$var`. This character is allowed to appear anywhere in a variable name, although previous versions of the ECMA standard discouraged its use in handwritten programs and suggested it should only be used in generated code (programs written by other programs). This suggestion is not well respected by the JavaScript community, and `$` is in fact commonly used in practice as a function name.

Variables are case sensitive

Variable names are case sensitive. You can easily verify this statement using your JavaScript console. Try typing the following code by pressing *Enter* after each line:

```
var case_matters = 'lower';
var CASE_MATTERS = 'upper';
case_matters;
CASE_MATTER;
```

To save keystrokes when you enter the third line, you can type `case` and press the *Tab* or right arrow key. **Console** autocompletes the variable name to `case_matters`. Similarly, for the last line, type `CASE` and press the *Tab* key. The end result is shown in the following figure:

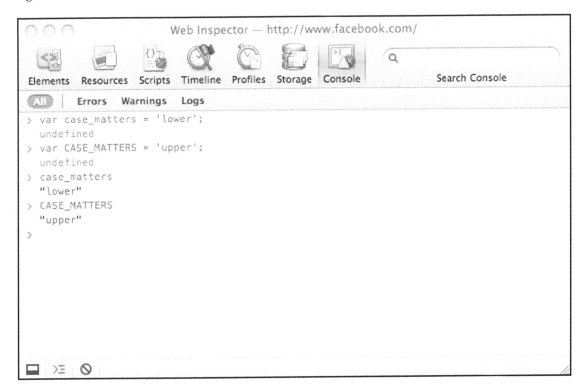

Throughout the rest of this book, only the code for the examples is given instead of a screenshot, as follows:

```
> var case_matters = 'lower';
> var CASE_MATTERS = 'upper';
```

```
> case_matters;
"lower"
> CASE_MATTERS;
"upper"
```

The greater-than signs (>) show the code that you type; the rest is the result as printed in **Console**. Again, remember that when you see such code examples, you're strongly encouraged to type in the code yourself. Then, you can experiment by tweaking it a little here and there to get a better feeling of how exactly it works.

 You can see in the preceding screenshot that sometimes what you type in **Console** results in the word **undefined**. You can simply ignore this, but if you're curious, here's what happens when evaluating (executing) what you type–the **Console** prints the returned value. Some expressions, such as var a = 1;, don't return anything explicitly, in which case, they implicitly return the special value **undefined** (more on in a bit). When an expression returns some value (for example, case_matters in the previous example or something such as 1 + 1), the resulting value is printed out. Not all consoles print the **undefined** value; for example, the Firebug console.

Operators

Operators take one or two values (or variables), perform an operation, and return a value. Let's check out a simple example of using an operator, just to clarify the terminology:

```
> 1 + 2;
3
```

In the preceding code:

- The + symbol is the operator
- The operation is addition
- The input values are 1 and 2 (they are also called operands)
- The result value is 3
- The whole thing is called an expression

Instead of using the values 1 and 2 directly in the expression, you can use variables. You can also use a variable to store the result of the operation as the following example demonstrates:

```
> var a = 1;
> var b = 2;
> a + 1;
2
> b + 2;
4
> a + b;
3
> var c = a + b;
> c;
3
```

The following table lists the basic arithmetic operators:

Operator symbol	Operation	Example
+	Addition	```> 1 + 2;``` ```3```
−	Subtraction	```> 99.99 - 11;``` ```88.99```
*	Multiplication	```> 2 * 3;``` ```6```
/	Division	```> 6 / 4;``` ```1.5```

%	Modulo, the remainder of a division	```> 6 % 3;```
		```0```
		```> 5 % 3;```
		```2```
		It's sometimes useful to test if a number is even or odd. Using the modulo operator, it's easy to do just that. All odd numbers return 1 when divided by 2, while all even numbers return 0, for example:
		```> 4 % 2;```
		```0```
		```> 5 % 2;```
		```1```

++	Increment a value by 1	Post increment is when the input value is incremented after it's returned, for example:
| | | ```
> var a = 123;
> var b = a++;
> b;
123
> a;
124
``` |
| | | The opposite is pre-increment. The input value is incremented by 1 first and then returned, for example: |
| | | ```
> var a = 123;
> var b = ++a;
> b;
124
> a;
124
``` |
| -- | Decrement a value by 1 | Post-decrement: |
| | | ```
> var a = 123;
> var b = a--;
> b;
123
> a;
122
``` |
| | | Pre-decrement: |
| | | ```
> var a = 123;
> var b = --a;
> b;
122
> a;
122
``` |

The `var a = 1;` is also an operation; it's the simple assignment operation, and = is the **simple assignment operator**.

There is also a family of operators that are a combination of an assignment and an arithmetic operator. These are called **compound operators**. They can make your code more compact. Let's see some of them with the following examples:

```
> var a = 5;
> a += 3;
8
```

In this example, `a += 3;` is just a shorter way of doing `a = a + 3;`. For example:

```
> a -= 3;
5
```

Here, `a -= 3;` is the same as `a = a - 3;`:

```
> a *= 2;
10
> a /= 5;
2
> a %= 2;
0
```

In addition to the arithmetic and assignment operators discussed previously, there are other types of operators, as you'll see later in this, and the following chapters.

Best practice

Always end your expressions with a semicolon. JavaScript has a semicolon insertion mechanism, where it can add the semicolon if you forget it at the end of a line. However, this can also be a source of errors, so it's best to make sure you always explicitly state where you want to terminate your expressions. In other words, both expressions `> 1 + 1` and `> 1 + 1;` will work; but throughout the book, you'll always see the second type, terminated with a semicolon, just to emphasize this habit.

Primitive data types

Any value that you use is of a certain type. In JavaScript, the following are just a few primitive data types:

1. **Number**: This includes floating point numbers as well as integers. For example, these values are all numbers–`1`, `100`, `3.14`.
2. **String**: These consist of any number of characters, for example, `a`, `one`, and `one 2 three`.
3. **Boolean**: This can be either `true` or `false`.

4. **Undefined**: When you try to access a variable that doesn't exist, you get the special value undefined. The same happens when you declare a variable without assigning a value to it yet. JavaScript initializes the variable behind the scenes with the value `undefined`. The undefined data type can only have one value–the special value `undefined`.

5. **Null**: This is another special data type that can have only one value–the `null` value. It means no value, an empty value, or nothing. The difference with undefined is that if a variable has a null value, it's still defined; it just so happens that its value is nothing. You'll see some examples shortly.

Any value that doesn't belong to one of the five primitive types listed here is an object. Even null is considered an object, which is a little awkward having an object (something) that is actually nothing. We'll learn more about objects in Chapter 4, *Objects*, but for the time being, just remember that in JavaScript, the data types are as follows:

- Primitive (the five types listed previously)
- Non-primitive (objects)

Finding out the value type – the typeof operator

If you want to know the type of a variable or a value, you can use the special typeof operator. This operator returns a string that represents the data type. The return values of using typeof are one of the following:

- number
- string
- boolean
- undefined
- object
- function

In the next few sections, you'll see typeof in action using examples of each of the five primitive data types.

Numbers

The simplest number is an integer. If you assign `1` to a variable, and then use the `typeof` operator, it returns the string `number`, as follows:

```
> var n = 1;
> typeof n;
"number"
> n = 1234;
> typeof n;
"number"
```

In the preceding example, you can see that the second time you set a variable's value, you don't need the `var` statement.

Numbers can also be floating point (decimals), for example:

```
> var n2 = 1.23;
> typeof n;
"number"
```

You can call `typeof` directly on the value without assigning it to a variable first, for example:

```
> typeof 123;
"number"
```

Octal and hexadecimal numbers

When a number starts with a `0`, it's considered an octal number. For example, the octal `0377` is the decimal `255`:

```
> var n3 = 0377;
> typeof n3;
"number"
> n3;
255
```

The last line in the preceding example prints the decimal representation of the octal value.

ES6 provides a prefix 0o (or 0O, but this looks very confusing in most monospace fonts) to represent octals. Consider the following line of code for example:

```
console.log(0o776); //510
```

While you may not be intimately familiar with octal numbers, you've probably used hexadecimal values to define colors in CSS stylesheets.

In CSS, you have several options to define a color, two of them are as follows:

- Using decimal values to specify the amount of R (red), G (green), and B (blue), ranging from 0 to 255. For example, *rgb(0, 0, 0)* is black and *rgb(255, 0, 0)* is red (maximum amount of red and no green or blue).
- Using hexadecimals and specifying two characters for each R, G, and B value. For example, *#000000* is black and *#ff0000* is red. This is because *ff* is the hexadecimal value for 255.

In JavaScript, you can put 0x before a hexadecimal value, also called hex for short, for example:

```
> var n4 = 0x00;
> typeof n4;
"number"
> n4;
0
> var n5 = 0xff;
> typeof n5;
"number"
> n5;
255
```

Binary Literals

Untill ES6, if you needed binary representation of an integer, you had to pass them to the parseInt() function as a string with a radix of 2, as follows:

```
console.log(parseInt('111',2)); //7
```

In ES6 you can use 0b (or 0B) prefix to represent binary integers. For example:

```
console.log(0b111); //7
```

Exponent literals

`1e1` (also written as `1e+1` or `1E1` or `1E+1`) represents the number 1 with a 0 after it, or in other words, `10`. Similarly, `2e+3` represents the number **2** with three 0s after it, or `2000`, for example:

```
> 1e1;
10
> 1e+1;
10
> 2e+3;
2000
> typeof 2e+3;
"number"
```

`2e+3` means moving the decimal point three digits to the right of the number **2**. There's also `2e-3`, meaning you move the decimal point three digits to the left of the number **2**. Look at the following figure:

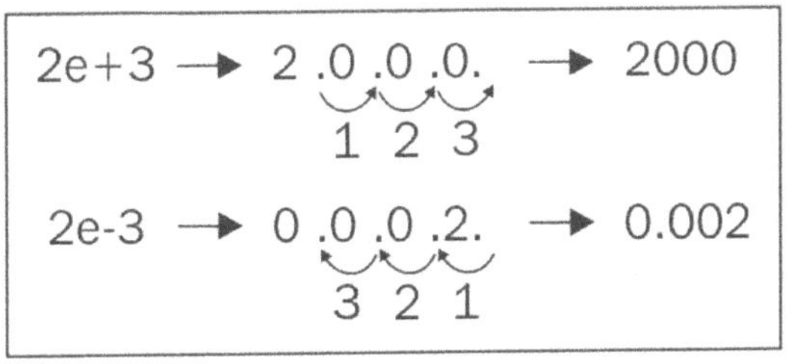

```
2e+3 ──► 2 .0 .0 .0.  ──► 2000
           1  2  3

2e-3 ──► 0 .0 .0 .2.  ──► 0.002
           3  2  1
```

The following is the code:

```
> 2e-3;
0.002
> 123.456E-3;
0.123456
> typeof 2e-3;
"number"
```

Infinity

There is a special value in JavaScript called Infinity. It represents a number too big for JavaScript to handle. Infinity is indeed a number, as typing `typeof Infinity` in the console will confirm. You can also quickly check that a number with 308 zeros is ok, but 309 zeros is too much. To be precise, the biggest number JavaScript can handle is `1.7976931348623157e+308`, while the smallest is `5e-324`, Look at the following example:

```
> Infinity;
Infinity
> typeof Infinity;
"number"
> 1e309;
Infinity
> 1e308;
1e+308
```

Dividing by zero gives you infinity, for example:

```
> var a = 6 / 0;
> a;
Infinity
```

`Infinity` is the biggest number (or rather a little bigger than the biggest), but how about the smallest? It's infinity with a minus sign in front of it; `-Infinity`, for example:

```
> var i = -Infinity;
> i;
-Infinity
> typeof i;
"number"
```

Does this mean you can have something that's exactly twice as big as Infinity, from 0 up to infinity and then from 0 down to minus infinity? Well, not really. When you sum `Infinity` and `-Infinity`, you don't get 0, but something that is called **Not a Number (NaN)**, For example:

```
> Infinity - Infinity;
NaN
> -Infinity + Infinity;
NaN
```

Any other arithmetic operation with `Infinity` as one of the operands gives you `Infinity`, for example:

```
> Infinity - 20;
Infinity
> -Infinity * 3;
-Infinity
> Infinity / 2;
Infinity
> Infinity - 9999999999999999;
Infinity
```

There is a lesser known global method, `isFinite()`, that tells you if the value is infinity or not. ES6 adds a `Number.isFinite()` method to do just that. Why another method, you may ask. The global variant of `isFinite()` tries to cast the value through Number(value), while `Number.isFinite()` doesn't, hence it's more accurate.

NaN

What was this `NaN` in the previous example? It turns out that despite its name, Not a Number, `NaN` is a special value that is also a number:

```
> typeof NaN;
"number"
> var a = NaN;
> a;
NaN
```

You get `NaN` when you try to perform an operation that assumes numbers, but the operation fails. For example, if you try to multiply `10` by the character `"f"`, the result is `NaN`, because `"f"` is obviously not a valid operand for a multiplication:

```
> var a = 10 * "f";
> a;
NaN
```

`NaN` is contagious, so if you have even one `NaN` in your arithmetic operation, the whole result goes down the drain, for example:

```
> 1 + 2 + NaN;
NaN
```

Number.isNaN

ES5 has a global method–`isNaN()`. It determines if a value is `NaN` or not. ES6 provides a very similar method–`Number.isNaN()` (Notice that this method is not global).

The difference between the global `isNaN()` and `Number.isNaN()` is that global `isNaN()` casts non-numeric values before evaluating them to be `NaN`. Let's look at the following example. We are using the ES6 `Number.isNaN()` method to test if something is a `NaN` or not:

```
console.log(Number.isNaN('test')); //false : Strings are not NaN
console.log(Number.isNaN(123)); //false : integers are not NaN
console.log(Number.isNaN(NaN)); //true : NaNs are NaNs
console.log(Number.isNaN(123/'abc')); //true : 123/'abc' results in an
NaN
```

We saw that ES5's global `isNaN()` method first casts non-numeric values and then does the comparison; the following result will be different from its ES6 counterpart:

```
console.log(isNaN('test')); //true
```

In general, compared to its global variant, `Number.isNaN()` is more correct. However, neither of them can be used to figure out if something is not a number–they just answer if the value is a `NaN` or not. Practically, you are interested in knowing if a value identifies as a number or not. Mozilla suggests the following polyfill method to do just that:

```
function isNumber(value) {
  return typeof value==='number' && !Number.isNaN(value);
}
```

Number.isInteger

This is a new method in ES6. It returns `true` if the number is finite and does not contain any decimal points (is an integer):

```
console.log(Number.isInteger('test')); //false
console.log(Number.isInteger(Infinity)); //false
console.log(Number.isInteger(NaN)); //false
console.log(Number.isInteger(123)); //true
console.log(Number.isInteger(1.23)); //false
```

Strings

A string is a sequence of characters used to represent text. In JavaScript, any value placed between single or double quotes is considered a string. This means that 1 is a number, but "1" is a string. When used with strings, typeof returns the string "string", for example:

```
> var s = "some characters";
> typeof s;
"string"
> var s = 'some characters and numbers 123 5.87';
> typeof s;
"string"
```

Here's an example of a number used in the string context:

```
> var s = '1';
> typeof s;
"string"
```

If you put nothing in quotes, it's still a string (an empty string), for example:

```
> var s = ""; typeof s;
"string"
```

As you already know, when you use the plus sign with two numbers, this is the arithmetic addition operation. However, if you use the plus sign with strings, this is a string concatenation operation, and it returns the two strings glued together:

```
> var s1 = "web";
> var s2 = "site";
> var s = s1 + s2;
> s;
"website"
> typeof s;
"string"
```

The dual purpose of the + operator is a source of errors. Therefore, if you intend to concatenate strings, it's always best to make sure that all of the operands are strings. The same applies for addition; if you intend to add numbers then make sure the operands are numbers. You'll learn various ways to do so further in the chapter and the book.

String conversions

When you use a number-like string, for example, `"1"`, as an operand in an arithmetic operation, the string is converted to a number behind the scenes. This works for all arithmetic operations except addition, because of its ambiguity. Consider the following example:

```
> var s = '1';
> s = 3 * s;
> typeof s;
"number"
> s;
3
> var s = '1';
> s++;
> typeof s;
"number"
> s;
2
```

A lazy way to convert any number-like string to a number is to multiply it by 1 (another way is to use a function called `parseInt()`, as you'll see in the next chapter):

```
> var s = "100"; typeof s;
"string"
> s = s * 1;
100
> typeof s;
"number"
```

If the conversion fails, you'll get `NaN`:

```
> var movie = '101 dalmatians';
> movie * 1;
NaN
```

You can convert a string to a number by multiplying it by 1. The opposite–converting anything to a string–can be done by concatenating it with an empty string, as follows:

```
> var n = 1;
> typeof n;
"number"
> n = "" + n;
"1"
> typeof n;
"string"
```

Special strings

There are also strings with special meanings, as listed in the following table:

String	Meaning	Example

`\\`
`'`
`"`
	The \ is the escape character. When you want to have quotes inside your string, you can escape them so that JavaScript doesn't think they mean the end of the string.
	If you want to have an actual backslash in the string, escape it with another backslash.
		`> var s = 'I don't know';`: This is an error because JavaScript thinks the string is `I don` and the rest is invalid code. The following codes are valid:
		`> var s = 'I don\'t know';`
		`> var s = "I don't know";`
		`> var s = "I don\'t know";`
		`> var s = '"Hello",   he said.';`
		`> var s = "\"Hello\",   he said.";`
		`Escaping the escape:`
		`> var s = "1\\2"; s;`
		`"1\2"`

`\n`	End of line.	`> var s = '\n1\n2\n3\n';`
		`> s;`
		`"`
		`1`
		`2`
		`3`
		`"`

`\r`	Carriage return.	Consider the following statements:
		`> var s = '1\r2';`
		`> var s = '1\n\r2';`
		`> var s = '1\r\n2';`
		The result of all of these is as follows:
		`> s;`
		`"1`
		`2"`

`\t`	Tab.	`> var s = "1\t2";`
		`> s;`
		`"1  2"`

`\u`	The \u followed by a character code allows you to use Unicode.	Here's my name in Bulgarian written with Cyrillic characters:
		`> "\u0421\u0442\u043E\u044F\u043D";`
		`"Стоян"`

There are also additional characters that are rarely used: \b (backspace), \v (vertical tab), and \f (form feed).

String template literals

ES6 introduced template literals. If you are familiar with other programming languages, Perl and Python have supported template literals for a while now. Template literals allow expressions to be embedded within regular strings. ES6 has two kinds of literals: template literals and tagged literals.

Template literals are single or multiple line strings with embedded expressions. For example, you must have done something similar to this:

```
var log_level="debug";
var log_message="meltdown";
console.log("Log level: "+ log_level +
  " - message : " + log_message);
//Log level: debug - message : meltdown
```

You can accomplish the same using template literals, as follows:

```
console.log(`Log level: ${log_level} - message: ${log_message}`)
```

Template literals are enclosed by the back-tick (` `) (grave accent) character instead of the usual double or single quotes. Template literal place holders are indicated by the dollar sign and curly braces (${expression}). By default, they are concatenated to form a single string. The following example shows a template literal with a slightly complex expression:

```
var a = 10;
var b = 10;
console.log(`Sum is ${a + b} and Multiplication would be ${a * b}.`);
//Sum is 20 and Multiplication would be 100.
```

How about embedding a function call?

```
var a = 10;
var b = 10;
function sum(x,y){
  return x+y
}
function multi(x,y){
  return x*y
}
console.log(`Sum is ${sum(a,b)} and Multiplication
  would be ${multi(a,b)}.`);
```

Template literals also simplify multiline string syntax. Instead of writing the following line of code:

```
console.log("This is line one \n" + "and this is line two");
```

You can have a much cleaner syntax using template literals, which is as follows:

```
console.log(`This is line one and this is line two`);
```

ES6 has another interesting literal type called **Tagged Template Literals**. Tagged templates allow you to modify the output of template literals using a function. If you prefix an expression to a template literal, that prefix is considered to be a function to be invoked. The function needs to be defined before we can use the tagged template literal. For example, the following expression:

```
transform`Name is ${lastname}, ${firstname} ${lastname}`
```

The preceding expression is converted into a function call:

```
transform([["Name is ", ", ", " "],firstname, lastname)
```

The tag function, 'transform', gets two parameters–template strings like `Name is` and substitutions defined by `${}`. The substitutions are only known at runtime. Let's expand the `transform` function:

```
function transform(strings, ...substitutes){
  console.log(strings[0]); //"Name is"
  console.log(substitutes[0]); //Bond
}
var firstname = "James";
var lastname = "Bond"
transform`Name is ${lastname}, ${firstname} ${lastname}`
```

When template strings (`Name is`) are passed to the tag function, there are two forms of each template string, as follows:

- The raw form where the backslashes are not interpreted
- The cooked form where the backslashes has special meaning

You can access the raw string form using raw property, as the following example shows:

```
function rawTag(strings,...substitutes){
  console.log(strings.raw[0])
}
rawTag`This is a raw text and \n are not treated differently`
//This is a raw text and \n are not treated differently
```

Booleans

There are only two values that belong to the Boolean data type–the `true` and `false` values used without quotes:

```
> var b = true;
> typeof b;
"boolean"
> var b = false;
> typeof b;
"boolean"
```

If you quote `true` or `false`, they become strings, as shown in the following example:

```
> var b = "true";
> typeof b;
"string"
```

Logical operators

There are three operators, called logical operators, that work with Boolean values. These are as follows:

```
! - logical NOT (negation)
&& - logical AND
|| - logical OR
```

You know that when something is not true, it must be false. Here's how this is expressed using JavaScript and the logical ! operator:

```
> var b = !true;
> b;
false
```

If you use the logical NOT twice, you will get the original value, which is as follows:

```
> var b = !!true;
> b;
true
```

If you use a logical operator on a non-Boolean value, the value is converted to Boolean behind the scenes, as follows:

```
> var b = "one";
> !b;
false
```

In the preceding case, the string value "one" is converted to a Boolean, true, and then negated. The result of negating true is false. In the following example, there's a double negation, so the result is true:

```
> var b = "one";
> !!b;
true
```

You can convert any value to its Boolean equivalent using a double negation. Understanding how any value converts to a Boolean is important. Most values convert to true with the exception of the following, which convert to false:

- The empty string ""
- null
- undefined
- The number 0
- The number NaN
- The Boolean false

These six values are referred to as falsy, while all others are truthy, (including, for example, the strings "0", " ", and "false").

Let's see some examples of the other two operators–the logical AND (&&) and the logical OR (||). When you use &&, the result is true only if all of the operands are true. When you use ||, the result is true if at least one of the operands is true:

```
> var b1 = true, b2 = false;
> b1 || b2;
true
> b1 && b2;
false
```

Here's a list of the possible operations and their results:

Operation	Result
true && true	true
true && false	false
false && true	false
false && false	false
true || true	true

true		false	true
false		true	true
false		false	false

You can use several logical operations one after the other, as follows:

```
> true && true && false && true;
false
> false || true || false;
true
```

You can also mix `&&` and `||` in the same expression. In such cases, you should use parentheses to clarify how you intend the operation to work. Consider the following example:

```
> false && false || true && true;
true
> false && (false || true) && true;
false
```

Operator precedence

You might wonder why the previous expression (`false && false || true && true`) returned `true`. The answer lies in the operator precedence, as you know from mathematics:

```
> 1 + 2 * 3;
7
```

This is because multiplication has a higher precedence over addition, so `2 * 3` is evaluated first, as if you typed:

```
> 1 + (2 * 3);
7
```

Similarly for logical operations, ! has the highest precedence and is executed first, assuming there are no parentheses that demand otherwise. Then, in the order of precedence, comes `&&` and finally, `||`. In other words, the following two code snippets are the same. The first one is as follows:

```
> false && false || true && true;
true
```

And the second one is as follows:

```
> (false && false) || (true && true);
true
```

Best practice
Use parentheses instead of relying on operator precedence. This makes your code easier to read and understand.

The ECMAScript standard defines the precedence of operators. While it may be a good memorization exercise, this book doesn't offer it. First of all, you'll forget it, and second, even if you manage to remember it, you shouldn't rely on it. The person reading and maintaining your code will likely be confused.

Lazy evaluation

If you have several logical operations one after the other, but the result becomes clear at some point before the end, the final operations will not be performed because they don't affect the end result. Consider the following line of code as an example:

```
> true || false || true || false || true;
true
```

As these are all OR operations and have the same precedence, the result will be true if at least, one of the operands is true. After the first operand is evaluated, it becomes clear that the result will be true, no matter what values follow. So, the JavaScript engine decides to be lazy (OK, efficient) and avoids unnecessary work by evaluating code that doesn't affect the end result. You can verify this short-circuiting behavior by experimenting in the console, as shown in the following code block:

```
> var b = 5;
> true || (b = 6);
true
> b;
5
> true && (b = 6);
6
> b;
6
```

This example also shows another interesting behavior–if JavaScript encounters a non-Boolean expression as an operand in a logical operation, the non-Boolean is returned as a result:

```
> true || "something";
true
> true && "something";
"something"
> true && "something" && true;
true
```

This behavior is not something you should rely on because it makes the code harder to understand. It's common to use this behavior to define variables when you're not sure whether they were previously defined. In the next example, if the `mynumber` variable is defined, its value is kept; otherwise, it's initialized with the value `10`:

```
> var mynumber = mynumber || 10;
> mynumber;
10
```

This is simple and looks elegant, but be aware that it's not completely foolproof. If `mynumber` is defined and initialized to `0`, or to any of the six falsy values, this code might not behave as you expect, as shown in the following piece of code:

```
> var mynumber = 0;
> var mynumber = mynumber || 10;
> mynumber;
10
```

Comparison

There's another set of operators that all return a Boolean value as a result of the operation. These are the comparison operators. The following table lists them together with example uses:

Operator symbol	Description	Example

==	**Equality comparison**: This returns `true` when both operands are equal. The operands are converted to the same type before being compared. They're also called loose comparison.	`> 1 == 1;`
		`true`
		`> 1 == 2;`
		`false`
		`> 1 =='1';`
		`true`

===	**Equality and type comparison**: This returns `true` if both operands are equal and of the same type. It's better and safer to compare this way because there's no behind-the-scenes type conversions. It is also called strict comparison.	```> 1 === '1';```
		```false```
		```> 1 === 1;```
		```true```

!=	**Non-equality comparison**: This returns `true` if the operands are not equal to each other (after a type conversion).	```> 1 != 1;```
		```false```
		```> 1 != '1';```
		```false```
		```> 1 != '2';```
		```true```

!==	**Non-equality comparison without type conversion**: Returns `true` if the operands are not equal or if they are of different types.	```> 1 !== 1;```
		```false```
		```> 1 !== '1';```
		```true```

>	This returns `true` if the left operand is greater than the right one.	```> 1 > 1;```
		```false```
		```> 33 > 22;```
		```true```

>=	This returns `true` if the left operand is greater than or equal to the right one.	```> 1 >= 1;``` ```true```

<	This returns `true` if the left operand is less than the right one.	```> 1 < 1;```
		```false```
		```> 1 < 2;```
		```true```

<=	This returns `true` if the left operand is less than or equal to the right one.	```> 1 <= 1;```
		```true```
		```> 1 <= 2;```
		```true```

Note that `NaN` is not equal to anything, not even itself. Take a look at the following line of code:

```
> NaN == NaN;
false
```

Undefined and null

If you try to use a non-existing variable, you'll get the following error:

```
> foo;
ReferenceError: foo is not defined
```

Using the `typeof` operator on a non-existing variable is not an error. You will get the "undefined" string back, as follows:

```
> typeof foo;
"undefined"
```

If you declare a variable without giving it a value, this is, of course, not an error. But, the `typeof` still returns "undefined":

```
> var somevar;
> somevar;
> typeof somevar;
"undefined"
```

This is because, when you declare a variable without initializing it, JavaScript automatically initializes it with the `undefined` value, as shown in the following lines of code:

```
> var somevar;
> somevar === undefined;
true
```

The `null` value, on the other hand, is not assigned by JavaScript behind the scenes; it's assigned by your code, which is as follows:

```
> var somevar = null;
null
> somevar;
null
> typeof somevar;
"object"
```

Although the difference between `null` and `undefined` is small, it can be critical at times. For example, if you attempt an arithmetic operation, you will get different results:

```
> var i = 1 + undefined;
> i;
NaN
> var i = 1 + null;
> i;
1
```

This is because of the different ways `null` and `undefined` are converted to the other primitive types. The following examples show the possible conversions:

- Conversion to a number:

```
> 1 * undefined;
```

- Conversion to NaN:

```
> 1 * null;
0
```

- Conversion to a Boolean:

```
> !!undefined;
false
> !!null;
false
```

- Conversion to a string:

```
> "value: " + null;
"value: null"
> "value: " + undefined;
"value: undefined"
```

Symbols

ES6 introduced a new primitive type–symbols. Several languages have a similar notion. Symbols look very similar to regular strings, but they are very different. Let's see how these symbols are created:

```
var atom = Symbol()
```

Notice that we don't use `new` operator while creating symbols. You will get an error when you do use it:

```
var atom = new Symbol() //Symbol is not a constructor
```

You can describe `Symbol` as well:

```
var atom = Symbol('atomic symbol')
```

Describing symbols comes in very handy while debugging large programs where there are lots of symbols scattered across.

The most important property of `Symbol` (and hence the reason of their existence) is that they are unique and immutable:

```
console.log(Symbol() === Symbol()) //false
console.log(Symbol('atom') === Symbol('atom')) // false
```

For now, we will have to pause this discussion on symbols. Symbols are used as property keys and places where you need unique identifiers. We will discuss symbols in a later part of this book.

Primitive data types recap

Let's quickly summarize some of the main points discussed so far:

- There are five primitive data types in JavaScript:
  - Number
  - String
  - Boolean
  - Undefined
  - Null
- Everything that is not a primitive data type is an object.

  The primitive number data type can store positive and negative integers or floats, hexadecimal numbers, octal numbers, exponents, and the special numbers–NaN, Infinity, and -Infinity.

- The string data type contains characters in quotes. Template literals allow embedding of expressions inside a string.
- The only values of the Boolean data type are `true` and `false`.

- The only value of the null data type is the `null` value.
- The only value of the undefined data type is the `undefined` value.
- All values become `true` when converted to a Boolean, with the exception of the following six falsy values:
  - `""`
  - `null`
  - `undefined`
  - `0`
  - `NaN`
  - `false`

Arrays

Now that you know about the basic primitive data types in JavaScript, it's time to move to a more powerful data structure–the array.

So, what is an array? It's simply a list (a sequence) of values. Instead of using one variable to store one value, you can use one array variable to store any number of values as elements of the array.

To declare a variable that contains an empty array, you can use square brackets with nothing between them, as shown in the following line of code:

```
> var a = [];
```

To define an array that has three elements, you can write the following line of code:

```
> var a = [1, 2, 3];
```

When you simply type the name of the array in the console, you can get the contents of your array:

```
> a;
[1, 2, 3]
```

Now the question is how to access the values stored in these array elements. The elements contained in an array are indexed with consecutive numbers, starting from zero. The first element has index (or position) 0, the second has index 1, and so on. Here's the three-element array from the previous example:

Index	Value
0	1
1	2
2	3

To access an array element, you can specify the index of that element inside square brackets. So, a[0] gives you the first element of the array a, a[1] gives you the second, and so on, as shown in the following example:

```
> a[0];
1
> a[1];
2
```

Adding/updating array elements

Using the index, you can also update the values of the elements of the array. The next example updates the third element (index 2) and prints the contents of the new array, as follows:

```
> a[2] = 'three';
"three"
> a;
[1, 2, "three"]
```

You can add more elements by addressing an index that didn't exist before, as shown in the following lines of code:

```
> a[3] = 'four';
"four"
> a;
[1, 2, "three", "four"]
```

If you add a new element but leave a gap in the array, those elements in between don't exist and return the `undefined` value if accessed. Check out the following example:

```
> var a = [1, 2, 3];
> a[6] = 'n`xew';
"new"
> a;
[1, 2, 3, undefined x 3, "new"]
```

Deleting elements

To delete an element, you can use the `delete` operator. However, after the deletion, the length of the array does not change. In a sense, you may get a hole in the array:

```
> var a = [1, 2, 3];
> delete a[1];
true
> a;
[1, undefined, 3]
> typeof a[1];
"undefined"
```

Arrays of arrays

Arrays can contain all types of values, including other arrays:

```
> var a = [1, "two", false, null, undefined];
> a;
[1, "two", false, null, undefined]
> a[5] = [1, 2, 3];
[1, 2, 3]
> a;
[1, "two", false, null, undefined, Array[3]]
```

The `Array[3]` in the result is clickable in the console and it expands the array values. Let's look at an example where you have an array of two elements, both of them being other arrays:

```
> var a = [[1, 2, 3], [4, 5, 6]];
> a;
[Array[3], Array[3]]
```

The first element of the array is `[0]`, and it's also an array:

```
> a[0];
[1, 2, 3]
```

To access an element in the nested array, you can refer to the element index in another set of square brackets, as follows:

```
> a[0][0];
1
> a[1][2];
6
```

Note that you can use the array notation to access individual characters inside a string, as shown in the following code block:

```
> var s = 'one';
> s[0];
"o"
> s[1];
"n"
> s[2];
"e"
```

 Array access to strings was supported by many browsers for a while (not older IEs), but it was officially recognized only as late as ECMAScript 5.

There are more ways to have fun with arrays (and we get to those in `Chapter 4`, *Objects*), but let's stop here for now, remembering the following points:

* An array is a data store
* An array contains indexed elements
* Indexes start from zero and increment by one for each element in the array
* To access an element of an array, you can use its index in square brackets
* An array can contain any type of data, including other arrays

Conditions and loops

Conditions provide a simple but powerful way to control the flow of code execution. Loops allow you to perform repetitive operations with less code. Let's take a look at:

- `if` conditions
- `switch` statements
- `while`, `do...while`, `for`, and `for...in` loops

 The examples in the following sections require you to switch to the multiline Firebug console. Or, if you use the WebKit console, press *Shift + Enter* instead of *Enter* to add a new line.

Code blocks

In the preceding examples, you saw the use of code blocks. Let's take a moment to clarify what a block of code is, because you will use blocks extensively when constructing conditions and loops.

A block of code consists of zero or more expressions enclosed in curly brackets, which is shown in the following lines of code:

```
{
  var a = 1;
  var b = 3;
}
```

You can nest blocks within each other indefinitely, as shown in the following example:

```
{
  var a = 1;
  var b = 3;
  var c, d;
  {
    c = a + b;
    {
      d = a - b;
    }
  }
}
```

Best practice tips

Use end-of-line semicolons, as discussed previously in the chapter. Although the semicolon is optional when you have only one expression per line, it's good to develop the habit of using them. For best readability, the individual expressions inside a block should be placed one per line and separated by semicolons.

Indent any code placed within curly brackets. Some programmers like one tab indentation, some use four spaces, and some use two spaces. It really doesn't matter, as long as you're consistent. In the preceding example, the outer block is indented with two spaces, the code in the first nested block is indented with four spaces, and the innermost block is indented with six spaces.

Use curly brackets. When a block consists of only one expression, the curly brackets are optional, but for readability and maintainability, you should get into the habit of always using them, even when they're optional.

The if condition

Here's a simple example of an `if` condition:

```
var result = '', a = 3;
if (a > 2) {
   result = 'a is greater than 2';
}
```

The parts of the `if` condition are as follows:

- The `if` statement
- A condition in parentheses–`is a greater than 2`?
- A block of code wrapped in `{}` that executes if the condition is satisfied

The condition (the part in parentheses) always returns a Boolean value, and may also contain the following:

- A logical operation–`!`, `&&`, or `||`
- A comparison, such as `===`, `!=`, `>`, and so on
- Any value or variable that can be converted to a Boolean
- A combination of the above

The else clause

There can also be an optional else part of the `if` condition. The `else` statement is followed by a block of code that runs if the condition evaluates to `false`:

```
if (a > 2) {
  result = 'a is greater than 2';
} else {
  result = 'a is NOT greater than 2';
}
```

In between the `if` and the `else` statements, there can also be an unlimited number of `else...if` conditions. Here's an example:

```
if (a > 2 || a < -2) {
  result = 'a is not between -2 and 2';
} else if (a === 0 && b === 0) {
  result = 'both a and b are zeros';
} else if (a === b) {
  result = 'a and b are equal';
} else {
  result = 'I give up';
}
```

You can also nest conditions by putting new conditions within any of the blocks, as shown in the following piece of code:

```
if (a === 1) {
  if (b === 2) {
    result = 'a is 1 and b is 2';
  } else {
    result = 'a is 1 but b is definitely not 2';
  }
} else {
  result = 'a is not 1, no idea about b';
}
```

Checking if a variable exists

Let's apply the new knowledge about conditions for something practical. It's often necessary to check whether a variable exists. The laziest way to do this is to simply put the variable in the condition part of the `if` statement, for example, `if (somevar) {...}`. But, this is not necessarily the best method. Let's take a look at an example that tests whether a variable called `somevar` exists, and if so, sets the `result` variable to `yes`:

```
> var result = '';
```

```
> if (somevar) {
    result = 'yes';
  }
ReferenceError: somevar is not defined
> result;
""
```

This code obviously works because the end result was not `yes`. But firstly, the code generated an error—`somevar` is not defined, and you don't want your code to behave like that. Secondly, just because `if (somevar)` returns `false`, it doesn't mean that `somevar` is not defined. It could be that `somevar` is defined and initialized but contains a falsy value like `false` or 0.

A better way to check if a variable is defined is to use `typeof`:

```
> var result = "";
> if (typeof somevar !== "undefined") {
    result = "yes";
  }
> result;
""
```

The `typeof` operator always returns a string, and you can compare this string with the string `"undefined"`. Note that the `somevar` variable may have been declared but not assigned a value yet and you'll still get the same result. So, when testing with `typeof` like this, you're really testing whether the variable has any value other than the `undefined` value:

```
> var somevar;
> if (typeof somevar !== "undefined") {
    result = "yes";
  }
> result;
""
> somevar = undefined;
> if (typeof somevar !== "undefined") {
    result = "yes";
  }
> result;
""
```

If a variable is defined and initialized with any value other than `undefined`, its type returned by `typeof` is no longer `"undefined"`, as shown in the following piece of code:

```
> somevar = 123;
> if (typeof somevar !== "undefined") {
```

```
    result = 'yes';
  }
> result;
"yes"
```

Alternative if syntax

When you have a simple condition, you can consider using an alternative `if` syntax. Take a look at this:

```
var a = 1;
var result = '';
if (a === 1) {
  result = "a is one";
} else {
  result = "a is not one";
}
```

You can also write this as:

```
> var a = 1;
> var result = (a === 1) ? "a is one" : "a is not one";
```

You should only use this syntax for simple conditions. Be careful not to abuse it, as it can easily make your code unreadable. Here's an example.

Let's say you want to make sure a number is within a certain range, say between `50` and `100`:

```
> var a = 123;
> a = a > 100 ? 100 : a < 50 ? 50: a;
> a;
100
```

It may not be clear how this code works exactly because of the multiple ?. Adding parentheses makes it a little clearer, as shown in the following code block:

```
> var a = 123;
> a = (a > 100 ? 100 : a < 50) ? 50 : a;
> a;
50
> var a = 123;
> a = a > 100 ? 100 : (a < 50 ? 50 : a);
> a;
100
```

`?:` is called a ternary operator because it takes three operands.

Switch

If you find yourself using an `if` condition and having too many `else...if` parts, you can consider changing the `if` to a `switch`, as follows:

```
var a = '1',
    result = '';
switch (a) {
case 1:
  result = 'Number 1';
  break;
case '1':
  result = 'String 1';
  break;
default:
  result = 'I don't know';
  break;
}
```

The result after executing this is "`String 1`". Let's see what the parts of a `switch` are:

- The `switch` statement.
- An expression in parentheses. The expression most often contains a variable, but can be anything that returns a value.
- A number of `case` blocks enclosed in curly brackets.
- Each `case` statement is followed by an expression. The result of the expression is compared to the expression found after the `switch` statement. If the result of the comparison is `true`, the code that follows the colon after the `case` is executed.
- There is an optional `break` statement to signal the end of the `case` block. If this `break` statement is reached, the `switch` statement is all done. Otherwise, if the `break` is missing, the program execution enters the next `case` block.
- There's an optional default case marked with the `default` statement and followed by a block of code. The `default` case is executed if none of the previous cases evaluated to `true`.

In other words, the step-by-step procedure to execute a `switch` statement is as follows:

1. Evaluate the `switch` expression found in parentheses; remember it.
2. Move to the first case and compare its value with the one from Step 1.
3. If the comparison in Step 2 returns `true`, execute the code in the `case` block.
4. After the `case` block is executed, if there's a `break` statement at the end of it, exit `switch`.
5. If there's no `break` or Step 2 returned `false`, move on to the next `case` block.
6. Repeat steps 2 to 5.
7. If you are still here (no exit in Step 4), execute the code following the `default` statement.

 Indent the code that follows the case lines. You can also indent case from the switch, but that doesn't give you much in terms of readability.

Don't forget to break

Sometimes, you may want to omit the break intentionally, but that's rare. It's called a fall-through and should always be documented because it may look like an accidental omission. On the other hand, sometimes you may want to omit the whole code block following a case and have two cases sharing the same code. This is fine, but it doesn't change the rule that if there's code that follows a case statement, this code should end with a break. In terms of indentation, aligning the break with the case or with the code inside the case is a personal preference; again, being consistent is what matters.

Use the default case. This helps you make sure that you always have a meaningful result after the switch statement, even if none of the cases matches the value being switched.

Loops

The `if...else` and `switch` statements allow your code to take different paths, as if you're at a crossroad, and decide which way to go depending on a condition. Loops, on the other hand, allow your code to take a few roundabouts before merging back into the main road. How many repetitions? That depends on the result of evaluating a condition before (or after) each iteration.

Let's say you are (your program execution is) traveling from **A** to **B**. At some point, you will reach a place where you have to evaluate a condition, **C**. The result of evaluating **C** tells you whether you should go into a loop, **L**. You make one iteration and arrive at **C** again. Then, you evaluate the condition once again to see if another iteration is needed. Eventually, you move on your way to **B**:

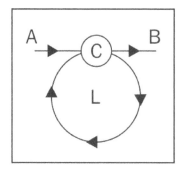

An infinite loop is when the condition is always `true`, and your code gets stuck in the loop forever. This is, of course, a logical error, and you should look out for such scenarios.

In JavaScript, the following are the four types of loops:

- `while` loops
- `do-while` loops
- `for` loops
- `for-in` loops

While loops

The `while` loops are the simplest type of iteration. They look like the following:

```
var i = 0;
while (i < 10) {
   i++;
}
```

The `while` statement is followed by a condition in parentheses and a code block in curly brackets. As long as the condition evaluates to `true`, the code block is executed over and over again.

Do-while loops

The do...while loops are a slight variation of while loops. An example is shown as follows:

```
var i = 0;
do {
  i++;
} while (i < 10);
```

Here, the do statement is followed by a code block and a condition after the block. This means that the code block is always executed, at least once, before the condition is evaluated.

If you initialize i to 11 instead of 0 in the last two examples, the code block in the first example (the while loop) will not be executed, and i will still be 11 at the end, while in the second (the do...while loop), the code block will be executed once and i will become 12.

For loops

The for loop is the most widely used type of loop, and you should make sure you're comfortable with this one. It requires just a little bit more in terms of syntax:

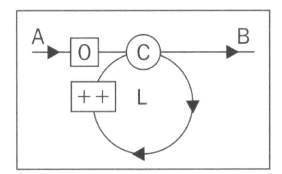

In addition to the **C** condition and the **L** code block, you have the following:

- **Initialization**: This is the code that is executed before you even enter the loop (marked with **0** in the diagram)
- **Increment**: This is the code that is executed after every iteration (marked with **++** in the diagram)

The following is the most widely used `for` loop pattern:

- In the initialization part, you can define a variable (or set the initial value of an existing variable), most often called `i`
- In the condition part, you can compare `i` to a boundary value, such as `i < 100`
- In the increment part, you can increase `i` by 1, such as `i++`

Here's an example:

```
var punishment = '';
for (var i = 0; i < 100; i++) {
  punishment += 'I will never do this again, ';
}
```

All three parts (initialization, condition, and increment) can contain multiple expressions separated by commas. Say you want to rewrite the example and define the variable `punishment` inside the initialization part of the loop:

```
for (var i = 0, punishment = ''; i < 100; i++) {
  punishment += 'I will never do this again, ';
}
```

Can you move the body of the loop inside the increment part? Yes, you can, especially as it's a one-liner. This gives you a loop that looks a little awkward, as it has no body. Note that this is just an intellectual exercise; it's not recommended that you write awkward-looking code:

```
for (
  var i = 0, punishment = '';
  i < 100;
  i++, punishment += 'I will never do this again, ') {

  // nothing here

}
```

These three parts are all optional. Here's another way of rewriting the same example:

```
var i = 0, punishment = '';
for (;;) {
  punishment += 'I will never do this again, ';
  if (++i == 100) {
    break;
  }
}
```

Although the last rewrite works exactly the same way as the original, it's longer and harder to read. It's also possible to achieve the same result using a `while` loop. But, the `for` loops make the code tighter and more robust because the mere syntax of the `for` loop makes you think about the three parts (initialization, condition, and increment), and thus helps you reconfirm your logic and avoid situations such as being stuck in an infinite loop.

The `for` loops can be nested within each other. Here's an example of a loop that is nested inside another loop and assembles a string containing ten rows and ten columns of asterisks. Think of `i` being the row and `j` being the column of an image:

```
var res = '\n';
for (var i = 0; i < 10; i++) {
  for (var j = 0; j < 10; j++) {
    res += '* ';
  }
  res += '\n';
}
```

The result is a string, as shown here:

```
"
* * * * * * * * * *
* * * * * * * * * *
* * * * * * * * * *
* * * * * * * * * *
* * * * * * * * * *
* * * * * * * * * *
* * * * * * * * * *
* * * * * * * * * *
* * * * * * * * * *
* * * * * * * * * *
"
```

Here's another example that uses nested loops and a modulo operation to draw a snowflake-like result:

```
var res = '\n', i, j;
for (i = 1; i <= 7; i++) {
  for (j = 1; j <= 15; j++) {
    res += (i * j) % 8 ? ' ' : '*';
  }
  res += '\n';
}
```

The result is as follows:

```
"
             *
      *      *      *
             *
   *  *  *  *  *  *  *
             *
      *      *      *
             *

"
```

For...in loops

The `for...in` loop is used to iterate over the elements of an array, or an object, as you'll see later. This is its only use; it cannot be used as a general-purpose repetition mechanism to replace `for` or `while`. Let's see an example of using a `for-in` to loop through the elements of an array. But, bear in mind that this is for informational purposes only, as `for...in` is mostly suitable for objects and the regular `for` loop should be used for arrays.

In this example, you can iterate over all of the elements of an array and print out the index (the key) and the value of each element, for example:

```
// example for information only
// for-in loops are used for objects
// regular for is better suited for arrays

var a = ['a', 'b', 'c', 'x', 'y', 'z'];

var result = '\n';

for (var i in a) {
   result += 'index: ' + i + ', value: ' + a[i] + '\n';
}
The result is:
"
index: 0, value: a
index: 1, value: b
index: 2, value: c
index: 3, value: x
index: 4, value: y
index: 5, value: z
"
```

Comments

One last thing for this chapter–comments. Inside your JavaScript program, you can put comments. These are ignored by the JavaScript engine and don't have any effect on how the program works. But they can be invaluable when you revisit your code after a few months, or transfer the code to someone else for maintenance.

The following two types of comments are allowed:

- Single line comments start with `//` and end at the end of the line.
- Multiline comments start with `/*` and end with `*/` on the same line or any subsequent line. Note that any code in between the comment start and the comment end is ignored.

Some examples are as follows:

```
// beginning of line

var a = 1; // anywhere on the line

/* multi-line comment on a single line */

/*
   comment that spans several lines
*/
```

There are even utilities, such as JSDoc and YUIDoc, that can parse your code and extract meaningful documentation based on your comments.

Exercises

1. What is the result of executing each of these lines in the console? Why?

```
> var a; typeof a;
> var s = '1s'; s++;
> !!"false";
> !!undefined;
> typeof -Infinity;
> 10 % "0";
> undefined == null;
> false === "";
> typeof "2E+2";
> a = 3e+3; a++;
```

2. What is the value of v after the following?

```
> var v = v || 10;
```

   Experiment by first setting v to 100, 0, or null.

3. Write a small program that prints out the multiplication table. Hint: use a loop nested inside another loop.

Summary

In this chapter, you learned a lot about the basic building blocks of a JavaScript program. Now you know the following primitive data types:

- Number
- String
- Boolean
- Undefined
- Null

You also know quite a few operators, which are as follows:

- **Arithmetic operators**: +, -, *, /, and %
- **Increment operators**: ++ and --
- **Assignment operators**: =, +=, -=, *=, /=, and %=
- **Special operators**: typeof and delete
- **Logical operators**: &&, ||, and !
- **Comparison operators**: ==, ===, !=, !==, <, >, >=, and <=
- **The ternary operator**: ?

Then you learned how to use arrays to store and access data, and finally you saw different ways to control the flow of your program using conditions (if...else or switch) and loops (while, do...while, for, and for...in).

This is quite a bit of information; give yourself a well-deserved pat on the back before diving into the next chapter. More fun is coming up!

3
Functions

Mastering functions is an important skill when you learn any programming language, and even more so when it comes to JavaScript. This is because JavaScript has many uses for functions, and much of the language's flexibility and expressiveness comes from them. Where most programming languages have a special syntax for some object-oriented features, JavaScript just uses functions. This chapter will cover the following topics:

- How to define and use a function
- Passing arguments to a function
- Predefined functions that are available to you for free
- The scope of variables in JavaScript
- The concept that functions are just data, albeit a special type of data

Understanding these topics will provide a solid base that will allow you to dive into the second part of the chapter, which shows some interesting applications of functions, as follows:

- Using anonymous functions
- Callbacks
- Immediate (self-invoking) functions
- Inner functions (functions defined inside other functions)
- Functions that return functions
- Functions that redefine themselves
- Closures

What is a function?

Functions allow you to group together a code, give it a name, and reuse it later, addressing it by the name you gave it. Let's consider the following code as an example:

```
function sum(a, b) {
  var c = a + b;
  return c;
}
```

The parts that make up a function are shown as follows:

- The `function` keyword.
- The name of the function; in this case, `sum`.
- The function parameters; in this case, `a` and `b`. A function can take any number of parameters, or no parameters, separated by commas.
- A code block, also called the body of the function.
- The `return` statement. A function always returns a value. If it doesn't return a value explicitly, it implicitly returns the value `undefined`.

Note that a function can only return a single value. If you need to return more values, you can simply return an array that contains all of the values you need as elements of this array.

The preceding syntax is called a function declaration. It's just one of the ways to create a function in JavaScript, and more ways are coming up.

Calling a function

In order to make use of a function, you will need to call it. You can call a function simply using its name, optionally, followed by any number of values in parentheses. To invoke a function is another way of saying to call.

Let's call the `sum()` function, passing two arguments and assigning the value that the function returns to the variable `result`:

```
> var result = sum(1, 2);
> result;
3
```

Parameters

When defining a function, you can specify what parameters the function expects to receive when it's called. A function may not require any parameters, but if it does, and you forget to pass them, JavaScript will assign the undefined value to the ones you skipped. In the next example, the function call returns NaN because it tries to sum 1 and undefined:

```
> sum(1);
NaN
```

Technically speaking, there is a difference between parameters and arguments, although the two are often used interchangeably. Parameters are defined together with the function, while arguments are passed to the function when it's called. Consider the following example:

```
> function sum(a, b) {
    return a + b;
  }
> sum(1, 2);
```

Here, a and b are parameters, while 1 and 2 are arguments.

JavaScript is not picky at all when it comes to accepting arguments. If you pass more than the function expects, the extra ones will be silently ignored, as shown in the following example:

```
> sum(1, 2, 3, 4, 5);
3
```

What's more, you can create functions that are flexible about the number of parameters they accept. This is possible thanks to the special value arguments that are created automatically inside each function. Here's a function that simply returns whatever arguments are passed to it:

```
> function args() {
    return arguments;
  }
> args();
[]
> args( 1, 2, 3, 4, true, 'ninja');
[1, 2, 3, 4, true, "ninja"]
```

Using `arguments`, you can improve the `sum()` function to accept any number of arguments and add them all up, as shown in the following example:

```
function sumOnSteroids() {
  var i,
      res = 0,
      number_of_params = arguments.length;
  for (i = 0; i < number_of_params; i++) {
    res += arguments[i];
  }
  return res;
}
```

If you test this function by calling it with a different number of arguments, or even none at all, you can verify that it works as expected, as you can see in the following example:

```
> sumOnSteroids(1, 1, 1);
3
> sumOnSteroids(1, 2, 3, 4);
10
> sumOnSteroids(1, 2, 3, 4, 4, 3, 2, 1);
20
> sumOnSteroids(5);
5
> sumOnSteroids();
0
```

The `arguments.length` expression returns the number of arguments passed when the function was called. Don't worry if the syntax is unfamiliar, we'll examine it in detail in the next chapter. You'll also see that `arguments` is not an array (although it sure looks like one), but an array-like object.

ES6 introduces several important improvements around function parameters. ES6 function parameters can now have default values, rest parameters, and allows destructuring. The next section discusses each of these concepts in detail.

Default parameters

Function parameters can be assigned default values. While calling the function, if a parameter is omitted, the default value assigned to the parameter is used:

```
function render(fog_level=0, spark_level=100){
  console.log(`Fog Level: ${fog_level} and spark_level:
   ${spark_level}`)
}
render(10); //Fog Level: 10 and spark_level: 100
```

In this example, we are omitting the `spark_level` parameter, and hence the default value assigned to the parameter is used. It is important to note that `undefined` is considered as an absence of parameter value; consider the following line of code, for example:

```
render(undefined,10); //Fog Level: 0 and spark_level: 10
```

While providing default values of parameters, it is possible to refer to other parameters as well:

```
function t(fog_level=1, spark_level=fog_level){
  console.log(`Fog Level: ${fog_level} and spark_level:
   ${spark_level}`)
  //Fog Level: 10 and spark_level: 10
}
function s(fog_level=10, spark_level = fog_level*10){
  console.log(`Fog Level: ${fog_level} and spark_level:
   ${spark_level}`)
  //Fog Level: 10 and spark_level: 100
}
t(10);
s(10);
```

Default parameters have their own scope; this scope is sandwiched between the outer function scope and the inner scope of the function. If the parameter is shadowed by a variable in inner scope, surprisingly, the inner variable is not available. The following example will help explain this:

```
var scope="outer_scope";
function scoper(val=scope){
  var scope="inner_scope";
  console.log(val); //outer_scope
}
scoper();
```

You may expect `val` to get shadowed by the inner definition of the `scope` variable, but as the default parameters have their own scope, the value assigned to `val` is unaffected by the inner scope.

Rest parameters

ES6 introduces rest parameters. Rest parameters allow us to send an arbitrary number of parameters to a function in the form of an array. Rest parameter can only be the last one in the list of parameters, and there can only be one rest parameter. Putting a rest operator(. . .) before the last formal parameter indicates that parameter is a rest parameter. The following example shows adding a rest operator before the last formal parameter:

```
function sayThings(tone, ...quotes){
  console.log(Array.isArray(quotes)); //true
  console.log(`In ${tone} voice, I say ${quotes}`)
}
sayThings("Morgan Freeman","Something serious","
 Imploding Universe"," Amen");
//In Morgan Freeman voice, I say Something serious,
 Imploding Universe,Amen
```

The first parameter passed to the function is received in `tone`, while the rest of the parameters are received as an array. Variable arguments (var-args) have been part of several other languages and a welcome edition to ES6. Rest parameters can replace the slightly controversial `arguments` variable. The major difference between rest parameters and the `arguments` variable is that the rest parameters are real arrays. All array methods are available to rest parameters.

Spread operators

A spread operator looks exactly like a rest operator but performs the exact opposite function. Spread operators are used while providing arguments while calling a function or defining an array. The spread operator takes an array and splits its element into individual variables. The following example illustrates how the spread operator provides a much clearer syntax while calling functions that take an array as an argument:

```
function sumAll(a,b,c){
  return a+b+c
}
var numbers = [6,7,8]
//ES5 way of passing array as an argument of a function
console.log(sumAll.apply(null,numbers)); //21
//ES6 Spread operator
console.log(sumAll(...numbers))//21
```

In ES5, it is common to use the `apply()` function when passing an array as an argument to a function. In the preceding example, we have an array we need to pass to a function where the function accepts three variables. The ES5 method of passing an array to this function uses the `apply()` function, where the second argument allows an array to be passed to the function being called. ES6 spread operators give a much cleaner and precise way to deal with this situation. While calling `sumAll()`, we use the spread operator(`...`) and pass the `numbers` array to the function call. The array is then split into individual variables–`a`, `b`, and `c`.

Spread operators improve the capabilities of arrays in JavaScript. If you want to create an array that is made up of another array, the existing array syntax does not support this. You have to use `push`, `splice`, and `concat` to achieve this. However, using spread operators, this becomes trivial:

```
var midweek = ['Wed', 'Thu'];
var weekend = ['Sat', 'Sun'];
var week = ['Mon','Tue', ...midweek, 'Fri', ...weekend];
 //["Mon","Tue","Wed","Thu","Fri","Sat","Sun"]
console.log(week);
```

In the preceding example, we are constructing a `week` array using two arrays, `midweek` and `weekend`, using the spread operator.

Predefined functions

There are a number of functions that are built into the JavaScript engine and are available for you to use. Let's take a look at them. While doing so, you'll have a chance to experiment with functions, their arguments and return values, and become comfortable working with functions. The following is a list of the built-in functions:

- parseInt()
- parseFloat()
- isNaN()
- isFinite()
- encodeURI()
- decodeURI()
- encodeURIComponent()
- decodeURIComponent()
- eval()

The black box function

Often, when you invoke functions, your program doesn't need to know how these functions work internally. You can think of a function as a black box, give it some values (as input arguments), and then take the output result it returns. This is true for any function–one that's built into the JavaScript engine, one that you create, or one that a co-worker or someone else created.

parseInt()

The `parseInt()` function takes any type of input (most often a string) and tries to make an integer out of it. If it fails, it returns `NaN`, as shown in the following code:

```
> parseInt('123');
123
> parseInt('abc123');
NaN
> parseInt('1abc23');
1
> parseInt('123abc');
123
```

The function accepts an optional second parameter, which is the radix, telling the function what type of number to expect—decimal, hexadecimal, binary, and so on. For example, trying to extract a decimal number out of the FF string makes no sense, so the result is NaN, but if you try FF as a hexadecimal, then you get 255, as shown in the following piece of code:

```
> parseInt('FF', 10);
NaN
> parseInt('FF', 16);
255
```

Another example would be parsing a string with a base 10 (decimal) and base 8 (octal):

```
> parseInt('0377', 10);
377
> parseInt('0377', 8);
255
```

If you omit the second argument when calling parseInt(), the function will assume 10 (a decimal), with the following exceptions:

- If you pass a string beginning with 0x, then the radix is assumed to be 16 (a hexadecimal number is assumed).
- If the string you pass starts with 0, the function assumes radix 8 (an octal number is assumed). Consider the following examples:

```
> parseInt('377');
377
> console.log(0o377);
255
> parseInt('0x377');
887
```

The safest thing to do is to always specify the radix. If you omit the radix, your code will probably still work in 99 percent of cases (because most often you parse decimals); however, every once in a while, it might cause you a bit of hair loss while debugging some edge cases. For example, imagine you have a form field that accepts calendar days or months and the user types 06 or 08.

ECMAScript 5 removes the octal literal values and avoids the confusion with parseInt() and unspecified radix.

parseFloat()

The parseFloat() function is similar to the parseInt() function, but it also looks for decimals when trying to figure out a number from your input. This function takes only one parameter, which is as follows:

```
> parseFloat('123');
123
> parseFloat('1.23');
1.23
> parseFloat('1.23abc.00');
1.23
> parseFloat('a.bc1.23');
NaN
```

As with parseInt(), parseFloat() gives up at the first occurrence of an unexpected character, even though the rest of the string might have usable numbers in it:

```
> parseFloat('a123.34');
NaN
> parseFloat('12a3.34');
12
```

The parseFloat() function understands exponents in the input (unlike parseInt()):

```
> parseFloat('123e-2');
1.23
> parseFloat('1e10');
10000000000
> parseInt('1e10');
1
```

isNaN()

Using `isNaN()`, you can check if an input value is a valid number that can safely be used in arithmetic operations. This function is also a convenient way to check whether `parseInt()`, `parseFloat()`, or any arithmetic operation succeeded:

```
> isNaN(NaN);
true
> isNaN(123);
false
> isNaN(1.23);
false
> isNaN(parseInt('abc123'));
true
```

The function will also try to convert the input to a number:

```
> isNaN('1.23');
false
> isNaN('a1.23');
true
```

The `isNaN()` function is useful because the special value `NaN` is not equal to anything, including itself. In other words, `NaN === NaN` is `false`. So, `NaN` cannot be used to check if a value is a valid number.

isFinite()

The `isFinite()` function checks whether the input is a number that is neither `Infinity` nor `NaN`:

```
> isFinite(Infinity);
false
> isFinite(-Infinity);
false
> isFinite(12);
true
> isFinite(1e308);
true
> isFinite(1e309);
false
```

If you are wondering about the results returned by the last two calls, remember from the previous chapter that the biggest number in JavaScript is `1.7976931348623157e+308`, so `1e309` is effectively infinity.

Encode/decode URIs

In a **Uniform Resource Locator** (**URL**) or a **Uniform Resource Identifier** (**URI**), some characters have special meanings. If you want to escape those characters, you can use the encodeURI() or encodeURIComponent() functions. The first one will return a usable URL, while the second one assumes you're only passing a part of the URL, such as a query string for example, and will encode all applicable characters, as follows:

```
> var url = 'http://www.packtpub.com/script.php?q=this and that';
> encodeURI(url);
"http://www.packtpub.com/script.php?q=this%20and%20that"
> encodeURIComponent(url);
"http%3A%2F%2Fwww.packtpub.com%2Fscript.php%3Fq%3Dthis%20and%20that"
```

The opposites of encodeURI() and encodeURIComponent() are decodeURI() and decodeURIComponent(), respectively.

Sometimes, in legacy code, you might see the functions escape() and unescape() used to encode and decode URLs, but these functions have been deprecated; they encode differently and should not be used.

eval()

The eval() function takes a string input and executes it as a JavaScript code, as follows:

```
> eval('var ii = 2;');
> ii;
2
```

So, eval('var ii = 2;') is the same as var ii = 2;

The eval() function can be useful sometimes, but it should be avoided if there are other options. Most of the time, there are alternatives, and in most cases, the alternatives are more elegant and easier to write and maintain. *Eval is evil* is a mantra you can often hear from seasoned JavaScript programmers. The drawbacks of using eval() are as follows:

- **Security**: JavaScript is powerful, which also means it can cause damage. If you don't trust the source of the input you pass to eval(), just don't use it.
- **Performance**: It's slower to evaluate live code than to have the code directly in the script.

A bonus – the alert() function

Let's take a look at another common function–`alert()`. It's not part of the core JavaScript (it's nowhere to be found in the ECMA specification), but it's provided by the host environment–the browser. It shows a string of text in a message box. It can also be used as a primitive debugging tool, although the debuggers in modern browsers are much better suited for this purpose.

Here's a screenshot showing the result of executing the `alert("Hi There")` code:

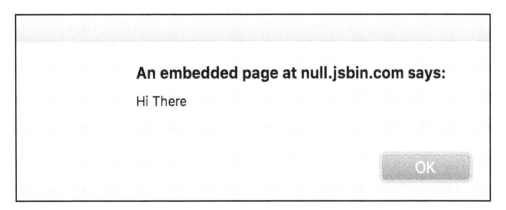

Before using this function, bear in mind that it blocks the browser thread, meaning that no other code will be executed until the user closes the alert. If you have a busy Ajax-type application, it's generally not a good idea to use `alert()`.

Scope of variables

It's important to note, especially if you have come to JavaScript from another language, that variables in JavaScript are not defined in a block scope, but in a function scope. This means that if a variable is defined inside a function, it's not visible outside of the function. However, if it's defined inside an `if` or a `for` code block, it's visible outside the block. The term global variables describes variables you define outside of any function (in the global program code), as opposed to local variables, which are defined inside a function. The code inside a function has access to all global variables as well as to its own local ones.

In the next example:

- The f() function has access to the global variable
- Outside the f() function, the local variable doesn't exist

```
var global = 1;
function f() {
   var local = 2;
   global++;
   return global;
}
```

Let's test this:

```
> f();
2
> f();
3
> local;
ReferenceError: local is not defined
```

It's also important to note that if you don't use var to declare a variable, this variable is automatically assigned a global scope. Let's see an example:

What happened? The `f()` function contains the `local` variable. Before calling the function, the variable doesn't exist. When you call the function for the first time, the `local` variable is created with a global scope. Then, if you access the `local` variable outside the function, it will be available.

Best practice tips
Minimize the number of global variables in order to avoid naming collisions. Imagine two people working on two different functions in the same script, and they both decide to use the same name for their global variable. This could easily lead to unexpected results and hard-to-find bugs. Always declare your variables with the `var` statement. Consider a single `var` pattern. Define all variables needed in your function at the very top of the function so you have a single place to look for variables and, hopefully, prevent accidental globals.

Variable hoisting

Here's an interesting example that shows an important aspect of local versus global scoping:

```
var a = 123;

function f() {
  alert(a);
  var a = 1;
  alert(a);
}

f();
```

You might expect that the first `alert()` function will display `123` (the value of the global variable a) and the second will display `1` (the local variable a). But, this is not the case. The first alert will show `undefined`. This is because, inside the function, the local scope is more important than the global scope. So, a local variable overwrites any global variable with the same name. At the time of the first `alert()`, the a variable was not yet defined (hence the `undefined` value), but it still existed in the local space due to the special behavior called **hoisting**.

When your JavaScript program execution enters a new function, all the variables declared anywhere in the function are moved, elevated, or hoisted to the top of the function. This is an important concept to keep in mind. Further, only the declaration is hoisted, meaning only the presence of the variable is moved to the top. Any assignments stay where they are. In the preceding example, the declaration of the local variable a was hoisted to the top. Only the declaration was hoisted, but not the assignment to 1. It's as if the function was written in the following way:

```
var a = 123;

function f() {
  var a; // same as: var a = undefined;
  alert(a); // undefined
  a = 1;
  alert(a); // 1
}
```

You can also adopt the single var pattern mentioned previously in the best practice section. In this case, you'll be doing a sort of manual variable hoisting to prevent confusion with the JavaScript hoisting behavior.

Block scope

ES6 provides additional scope while declaring variables. We looked at function scope and how it affects variables declared with the var keyword. If you are coding in ES6, block scope will mostly replace your need to use variables declared using var. Although, if you are still with ES5, we want you to make sure that you look at hoisting behavior carefully.

ES6 introduces the let and const keywords that allow us to declare variables.

Variables declared with let are block-scoped. They exist only within the current block. Variables declared with var are function scoped, as we saw earlier. The following example illustrates the block scope:

```
var a = 1;
{
    let a = 2;
    console.log( a );    // 2
}
console.log( a );        // 1
```

The scope between an opening brace' { ' and a closing brace ' } ' is a block. If you are coming from a background in Java or C/C++, the concept of a block scope will be very familiar to you. In those languages, programmers introduced blocks just to define a scope. In JavaScript, however, there was a need to idiomatically introduce blocks as they didn't have a scope associated to it. However, ES6 allows you to create block-scoped variables using the `let` keyword. As you can see in the preceding example, variable `a` created inside the block is available within the block. While declaring block-scoped variables, it is generally recommended to add the `let` declaration at the top of the block. Let's look at another example to clearly distinguish function and block scope:

```
function swap(a,b){ // <--function scope starts here
  if(a>0 && b>0){   // <--block scope starts here
    let tmp=a;
    a=b;
    b=tmp;
  }                 // <--block scope ends here
  console.log(a,b);
  console.log(tmp); // tmp is not defined as it is available
   only in the block scope
  return [a,b];
}
swap(1,2);
```

As you can see, `tmp` is declared with `let` and is available only in the block in which it was defined. For all practical purposes, you should maximize your use of block-scoped variables. Unless there is something very specific you are trying to do that makes it necessary for you to use `var` declarations, make sure you prefer block scoped variables. However, incorrectly using the `let` keyword can cause a couple of problems. First, you cannot redeclare the same variable within the same function or block scope using the `let` keyword:

```
function blocker(x){
  if(x){
    let f;
    let f; //duplicate declaration "f"
  }
}
```

In ES6, variables declared by the `let` keyword are hoisted to block scope. However, referencing the variable before its declaration is an error.

Another keyword introduced in ES6 is `const`. A variable declared with the `const` keyword creates a read-only reference to a value. This does not mean that the value held by the reference is immutable. However, the variable identifier cannot be reassigned. Constants are block-scoped just like variables created using the `let` keyword. Also, you have to assign a value to the variable while declaring them.

Although it sounds like it does, `const` has nothing to do with immutable values. Constants create immutable binding. This is an important distinction and needs to be understood correctly. Let's consider the following example:

```
const car = {}
car.tyres = 4
```

This is a valid code; here we are assigning value `{}` to a constant `car`. Once assigned, this reference cannot be changed. In ES6, you should do the following:

- Use `const` where possible. Use them for all variables whose values don't change:

```
Use let
```

- Avoid `var`.

Functions are data

Functions in JavaScript are actually data. This is an important concept that we'll need later on. This means that you can create a function and assign it to a variable, as follows:

```
var f = function () {
  return 1;
};
```

This way of defining a function is sometimes referred to as **function literal notation**.

The `function () { return 1; }` part is a **function expression**. A function expression can optionally have a name, in which case it becomes a **named function expression** (NFE). So, this is also allowed, although rarely seen in practice (and causes IE to mistakenly create two variables in the enclosing scope–f and `myFunc`):

```
var f = function myFunc() {
  return 1;
};
```

As you can see, there's no difference between a named function expression and a function declaration. But they are, in fact, different. The only way to distinguish between the two is to look at the context in which they are used. Function declarations may only appear in program code (in a body of another function or in the main program). You'll see many more examples of functions later on in the book that will clarify these concepts.

When you use the `typeof` operator on a variable that holds a function value, it returns the string "`function`" as shown in the following example:

```
> function define() {
    return 1;
  }

> var express = function () {
    return 1;
  };

> typeof define;
"function"

> typeof express;
"function"
```

So, JavaScript functions are data, but a special kind of data with the following two important features:

- They contain code
- They are executable (they can be invoked)

As you have seen before, the way to execute a function is by adding parentheses after its name. As the next example demonstrates, this works regardless of how the function was defined. In the example, you can also see how a function is treated as a regular value; it can be copied to a different variable, as follows:

```
> var sum = function (a, b) {
    return a + b;
  };

> var add = sum;
> typeof add;
function
> add(1, 2);
3
```

As functions are data assigned to variables, the same rules for naming functions apply as for naming variables–a function name cannot start with a number and it can contain any combination of letters, numbers, the underscore character, and the dollar sign.

Anonymous functions

As you now know, there exists a function expression syntax where you can have a function defined like the following:

```
var f = function (a) {
  return a;
};
```

This is also often called an **anonymous function** (as it doesn't have a name), especially when such a function expression is used even without assigning it to a variable. In this case, there can be two elegant uses for such anonymous functions, which are as follows:

- You can pass an anonymous function as a parameter to another function. The receiving function can do something useful with the function that you pass.
- You can define an anonymous function and execute it right away.

Let's see these two applications of anonymous functions in more detail.

Callback functions

As a function is just like any other data assigned to a variable, it can be defined, copied, and also passed as an argument to other functions.

Here's an example of a function that accepts two functions as parameters, executes them, and returns the sum of what each of them returns:

```
function invokeAdd(a, b) {
  return a() + b();
}
```

Now, let's define two simple additional functions using a function declaration pattern that only returns hardcoded values:

```
function one() {
    return 1;
}
function two() {
    return 2;
}
```

Now you can pass those functions to the original function, `invokeAdd()`, and get the following result:

```
> invokeAdd(one, two);
3
```

Another example of passing a function as a parameter is to use anonymous functions (function expressions). Instead of defining `one()` and `two()`, you can simply do the following:

```
> invokeAdd(function () {return 1; }, function () {return 2; });
3
```

Or, you can make it more readable, as shown in the following code:

```
> invokeAdd(
    function () { return 1; },
    function () { return 2; }
);
3
```

Or, you can do the following:

```
> invokeAdd(
    function () {
      return 1;
    },
    function () {
      return 2;
    }
);
3
```

When you pass a function, A, to another function, B, and then B executes A, it's often said that A is a **callback** function. If A doesn't have a name, then you can say that it's an anonymous callback function.

When are callback functions useful? Let's see some examples that demonstrate the benefits of callback functions, namely:

- They let you pass functions without the need to name them, which means there are fewer variables floating around
- You can delegate the responsibility of calling a function to another function, which means there is less code to write
- They can help with performance by deferring the execution or by unblocking calls

Callback examples

Take a look at this common scenario–you have a function that returns a value, which you then pass to another function. In our example, the first function, `multiplyByTwo()`, accepts three parameters, loops through them, multiplies them by two, and returns an array containing the result. The second function, `addOne()`, takes a value, adds one to it, and returns it, as follows:

```
function multiplyByTwo(a, b, c) {
  var i, ar = [];
  for (i = 0; i < 3; i++) {
    ar[i] = arguments[i] * 2;
  }
  return ar;
}

function addOne(a) {
  return a + 1;
}
```

Let's test these functions:

```
> multiplyByTwo(1, 2, 3);
[2, 4, 6]
> addOne(100);
101
```

Now, let's say you want to have an array, `myarr`, that contains three elements, and each of the elements is to be passed through both functions. First, let's start with a call to `multiplyByTwo()`:

```
> var myarr = [];
> myarr = multiplyByTwo(10, 20, 30);
[20, 40, 60]
```

Now, loop through each element, passing it to addOne():

```
> for (var i = 0; i < 3; i++) {
    myarr[i] = addOne(myarr[i]);
  }
> myarr;
[21, 41, 61]
```

As you can see, everything works fine, but there's room for improvement. For example, there were two loops. Loops can be expensive if they go through a lot of repetitions. You can achieve the same result with only one loop. Here's how to modify multiplyByTwo() so that it accepts a callback function and invokes that callback on every iteration:

```
function multiplyByTwo(a, b, c, callback) {
  var i, ar = [];
  for (i = 0; i < 3; i++) {
    ar[i] = callback(arguments[i] * 2);
  }
  return ar;
}
```

Using the modified function, all the work is done with just one function call, which passes the start values and the callback function, as follows:

```
> myarr = multiplyByTwo(1, 2, 3, addOne);
[3, 5, 7]
```

Instead of defining addOne(), you can use an anonymous function, therefore saving an extra global variable:

```
> multiplyByTwo(1, 2, 3, function (a) {
    return a + 1;
  });
[3, 5, 7]
```

Anonymous functions are easy to change should the need arise:

```
> multiplyByTwo(1, 2, 3, function (a) {
    return a + 2;
  });
[4, 6, 8]
```

Immediate functions

So far, we have discussed using anonymous functions as callbacks. Let's see another application of an anonymous function–calling a function immediately after it's defined. Here's an example:

```
(
  function () {
    alert('boo');
  }
)();
```

The syntax may look a little scary at first, but all you do is simply place a function expression inside parentheses followed by another set of parentheses. The second set says execute now and is also the place to put any arguments that your anonymous function might accept, for example:

```
(
  function (name) {
    alert('Hello ' + name + '!');
  }
)('dude');
```

Alternatively, you can move the closing of the first set of parentheses to the end. Both of these work:

```
(function () {
  // ...
}());

// vs.

(function () {
  // ...
})();
```

One good application of immediate (self-invoking) anonymous functions is when you want to have some work done without creating extra global variables. A drawback, of course, is that you cannot execute the same function twice. This makes immediate functions best suited for one-off or initialization tasks.

An immediate function can also optionally return a value if you need one. It's not uncommon to see code that looks like the following:

```
var result = (function () {
  // something complex with
  // temporary local variables...
  // ...
  // return something;
}());
```

In this case, you don't need to wrap the function expression in parentheses; you only need the parentheses that invoke the function. So, the following piece of code also works:

```
var result = function () {
  // something complex with
  // temporary local variables
  // return something;
}();
```

This syntax works, but may look slightly confusing; without reading the end of the function, you don't know if `result` is a function or the return value of the immediate function.

Inner (private) functions

Bearing in mind that a function is just like any other value, there's nothing that stops you from defining a function inside another function, here's the example:

```
function outer(param) {
  function inner(theinput) {
    return theinput * 2;
  }
  return 'The result is ' + inner(param);
}
```

Using a function expression, this can also be written as follows:

```
var outer = function (param) {
  var inner = function (theinput) {
    return theinput * 2;
  };
  return 'The result is ' + inner(param);
};
```

When you call the global `outer()` function, it will internally call the local `inner()` function. As `inner()` is local, it's not accessible outside `outer()`, so you can say it's a private function:

```
> outer(2);
"The result is 4"
> outer(8);
"The result is 16"
> inner(2);
ReferenceError: inner is not defined
```

The benefits of using private functions are as follows:

- You can keep the global namespace clean, which is less likely to cause naming collisions
- Privacy–you can expose only those functions to the outside world that you decide, and keep the functionality that is not meant to be consumed by the rest of the application to yourself

Functions that return functions

As mentioned earlier, a function always returns a value, and if it doesn't do it explicitly with `return`, then it does so implicitly by returning `undefined`. A function can return only one value, and this value can just as easily be another function, for example:

```
function a() {
  alert('A!');
  return function () {
    alert('B!');
  };
}
```

In this example, the `a()` function does its job (says `A!`) and returns another function that does something else (says `B!`). You can assign the return value to a variable and then use this variable as a normal function, as follows:

```
> var newFunc = a();
> newFunc();
```

Here, the first line will alert A! and the second will alert B!.

If you want to execute the returned function immediately without assigning it to a new variable, you can simply use another set of parentheses. The end result will be the same:

```
> a()();
```

Function, rewrite thyself!

As a function can return a function, you can use the new function to replace the old one. Continuing with the previous example, you can take the value returned by the call to a() to overwrite the actual a() function:

```
> a = a();
```

The preceding line of code alerts A!, but the next time you call a() it alerts B!. This is useful when a function has some initial one-off work to do. The function overwrites itself after the first call in order to avoid doing unnecessary repetitive work every time it's called.

In the preceding example, the function was redefined from the outside and the returned value was assigned back to the function. But, the function can actually rewrite itself from the inside, as shown in the following example:

```
function a() {
  alert('A!');
  a = function () {
    alert('B!');
  };
}
```

If you call this function for the first time, it will do the following:

- Alert A! (consider this as being the one-off preparatory work)
- Redefine the global variable a and assigning a new function to it

Every subsequent time that the function is called, it will alert B!.

Here's another example that combines several of the techniques discussed in the last few sections of this chapter:

```
var a = (function () {

    function someSetup () {
        var setup = 'done';
    }

    function actualWork () {
        alert ('Worky-worky');
    }

    someSetup ();
    return actualWork;

}());
```

From this example, you can note the following things:

- You have private functions; `someSetup()` and `actualWork()`.
- You have an immediate function: an anonymous function that calls itself using the parentheses following its definition.
- The function executes for the first time, calls `someSetup()`, and then returns a reference to the `actualWork` variable, which is a function. Notice that there are no parentheses in the `return` statement because you're returning a function reference, not the result of invoking this function.
- As the whole thing starts with `var a =`, the value returned by the self-invoked function is assigned to `a`.

If you want to test your understanding of the topics just discussed, answer the following questions. What will the preceding code alert be in the following cases:

- It is initially loaded?
- You call `a()` afterwards?

These techniques could be really useful when working in the browser environment. Different browsers can have different ways of achieving the same result. If you know that the browser features won't change between function calls, you can have a function determine the best way to do the work in the current browser, then redefine itself so that the browser capability detection is done only once. You'll see concrete examples of this scenario later in this book.

Closures

The rest of the chapter is about closures (what better way to close a chapter?). Closures can be a little hard to grasp initially, so don't feel discouraged if you don't get it during the first read. You should go through the rest of the chapter and experiment with the examples on your own, but if you feel you don't fully understand the concept, you can come back to it later when the topics discussed previously in this chapter have had a chance to sink in.

Before moving on to closures, let's first review and expand on the concept of scope in JavaScript.

Scope chain

As you know, in JavaScript, there is no curly braces scope, but there is a function scope. A variable defined in a function is not visible outside the function, but a variable defined in a code block (for example an `if` or a `for` loop) is visible outside the block, for example:

```
> var a = 1;
> function f() {
    var b = 1;
    return a;
  }
> f();
1
> b;
ReferenceError: b is not defined
```

The `a` variable is in the global space, while `b` is in the scope of the function `f()`. So, we have the following:

- Inside `f()`, both `a` and `b` are visible
- Outside `f()`, `a` is visible, but `b` is not

If you define an `inner()` function nested inside `outer()`, it will have access to variables in its own scope, plus the scope of its parents. This is known as a scope chain, and the chain can be as long (deep) as you need it to be:

```
var global = 1;
function outer() {
  var outer_local = 2;
  function inner() {
    var inner_local = 3;
    return inner_local + outer_local + global;
  }
  return inner();
}
```

Let's test if the `inner()` function has access to all variables:

```
> outer();
6
```

Breaking the chain with a closure

Let's introduce closures with an illustration and look at the following code and see what's happening there:

```
var a = "global variable";
var F = function () {
  var b = "local variable";
  var N = function () {
    var c = "inner local";
  };
};
```

First, there is the global scope **G**. Think of it as the universe, as if it contains everything:

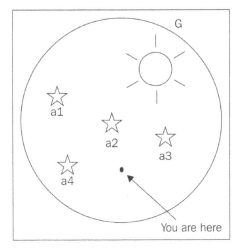

It can contain global variables such as **a1** and **a2** and global functions such as **F**:

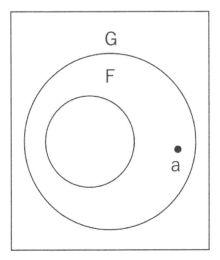

Functions have their own private space and can use it to store other variables, such as **b**, and inner functions, such as **N** (for inner). At some point, you will end up with a picture like the following:

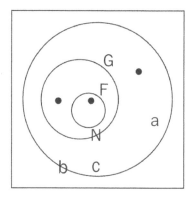

If you're at point a, you're inside the global space. If you're at point **b**, which is inside the space of the **F** function, then you have access to the global space and to the **F** space. If you're at point **c**, which is inside the **N** function, then you can access the global space, the **F** space, and the **N** space. You cannot reach from **a** to **b**, because **b** is invisible outside **F**. But, you can get from **c** to **b** if you want or from **N** to **b**. The interesting part is that the closure effect happens when somehow **N** breaks out of **F** and ends up in the global space.

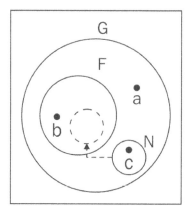

What happens then? **N** is in the same global space as **a**. And, as functions remember the environment in which they were defined, **N** will still have access to the **F** space, and hence, can access **b**. This is interesting, because **N** is where **a** is and yet **N** does have access to **b**, but **a** doesn't.

Additionally, how does **N** break the chain? By making itself global (omitting `var`) or by having **F** deliver (or `return`) it to the global space. Let's see how this is done in practice.

Closure #1

Take a look at the following function, which is the same as before, only F returns N and also N returns b, to which it has access via the scope chain:

```
var a = "global variable";
var F = function () {
  var b = "local variable";
  var N = function () {
    var c = "inner local";
    return b;
  };
  return N;
};
```

The F function contains the b variable, which is local, and therefore inaccessible from the global space:

```
> b;
ReferenceError: b is not defined
```

The N function has access to its private space, to the F() function's space, and to the global space. So, it can see b. As F() is callable from the global space (it's a global function), you can call it and assign the returned value to another global variable. The result – a new global function that has access to the F() function's private space:

```
> var inner = F();
> inner();
"local variable"
```

Closure #2

The final result of the next example will be the same as the previous example, but the way to achieve it is a little different. F() doesn't return a function, but instead it creates a new global function, inner(), inside its body.

Let's start by declaring a placeholder for the global function-to-be. This is optional, but it's always good to declare your variables. Then, you can define the F() function as follows:

```
var inner; // placeholder
var F = function () {
  var b = "local variable";
  var N = function () {
    return b;
  };
  inner = N;
};
```

Now, let's see what happens if you invoke F():

```
> F();
```

A new function, N(),is defined inside F() and assigned to the global inner function. During definition time, N() was inside F(), so it had access to the F() function's scope. The inner() function will keep its access to the F() function's scope, even though it's part of the global space, for example:

```
> inner();
"local variable".
```

A definition and closure #3

Every function can be considered a closure. This is because every function maintains a secret link to the environment (the scope) in which it was created. But, most of the time, this scope is destroyed unless something interesting happens (as shown in the preceding code) that causes it to be maintained.

Based on what you've seen so far, you can say that a closure is created when a function keeps a link to its parent scope even after the parent has returned. And, every function is a closure because, at the very least, every function maintains access to the global scope, which is never destroyed.

Let's see one more example of a closure, this time using the function parameters. Function parameters behave like local variables to this function, but they are implicitly created; you don't need to use `var` for them. You can create a function that returns another function, which in turn returns its parent's parameter, as follows:

```
function F(param) {
  var N = function () {
    return param;
  };
  param++;
  return N;
}
```

You can use the function as follows:

```
> var inner = F(123);
> inner();
124
```

Notice how `param++` was incremented after the function was defined and yet, when called, `inner()` returned the updated value. This demonstrates that the function maintains a reference to the scope where it was defined, and not to the variables and their values found in the scope during the function execution.

Closures in a loop

Let's take a look at a canonical rookie mistake when it comes to closures. It can easily lead to hard-to-spot bugs, because on the surface, everything looks normal.

Let's loop three times, each time creating a new function that returns the loop sequence number. The new functions will be added to an array and the array is returned at the end. Here's the function:

```
function F() {
  var arr = [], i;
  for (i = 0; i < 3; i++) {
    arr[i] = function () {
      return i;
    };
  }
  return arr;
}
```

Let's run the function, assigning the result to the `arr` array:

```
> var arr = F();
```

Now you have an array of three functions. Let's invoke them by adding parentheses after each array element. The expected behavior is to see the loop sequence printed out as 0, 1, and 2. Let's try:

```
> arr[0]();
3
> arr[1]();
3
> arr[2]();
3
```

Hmm, not quite as expected. What happened here? All three functions point to the same local variable: `i`. Why? The functions don't remember values, they only keep a link (reference) to the environment where they were created. In this case, the `i` variable happens to live in the environment where the three functions were defined. So, all functions, when they need to access the value, reach back to the environment and find the most current value of `i`. After the loop, the `i` variable's value is 3. So, all three functions point to the same value.

Why three and not two is another good question to think about for better understanding the `for` loop.

So, how do you implement the correct behavior? The answer is to use another closure, as shown in the following piece of code:

```
function F() {
  var arr = [], i;
  for (i = 0; i < 3; i++) {
    arr[i] = (function (x) {
      return function () {
        return x;
      };
    }(i));
  }
  return arr;
}
```

This gives you the expected result as follows:

```
> var arr = F();
> arr[0]();
0
> arr[1]();
1
> arr[2]();
2
```

Here, instead of just creating a function that returns i, you pass the i variable's current value to another immediate function. In this function, i becomes the local value x, and x has a different value every time.

Alternatively, you can use a normal (as opposed to an immediate) inner function to achieve the same result. The key is to use the middle function to localize the value of i at every iteration, as follows:

```
function F() {
   function binder(x) {
      return function () {
         return x;
      };
   }

   var arr = [], i;
   for (i = 0; i < 3; i++) {
      arr[i] = binder(i);
   }
   return arr;
}
```

Getter and setter

Let's see two more examples of using closures. The first one involves the creation of the getter and setter functions. Imagine that you have a variable that should contain a specific type of value or a specific range of values. You don't want to expose this variable because you don't want just any part of the code to be able to alter its value. You can protect this variable inside a function and provide two additional functions—one to get the value and one to set it. The one that sets it could contain some logic to validate a value before assigning it to the protected variable. Let's make the validation part simple (for the sake of keeping the example short) and only accept number values.

You can place both the getter and the setter functions inside the same function that contains the `secret` variable so that they share the same scope:

```
var getValue, setValue;

(function () {

  var secret = 0;

  getValue = function () {
    return secret;
  };

  setValue = function (v) {
    if (typeof v === "number") {
      secret = v;
    }
  };

}());
```

In this case, the function that contains everything is an immediate function. It defines `setValue()` and `getValue()` as global functions, while the `secret` variable remains local and inaccessible directly, as shown in the following example:

```
> getValue();
0
> setValue(123);
> getValue();
123
> setValue(false);
> getValue();
123
```

Iterator

The last closure example (also the last example in this chapter) shows the use of a closure to accomplish an iterator functionality.

You already know how to loop through a simple array, but there might be cases where you have a more complicated data structure with different rules as to what the sequence of values has. You can wrap the complicated who's next logic into an easy-to-use `next()` function. Then, you can simply call `next()` every time you need the consecutive value.

For this example, let's just use a simple array and not a complex data structure. Here's an initialization function that takes an input array and also defines a secret pointer, `i`, that will always point to the next element in the array:

```
function setup(x) {
  var i = 0;
  return function () {
    return x[i++];
  };
}
```

Calling the `setup()` function with a data array will create the `next()` function for you, as follows:

```
> var next = setup(['a', 'b', 'c']);
```

From there it's easy and fun; calling the same function over and over again gives you the next element, which is as follows:

```
> next();
"a"
> next();
"b"
> next();
"c"
```

IIFE versus blocks

As ES5 did not provide block scope, a popular pattern to achieve block scope was to use **immediately invoked function expressions (IIFE)**, for example:

```
(function () {
  var block_scoped=0;
}());
console.log(block_scoped); //reference error
```

With ES6's support for block scopes, you can simply use a `let` or `const` declaration.

Arrow functions

JavaScript uses almost all variations of arrows. With ES6, it introduces a new syntax for writing functions. We have always written function expressions in JavaScript. It is idiomatic to write code like this in JavaScript (this example is in jQuery):

```
$("#submit-btn").click(function (event) {
  validateForm();
  submitMessage();
});
```

This is a typical jQuery event handler. The event handler `click()` function accepts a function as a parameter and we will simply create an inline anonymous function expression and pass it to the click function. This style of writing anonymous function expressions is known as **Lambda functions**. Several other languages support this feature. Though lambdas are more or less standard in new languages, JavaScript was responsible for popularizing their usage. However, the lambda syntax in JavaScript has not been very concise. ES6 arrow functions fill that gap and provide a concise syntax to write functions.

Arrow function provide a more concise syntax than the traditional function expressions; for example, consider the following piece of code:

```
const num = [1,2,3]
const squares = num.map(function(n){
  return n*n;
});
console.log(squares); //[1,4,9]
```

Arrow functions syntax can simplify the function to the following line of code:

```
const squares_6 =num.map( n=> n*n)
```

As you can see, there is no `function` or `return` keyword anywhere. If your function has only one argument, you will end up writing the function as `identifer => expression`.

When you need multiple arguments, you need to wrap the argument list in braces:

- **No parameters**: `() => {...}`
- **One parameter**: `a => {...}`
- **More than one parameters**: `(a,b) => {...}`

Arrow functions can have both the statement block bodies as well as expression bodies:

```
n => { return n+n}   //statement block
n =>n+n              //expression
```

Both are equivalent but the second variation is concise and preferred. Arrow functions are always anonymous. One important aspect of arrow functions that we will discuss a little later is that arrow functions do not bind their own values of the `this` keyword–the value is lexically derived from the surrounding scope. As we have not yet looked at the `this` keyword in detail, we will defer the discussion to a later part of this book.

Exercises

1. Write a function that converts a hexadecimal color, for example blue (`#0000FF`), into its RGB representation, `rgb(0, 0, 255)`. Name your function `getRGB()` and test it with the following code (hint: treat the string as an array of characters):

```
> var a = getRGB("#00FF00");
> a;
"rgb(0, 255, 0)"
```

2. What do each of these following lines print in the console?

```
> parseInt(1e1);
> parseInt('1e1');
> parseFloat('1e1');
> isFinite(0/10);
> isFinite(20/0);
> isNaN(parseInt(NaN));
```

3. What does this following code alert?

```
var a = 1;

function f() {
 function n() {
    alert(a);
  }
  var a = 2;
  n();
}

f();
```

4. All these following examples alert `"Boo!"`. Can you explain why?

- Example 1:

```
var f = alert;
eval('f("Boo!")');
```

- Example 2:

```
var e;
var f = alert;
eval('e=f')('Boo!');
```

- Example 3:

```
(function(){
  return alert;}
)()('Boo!');
```

Summary

You have now completed the introduction to the fundamental concepts related to functions in JavaScript. This has laid the groundwork that will allow you to quickly grasp the concepts of object-oriented JavaScript and the patterns used in modern JavaScript programming. So far, we've been avoiding the OO features, but as you have reached this point in the book, it's only going to get more interesting from here on in. Let's take a moment to review the topics discussed in this chapter:

- The basics of how to define and invoke (call) a function using either a function declaration syntax or a function expression
- Function parameters and their flexibility
- Built-in functions–`parseInt()`, `parseFloat()`, `isNaN()`, `isFinite()`, and `eval()`–and the four functions to encode/decode a URL
- The scope of variables in JavaScript–no curly braces scope, variables have only function scope and the scope chain

- Functions as data–a function is like any other piece of data that you assign to a variable and a lot of interesting applications follow from this, such as:
    - Private functions and private variables
    - Anonymous functions
    - Callbacks
    - Immediate functions
    - Functions overwriting themselves
- Closures
- Arrow functions

4
Objects

Now that you've mastered JavaScript's primitive data types, arrays, and functions, it's time to stay true to the promise of the book title and talk about objects.

JavaScript has an eccentric take on the classical Object-oriented programming. Object-oriented programming is one of the most popular programming paradigms and has been a mainstay in most of programming languages like Java and C++. There are well defined ideas proposed by classical OOP that most of these languages adopt. JavaScript, however, has a different take on it. We will look JavaScript's way of supporting OOP.

In this chapter, you will learn the following topics:

- How to create and use objects
- What are the constructor functions
- What types of built-in JavaScript objects exist and what they can do for you

From arrays to objects

As you already know from Chapter 2, *Primitive Data Types, Arrays, Loops, and Conditions*, an array is just a list of values. Each value has an index (a numeric key) that starts from zero and increments by one for each value. Consider the following example:

```
> var myarr = ['red', 'blue', 'yellow', 'purple'];
> myarr;
["red", "blue", "yellow", "purple"].
> myarr[0];
"red"
> myarr[3];
"purple"
```

If you put the indexes in one column and the values in another, you'll end up with a table of key/value pairs shown as follows:

Key	Value
0	red
1	blue
2	yellow
3	purple

An object is similar to an array, but the difference is that you define the keys yourself. You're not limited to using only numeric indexes, and you can use friendlier keys such as `first_name`, `age`, and so on.

Let's take a look at a simple object and examine its parts:

```
var hero = {
  breed: 'Turtle',
  occupation: 'Ninja'
};
```

You can see that:

- The name of the variable that refers to the object is `hero`
- Instead of `[` and `]`, which you use to define an array, you use `{` and `}` for objects
- You separate the elements (called properties) contained in the object with commas
- The key/value pairs are divided by colons, as in `key:value`

The keys (names of the properties) can optionally be placed in quotation marks. For example, these keys are all the same:

```
var hero - {occupation: 1};
var hero = {"occupation": 1};
var hero = {'occupation': 1};
```

It's recommended that you don't quote the names of the properties (it's less typing), but there are cases when you must use quotes. Some of the cases are stated here:

- If the property name is one of the reserved words in JavaScript (see `Appendix A`, *Reserved Words*)
- If it contains spaces or special characters (anything other than letters, numbers, and the _ and $ characters)
- If it starts with a number

In other words, if the name you have chosen for a property is not a valid name for a variable in JavaScript, then you need to wrap it in quotes.

Have a look at this bizarre-looking object:

```
var o = {
  $omething: 1,
  'yes or no': 'yes',
  '!@#$%^&*': true
};
```

This is a valid object. The quotes are required for the second and the third properties; otherwise, you'll get an error.

Later in this chapter, you'll see other ways to define objects and arrays, in addition to `[]` and `{}`. However, first, let's introduce this bit of terminology – defining an array with `[]` is called **array literal notation**, and defining an object using curly braces `{}` is called **object literal notation**.

Elements, properties, methods, and members

When talking about arrays, you say that they contain elements. When talking about objects, you say that they contain properties. There isn't any significant difference in JavaScript; it's just the terminology that people are used to, probably from other programming languages.

A property of an object can point to a function, because functions are just data. Properties that point to functions are also called methods. In the following example, `talk` is a method:

```
var dog = {
  name: 'Benji',
  talk: function () {
    alert('Woof, woof!');
  }
};
```

As you have seen in the previous chapter, it's also possible to store functions as array elements and invoke them, but you'll not see much code like this in practice:

```
> var a = [];
> a[0] = function (what) { alert(what); };
> a[0]('Boo!');
```

You can also see people using the word members to refer to the properties of an object, most often when it doesn't matter if the property is a function or not.

Hashes and associative arrays

In some programming languages, there is a distinction between:

- A regular array, also called an **indexed** or **enumerated** array (the keys are numbers)
- An associative array, also called a **hash** or a **dictionary** (the keys are strings)

JavaScript uses arrays to represent indexed arrays and objects to represent associative arrays. If you want a hash in JavaScript, you use an object.

Accessing an object's properties

There are two ways to access the property of an object:

- Using the square bracket notation, for example, `hero['occupation']`
- Using the dot notation, for example, `hero.occupation`

The dot notation is easier to read and write, but it cannot always be used. The same rules apply for quoting property names. If the name of the property is not a valid variable name, you cannot use the dot notation.

Let's take the `hero` object again:

```
var hero = {
  breed: 'Turtle',
  occupation: 'Ninja'
};
```

Following is an example for accessing a property with the dot notation:

```
> hero.breed;
"Turtle"
```

Let's see an example for accessing a property with the bracket notation:

```
> hero['occupation'];
"Ninja"
```

Consider the following example for accessing a non-existing property returns `undefined`:

```
> 'Hair color is ' + hero.hair_color;
"Hair color is undefined"
```

Objects can contain any data, including other objects:

```
var book = {
  name: 'Catch-22',
  published: 1961,
  author: {
    firstname: 'Joseph',
    lastname: 'Heller'
  }
};
```

To get to the `firstname` property of the object contained in the `author` property of the `book` object, you can use the following lines of code:

```
> book.author.firstname;
"Joseph"
```

Let see an example using the square brackets notation:

```
> book['author']['lastname'];
"Heller"
```

It works even if you mix both:

```
> book.author['lastname'];
"Heller"
> book['author'].lastname;
"Heller"
```

Another case where you need square brackets is when the name of the property you need to access is not known beforehand. During runtime, it's dynamically stored in a variable:

```
> var key = 'firstname';
> book.author[key];
"Joseph"
```

Calling an object's methods

You know a method is just a property that happens to be a function, so you access methods in the same way in which you would access properties–using the dot notation or using square brackets. Calling (invoking) a method is the same as calling any other function – you just add parentheses after the method name, which effectively says Execute!:

```
> var hero = {
    breed: 'Turtle',
    occupation: 'Ninja',
    say: function () {
      return 'I am ' + hero.occupation;
    }
  };
> hero.say();
"I am Ninja"
```

If there are any parameters that you want to pass to a method, you would proceed as you would with normal functions:

```
> hero.say('a', 'b', 'c');
```

As you can use the array-like square brackets to access a property, it means you can also use brackets to access and invoke methods:

```
> hero['say']();
```

This is not a common practice, unless the method name is not known at the time of writing code, but it is instead defined at runtime:

```
var method = 'say';
hero[method]();
```

 No quotes unless you have to use the dot notation to access methods and properties, and don't quote properties in your object literals.

Altering properties/methods

JavaScript allows you to alter the properties and methods of existing objects at any time. This includes adding new properties or deleting them. You can start with a blank object and add properties later. Let's see how you can go about doing this.

An object without properties is shown as follows:

```
> var hero = {};
```

 A "blank" object
In this section, you started with a "blank" object, `var hero = {}`. Blank is in quotes because this object is not really empty and useless. Although at this stage it has no properties of its own, it has already inherited some. You'll learn more about own versus inherited properties later. So, an object in ES3 is never really blank or empty. In ES5 though, there is a way to create a completely blank object that doesn't inherit anything, but let's not get ahead too much.

1. Following is the code to access an non-existing property:

```
> typeof hero.breed;
"undefined"
```

2. Adding two properties and a method:

```
> hero.breed = 'turtle';
> hero.name = 'Leonardo';
> hero.sayName = function () {
    return hero.name;
  };
```

3. Calling the method:

```
> hero.sayName();
"Leonardo"
```

4. Deleting a property:

```
> delete hero.name;
true
```

5. If you call the method again, it will no longer find the deleted `name` property:

```
> hero.sayName();
"undefined"
```

Malleable objects

You can always change any object at any time, such as adding and removing properties and changing their values. However, there are exceptions to this rule. A few properties of some built-in objects are not changeable (for example, `Math.PI`, as you'll see later). Also, ES5 allows you to prevent changes to objects. You'll learn more about it in `Appendix C`, *Built-in Objects*.

Using the this value

In the previous example, the `sayName()` method used `hero.name` to access the `name` property of the `hero` object. When you're inside a method though, there is another way to access the object the method belongs to. This method is using the special value `this`:

```
> var hero = {
    name: 'Rafaelo',
    sayName: function () {
      return this.name;
    }
  };
> hero.sayName();
"Rafaelo"
```

So, when you say `this`, you're actually saying–this object or the current object.

Constructor functions

There is another way to create objects–using constructor functions. Let's look at an example:

```
function Hero() {
  this.occupation = 'Ninja';
}
```

In order to create an object using this function, you can use the new operator as follows:

```
> var hero = new Hero();
> hero.occupation;
"Ninja"
```

A benefit of using constructor functions is that they accept parameters, which can be used when creating new objects. Let's modify the constructor to accept one parameter and assign it to the name property:

```
function Hero(name) {
  this.name = name;
  this.occupation = 'Ninja';
  this.whoAreYou = function () {
    return "I'm " +
           this.name +
           " and I'm a " +
           this.occupation;
  };
}
```

Now, you can create different objects using the same constructor:

```
> var h1 = new Hero('Michelangelo');
> var h2 = new Hero('Donatello');
> h1.whoAreYou();
"I'm Michelangelo and I'm a Ninja"
> h2.whoAreYou();
"I'm Donatello and I'm a Ninja"
```

 By convention, you should capitalize the first letter of your constructor functions so that you have a visual clue that they are not intended to be called as regular functions.

If you call a function that is designed to be a constructor but you omit the `new` operator, it is not an error. However, it doesn't give you the expected result:

```
> var h = Hero('Leonardo');
> typeof h;
"undefined"
```

What happened here? There is no `new` operator, so a new object was not created. The function was called like any other function, so the variable `h` contains the value that the function returns. The function does not return anything (there's no `return` function), so it actually returns `undefined`, which gets assigned to the variable `h`.

In this case, what does `this` refer to? It refers to the global object.

The global object

You have already learned a bit about global variables (and how you should avoid them). You also know that JavaScript programs run inside a host environment (the browser, for example). Now that you know about objects, it's time for the whole truth, the host environment provides a global object, and all global variables are accessible as properties of the global object.

If your host environment is the web browser, the global object is called **window**. Another way to access the global object (and this is also true in most other environments) is to use `this` keyword outside a constructor function, for example in the global program code outside any function.

As an illustration, you can declare a global variable outside any function as follows:

```
> var a = 1;
```

Then, you can access this global variable in various ways:

- As a variable `a`
- As a property of the global object, for example, `window['a']` or `window.a`
- As a property of the global object referred to as `this`:

```
> var a = 1;
> window.a;
1
> this.a;
1
```

Let's go back to the case where you define a constructor function and call it without the `new` operator. In such cases, `this` refers to the global object and all the properties set to `this` become properties of `window`.

Declaring a constructor function and calling it without new returns `"undefined"`:

```
> function Hero(name) {
    this.name = name;
  }
> var h = Hero('Leonardo');
> typeof h;
"undefined"
> typeof h.name;
TypeError: Cannot read property 'name' of undefined
```

As you had `this` keyword inside the function `Hero`, a global variable (a property of the global object) called `name` was created:

```
> name;
"Leonardo"
> window.name;
"Leonardo"
```

If you call the same constructor function using `new`, then a new object is returned, and `this` refers to it:

```
> var h2 = new Hero('Michelangelo');
> typeof h2;
"object"
> h2.name;
"Michelangelo"
```

The built-in global functions you have seen in `Chapter 3`, *Functions*, can also be invoked as methods of the `window` object. So, the following two calls have the same result:

```
> parseInt('101 dalmatians');
101
> window.parseInt('101 dalmatians')
101
```

The constructor property

When an object is created, a special property is assigned to it behind the scenes–the `constructor` property. It contains a reference to the constructor function used to create this object.

Continuing from the previous example:

```
> h2.constructor;
function Hero(name) {
   this.name = name;
}
```

As the `constructor` property contains a reference to a function, you might as well call this function to produce a new object. The following code is like saying, "I don't care how object h2 was created, but I want another one just like it":

```
> var h3 = new h2.constructor('Rafaello');
> h3.name;
"Rafaello"
```

If an object was created using the object literal notation, its constructor is the built-in `Object()` constructor function (there is more about this later in this chapter):

```
> var o = {};
> o.constructor;
function Object() { [native code] }
> typeof o.constructor;
"function"
```

The instanceof operator

With the `instanceof` operator, you can test whether an object was created with a specific `constructor` function:

```
> function Hero() {}
> var h = new Hero();
> var o = {};
> h instanceof Hero;
true
> h instanceof Object;
true
> o instanceof Object;
true
```

Note that you don't put parentheses after the function name (you don't use `h instanceof Hero()`). This is because you're not invoking this function, but just referring to it by name, as with any other variable.

Functions that return objects

In addition to using `constructor` functions and the `new` operator to create objects, you can also use a normal function to create objects without the `new` operator. You can have a function that does a bit of preparatory work and has an object as a return value.

For example, here's a simple `factory()` function that produces objects:

```
function factory(name) {
  return {
    name: name
  };
}
```

Consider the following example using the `factory()` function:

```
> var o = factory('one');
> o.name;
"one"
> o.constructor;
function Object() { [native code] }
```

In fact, you can also use `constructor` functions and `return` objects different from `this` keyword. This means you can modify the default behavior of the `constructor` function. Let's see how.

Here's the normal constructor scenario:

```
> function C() {
    this.a = 1;
  }
> var c = new C();
> c.a;
1
```

However, now, look at this scenario:

```
> function C2() {
    this.a = 1;
    return {b: 2};
  }
> var c2 = new C2();
> typeof c2.a;
"undefined"
> c2.b;
2
```

What happened here? Instead of returning the `this` object, which contains the property `a`, the constructor returned another object that contains the property `b`. This is possible only if the return value is an object. Otherwise, if you try to return anything that is not an object, the constructor will proceed with its usual behavior and return `this`.

If you think about how objects are created inside constructor functions, you can imagine that a variable called `this` is defined at the top of the function and then returned at the end. Consider the following code:

```
function C() {
  // var this = {}; // pseudo code, you can't do this
  this.a = 1;
  // return this;
}
```

Passing objects

When you assign an object to a different variable or pass it to a function, you only pass a reference to that object. Consequently, if you make a change to the reference, you're actually modifying the original object.

Here's an example of how you can assign an object to another variable and then make a change to the copy. As a result, the original object is also changed:

```
> var original = {howmany: 1};
> var mycopy = original;
> mycopy.howmany;
1
> mycopy.howmany = 100;
100
> original.howmany;
100
```

The same thing applies when passing objects to functions:

```
> var original = {howmany: 100};
> var nullify = function (o) { o.howmany = 0; };
> nullify(original);
> original.howmany;
0
```

Comparing objects

When you compare objects, you'll get `true` only if you compare two references to the same object. If you compare two distinct objects that happen to have the exact same methods and properties, the result would be `false`.

Let's create two objects that look the same:

```
> var fido  = {breed: 'dog'};
> var benji = {breed: 'dog'};
```

Comparing them returns `false`:

```
> benji === fido;
false
> benji == fido;
false
```

You can create a new variable, `mydog`, and assign one of the objects to it. This way, the variable `mydog` actually points to the same object:

```
> var mydog = benji;
```

In this case, `benji` is `mydog` because they are the same object (changing the `mydog` variable's properties will change the `benji` variable's properties). The comparison returns `true`:

```
> mydog === benji;
true
```

As `fido` is a different object, it does not compare to `mydog`:

```
> mydog === fido;
false
```

Objects in the WebKit console

Before diving into the built-in objects in JavaScript, let's quickly say a few words about working with objects in the WebKit console.

After playing around with the examples in this chapter, you might have already noticed how objects are displayed in the console. If you create an object and type its name, you'll get an arrow pointing to the word object.

The object is clickable and expands to show you a list of all of the properties of the object. If a property is also an object, there is an arrow next to it too, so you can expand this as well. This is handy as it gives you an insight into exactly what this object contains. Consider the following example:

```
⊖ ○ ○          Developer Tools – http://www.phpied.com/files/imaje/verbose.html

  Elements  Resources  Network  Scripts  Timeline  Profiles  Audits  Console      Search Console
> var benji = {name: 'Benji', breed: 'dog', obj: {prop: 1}};
  undefined
> benji
  ▼ Object
      breed: "dog"
      name: "Benji"
    ▼ obj: Object
        prop: 1
      ▶ __proto__: Object
    ▶ __proto__: Object
>

  ⊡  ⟩≡  Q  ⊘   <top frame> ⬍  (All) │  Errors   Warnings   Logs                          ✿
```

You can ignore __proto__ for now; there's more about it in the next chapter.

Logging using the console.log method

The console also offers you an object called `console` and a few methods, such as `console.log()` and `console.error()`, which you can use to display any value you want in the console.

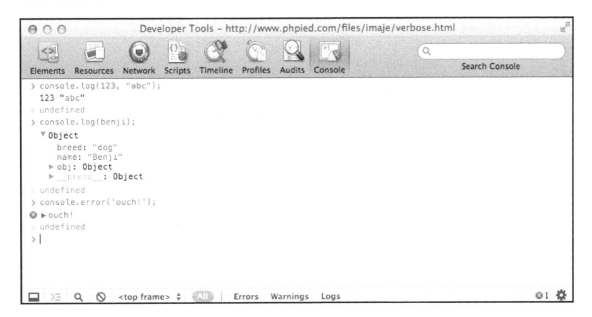

The `console.log()` method is convenient when you want to quickly test something, as well as when you want to dump some intermediate debugging information in your real scripts. Here's how you can experiment with loops, for example:

```
> for (var i = 0; i < 5; i++) {
    console.log(i);
}
0
1
2
3
4
```

ES6 object literals

ES6 introduces a much succinct syntax while using object literals. ES6 offers several shorthands for property initialization and function definitions. ES6 shorthands closely resemble a familiar JSON syntax. Consider the following code fragment:

```
let a = 1
let b = 2
let val = {a: a, b: b}
console.log(val) //{"a":1,"b":2}
```

This is a typical way to assign property values. If the name of the variable and the property key is the same, ES6 allows you to use shorthand syntax. The preceding code can be written as follows:

```
let a = 1
let b = 2
let val = {a, b}
console.log(val) //{"a":1,"b":2}
```

Similar syntax is available for method definitions as well. As we have discussed, methods are simply properties of an object whose values are functions. Consider the following example:

```
var obj = {
  prop: 1,
  modifier:  function() {
    console.log(this.prop);
  }
}
```

There is a compact way to define methods in ES6. You simply drop the `function` keyword and `:`. The equivalent code in ES6 would look like the following:

```
var obj = {
  prop: 1,
  modifier () {
    console.log(this.prop);
  }
}
```

ES6 allows you to compute the key of a property. Until ES6, you could only use fixed property names. Here is an example:

```
var obj = {
  prop: 1,
  modifier: function () {
    console.log(this.prop);
  }
}
obj.prop = 2;
obj.modifier(); //2
```

As you can see, we are limited to using fixed key names: `prop` and `modifier` in this case. However, ES6 allows you to use computed property keys. It is possible to create property keys dynamically using values returned by a function as well:

```
let vehicle = "car"
function vehicleType(){
  return "truck"
}
let car = {
  [vehicle+"_model"]: "Ford"
}
let truck= {
  [vehicleType() + "_model"]: "Mercedez"
}
console.log(car) //{"car_model":"Ford"}
console.log(truck) //{"truck_model":"Mercedez"}
```

We are using the value of variable `vehicle` to concatenate with a fixed string to derive the property key while creating the `car` object. In the second snippet, we are creating a property by concatenating a fixed string with the value returned by a function. This way of computing property keys provides great flexibility while creating objects, and a lot of boilerplate and repetitive code can be eliminated.

This syntax is applicable to method definition as well:

```
let object_type = "Vehicle"
let obj = {
  ["get"+object_type]() {
    return "Ford"
  }
}
```

Object properties and attributes

Each object has a few properties. Each property, in turn, has a key and attributes. A property's state is stored in these attributes. All properties have the following attributes:

- **Enumerable (boolean)**: This indicates if you can enumerate the properties of the object. System properties are non-enumerable while user properties are enumerable. Unless there is a strong reason, this property should remain untouched.
- **Configurable(boolean)**: If this attribute is `false`, the property cannot be deleted or edited (it cannot change any of its attribute).

You can use the `Object.getOwnPropertyDescriptor()` method to retrieve an object's own properties:

```
let obj = {
  age: 25
}
console.log(Object.getOwnPropertyDescriptor(obj, 'age'));
//{"value":25,"writable":true,"enumerable":true,"configurable":true}
```

Meanwhile, the property can be defined using the `Object.defineProperty()` method:

```
let obj = {
  age: 25
}
Object.defineProperty(obj, 'age', { configurable: false })
console.log(Object.getOwnPropertyDescriptor(obj, 'age'));
//{"value":25,"writable":true,"enumerable":true,"configurable":false}
```

Though you would never use these methods, it is important to understand object properties and attributes. In the next section, we will discuss how some of the `object` methods are used in context of some of these properties.

ES6 object methods

ES6 introduces a few static helper methods for objects. `Object.assign` is a helper method that replaces popular mixins to perform a shallow copy of an object.

Copy properties using Object.assign

This method is used to copy properties of the target object into the source object. In other words, this method merges the source object with the target object and modifies the target object:

```
let a = {}
Object.assign(a, { age: 25 })
console.log(a)   //{"age":25}
```

The first parameter to `Object.assign` is the target on which source properties are copied. The same target object is returned to the caller. Existing properties are overwritten, while properties that aren't part of the source object are ignored:

```
let a = {age : 23, gender: "male"}
Object.assign(a, { age: 25 })    // age overwritten, but gender ignored
console.log(a)   //{"age":25, "gender":"male"}
```

`Object.assign` can take multiple source objects. You can write `Object.assign(target, source1, source2)`. Here is an example:

```
console.log(Object.assign({a:1, b:2}, {a: 2}, {c: 4}, {b: 3}))
//Object {
//"a": 2,
//"b": 3,
//"c": 4
//
```

In this snippet, we are assigning properties from multiple source objects. Also, notice how `Object.assign()` returns the target object, which we in turn use inside `console.log()`.

One point to note is that only enumerable own (non-inherited) properties can be copied using `Object.assign()`. Properties from the prototype chain (will be discussed later in this chapter when we talk about Inheritance) are not considered. Our earlier discussion of enumerable properties will help you understand this distinction.

In the following example, we will create a non-enumerable property using `defineProperty()` and validate the fact that `Object.assign()` ignores that property:

```
let a = {age : 23, gender: "male"}
Object.defineProperty(a, 'superpowers', {enumerable:false, value:
'ES6'})
console.log(
```

The property defined as `superpowers` has the enumerable attribute set to `false`. While copying properties, this property is ignored.

Compare values with Object.is

ES6 provides a slightly precise way of comparing values. We have discussed the strict equality operator ===. However, for `NaN` and −0 and +0, the strict equality operator behaves inconsistently. Here is an example:

```
console.log(NaN===NaN) //false
console.log(-0===+0) //true
//ES6 Object.is
console.log(Object.is(NaN,NaN)) //true
console.log(Object.is(-0,+0)) //false
```

Apart from these two cases, `Object.is()` can safely be replaced with the === operator.

Destructuring

You will be working with objects and arrays all the time when you code. JavaScript object and array notations resemble the JSON format. You will define objects and arrays, and then retrieve elements from them. ES6 gives a convenient syntax that significantly improves the way we access properties/members from objects and arrays. Let's consider a typical code you would often write:

```
var config = {
  server: 'localhost',
  port: '8080'
}
var server = config.server;
var port = config.port;
```

Here, we extracted values of server and port from the `config` object and assigned them to local variables. Pretty straightforward! However, when this object has a bunch of properties, some of them nested, this simple operation can get very tedious to write.

ES6 destructuring syntax allows an object literal on the left-hand side of an assignment statement. In the following example, we will define an object `config` with a few properties. Later, we will use destructuring to assign the object `config` to assign values to individual properties on the left-hand side of the assignment statement:

```
let config = {
  server: 'localhost',
  port: '8080',
  timeout: 900,
}
let {server,port} = config
console.log(server, port) //"localhost" "8080"
```

As you can see `server` and `port` are local variables that got assigned properties from the `config` object because the name of the properties were the same as that of the local variables. You can also pick particular properties while you assign them to local variables. Here is an example:

```
let {timeout : t} =config
console.log(t) //900
```

Here, we are only picking `timeout` from the `config` object and assign it to a local variable `t`.

You can also use the destructuring syntax to assign values to already declared variables. In this case, you have to put parentheses around the assignment:

```
let config = {
  server: 'localhost',
  port: '8080',
  timeout: 900,
}
let server = '127.0.0.1';
let port = '80';
({server,port} = config) //assignment surrounded by ()
console.log(server, port) //"localhost" "8080"
```

As the destructuring expression evaluates to the right-hand side of the expression, it's possible to use it anywhere you would expect a value. For example, in a function call, as shown here:

```
let config = {
  server: 'localhost',
  port: '8080',
  timeout: 900,
}
let server='127.0.0.1';
let port ='80';
let timeout ='100';

function startServer(configValue){
  console.log(configValue)
}
startServer({server,port,timeout} = config)
```

If you specify a local variable with a property name that does not exist in the object, the local variable gets an undefined value. However, while using variables in the destructuring assignment, you can optionally specify default values:

```
let config = {
  server: 'localhost',
  port: '8080'
}
let {server,port,timeout=0} = config
console.log(timeout)
```

In this example, for a non-existent property timeout, we provided a default value to prevent getting undefined values assigned to local variables.

Destructuring works on arrays as well, and the syntax is also very similar to that of the objects. We just need to replace object literal syntax with array:literals:

```
const arr = ['a','b']
const [x,y] = arr
console.log (x,y) /"a" "b"
```

As you can see, this is the exact same syntax we saw earlier. We defined an array `arr` and later used the destructuring syntax to assign elements of that array to two local variables, `x` and `y`. Here, the assignment happens based on the order of elements in the array. As you only care about the position of elements, you can skip some of them if you want to. Here is an example:

```
const days = ['Thursday','Friday','Saturday','Sunday']
const [,,sat,sun] = days
console.log (sat,sun) //"Saturday" "Sunday"
```

Here, we know that we need elements from positions 2 and 3 (an array's index starts from 0), and hence, we ignore elements at positions 0 and 1. Array destructuring can eliminate the use of a `temp` variable while swapping values of two variables. Consider the following:

```
let a=1, b=2;
[b,a] = [a,b]
console.log(a,b) //2 1
```

You can use the rest operator (. . .) to extract remaining elements and assign them to an array. The rest operator can only be used as the last operator during destructuring:

```
const [x, ...y] = ['a', 'b', 'c']; // x='a'; y=['b', 'c']
```

Built-in objects

Earlier in this chapter, you came across the `Object()` constructor function. It's returned when you create objects with the object literal notation and access their `constructor` property. `Object()` is one of the built-in constructors; there are a few others, and in the rest of this chapter you'll see all of them.

The built-in objects can be divided into three groups:

- **Data wrapper objects**: These are `Object`, `Array`, `Function`, `Boolean`, `Number`, and `String`. These objects correspond to the different data types in JavaScript. There is a data wrapper object for every different value returned by `typeof` (discussed in `Chapter 2`, *Primitive Data Types, Arrays, Loops, and Conditions*), with the exception of `undefined` and `null`.
- **Utility objects**: These are `Math`, `Date`, and `RegExp`, and can come in handy.
- **Error objects**: These include the generic `Error` object as well as other more specific objects that can help your program recover its working state when something unexpected happens.

Only a handful of methods of the built-in objects will be discussed in this chapter. For a full reference, see `Appendix C`, *Built-in Objects*.

If you're confused about what a built-in object is and what a built-in constructor is, well, they are the same thing. In a moment, you'll see how functions and, therefore, constructor functions, are also objects.

Object

Object is the parent of all JavaScript objects, which means that every object you create inherits from it. To create a new empty object, you can use the literal notation or the `Object()` constructor function. The following two lines are equivalent:

```
> var o = {};
> var o = new Object();
```

As mentioned before, an empty (or blank) object is not completely useless, because it already contains several inherited methods and properties. In this book, empty means an object like `{}` that has no properties of its own, other than the ones it automatically gets. Let's look at a few of the properties that even blank objects already have:

- The `o.constructor` property returns a reference to the constructor function
- The `o.toString()` is a method that returns a string representation of the object
- The `o.valueOf()` returns a single-value representation of the object; often, this is the object itself

Let's see these methods in action. First, create an object:

```
> var o = new Object();
```

Calling `toString()` returns a string representation of the object:

```
> o.toString();
"[object Object]"
```

The `toString()` method will be called internally by JavaScript when an object is used in a string context. For example, `alert()` works only with strings, so if you call the `alert()` function passing an object, the `toString()` method will be called behind the scenes. These two lines produce the same result:

```
> alert(o);
> alert(o.toString());
```

Another type of string context is the string concatenation. If you try to concatenate an object with a string, the object's `toString()` method is called first:

```
> "An object: " + o;
"An object: [object Object]"
```

The `valueOf()` method is another method that all objects provide. For the simple objects (whose constructor is `Object()`), the `valueOf()` method returns the object itself:

```
> o.valueOf() === o;
true
```

To summarize:

- You can create objects either with `var o = {};` (object literal notation, the preferred method) or with `var o = new Object();`
- Any object, no matter how complex, inherits from the `Object` object and therefore, offers methods such as `toString()` and properties such as a constructor

Array

`Array()` is a built-in function that you can use as a constructor to create arrays:

```
> var a = new Array();
```

This is equivalent to the array literal notation:

```
> var a = [];
```

No matter how the array is created, you can add elements to it as usual:

```
> a[0] = 1;
> a[1] = 2;
> a;
[1, 2]
```

When using the `Array()` constructor, you can also pass values that will be assigned to the new array's elements:

```
> var a = new Array(1, 2, 3, 'four');
> a;
[1, 2, 3, "four"]
```

An exception to this is when you pass a single number to the constructor. In this case, the number is considered to be the length of the array:

```
> var a2 = new Array(5);
> a2;
  [undefined x 5]
```

As arrays are created with a constructor, does this mean that arrays are in fact objects? Yes, and you can verify this using the `typeof` operator:

```
> typeof [1, 2, 3];
"object"
```

As arrays are objects, this means that they inherit the properties and methods of the parent object:

```
> var a = [1, 2, 3, 'four'];
> a.toString();
"1,2,3,four"
> a.valueOf();
[1, 2, 3, "four"]
> a.constructor;
function Array() { [native code] }
```

Arrays are objects, but of a special type because:

* The names of their properties are automatically assigned using numbers starting from 0.
* They have a `length` property that contains the number of elements in the array.
* They have more built-in methods in addition to those inherited from the parent object.

Let's examine the differences between an array and an object, starting by creating the empty array `a` and the empty object `o`:

```
> var a = [], o = {};
```

Array objects have a `length` property automatically defined for them, while normal objects do not:

```
> a.length;
0
> typeof o.length;
"undefined"
```

It's ok to add both numeric and non-numeric properties to both arrays and objects:

```
> a[0] = 1;
> o[0] = 1;
> a.prop = 2;
> o.prop = 2;
```

The `length` property is always up to date with the number of numeric properties, while it ignores the non-numeric ones:

```
> a.length;
1
```

The `length` property can also be set by you. Setting it to a greater value than the current number of items in the array makes room for additional elements. If you try to access these non-existing elements, you'll get the value `undefined`:

```
> a.length = 5;
5
> a;
[1, undefined x 4]
```

Setting the `length` property to a lower value removes the trailing elements:

```
> a.length = 2;
2
> a;
[1, undefined x 1]
```

A few array methods

In addition to the methods inherited from the parent object, array objects also have specialized methods for working with arrays, such as `sort()`, `join()`, and `slice()`, among others (see `Appendix C`, *Built-in Objects*, for the complete list).

Let's take an array and experiment with some of these methods:

```
> var a = [3, 5, 1, 7, 'test'];
```

The `push()` method appends a new element to the end of the array. The `pop()` method removes the last element. The `a.push('new')` method works like `a[a.length] = 'new'`, and `a.pop()` is like `a.length--`.

The push() method returns the length of the changed array, whereas pop() returns the removed element:

```
> a.push('new');
6
> a;
[3, 5, 1, 7, "test", "new"]
> a.pop();
"new"
> a;
[3, 5, 1, 7, "test"]
```

The sort() method sorts the array and returns it. In the next example, after sort, both a and b point to the same array:

```
> var b = a.sort();
> b;
[1, 3, 5, 7, "test"]
> a === b;
true
```

The join() method returns a string containing the values of all the elements in the array glued together using the string parameter passed to join():

```
> a.join(' is not ');
"1 is not 3 is not 5 is not 7 is not test"
```

The slice() method returns a piece of the array without modifying the source array. The first parameter to slice() is the start index (zero-based), and the second is the end index (both indices are zero-based). Start index is included, while the end index is not. Take a look at the following example:

```
> b = a.slice(1, 3);
[3, 5]
> b = a.slice(0, 1);
[1]
> b = a.slice(0, 2);
[1, 3]
```

After all the slicing, the source array is still the same:

```
> a;
[1, 3, 5, 7, "test"]
```

The `splice()` method modifies the source array. It removes a slice, returns it, and optionally fills the gap with new elements. The first two parameters define the start index and length (number of elements) of the slice to be removed; the other parameters pass the new values:

```
> b = a.splice(1, 2, 100, 101, 102);
[3, 5]
> a;
[1, 100, 101, 102, 7, "test"]
```

Filling the gap with new elements is optional, so you can skip it:

```
> a.splice(1, 3);
[100, 101, 102]
> a;
[1, 7, "test"]
```

ES6 array methods

Arrays get a bunch of useful methods. Libraries such as **lodash** and **underscore** provided features missing in the language so far. With the new helper methods, array creation and manipulation is much more functional and easy to code.

Array.from

Converting array-like values to arrays has always been a bit of a challenge in JavaScript. People have employed several hacks and written libraries to just let you handle arrays effectively.

ES6 introduces a very helpful method to convert array-like objects and iterable values into arrays. Array-like values are objects that have a length property and indexed elements. Every function has an implicit arguments variable that contains a list of all arguments passed to the function. This variable is an array-like object. Before ES6, the only way we could convert the `arguments` object to an array was to iterate through it and copy the values over to a new array:

```
function toArray(args) {
    var result = [];
    for (var i = 0, len = args.length; i < len; i++) {
        result.push(args[i]);
    }
    return result;
```

```
    }
    function doSomething() {
        var args = toArray(arguments);
        console.log(args)
    }
    doSomething("hellow", "world")
    //Array [
    //  "hellow",
    //  "world"
    //]
```

Here, we are creating a new array to copy over all elements of the `arguments` object. This is wasteful and needs a lot of unnecessary coding. `Array.from()` is a concise way to convert array-like objects into arrays. We can convert this example to a more succinct one using `Array.from()`:

```
    function doSomething() {
        console.log(Array.from(arguments))
    }
    doSomething("hellow", "world")
    //Array [
    //  "hellow",
    //  "world"
    //]
```

You can provide your own mapping scheme while calling `Array.from()` by providing a mapping function. This function is invoked on all the elements of the object and converts it. This is a useful construct for many common usecases, for example:

```
    function doSomething() {
      console.log(Array.from(arguments, function(elem)
    { return elem + " mapped"; }));
    }
```

In this example, we are deconstructing the `arguments` object using `Array.from` and for each element in `arguments` object, we are calling a function.

Creating arrays using Array.of

Creating an array using the `Array()` constructor causes a bit of a problem. The constructor behaves differently based on the number and type of arguments. When you pass a single numeric value to the `Array()` constructor, an array of undefined elements is created, with the value of the length assigned to the value of the argument:

```
let arr = new Array(2)
console.log(arr) //[undefined, undefined]
console.log(arr.length) //2
```

On the other hand, if you pass only one non-numeric value, it becomes the only item in the array:

```
let arr = new Array("2")
console.log(arr) //["2"]
console.log(arr.length) //1
```

This is not all. If you pass multiple values, they become elements of the array:

```
let arr = new Array(1,"2",{obj: "3"})
console.log(arr.length) //3
```

So, clearly, there needs to be a better way to create arrays to avoid such confusion. ES6 introduces the `Array.of` method that works like the `Array()` constructor, but guarantees one standard behavior. `Array.of` creates an array from its arguments, regardless of their number and type:

```
let arr = Array.of(1,"2",{obj: "3"})
console.log(arr.length) //3
```

Array.prototype methods

ES6 introduces several interesting methods as part of array instances. These methods help with array iteration and searching elements in the array, both of which are very frequent and useful operations.

Here are the methods used for iterating over arrays:

- `Array.prototype.entries()`
- `Array.prototype.values()`
- `Array.prorotype.keys()`

All three methods return an iterator. This iterator can be used to create arrays using `Array.from()` and can be used in for loops for iteration:

```
let arr = ['a','b','c']
for (const index of arr.keys()){
  console.log(index) //0 1 2
}
for (const value of arr.values()){
  console.log(value) //a b c
}
for (const [index,value] of arr.entries()){
  console.log(index,value)
}
//0 "a"
//1 "b"
//2 "c"
```

Similarly, there are new methods for searching within arrays. Looking for an element in an array usually involved iterating through the entire list and comparing them with a value, as there were no built-in methods for this. Though `indexOf()` and `lastIndexOf()` helped find a single value, there was no way to find elements based on complex conditions. With ES6, the following build-in methods help with `this` keyword.

- `Array.prototype.find`
- `Array.prototype.findIndex`

Both these methods accept two arguments–first is the `callback` function(which contains the predicate condition) and the second is an optional `this` keyword. The `callback` accepts three arguments: the array element, index of that element, and the array. The `callback` returns `true` if the element matches the predicate:

```
let numbers = [1,2,3,4,5,6,7,8,9,10];
console.log(numbers.find(n => n > 5)); //6
console.log(numbers.findIndex(n => n > 5)); //5
```

Function

You already know that functions are a special data type. However, it turns out that there's more to it than that: functions are actually objects. There is a built-in `constructor` function called `Function()` that allows for an alternative (but not necessarily recommended) way to create a function.

The following example shows three ways to define a function:

```
> function sum(a, b) { // function declaration
    return a + b;
  }
> sum(1, 2);
3
> var sum = function (a, b) { // function expression
    return a + b;
  };
> sum(1, 2)
3
> var sum = new Function('a', 'b', 'return a + b;');
> sum(1, 2)
3
```

When using the `Function()` constructor, you pass the parameter names first (as strings) and then the source code for the body of the function (again as a string). The JavaScript engine needs to evaluate the source code you pass and create the new function for you. This source code evaluation suffers from the same drawbacks as the `eval()` function, so defining functions using the `Function()` constructor should be avoided when possible.

If you use the `Function()` constructor to create functions that have lots of parameters, bear in mind that the parameters can be passed as a single comma-delimited list; so, for example, these are the same:

```
> var first = new Function(
    'a, b, c, d',
    'return arguments;'
  );
> first(1, 2, 3, 4);
    [1, 2, 3, 4]
> var second = new Function(
    'a, b, c',
    'd',
    'return arguments;'
  );
> second(1, 2, 3, 4);
    [1, 2, 3, 4]
```

```
> var third = new Function(
    'a',
    'b',
    'c',
    'd',
    'return arguments;'
);
> third(1, 2, 3, 4);
    [1, 2, 3, 4]
```

> Do not use the Function() constructor. As with eval() and
> setTimeout() (discussed later in the book), always try to stay away from
> passing JavaScript code as a string.

Properties of function objects

Like any other object, functions have a constructor property that contains a reference to
the Function() constructor function. This is true no matter which syntax you used to
create the function:

```
> function myfunc(a) {
    return a;
}
> myfunc.constructor;
function Function() { [native code] }
```

Functions also have a length property, which contains the number of formal parameters
the function expects:

```
> function myfunc(a, b, c) {
    return true;
}
> myfunc.length;
    3
```

Using the prototype property

One of the most widely used properties of function objects is the `prototype` property.
You'll see this property discussed in detail in the next chapter, but for now, let's just say:

- The `prototype` property of a `function` object points to another object
- Its benefits shine only when you use this `function` as a constructor
- All objects created with this `function` keep a reference to the `prototype` property and can use its properties as their own

Let's look at a quick example to demonstrate the `prototype` property. Take a simple object that has a property name and a method `say()` method:

```
var ninja = {
  name: 'Ninja',
  say: function () {
    return 'I am a ' + this.name;
  }
};
```

When you create a function (even one without a body), you can verify that it automatically has a `prototype` property that points to a new object:

```
> function F() {}
> typeof F.prototype;
"object"
```

It gets interesting when you modify the `prototype` property. You can add properties to it, or you can replace the default object with any other object. Let's assign `ninja` to the `prototype`:

```
> F.prototype = ninja;
```

Now, and here's where the magic happens, using the `F()` function as a `constructor` function, you can create a new object, `baby_ninja`, which will have access to the properties of `F.prototype` (which points to `ninja`) as if it were its own:

```
> var baby_ninja = new F();
> baby_ninja.name;
"Ninja"
> baby_ninja.say();
"I am a Ninja"
```

There will be much more on this topic later. In fact, the next chapter is all about the `prototype` property.

Methods of function objects

Function objects, being a descendant of the top parent object, get the default methods such as `toString()`. When invoked on a function, the `toString()` method returns the source code of the function:

```
> function myfunc(a, b, c) {
    return a + b + c;
  }
> myfunc.toString();
"function myfunc(a, b, c) {
  return a + b + c;
}"
```

If you try to peek into the source code of the built-in functions, you'll get the `[native code]` string instead of the body of the function:

```
> parseInt.toString();
"function parseInt() { [native code] }"
```

As you can see, you can use `toString()` to differentiate between native methods and developer-defined ones.

 The behavior of the function's `toString()` is environment dependent, and it differs among browsers in terms of spacing and new lines.

Call and apply

Function objects have `call()` and `apply()` methods. You can use them to invoke a function and pass any arguments to it.

These methods also allow your objects to borrow methods from other objects and invoke them as their own. This is an easy and powerful way to reuse code.

Let's say you have a `some_obj` object, which contains the `say()` method:

```
var some_obj = {
  name: 'Ninja',
  say: function (who) {
```

```
            return 'Haya ' + who + ', I am a ' + this.name;
    }
};
```

You can call the `say()` method, which internally uses `this.name` to gain access to its own name property:

```
> some_obj.say('Dude');
"Haya Dude, I am a Ninja"
```

Now, let's create a simple object, `my_obj`, which only has a name property:

```
> var my_obj = {name: 'Scripting guru'};
```

The `my_obj` likes the `some_obj` object's `say()` method so much that it wants to invoke it as its own. This is possible using the `call()` method of the `say()` function object:

```
> some_obj.say.call(my_obj, 'Dude');
"Haya Dude, I am a Scripting guru"
```

It worked! But what happened here? You invoked the `call()` method of the `say()` function object by passing two parameters–the `my_obj` object and the `Dude` string. The result is that when `say()` is invoked, the references to the this value that it contains point to `my_obj`. This way, `this.name` doesn't return `Ninja`, but `Scripting guru` instead.

If you have more parameters to pass when invoking the `call()` method, you just keep adding them:

```
some_obj.someMethod.call(my_obj, 'a', 'b', 'c');
```

If you don't pass an object as a first parameter to `call()` or you pass `null`, the global object is assumed.

The method `apply()` works the same way as `call()`, but with the difference that all parameters you want to pass to the method of the other object are passed as an array. The following two lines are equivalent:

```
some_obj.someMethod.apply(my_obj, ['a', 'b', 'c']);
some_obj.someMethod.call(my_obj, 'a', 'b', 'c');
```

Continuing the previous example, you can use the following line of code:

```
> some_obj.say.apply(my_obj, ['Dude']);
"Haya Dude, I am a Scripting guru"
```

The arguments object revisited

In the previous chapter, you have seen how, from inside a function, you have access to something called `arguments`, which contains the values of all the parameters passed to the function:

```
> function f() {
    return arguments;
  }
> f(1, 2, 3);
[1, 2, 3]
```

The `arguments` looks like an array, but it is actually an array-like object. It resembles an array because it contains indexed elements and a `length` property. However, the similarity ends there, as arguments doesn't provide any of the array methods, such as `sort()` or `slice()`.

However, you can convert `arguments` to an array and benefit from all the array goodies. Here's what you can do, practicing your newly-learned `call()` method:

```
> function f() {
    var args = [].slice.call(arguments);
    return args.reverse();
  }

> f(1, 2, 3, 4);
  [4, 3, 2, 1]
```

As you can see, you can borrow `slice()` using `[].slice` or the more verbose `Array.prototype.slice`.

Lexical this in arrow functions

We discussed ES6 arrow functions and the syntax in detail in the last chapter. However, an important aspect of arrow functions is that they behave differently from normal functions. The difference is subtle but important. Arrow functions do not have their own value of `this`. The value of `this` in an arrow function is inherited from the enclosing (lexical) scope.

Functions have a special variable `this` that refers to the object via which the method was invoked. As the value of `this` is dynamically given based on the function invocation, it is sometimes called dynamic `this`. A function is executed in two scopes–lexical and dynamic. A lexical scope is a scope that surrounds the function scope, and the dynamic scope is the scope that called the function (usually an object)

In JavaScript, traditional functions play several roles. They are non-method functions (aka subroutines or functions), methods (part of an object), and constructors. When functions do the duty of a subroutine, there is a small problem due to dynamic `this`. As subroutines are not called on an object, the value of `this` is undefined in a strict mode and set to the global scope otherwise. This makes writing `callbacks` difficult. Consider the following example:

```
var greeter = {
  default: "Hello ",
  greet: function (names){
    names.forEach(function(name) {
console.log(this.default + name); //Cannot read property
  'default' of undefined
    })
  }
}
console.log(greeter.greet(['world', 'heaven']))
```

We are passing a subroutine to the `forEach()` function on the `names` array. This subroutine has an undefined value of `this`, and unfortunately, it does not have access to `this` of the outer method `greet`. Clearly, this subroutine needs a lexical `this`,derive `this` from the surrounding scope of the `greet` method. Traditionally, to fix this limitation, we assign the lexical `this` into a variable, which is then accessible to the subroutine via closure.

We can fix the earlier example as follows:

```
var greeter = {
  default: "Hello ",
  greet: function (names){
    let that = this
    names.forEach(function(name) {
      console.log(that.default + name);
    })
  }
}
console.log(greeter.greet(['world', 'heaven']))
```

This is a reasonable hack to simulate lexical `this`. However, the problem with such hacks is that it creates too much noise for the person writing or reviewing `this` code. First, you have to understand the quirk of the behavior of `this`. Even if you understand `this` behavior well, you will need to continuously remain on the lookout for such hacks in your code.

Arrow functions have lexical `this` and do not require such a hack. They are more suited as subroutines because of `this`. We can covert the preceding example to use lexical `this` using the arrow function:

```
var greeter = {
  default: "Hello ",
  greet: function (names){
    names.forEach(name=> {
      console.log(this.default + name);   //lexical 'this'
        available for this subroutine
    })
  }
}
console.log(greeter.greet(['world', 'heaven']))
```

Inferring object types

You can see that you have this array-like arguments object looking so much like an array object. How can you reliably tell the difference between the two? Additionally, `typeof` returns an object when used with arrays. Therefore, how can you tell the difference between an object and an array?

The silver bullet is the `Object` object's `toString()` method. It gives you the internal class name used to create a given object:

```
> Object.prototype.toString.call({});
"[object Object]"
> Object.prototype.toString.call([]);
"[object Array]"
```

You have to call the original `toString()` method as defined in the prototype of the `Object` constructor. Otherwise, if you call the `Array` function's `toString()`, it will give you a different result, as it's been overridden for the specific purposes of the array objects:

```
> [1, 2, 3].toString();
"1,2,3"
```

The preceding code is same as:

```
> Array.prototype.toString.call([1, 2, 3]);
"1,2,3"
```

Let's have some more fun with `toString()`. Make a handy reference to save typing:

```
> var toStr = Object.prototype.toString;
```

The following example shows how we can differentiate between an array and the array-like object `arguments`:

```
> (function () {
    return toStr.call(arguments);
  }());
"[object Arguments]"
```

You can even inspect DOM elements:

```
> toStr.call(document.body);
"[object HTMLBodyElement]"
```

Boolean

Your journey through the built-in objects in JavaScript continues, and the next three are fairly straightforward. They are Boolean, number, and string. They merely wrap the primitive data types.

You already know a lot about Booleans from Chapter 2, *Primitive Data Types, Arrays, Loops, and Conditions*. Now, let's meet the `Boolean()` constructor:

```
> var b = new Boolean();
```

It's important to note that this creates a new object, b, and not a primitive Boolean value. To get the primitive value, you can call the `valueOf()` method (inherited from `Object` class and customized):

```
> var b = new Boolean();
> typeof b;
"object"
> typeof b.valueOf();
"boolean"
> b.valueOf();
false
```

Overall, objects created with the `Boolean()` constructor are not too useful, as they don't provide any methods or properties other than the inherited ones.

The `Boolean()` function, when called as a normal function without `new`, converts non-Booleans to Booleans (which is like using a double negation `!!`value):

```
> Boolean("test");
true
> Boolean("");
false
> Boolean({});
true
```

Apart from the six `false` values, everything else is `true` in JavaScript, including all objects. This also means that all Boolean objects created with `new Boolean()` are also `true`, as they are objects:

```
> Boolean(new Boolean(false));
true
```

This can be confusing, and since Boolean objects don't offer any special methods, it's best to just stick with regular primitive Boolean values.

Number

Similar to `Boolean()`, the `Number()` function can be used as:

- A `constructor` function (with `new`) to create objects.
- A normal function in order to try to convert any value to a number. This is similar to the use of `parseInt()` or `parseFloat()`:

```
> var n = Number('12.12');
> n;
12.12
> typeof n;
"number"
> var n = new Number('12.12');
> typeof n;
"object"
```

As functions are objects, they can also have properties. The `Number()` function has constant built-in properties that you cannot modify:

```
> Number.MAX_VALUE;
1.7976931348623157e+308
> Number.MIN_VALUE;
5e-324
> Number.POSITIVE_INFINITY;
Infinity
> Number.NEGATIVE_INFINITY;
-Infinity
> Number.NaN;
NaN
```

The number objects provide three methods—`toFixed()`, `toPrecision()`, and `toExponential()` (see `Appendix C`, *Built-in Objects*, for more details):

```
> var n = new Number(123.456);
> n.toFixed(1);
"123.5"
```

Note that you can use these methods without explicitly creating a `Number` object first. In such cases, the `Number` object is created (and destroyed) for you behind the scenes:

```
> (12345).toExponential();
"1.2345e+4"
```

Like all objects, the `Number` object also provide the `toString()` method. When used with `Number` object, this method accepts an optional radix parameter (10 being the default):

```
> var n = new Number(255);
> n.toString();
"255"
> n.toString(10);
"255"
> n.toString(16);
"ff"
> (3).toString(2);
"11"
> (3).toString(10);
"3"
```

String

You can use the `String()` constructor function to create string objects. String objects provide convenient methods for text manipulation.

Here's an example that shows the difference between a `String` object and a `primitive` string data type:

```
> var primitive = 'Hello';
> typeof primitive;
"string"
> var obj = new String('world');
> typeof obj;
"object"
```

A `String` object is similar to an array of characters. String objects have an indexed property for each character (introduced in ES5, but long supported in many browsers, except old IEs), and they also have a `length` property.

```
> obj[0];
"w"
> obj[4];
"d"
> obj.length;
5
```

To extract the `primitive` value from the `String` object, you can use the `valueOf()` or `toString()` method inherited from `Object`. You'll probably never need to do this, as `toString()` is called behind the scenes if you use an object in a `primitive` string context:

```
> obj.valueOf();
"world"
> obj.toString();
"world"
> obj + "";
"world"
```

The `primitive` strings are not objects, so they don't have any methods or properties. However, JavaScript also offers you the syntax to treat `primitive` strings as objects (just like you already saw with primitive numbers).

In the following example, `String` objects are being created (and then destroyed) behind the scenes every time you treat a `primitive` string as if it were an object:

```
> "potato".length;
6
> "tomato"[0];
"t"
> "potatoes"["potatoes".length - 1];
"s"
```

Here is one final example to illustrate the difference between a `primitive` string and a `String` object. In this example, we are converting them to Boolean. The empty string is a falsy value, but any string object is truthy (because all objects are truthy):

```
> Boolean("");
false
> Boolean(new String(""));
true
```

Similar to `Number()` and `Boolean()`, if you use the `String()` function without `new`, it converts the parameter to a primitive:

```
> String(1);
"1"
```

If you pass an object to `String()`, this object's `toString()` method will be called first:

```
> String({p: 1});
  "[object Object]"
> String([1, 2, 3]);
  "1,2,3"
> String([1, 2, 3]) === [1, 2, 3].toString();
  true
```

A few methods of string objects

Let's experiment with a few of the methods you can call on string objects (see `Appendix C, Built-in Objects`, for the complete list).

Start off by creating a string object:

```
> var s = new String("Couch potato");
```

The toUpperCase() and toLowerCase() methods transform the capitalization of the string:

```
> s.toUpperCase();
"COUCH POTATO"
> s.toLowerCase();
"couch potato"
```

The charAt() method tells you the character found at the position you specify, which is the same as using square brackets (treating a string as an array of characters):

```
> s.charAt(0);
"C"
> s[0];
"C"
```

If you pass a non-existent position to charAt(), you get an empty string:

```
> s.charAt(101);
""
```

The indexOf() method allows you to search within a string. If there is a match, the method returns the position at which the first match is found. The position count starts at 0, so the second character in Couch is o at position 1:

```
> s.indexOf('o');
1
```

You can optionally specify where (at what position) to start the search. The following finds the second o, because indexOf() is instructed to start the search at position 2:

```
> s.indexOf('o', 2);
7
```

The lastIndexOf() starts the search from the end of the string (but the position of the match is still counted from the beginning):

```
> s.lastIndexOf('o');
11
```

You can search , not only for characters, but also for strings, and the search is case sensitive:

```
> s.indexOf('Couch');
0
```

If there is no match, the function returns position −1:

```
> s.indexOf('couch');
-1
```

For a case-insensitive search, you can transform the string to lowercase first and then search:

```
> s.toLowerCase().indexOf('couch'.toLowerCase());
0
```

If you get 0, this means that the matching part of the string starts at position 0. This can cause confusion when you check with `if`, because `if` converts the position 0 to a Boolean `false` value. So, while this is syntactically correct, it is logically wrong:

```
if (s.indexOf('Couch')) {...}
```

The proper way to check whether a string contains another string is to compare the result of `indexOf()` to the number −1:

```
if (s.indexOf('Couch') !== -1) {...}
```

The `slice()` and `substring()` return a piece of the string when you specify the start and end positions:

```
> s.slice(1, 5);
"ouch"
> s.substring(1, 5);
"ouch"
```

Note that the second parameter you pass is the end position, not the length of the piece. The difference between these two methods is how they treat negative arguments. `substring()` treats them as zeros, while `slice()` adds them to the length of the string. So, if you pass parameters (1, −1) to both methods, it's the same as `substring(1,0)` and `slice(1,s.length−1)`:

```
> s.slice(1, -1);
"ouch potat"
> s.substring(1, -1);
"c"
```

There's also the non-standard method `substr()`, but you should try to avoid it in favor of `substring()`.

The `split()` method creates an array from the string using another string that you pass as a separator:

```
> s.split(" ");
["Couch", "potato"]
```

The `split()` method is the opposite of the `join()` method, which creates a string from an array:

```
> s.split(' ').join(' ');
"Couch potato"
```

The `concat()` glues strings together, in the same way in which the + operator does for `primitive` strings:

```
> s.concat("es");
"Couch potatoes"
```

Note that while some of the preceding methods discussed return new `primitive` strings, none of them modify the source string. After all the method calls listed previously, the initial string is still the same:

```
> s.valueOf();
"Couch potato"
```

You have seen how to use `indexOf()` and `lastIndexOf()` to search within strings, but there are more powerful methods (`search()`, `match()`, and `replace()`) that take regular expressions as parameters. You'll see these later in the `RegExp()` constructor function.

At this point, you're done with all of the data wrapper objects, so let's move on to the utility objects `Math`, `Date`, and `RegExp`.

Math

`Math` is a little different from the other built-in global objects you have seen previously. It's not a function, and, therefore, cannot be used with `new` to create objects. `Math` is a built-in global object that provides a number of methods and properties for mathematical operations.

The `Math` object's properties are constants, so you can't change their values. Their names are all in uppercase to emphasize the difference between them and a normal property (similar to the constant properties of the `Number()` constructor). Let's see a few of these constant properties:

- The constant PI:

```
> Math.PI;
  3.141592653589793
```

- Square root of 2:

```
> Math.SQRT2;
  1.4142135623730951
```

- Euler's constant:

```
> Math.E;
  2.718281828459045
```

- Natural logarithm of 2:

```
> Math.LN2;
  0.6931471805599453
```

- Natural logarithm of 10:

```
> Math.LN10;
  2.302585092994046
```

Now, you know how to impress your friends the next time they (for whatever reason) start wondering, "What was the value of *e*? I can't remember." Just type `Math.E` in the console and you have the answer.

Let's take a look at some of the methods the `Math` object provides (the full list is in `Appendix` `C`, *Built-in Objects*).

Generating random numbers:

```
> Math.random();
  0.3649461670235814
```

The `random()` function returns a number between 0 and 1, so if you want a number between, let's say, 0 and 100, you can use the following line of code:

```
> 100 * Math.random();
```

For numbers between any two values, use the formula `((max-min) * Math.random())+min`. For example, a random number between 2 and 10 can be obtained using the formula as follows:

```
> 8 * Math.random() + 2;
9.175650496668485
```

If you only need an integer, you can use one of the following rounding methods:

- `floor()` to round down
- `ceil()` to round up
- `round()` to round to the nearest

For example, to get either 0 or 1, you can use the following line of code:

```
> Math.round(Math.random());
```

If you need the lowest or the highest among a set of numbers, you have the `min()` and `max()` methods. So, if you have a form on a page that asks for a valid month, you can make sure that you always work with sane data (a value between 1 and 12):

```
> Math.min(Math.max(1, input), 12);
```

The `Math` object also provides the ability to perform mathematical operations for which you don't have a designated operator. This means that you can raise to a power using `pow()`, find the square root using `sqrt()`, and perform all the trigonometric operations–`sin()`, `cos()`, `atan()`, and so on.

For example, to calculate 2 to the power of 8, you can use the following line of code:

```
> Math.pow(2, 8);
256
```

To calculate the square root of 9, you can use the following line of code:

```
> Math.sqrt(9);
3
```

Date

`Date()` is a constructor function that creates date objects. You can create a new object by passing:

- Nothing (defaults to today's date)
- A date-like string
- Separate values for day, month, time, and so on
- A timestamp

Here is an object instantiated with today's date/time (using the browser's timezone):

```
> new Date();
Wed Feb 27 2013 23:49:28 GMT-0800 (PST)
```

The console displays the result of the `toString()` method called on the `Date` object, so you get this long string `Wed Feb 27 2013 23:49:28 GMT-0800 (PST)` as a representation of the date object.

Here are a few examples of using strings to initialize a `Date` object. Note how many different formats you can use to specify the date:

```
> new Date('2015 11 12');
Thu Nov 12 2015 00:00:00 GMT-0800 (PST)
> new Date('1 1 2016');
Fri Jan 01 2016 00:00:00 GMT-0800 (PST)
> new Date('1 mar 2016 5:30');
Tue Mar 01 2016 05:30:00 GMT-0800 (PST)
```

The `Date` constructor can figure out a date from different strings, but this is not really a reliable way of defining a precise date, for example, when passing user input to the constructor. A better way is to pass numeric values to the `Date()` constructor representing:

- Year
- Month – 0 (January) to 11 (December)
- Day – 1 to 31
- Hour – 0 to 23
- Minutes – 0 to 59
- Seconds – 0 to 59
- Milliseconds – 0 to 999

Let's look at some examples.

Passing all the parameters by writing the following line of code:

```
> new Date(2015, 0, 1, 17, 05, 03, 120);
Tue Jan 01 2015 17:05:03 GMT-0800 (PST)
```

Passing date and hour by writing the following line of code:

```
> new Date(2015, 0, 1, 17);
Tue Jan 01 2015 17:00:00 GMT-0800 (PST)
```

Watch out for the fact that the month starts from 0, so 1 is February:

```
> new Date(2016, 1, 28);
Sun Feb 28 2016 00:00:00 GMT-0800 (PST)
```

If you pass a value greater than the one allowed, your date overflows forward. As there's no February 30 in 2016, this means it has to be March 1 (2016 is a leap year):

```
> new Date(2016, 1, 29);
Mon Feb 29 2016 00:00:00 GMT-0800 (PST)
> new Date(2016, 1, 30);
Tue Mar 01 2016 00:00:00 GMT-0800 (PST)
```

Similarly, December 32 becomes January 1 of the next year:

```
> new Date(2012, 11, 31);
Mon Dec 31 2012 00:00:00 GMT-0800 (PST)
> new Date(2012, 11, 32);
Tue Jan 01 2013 00:00:00 GMT-0800 (PST)
```

Finally, a date object can be initialized with a timestamp (the number of milliseconds since the UNIX epoch, where 0 milliseconds is January 1, 1970):

```
> new Date(1357027200000);
Tue Jan 01 2013 00:00:00 GMT-0800 (PST)
```

If you call `Date()` without `new`, you get a string representing the current date, whether or not you pass any parameters. The following example gives the current time (current when this example was run):

```
> Date();
Wed Feb 27 2013 23:51:46 GMT-0800 (PST)
> Date(1, 2, 3, "it doesn't matter");
Wed Feb 27 2013 23:51:52 GMT-0800 (PST)
> typeof Date();
"string"
> typeof new Date();
"object"
```

Methods to work with date objects

Once you've created a date object, there are lots of methods you can call on that object. Most of the methods can be divided into `set*()` and `get*()` methods, for example, `getMonth()`, `setMonth()`, `getHours()`, `setHours()`, and so on. Let's see some examples.

Creating a date object by writing the following code:

```
> var d = new Date(2015, 1, 1);
> d.toString();
Sun Feb 01 2015 00:00:00 GMT-0800 (PST)
```

Setting the month to March (months start from 0):

```
> d.setMonth(2);
1425196800000
> d.toString();
Sun Mar 01 2015 00:00:00 GMT-0800 (PST)
```

Getting the month by writing the following code:

```
> d.getMonth();
2
```

In addition to all the methods of date objects, there are also two methods (plus one more added in ES5) that are properties of the `Date()` function/object. These do not need a `date` object; they work just like the `Math` object methods. In class-based languages, such methods would be called static because they don't require an instance.

The `Date.parse()` method takes a string and returns a timestamp:

```
> Date.parse('Jan 11, 2018');
1515657600000
```

The `Date.UTC()` method takes all the parameters for year, month, day, and so on, and produces a timestamp in **Universal Time** (**UT**):

```
> Date.UTC(2018, 0, 11);
1515628800000
```

As the `new Date()` constructor can accept timestamps, you can pass the result of `Date.UTC()` to it. Using the following example, you can see how `UTC()` works with Universal Time, while `new Date()` works with local time:

```
> new Date(Date.UTC(2018, 0, 11));
Wed Jan 10 2018 16:00:00 GMT-0800 (PST)
> new Date(2018, 0, 11);
Thu Jan 11 2018 00:00:00 GMT-0800 (PST)
```

The ES5 addition to the `Date` constructor is the `now()` method, which returns the current timestamp. It provides a more convenient way to get the timestamp instead of using the `getTime()` method on a `Date` object as you would in ES3:

```
> Date.now();
1362038353044
> Date.now() === new Date().getTime();
true
```

You can think of the internal representation of the date being an integer timestamp and all other methods being sugar on top of it. So, it makes sense that `valueOf()` is a timestamp:

```
> new Date().valueOf();
1362418306432
```

Also, dates cast to integers with the + operator:

```
> +new Date();
1362418318311
```

Calculating birthdays

Let's look at one final example of working with `Date` objects. I was curious about which day my birthday falls on in 2016:

```
> var d = new Date(2016, 5, 20);
> d.getDay();
1
```

Starting the count from 0 (Sunday), 1 means Monday. Is that so?

```
> d.toDateString();
"Mon Jun 20 2016"
```

ok, good to know, but Monday is not necessarily the best day for a party. So, how about a loop that shows how many times June 20 is a Friday from year 2016 to year 3016, or better yet, let's see the distribution of all the days of the week. After all, with all the progress in DNA hacking, we're all going to be alive and kicking in 3016.

First, let's initialize an array with seven elements, one for each day of the week. These will be used as counters. Then, as a loop goes up to 3016, let's increment the counters:

```
var stats = [0, 0, 0, 0, 0, 0, 0];
```

Here is the loop:

```
for (var i = 2016; i < 3016; i++) {
    stats[new Date(i, 5, 20).getDay()]++;
}
```

Here is the result:

```
> stats;
[140, 146, 140, 145, 142, 142, 145]
```

142 Fridays and 145 Saturdays. Woo-hoo!

RegExp

Regular expressions provide a powerful way to search and manipulate text. Different languages have different implementations (think dialects) of the regular expression syntax. JavaScript uses the Perl 5 syntax.

Instead of saying regular expression, people often shorten it to regex or regexp.

A regular expression consists of:

- A pattern you use to match text
- Zero or more modifiers (also called flags) that provide more instructions on how the pattern should be used

The pattern can be as simple as literal text to be matched verbatim, but that's rare, and in such cases you're better off using `indexOf()`. Most of the time, the pattern is more complex and could be difficult to understand. Mastering regular expressions' patterns is a large topic, which won't be discussed in full detail here. Instead, you'll see what JavaScript provides in terms of syntax, objects, and methods in order to support the use of regular expressions. You can also refer to `Appendix D`, *Regular Expressions*, to help you when you're writing patterns.

JavaScript provides the `RegExp()` constructor, which allows you to create regular expression objects:

```
> var re = new RegExp("j.*t");
```

There is also the more convenient **regexp literal notation**:

```
> var re = /j.*t/;
```

In the preceding example, `j.*t` is the regular expression pattern. It means " matches any string that starts with `j`, ends with `t`, and has zero or more characters in between ". The asterisk (`*`) means " zero or more of the preceding, " and the dot (`.`) means " any character ". The pattern needs to be quoted when passed to a `RegExp()` constructor.

Properties of RegExp objects

Regular expression objects have the following properties:

- `global`: If this property is `false`, which is the default, the search stops when the first match is found. Set this to `true` if you want all matches.
- `ignoreCase`: When the match is case insensitive, this property defaults to `false` (meaning the default is a case-sensitive match).
- `multiline`: Search matches that may span over more than one line default to `false`.
- `lastIndex`: The position at which to start the search; this defaults to `0`.
- `source`: This contains the `RegExp` pattern.

None of these properties, except for `lastIndex`, can be changed once the object has been created.

The first three items in the preceding list represent the regex modifiers. If you create a regex object using the constructor, you can pass any combination of the following characters as a second parameter:

- g for `global`
- i for `ignoreCase`
- m for `multiline`

These letters can be in any order. If a letter is passed, the corresponding modifier property is set to `true`. In the following example, all modifiers are set to `true`:

```
> var re = new RegExp('j.*t', 'gmi');
```

Let's verify:

```
> re.global;
true
```

Once set, the modifier cannot be changed:

```
> re.global = false;
> re.global;
true
```

To set any modifiers using the regex literal, you add them after the closing slash:

```
> var re = /j.*t/ig;
> re.global;
true
```

Methods of RegExp objects

Regex objects provide two methods you can use to find matches–`test()` and `exec()`. They both accept a string parameter. The `test()` method returns a Boolean (`true` when there's a match, `false` otherwise), while `exec()` returns an array of matched strings. Obviously, `exec()` is doing more work, so use `test()` only if you really need to do something with the matches. People often use regular expressions to validate data. In this case, `test()` should be enough.

In the following example, there is no match because of the capital J:

```
> /j.*t/.test("Javascript");
false
```

A case-insensitive test gives a positive result:

```
> /j.*t/i.test("Javascript");
true
```

The same test using `exec()` returns an array, and you can access the first element as shown here:

```
> /j.*t/i.exec("Javascript")[0];
"Javascript"
```

String methods that accept regular expressions as arguments

Previously in this chapter, you learned about string objects and how you can use the `indexOf()` and `lastIndexOf()` methods to search within text. Using these methods, you can only specify literal string patterns to search. A more powerful solution would be to use regular expressions to find text. String objects offer you this ability.

String objects provide the following methods that accept regular expression objects as parameters:

- `match()`: Returns an array of matches
- `search()`: Returns the position of the first match
- `replace()`: Allows you to substitute matched text with another string
- `split()`: Accepts a regexp when splitting a string into array elements

search() and match()

Let's look at some examples of using the `search()` and `match()` methods. First, you create a string object:

```
> var s = new String('HelloJavaScriptWorld');
```

Using `match()`, you get an array containing only the first match:

```
> s.match(/a/);
["a"]
```

Using the `g` modifier, you perform a global search, so the result array contains two elements:

```
> s.match(/a/g);
["a", "a"]
```

A case-insensitive match is as follows:

```
> s.match(/j.*a/i);
["Java"]
```

The `search()` method gives you the position of the matching string:

```
> s.search(/j.*a/i);
5
```

replace()

The `replace()` method allows you to replace the matched text with some other string. The following example removes all capital letters (it replaces them with blank strings):

```
> s.replace(/[A-Z]/g, '');
"elloavacriptorld"
```

If you omit the `g` modifier, you're only going to replace the first match:

```
> s.replace(/[A-Z]/, '');
"elloJavaScriptWorld"
```

When a match is found, if you want to include the matched text in the replacement string, you can access it using `$&`. Here's how to add an underscore before the match while keeping the match:

```
> s.replace(/[A-Z]/g, "_$&");
"_Hello_Java_Script_World"
```

When the regular expression contains groups (denoted by parentheses), the matches of each group are available as $1 for the first group, $2 the second, and so on:

```
> s.replace(/([A-Z])/g, "_$1");
"_Hello_Java_Script_World"
```

Imagine you have a registration form on your web page that asks for an e-mail address, username, and password. The user enters their e-mail IDs, and then, your JavaScript kicks in and suggests the username, taking it from the e-mail address:

```
> var email = "stoyan@phpied.com";
> var username = email.replace(/(.*)@.*/, "$1");
> username;
"stoyan"
```

Replace callbacks

When specifying the replacement, you can also pass a function that returns a string. This gives you the ability to implement any special logic you may need before specifying the replacements:

```
> function replaceCallback(match) {
    return "_" + match.toLowerCase();
  }

> s.replace(/[A-Z]/g, replaceCallback);
"_hello_java_script_world"
```

The callback function receives a number of parameters (the previous example ignores all but the first one):

- The first parameter is the `match`
- The last is the string being searched
- The one before last is the position of the `match`
- The rest of the parameters contain any strings matched by any groups in your regex pattern

Let's test this. First, let's create a variable to store the entire arguments array passed to the callback function:

```
> var glob;
```

Next, define a regular expression that has three groups and matches e-mail addresses in the format `something@something.something`:

```
> var re = /(.*)@(.*)\.(.*)/;
```

Finally, let's define a callback function that stores the arguments in `glob` and then returns the replacement:

```
var callback = function () {
  glob = arguments;
  return arguments[1] + ' at ' +
    arguments[2] + ' dot ' + arguments[3];
};
```

Now, perform a test:

```
> "stoyan@phpied.com".replace(re, callback);
"stoyan at phpied dot com"
```

Here's what the callback function received as arguments:

```
> glob;
["stoyan@phpied.com", "stoyan", "phpied", "com", 0,
"stoyan@phpied.com"]
```

split()

You already know about the `split()` method, which creates an array from an input string and a delimiter string. Let's take a string of comma-separated values and split it:

```
> var csv = 'one, two,three ,four';
> csv.split(',');
["one", " two", "three ", "four"]
```

Because the input string happens to have random inconsistent spaces before and after the commas, the array result has spaces too. With a regular expression, you can fix this using `\s*`, which means zero or more spaces:

```
> csv.split(/\s*,\s*/);
["one", "two", "three", "four"]
```

Passing a string when a RegExp is expected

One last thing to note is that the four methods that you have just seen (`split()`, `match()`, `search()`, and `replace()`) can also take strings as opposed to regular expressions. In this case, the string argument is used to produce a new regex as if it were passed to `new RegExp()`.

An example of passing a string to `replace` is shown as follows:

```
> "test".replace('t', 'r');
"rest"
```

The preceding lines of code are the same as the following one:

```
> "test".replace(new RegExp('t'), 'r');
"rest"
```

When you pass a string, you cannot set modifiers the way you do with a normal constructor or regex literal. There's a common source of errors when using a string instead of a regular expression object for string replacements, and it's due to the fact that the `g` modifier is `false` by default. The outcome is that only the first string is replaced, which is inconsistent with most other languages and a little confusing. Here is an example:

```
> "pool".replace('o', '*');
"p*ol"
```

Most likely, you want to replace all occurrences:

```
> "pool".replace(/o/g, '*');
"p**l"
```

Error objects

Errors happen, and it's good to have the mechanisms in place so that your code can realize that there has been an error condition and can recover from it in a graceful manner. JavaScript provides the `try`, `catch`, and `finally` statements to help you deal with errors. If an error occurs, an error object is thrown. Error objects are created using one of these built-in constructors–`EvalError`, `RangeError`, `ReferenceError`, `SyntaxError`, `TypeError`, and `URIError`. All these constructors inherit from `Error`.

Let's just cause an error and see what happens. What's a simple way to cause an error? Just call a function that doesn't exist. Type this into the console:

```
> iDontExist();
```

You'll get something like the following:

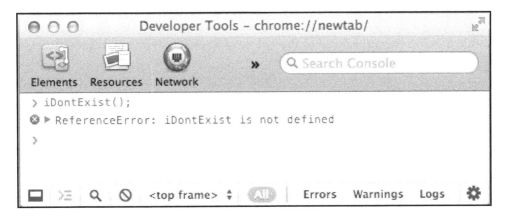

The display of errors can vary greatly between browsers and other host environments. In fact, most recent browsers tend to hide the errors from the users. However, you cannot assume that all of your users have disabled the display of errors, and it is your responsibility to ensure an error-free experience for them. The previous error propagated to the user, because the code didn't try to trap (catch) this error. The code didn't expect the error and was not prepared to handle it. Fortunately, it's trivial to trap the error. All you need is the `try` statement followed by a `catch` statement.

This code hides the error from the user:

```
try {
  iDontExist();
} catch (e) {
  // do nothing
}
```

Here you have:

- The `try` statement followed by a block of code.
- The `catch` statement followed by a variable name in parentheses and another block of code.

There can be an optional `finally` statement (not used in this example) followed by a block of code, which is executed regardless of whether there was an error or not.

In the previous example, the code block that follows the `catch` statement didn't do anything. However, this is the place where you put the code that can help recover from the error, or at least give feedback to the user that your application is aware that there was a special condition.

The variable `e` in the parentheses after the `catch` statement contains an error object. Like any other object, it contains properties and methods. Unfortunately, different browsers implement these methods and properties differently, but there are two properties that are consistently implemented–`e.name` and `e.message`.

Let's try this code now:

```
try {
  iDontExist();
} catch (e) {
  alert(e.name + ': ' + e.message);
} finally {
  alert('Finally!');
}
```

This will present an `alert()` showing `e.name` and `e.message` and then another `alert()` saying `Finally!`.

In Firefox and Chrome, the first alert will say **ReferenceError: iDontExist is not defined**. In Internet Explorer, it will be **TypeError: Object expected**. This tells us two things:

- The `e.name` method contains the name of the constructor that was used to create the error object
- As the error objects are not consistent across host environments (browsers), it would be somewhat tricky to have your code act differently depending on the type of error (the value of `e.name`)

You can also create error objects yourself using `new Error()` or any of the other error constructors and then let the JavaScript engine know that there's an erroneous condition using the `throw` statement.

For example, imagine a scenario where you call the `maybeExists()` function and after that make calculations. You want to trap all errors in a consistent way, no matter whether the error is that `maybeExists()` doesn't exist or that your calculations found a problem. Consider the following code:

```
try {
  var total = maybeExists();
  if (total === 0) {
    throw new Error('Division by zero!');
  } else {
    alert(50 / total);
  }
} catch (e) {
   alert(e.name + ': ' + e.message);
 } finally {
  alert('Finally!');
}
```

This code will alert different messages depending on whether or not `maybeExists()` is defined and the values it returns:

- If `maybeExists()` doesn't exist, you get **ReferenceError: maybeExists() is not defined** in Firefox and **TypeError: Object expected** in IE
- If `maybeExists()` returns 0, you get **Error: Division by zero!**
- If `maybeExists()` returns 2, you get an alert that says **25**

In all cases, there will be a second alert that says **Finally!**.

Instead of throwing a generic error, `thrownewError('Divisionbyzero!')`, you can be more specific if you choose to, for example, throw `thrownewRangeError('Divisionbyzero!')`. Alternatively, you don't need a constructor; you can simply throw a normal object:

```
throw {
  name: "MyError",
  message: "OMG! Something terrible has happened"
}
```

This gives you cross-browser control over the error name.

Exercises

Lets solve the following exercise:

1. Look at the following code:

    ```
    function F() {
      function C() {
        return this;
      }
      return C();
    }
    var o = new F();
    ```

    Does the value of `this` refer to the global object or the object `o`?

2. What's the result of executing this piece of code?

    ```
    function C(){
      this.a = 1;
      return false;
    }
    console.log(typeof new C());
    ```

3. What's the result of executing the following piece of code?

    ```
    > c = [1, 2, [1, 2]];
    > c.sort();
    > c.join('--');
    > console.log(c);
    ```

4. Imagine the `String()` constructor didn't exist. Create a constructor function, `MyString()`, that acts like `String()` as closely as possible. You're not allowed to use any built-in string methods or properties, and remember that the `String()` doesn't exist. You can use this code to test your constructor:

    ```
    > var s = new MyString('hello');
    > s.length;
          5
    > s[0];
          "h"
    > s.toString();
          "hello"
    > s.valueOf();
          "hello"
    > s.charAt(1);
    ```

```
           "e"
> s.charAt('2');
           "1"
> s.charAt('e');
           "h"
> s.concat(' world!');
           "hello world!"
> s.slice(1, 3);
           "el"
> s.slice(0, -1);
           "hell"
> s.split('e');
           ["h", "llo"]
> s.split('l');
           ["he", "", "o"]
```

You can use a `for` loop to loop through the input string, treating it as an array.

5. Update your `MyString()` constructor to include a `reverse()` method.

Try to leverage the fact that arrays have a `reverse()` method.

6. Imagine that `Array()` and the array literal notation don't exist. Create a constructor called `MyArray()` that behaves as close to `Array()` as possible. Test it with the following code:

```
> var a = new MyArray(1, 2, 3, "test");
> a.toString();
      "1,2,3,test"
> a.length;
      4
> a[a.length - 1];
      "test"
> a.push('boo');
      5
> a.toString();
      "1,2,3,test,boo"
> a.pop();
      "boo"
> a.toString();
```

```
            "1,2,3,test"
    > a.join(',');
            "1,2,3,test"
    > a.join(' isn't ');
            "1 isn't 2 isn't 3 isn't test"
```

- If you found this exercise amusing, don't stop with the `join()` method; go on with as many methods as possible.

7. Imagine `Math` didn't exist. Create a `MyMath` object that also provides the following additional methods:

- `MyMath.rand(min, max, inclusive)`: This generates a random number between `min` and `max`, inclusive if `inclusive` is `true` (default)
- `MyMath.min(array)`: This returns the smallest number in a given array
- `MyMath.max(array)`: This returns the largest number in a given array

Summary

In `Chapter 2`, *Primitive Data Types, Arrays, Loops, and Conditions*, you saw that there are five primitive data types (`number`, `string`, `Boolean`, `null`, and `undefined`), and we also said that everything that is not a primitive piece of data is an object. Now, you also know that:

- Objects are like arrays, but you specify the keys
- Objects contain properties
- Properties can be functions (functions are data; remember `var f = function () {};`). Properties that are functions are also called methods
- Arrays are actually objects with predefined numeric properties and an auto-incrementing `length` property
- Array objects have a number of convenient methods (such as `sort()` or `slice()`)
- Functions are also objects, and they have properties (such as `length` and `prototype`) and methods (such as `call()` and `apply()`)

Regarding the five primitive data types, apart from `undefined` and `null`, the other three have the corresponding constructor functions–`Number()`, `String()`, and `Boolean()`. Using these, you can create objects, called wrapper objects, which contain methods for working with primitive data elements.

`Number()`, `String()`, and `Boolean()` can be invoked:

- With the `new` operator, to create new objects.
- Without the `new` operator, to convert any value to the corresponding primitive data type.

Other built-in constructor functions you're now familiar with include `Object()`, `Array()`, `Function()`, `Date()`, `RegExp()`, and `Error()`. You're also familiar with `Math`—a global object that is not a constructor.

Now, you can see how objects have a central role in JavaScript programming, as pretty much everything is an object or can be wrapped by an object.

Finally, let's wrap up the literal notations you're now familiar with:

Name	Literal	Constructor	Example
Object	`{}`	`new Object()`	`{prop: 1}`
Array	`[]`	`new Array()`	`[1,2,3,'test']`
Regular expression	`/pattern/modifiers`	`new RegExp('pattern', 'modifiers')`	`/java.*/img`

5

ES6 Iterators and Generators

So far, we have discussed language constructs of JavaScript without looking at any specific language version. In this chapter, however, we will primarily focus on a few language features introduced in ES6. These features have a big impact on how you write JavaScript code. Not only do they improve the language significantly, they also offer several functional programming constructs unavailable to JavaScript programmers thus far.

In this chapter, we will take a look at newly introduced iterators and generators in ES6. With that knowledge, we will proceed to take a detailed look at the enhanced Collections constructs.

For...of loop

For...of loops are introduced in ES6 along with the iterable and iterator constructs. This new loop constructs replaces both the for...in and for...each loop constructs of ES5. As the for...of loop supports the iteration protocol, it can be used on built-in objects such as arrays, strings, maps, sets, and so on, and custom objects that are iterables. Consider the following piece of code as an example:

```
const iter = ['a', 'b'];
for (const i of iter) {
  console.log(i);
}
"a"
"b"
```

The `for...of` loop works with iterables and built-ins like arrays are iterables. If you notice, we are using `const` instead of `var` when we define the loop variable. This is a good practice because when you use `const`, a fresh variable is created with a new binding and storage space. You should use `const` over a `var` declaration with the `for...of` loop when you don't intend to modify the value of the loop variable inside the block.

Other collections support `for...of` loop too. For example, as a string is a sequence of Unicode characters, `for...of` loop works just fine:

```
for (let c of "String"){
  console.log(c);
}
//"s" "t" "r" "i" "n" "g"
```

The main difference between the `for...in` and `for...of` loop is that the `for...in` loop iterates through all enumerable properties of an object. `For...of` loop has a specific purpose, and that is to follow the iteration behavior based on how the object defines the iterable protocol.

Iterators and iterables

ES6 introduces a new mechanism of iterating over data. Traversing a list of data and doing something with it is a very common operation. ES6 enhances the iteration constructs. There are two primary concepts involved with this change–iterators and iterables.

Iterators

A JavaScript iterator is an object that exposes the `next()` method. This method returns the next item from the collection in the form of an object that has two properties–`done` and `value`. In the following example, we will return an iterator from an array by exposing the `next()` method:

```
//Take an array and return an iterator
function iter(array){
  var nextId= 0;
  return {
    next: function() {
      if(nextId < array.length) {
        return {value: array[nextId++], done: false};
      } else {
        return {done: true};
```

```
        }
      }
    }
  }
  var it = iter(['Hello', 'Iterators']);
  console.log(it.next().value); // 'Hello'
  console.log(it.next().value); // 'Iterators'
  console.log(it.next().done);  // true
```

In the preceding example, we are returning `value` and `done` till we have elements in the array. When we exhaust elements in the array to return, we will return `done` as `true`, indicating that the iteration has no more values. Elements from an iterator are accessed using the `next()` method repeatedly.

Iterables

An iterable is an object that defines its iteration behavior or internal iteration. Such objects can be used in the `for...of` loops introduced in ES6. Built-in types such as arrays and strings define default iteration behavior. For an object to be iterable, it must implement the `@@iterator` method, meaning the object must have a property with `'Symbol.iterator'` as key.

An object becomes iterable if it implements a method whose key is `'Symbol.iterator'`. This method must return an iterator via the `next()` method. Let's take a look at the following example to clarify this:

```
//An iterable object
//1. Has a method with key has 'Symbol.iterator'
//2. This method returns an iterator via method 'next'
let iter = {
  0: 'Hello',
  1: 'World of ',
  2: 'Iterators',
  length: 3,
  [Symbol.iterator]() {
    let index = 0;
    return {
      next: () => {
        let value = this[index];
        let done = index >= this.length;
        index++;
        return { value, done };
      }
    };
  }
```

```
};
for (let i of iter) {
  console.log(i);
}
"Hello"
"World of "
"Iterators"
```

Let's break this example down into smaller pieces. We are creating an iterable object. We will create an `iter` object using object literal syntax that we are already familiar with. One special aspect of this object is a `[Symbol.iterator]` method. This method definition uses a combination of computed properties and ES6 shorthand method definition syntax, which we already discussed in the last chapter. As this object contains a `[Symbol.iterator]` method, this object is iterable, or it follows an iterable protocol. This method also returns the iterator object that defines the iteration behavior via exposing the `next()` method. Now this object can be used with the `for...of` loop.

Generators

Closely linked with iterators and iterables, generators are one of the most talked about features of ES6. Generator functions return a generator object; this term sounds confusing at first. When you write a function, you also instinctively understand its behavior–the function starts execution, line-by-line, and finishes execution when the last line is executed. Once the function is linearly executed this way, the rest of the code that follows the function is executed.

In languages where multithreading is supported, such flow of execution can be interrupted and partially finished tasks can be shared between different threads, processes, and channels. JavaScript is single-threaded, and you don't need to deal with challenges around multithreading at the moment.

However, generator functions can be paused and resumed later. The important idea here is that the generator function chooses to pause itself, it cannot be paused by any external code. During execution, the function uses the `yield` keyword to pause. Once a generator function is paused, it can only be resumed by code outside the function.

You can pause and resume a generator function as many times you want to. With generator functions, a popular pattern is to write infinite loops and pause and resume them when needed. There are pros and cons of doing this, but the pattern has caught up already.

Another important point to understand is that generator functions also allow two-way message passing, in and out of it. Whenever you pause the function using `yield` keyword, the message is sent out of the generator function, and when the function is resumed, the message is passed back to the generator function.

Let's look at the following example to clarify how the generator functions work:

```
function* generatorFunc() {
    console.log('1'); //------------> A
    yield;             //-----------> B
    console.log('2'); //-----------> C
}
const generatorObj = generatorFunc();
console.log(generatorObj.next());
//"1"
//Object {
// "done": false,
// "value": undefined
//}
```

This is a very simple generator function. However, there are several interesting aspects that need careful understanding.

First, notice an asterix `*` immediately after the keyword function, this is the syntax to indicate that the function is a generator function. It is also okay to keep the asterix immediately preceding the function name. Both of the following are valid declarations:

```
function *f(){ }
function* f(){ }
```

Inside the function, the real magic is around the `yield` keyword. When the `yield` keyword is encountered, the function pauses itself. Before we move further, let's see how the function is invoked:

```
const generatorObj = generatorFunc();
generatorObj.next();   //"1"
```

When we invoke the generator function, it is not executed like a normal function, but it returns a generator object. You can use this generator object to control the execution of the generator function. The `next()` method on the generator object resumes the execution of the function.

When we call `next()` the first time, the execution proceeds up until the first line of the function (marked by 'A'), and pauses when the `yield` keyword is encountered. If we call the `next()` function again, it will resume the execution to the next line from the point the execution was paused last time:

```
console.log(generatorObj.next());
//"2"
//Object {
// "done": true,
// "value": undefined
//}
```

Once the entire function body is executed, any calls to `next()` on the generator object have no effect. We talked about generator functions allowing a two-way message passing. How does that work? In the previous example, you can see that whenever we resume the generator function, we receive an object with two values, `done` and `value`; in our case, we received `undefined` as the value. This is because we did not return any value with the `yield` keyword. When you return a value with the `yield` keyword, the calling function receives it. Consider the following example:

```
function* logger() {
  console.log('start')
  console.log(yield)
  console.log(yield)
  console.log(yield)
  return('end')
}

var genObj = logger();

// the first call of next executes from the
  start of the function until the first yield statement
console.log(genObj.next())
// "start", Object {"done": false,"value": undefined}
console.log(genObj.next('Save'))
// "Save", Object {"done": false,"value": undefined}
console.log(genObj.next('Our'))
// "Our", Object {"done": false,"value": undefined}
console.log(genObj.next('Souls'))
// "Souls",Object {"done": true,"value": "end"}
```

Let's trace the flow of execution of this example step by step. The generator function has three pauses or yields. We can create the generator object by writing the following line of code:

```
var genObj = logger();
```

We will start the execution of the generator function by calling the `next` method; this method starts the execution till the first yield. If you notice, we are not passing any value to the `next()` method in the first call. The purpose of this `next()` method is just to start the generator function. We will call the `next()` method again, but this time with a `"Save"` value passed as a parameter. This value is received by `yield` when the function execution is resumed, and we can see the value printed on console:

```
"Save", Object {"done": false,"value": undefined}
```

We will call the `next()` method again with two different values, and the output is similar to the one in the preceding code. When we call the `next()` method the last time, the execution ends and the generator function returns an `end` value to the calling piece of code. At the end of the execution, you will see `done` set as `true` and `value` assigned the value returned by the function, that is, `end`:

```
"Souls",Object {"done": true,"value": "end"}
```

It is important to note that the purpose of the first `next()` method is to start the execution of the generator function—it takes us to the first `yield` keyword and hence, any value passed to the first `next()` method is ignored.

From the discussion so far, it is apparent that generator objects conform to the iterator contract:

```
function* logger() {
  yield 'a'
  yield 'b'
}
var genObj = logger();
//the generator object is built using generator function
console.log(typeof genObj[Symbol.iterator] === 'function')    //true
// it is an iterable
console.log(typeof genObj.next === 'function') //true
// and an iterator (has a next() method)
console.log(genObj[Symbol.iterator]() === genObj) //true
```

This example confirms that generator functions also conform to the iterables contract.

Iterating over generators

Generators are iterators, and like all ES6 constructs that support iterables, they can be used to iterate over generators.

The first method is to use the `for...of` loop, as shown in the following code:

```
function* logger() {
  yield 'a'
  yield 'b'
}
for (const i of logger()) {
  console.log(i)
}
//"a" "b"
```

We are not creating a generator object here. The `For...of` loop has support for iterables and generators naturally fall into this loop.

The spread operator can be used to turn iterables into arrays. Consider the following example:

```
function* logger() {
  yield 'a'
  yield 'b'
}
const arr = [...logger()]
console.log(arr) //["a","b"]
```

Finally, you can use the destructuring syntax with generators, as follows:

```
function* logger() {
  yield 'a'
  yield 'b'
}
const [x,y] = logger()
console.log(x,y) //"a" "b"
```

Generators play an important role in asynchronous programming. Shortly, we will look at asynchronous programming and promises in ES6. JavaScript and Node.js offer a great environment to write asynchronous programs. Generators can help you write cooperative multitasking functions.

Collections

ES6 introduces four data structures–`Map`, `WeakMap`, `Set`, and `WeakSet`. JavaScript, when compared to other languages such as Python and Ruby, had a very weak standard library to support hash or Map data structures or dictionaries. Several hacks were invented to somehow achieve the behavior of a `Map` by mapping a string key with an object. There were side effects of such hacks. Language support for such data structures was sorely needed.

ES6 supports standard dictionary data structures; we will look at more details around these in the next section.

Map

`Map` allows arbitrary values as `keys`. The `keys` are mapped to values. Maps allow fast access to values. Let's look at some examples of maps:

```
const m = new Map(); //Creates an empty Map
m.set('first', 1);   //Set a value associated with a key
console.log(m.get('first'));  //Get a value using the key
```

We will create an empty `Map` using the constructor. You can use the `set()` method to add an entry to the `Map` associating key with value, and overwriting any existing entry with the same key. Its counterpart method, `get()`, gets the value associated with a key, or `undefined` if there is no such entry in the map.

There are other helper methods available with maps, which are as follows:

```
console.log(m.has('first')); //Checks for existence of a key
//true
m.delete('first');
console.log(m.has('first')); //false

m.set('foo', 1);
m.set('bar', 0);

console.log(m.size); //2
m.clear(); //clears the entire map
console.log(m.size); //0
```

You can create a `Map` using the following iterable *[key, value]* pairs as well:

```
const m2 = new Map([
    [ 1, 'one' ],
    [ 2, 'two' ],
    [ 3, 'three' ],
]);
```

You can chain the `set()` method for a compact syntax as follows:

```
const m3 = new Map().set(1, 'one').set(2, 'two').set(3, 'three');
```

We can use any value as a key. For objects, the key can only be strings, but with collections, this limitation is removed. We can use an object as a key as well, though such use is not very popular:

```
const obj = {}
const m2 = new Map([
  [ 1, 'one' ],
  [ "two", 'two' ],
  [ obj, 'three' ],
]);
console.log(m2.has(obj)); //true
```

Iterating over maps

One important thing to remember is that order is important with maps. Maps retain the order in which elements were added.

There are three iterables you can use to iterate over a `Map`, that is, `keys`, `values`, and `entries`.

The `keys()` method returns iterable over the keys of a `Map` as follows:

```
const m = new Map([
  [ 1, 'one' ],
  [ 2, 'two' ],
  [ 3, 'three' ],
]);
for (const k of m.keys()){
  console.log(k);
}
//1 2 3
```

Similarly, the `values()` method returns iterable over the values of a `Map`, as shown in the following example:

```
for (const v of m.values()){
  console.log(v);
}
//"one"
//"two"
//"three"
```

The `entries()` method returns entries of the `Map` in form of a *[key,value]* pair, as you can see in the following code:

```
for (const entry of m.entries()) {
  console.log(entry[0], entry[1]);
}
//1 "one"
//2 "two"
//3 "three"
```

You can use destructuring to make this concise as follows:

```
for (const [key, value] of m.entries()) {
  console.log(key, value);
}
//1 "one"
//2 "two"
//3 "three"
```

An even more succinct:

```
for (const [key, value] of m) {
  console.log(key, value);
}
//1 "one"
//2 "two"
//3 "three"
```

Converting maps to arrays

The spread operator (. . .) comes in handy if you want to convert a `Map` to an array:

```
const m = new Map([
  [ 1, 'one' ],
  [ 2, 'two' ],
  [ 3, 'three' ],
]);
const keys = [...m.keys()]
console.log(keys)
//Array [
//1,
//2,
//3
//]
```

As maps are iterable, you can convert the entire `Map` into an array using spread operators:

```
const m = new Map([
  [ 1, 'one' ],
  [ 2, 'two' ],
  [ 3, 'three' ],
]);
const arr = [...m]
console.log(arr)
//Array [
//[1,"one"],
//[2,"two"],
//[3,"three"]
//]
```

Set

A `Set` is a collection of values. You can add and remove values from it. Although this sounds similar to arrays, sets don't allow the same value twice. Value in a `Set` can be of any type. So far, you must be wondering how different is this from an Array? A `Set` is designed to do one thing quickly–membership testing. Arrays are relatively slower at this. `Set` operations are similar to `Map` operations:

```
const s = new Set();
s.add('first');
s.has('first'); // true
s.delete('first'); //true
s.has('first'); //false
```

Similar to maps, you can create a `Set` via an iterator:

```
const colors = new Set(['red', white, 'blue']);
```

When you add a value to the `Set`, and the value already existed, nothing happens. Similarly, if you delete a value from the `Set`, and the value didn't exist in the first place, nothing happens. There is no way to catch this scenario.

WeakMap and WeakSet

`WeakMap` and `WeakSet` have the similar, but restricted, APIs as the `Map` and `Set` respectively, and they work mostly like their strong counterparts. There are a few differences though, which are as follows:

- `WeakMap` only supports the `new`, `has()`, `get()`, `set()`, and `delete()` methods
- `WeakSet` only supports `new`, `has()`, `add()`, and `delete()`
- Keys of a `WeakMap` must be objects
- Values of a `WeakSet` must be objects
- You can't iterate over `WeakMap`; the only way you can access a value is via its key
- You can't iterate over a `WeakSet`
- You can't clear a `WeakMap` or a `WeakSet`

Let's understand `WeakMap` first. The difference between a `Map` and a `WeakMap` is that a `WeakMap` allows itself to be garbage collected. The keys in a `WeakMap` are weakly held. `WeakMap` keys are not counted when the garbage collector does a reference count (a technique to see all alive references), and they are garbage collected when possible.

WeakMaps are useful when you don't have any control over the life cycle of the object you are keeping in the Map. You don't need to worry about memory leak when using WeakMaps because the objects will not keep the memory occupied even if their life cycle is long.

Same implementation details apply to `WeakSet` as well. However, as you cannot iterate over a `WeakSet`, there are not many use cases for a `WeakSet`.

Summary

In this chapter, we took a detailed look at ES6 Generators. Generators are one of the most anticipated features of ES6. The ability to pause and resume execution of a function opens up a lot of possibilities around co-operative programming. The primary strength of generators is that they provide a single-threaded, synchronous-looking code style, while hiding the asynchronous nature away. This makes it easier for us to express in a very natural way what the flow of our program's steps/statements is without simultaneously having to navigate asynchronous syntax and gotchas. We achieve separation of concern using generators due to this.

Generators work hand-in-hand with the iterators and iterables contract. These are welcome addition to ES6 and significantly boosts the data structures the language offers. Iterators provide a simple way to return a (potentially unbounded) sequence of values. The `@@iterator` symbol is used to define default iterators for objects, making them an iterable.

The most important use case for iterators becomes evident when we want to use it in a construct that consumes iterables, such as the `for...of` loop. In this chapter we also looked at a new loop construct `for...of` introduced in ES6. `for...of` works with a lot of native objects because they have default `@@iterator` methods defined. We looked at new additions to the ES6 collections like–Maps, Sets, WeakMaps, and Weak Sets. These collections have additional iterator methods–`.entries()`, `.values()` and `.keys()`.

The next chapter will take a detailed look at JavaScript Prototypes.

6
Prototype

In this chapter, you'll learn about the prototype property of the function objects. Understanding how the prototype works is an important part of learning the JavaScript language. After all, JavaScript is often classified as having a prototype-based object model. There's nothing particularly difficult about the prototype, but it's a new concept, and as such, may sometimes take a bit of time to sink in. Like closures (see `Chapter 3`, *Functions*), the prototype is one of those things in JavaScript which, once you get, seem so obvious and make perfect sense. As with the rest of this book, you're strongly encouraged to type in and play around with the examples – this makes it much easier to learn and remember the concepts.

In this chapter, we will cover the following topics:

- Every function has a `prototype` property and it contains an object
- Adding properties to the prototype object
- Using the properties added to the prototype
- The difference between own properties and properties of the prototype
- The `__proto__` property, the secret link every object keeps to its prototype
- Methods such as `isPrototypeOf()`, `hasOwnProperty()`, and `propertyIsEnumerable()`
- Enhancing built-in objects, such as arrays or strings, and why that can be a bad idea

The prototype property

The functions in JavaScript are objects, and they contain methods and properties. Some of the methods that you're already familiar with are `apply()` and `call()`, and some of the other properties are `length` and `constructor`. Another property of the function objects is `prototype`.

If you define a simple function, `foo()`, you can access its properties as you would do with any other object. Consider the following code:

```
> function foo(a, b) {
    return a * b;
  }
> foo.length;
2
> foo.constructor;
function Function() { [native code] }
```

The `prototype` property is a property that is available to you as soon as you define the function. Its initial value is an empty object:

```
> typeof foo.prototype;
"object"
```

It's as if you have added this property yourself, as follows:

```
> foo.prototype = {};
```

You can augment this empty object with properties and methods. They won't have any effect on the `foo()` function itself; they'll only be used if you call `foo()` as a constructor.

Adding methods and properties using the prototype

In the previous chapter, you learned how to define constructor functions that you can use to create (construct) new objects. The main idea is that, inside a function invoked with `new`, you will have access to the `this` value, which refers to the object to be returned by the constructor. Augmenting, which is adding methods and properties to `this`, is how you can add functionality to the object being constructed.

Let's take a look at the constructor function, `Gadget()`, which uses `this` to add two properties and one method to the objects it creates, as follows:

```
function Gadget(name, color) {
  this.name = name;
  this.color = color;
  this.whatAreYou = function () {
    return 'I am a ' + this.color + ' ' + this.name;
  };
}
```

Adding methods and properties to the `prototype` property of the constructor function is another way to add functionality to the objects this constructor produces. Let's add two more properties, `price` and `rating`, as well as a `getInfo()` method. As `prototype` already points to an object, you can just keep adding properties and methods to it, as follows:

```
Gadget.prototype.price = 100;
Gadget.prototype.rating = 3;
Gadget.prototype.getInfo = function () {
  return 'Rating: ' + this.rating +
         ', price: ' + this.price;
};
```

Alternatively, instead of adding properties to the `prototype` object one by one, you can overwrite the `prototype` completely, replacing it with an object of your choice, as shown in the following example:

```
Gadget.prototype = {
  price: 100,
  rating: ...  /* and so on... */
};
```

Using the prototype's methods and properties

All the methods and properties you have added to the `prototype` are available as soon as you create a new object using the constructor. If you create a `newtoy` object using the `Gadget()` constructor, you can access all the methods and properties that are already defined, as you can see in the following code:

```
> var newtoy = new Gadget('webcam', 'black');
> newtoy.name;
"webcam"
> newtoy.color;
"black"
> newtoy.whatAreYou();
"I am a black webcam"
> newtoy.price;
100
> newtoy.rating;
3
> newtoy.getInfo();
"Rating: 3, price: 100"
```

It's important to note that the `prototype` is live. Objects are passed by reference in JavaScript, and therefore, the `prototype` is not copied with every new object instance. What does this mean in practice? It means that you can modify the `prototype` at any time, and all the objects, even those created before the modification, will see the changes.

Let's continue the example by adding a new method to the `prototype`:

```
Gadget.prototype.get = function (what) {
  return this[what];
};
```

Even though the `newtoy` object was created before the `get()` method was defined, the `newtoy` object still has access to the new method, which is as follows:

```
> newtoy.get('price');
100
> newtoy.get('color');
"black"
```

Own properties versus prototype properties

In the preceding example, `getInfo()` was used internally to access the properties of the object. It could've also used `Gadget.prototype` to achieve the same output, as follows:

```
Gadget.prototype.getInfo = function () {
  return 'Rating: ' + Gadget.prototype.rating +
         ', price: ' + Gadget.prototype.price;
};
```

What's the difference? To answer this question, let's examine in detail how the `prototype` works.

Let's take the `newtoy` object again:

```
var newtoy = new Gadget('webcam', 'black');
```

When you try to access a property of `newtoy`, say, `newtoy.name`, the JavaScript engine looks through all of the properties of the object searching for one called `name`, and if it finds it, it returns its value, as follows:

```
> newtoy.name;
"webcam"
```

What if you try to access the `rating` property? The JavaScript engine examines all of the properties of the `newtoy` object and doesn't find the one called `rating`. Then, the script engine identifies the `prototype` of the constructor function used to create this object (the same as if you do `newtoy.constructor.prototype`). If the property is found in the `prototype` object, the following property is used:

```
> newtoy.rating;
3
```

You can do the same and access the `prototype` directly. Every object has a `constructor` property, which is a reference to the function that created the object, so in this case look at the following code:

```
> newtoy.constructor === Gadget;
true
> newtoy.constructor.prototype.rating;
3
```

Now, let's take this lookup one step further. Every object has a constructor. The `prototype` is an object, so it must have a constructor too, which, in turn, has a `prototype`. You can go up the prototype chain, and you will eventually end up with the built-in `Object()` object, which is the highest-level parent. In practice, this means that if you try `newtoy.toString()` and `newtoy` doesn't have its own `toString()` method, and its `prototype` doesn't either, in the end, you'll get the object's `toString()` method:

```
> newtoy.toString();
"[object Object]"
```

Overwriting a prototype's property with an own property

As the preceding discussion demonstrates, if one of your objects doesn't have a certain property of its own, it can use one, if it exists, somewhere up the prototype chain. What if the object does have its own property and the prototype also has one with the same name? Then, the own property takes precedence over the prototype's.

Consider a scenario where a property name exists as both an own property and a property of the `prototype` object:

```
> function Gadget(name) {
    this.name = name;
  }
> Gadget.prototype.name = 'mirror';
```

Creating a new object and accessing its `name` property gives you the object's own `name` property, as follows:

```
> var toy = new Gadget('camera');
> toy.name;
"camera"
```

You can tell where the property was defined using `hasOwnProperty()`, which is as follows:

```
> toy.hasOwnProperty('name');
true
```

If you delete the `toy` object's own `name` property, the prototype's property with the same name shines through:

```
> delete toy.name;
true
> toy.name;
"mirror"
> toy.hasOwnProperty('name');
false
```

Of course, you can always recreate the object's own property as follows:

```
> toy.name = 'camera';
> toy.name;
"camera"
```

You can play around with the `hasOwnProperty()` method to find out the origins of a particular property you're curious about. The `toString()` method was mentioned earlier. Where is it coming from?

```
> toy.toString();
"[object Object]"
> toy.hasOwnProperty('toString');
false
> toy.constructor.hasOwnProperty('toString');
false
> toy.constructor.prototype.hasOwnProperty('toString');
false
> Object.hasOwnProperty('toString');
false
> Object.prototype.hasOwnProperty('toString');
true
```

Enumerating properties

If you want to list all the properties of an object, you can use a `for...in` loop. In Chapter 2, *Primitive Data Types, Arrays, Loops, and Conditions*, you saw that you can also loop through all the elements of an array with `for...in`, but as mentioned there, `for` is better suited for arrays and `for...in` for objects. Let's take an example of constructing a query string for a URL from an object:

```
var params = {
  productid: 666,
  section: 'products'
};
```

```
var url = 'http://example.org/page.php?',
    i,
    query = [];

for (i in params) {
    query.push(i + '=' + params[i]);
}

url += query.join('&');
```

This produces the `url` string as follows:

```
http://example.org/page.php?productid=666&section=products.
```

The following are a few details to be aware of:

- Not all properties show up in a `for...in` loop. For example, the length (for arrays) and constructor properties don't show up. The properties that do show up are called enumerable. You can check which ones are enumerable with the help of the `propertyIsEnumerable()` method that every object provides. In ES5, you can specify which properties are enumerable, while in ES3 you don't have that control.
- Prototypes that come through the prototype chain also show up, provided they are enumerable. You can check whether a property is an object's own property or a prototype's property using the `hasOwnProperty()` method.
- The `propertyIsEnumerable()` method returns `false` for all of the prototype's properties, even those that are enumerable and show up in the `for...in` loop.

Let's see these methods in action. Take this simplified version of `Gadget()`:

```
function Gadget(name, color) {
  this.name = name;
  this.color = color;
  this.getName = function () {
    return this.name;
  };
}
Gadget.prototype.price = 100;
Gadget.prototype.rating = 3;
```

Create a new object as follows:

```
var newtoy = new Gadget('webcam', 'black');
```

Now, if you loop using a `for...in` loop, you can see all of the object's properties, including those that come from the prototype:

```
for (var prop in newtoy) {
    console.log(prop + ' = ' + newtoy[prop]);
}
```

The result also contains the object's methods, as methods are just properties that happen to be functions:

```
name = webcam
color = black
getName = function () {
    return this.name;
}
price = 100
rating = 3
```

If you want to distinguish between the object's own properties and the prototype's properties, use `hasOwnProperty()`. Try the following first:

```
> newtoy.hasOwnProperty('name');
true
> newtoy.hasOwnProperty('price');
false
```

Let's loop again, but this time, showing only the object's own properties:

```
for (var prop in newtoy) {
    if (newtoy.hasOwnProperty(prop)) {
        console.log(prop + '=' + newtoy[prop]);
    }
}
```

The result is as follows:

```
name=webcam
color=black
getName = function () {
    return this.name;
}
```

Now, let's try `propertyIsEnumerable()`. This method returns `true` for the object's own properties that are not built in, for example:

```
> newtoy.propertyIsEnumerable('name');
true
```

Most built-in properties and methods are not enumerable:

```
> newtoy.propertyIsEnumerable('constructor');
false
```

Any properties coming down the prototype chain are not enumerable:

```
> newtoy.propertyIsEnumerable('price');
false
```

However, not that such properties are enumerable if you reach the object contained in the `prototype` and invoke its `propertyIsEnumerable()` method. Consider the following code:

```
> newtoy.constructor.prototype.propertyIsEnumerable('price');
true
```

Using isPrototypeOf() method

Objects also have the `isPrototypeOf()` method. This method tells you whether that specific object is used as a prototype of another object.

Let's take a simple object named `monkey`:

```
var monkey = {
  hair: true,
  feeds: 'bananas',
  breathes: 'air'
};
```

Now, let's create a `Human()` constructor function and set its `prototype` property to point to `monkey`:

```
function Human(name) {
  this.name = name;
}
Human.prototype = monkey;
```

Now, if you create a new `Human` object called `george` and ask If `monkey` the prototype of `george?`, you'll get `true`:

```
> var george = new Human('George');
> monkey.isPrototypeOf(george);
true
```

Note that you have to know, or suspect, who the prototype is and then ask is it true that your prototype is `monkey`? in order to confirm your suspicion. But, what if you don't suspect anything, and you have no idea? Can you just ask the object to tell you its prototype? The answer is, you can't in all browsers, but you can in most of them. Most recent browsers have implemented the addition to ES5 called `Object.getPrototypeOf()`.

```
> Object.getPrototypeOf(george).feeds;
"bananas"
> Object.getPrototypeOf(george) === monkey;
true
```

For some of the pre-ES5 environments that don't have `getPrototypeOf()`, you can use the special property, `__proto__`.

The secret __proto__ link

As you already know, the `prototype` property is consulted when you try to access a property that does not exist in the current object.

Consider another object called `monkey`, and use it as a prototype when creating objects with the `Human()` constructor:

```
> var monkey = {
    feeds: 'bananas',
    breathes: 'air'
  };
> function Human() {}
> Human.prototype = monkey;
```

Now, let's create a `developer` object, and give it the following properties:

```
> var developer = new Human();
> developer.feeds = 'pizza';
> developer.hacks = 'JavaScript';
```

Now, let's access these properties (for example, `hacks` is a property of the `developer` object):

```
> developer.hacks;
"JavaScript"
```

The `feeds` property can also be found in the object, as follows:

```
> developer.feeds;
"pizza"
```

The `breathes` property doesn't exist as a property of the `developer` object, so the prototype is looked up, as if there is a secret link or passageway that leads to the `prototype` object:

```
> developer.breathes;
"air"
```

The secret link is exposed in most modern JavaScript environments as the `__proto__` property, the word `proto` with two underscores before and after:

```
> developer.__proto__ === monkey;
true
```

You can use this secret property for learning purposes, but it's not a good idea to use it in your real scripts because it does not exist in all browsers (notably IE), so your scripts won't be portable.

Be aware that `__proto__` is not the same as `prototype`, as `__proto__` is a property of the instances (objects), whereas `prototype` is a property of the constructor functions used to create those objects:

```
> typeof developer.__proto__;
"object"
> typeof developer.prototype;
"undefined"
> typeof developer.constructor.prototype;
"object"
```

Once again, you should use `__proto__` only for learning or debugging purposes. Or, if you're lucky enough and your code only needs to work in ES5-compliant environments, you can use `Object.getPrototypeOf()`.

Augmenting built-in objects

The objects created by the built-in constructor functions, such as `Array`, `String`, and even `Object` and `Function`, can be augmented (or enhanced) through the use of prototypes. This means that you can, for example, add new methods to the `Array` prototype, and in this way you can make them available to all arrays. Let's see how to do this.

In PHP, there is a function called `in_array()`, which tells you whether a value exists in an array. In JavaScript, there is no `inArray()` method, although, in ES5, there's `indexOf()`, which you can use for the same purpose. So, let's implement it and add it to `Array.prototype`, as follows:

```
Array.prototype.inArray = function (needle) {
  for (var i = 0, len = this.length; i < len; i++) {
    if (this[i] === needle) {
      return true;
    }
  }
  return false;
};
```

Now, all arrays have access to the new method. Let's test the following code:

```
> var colors = ['red', 'green', 'blue'];
> colors.inArray('red');
true
> colors.inArray('yellow');
false
```

That was nice and easy! Let's do it again. Imagine your application often needs to spell words backward, and you feel there should be a built-in `reverse()` method for string objects. After all, arrays have `reverse()`. You can easily add a `reverse()` method to the `String` prototype by borrowing `Array.prototype.reverse()` (there was a similar exercise at the end of Chapter 4, *Objects*):

```
String.prototype.reverse = function () {
  return Array.prototype.reverse.
          apply(this.split('')).join('');
};
```

This code uses the `split()` method to create an array from a string, then calls the `reverse()` method on this array, which produces a reversed array. The resulting array is then turned back into a string using the `join()` method. Let's test the new method:

```
> "bumblebee".reverse();
  "eebelbmub"
```

Augmenting built-in objects – discussion

Augmenting built-in objects through the prototype is a powerful technique, and you can use it to shape JavaScript in any way you like. Because of its power, though, you should always thoroughly consider your options before using this approach.

The reason is that once you know JavaScript, you're expecting it to work the same way, no matter which third-party library or widget you're using. Modifying core objects can confuse the users and maintainers of your code and create unexpected errors.

JavaScript evolves and browser's vendors continuously support more features. What you consider a missing method today and decide to add to a core prototype could be a built-in method tomorrow. In this case, your method is no longer needed. Additionally, what if you have already written a lot of code that uses the method and your method is slightly different from the new built-in implementation?

The most common and acceptable use case to augment built-in prototypes is to add support for new features (ones that are already standardized by the ECMAScript committee and implemented in new browsers) to old browsers. One example will be adding an ES5 method to old versions of IE. These extensions are known as **shims** or **polyfills**.

When augmenting prototypes, you will first check if the method exists before implementing it yourself. This way, you can use the native implementation in the browser if one exists. For example, let's add the `trim()` method for strings, which is a method that exists in ES5 but is missing in older browsers:

```
if (typeof String.prototype.trim !== 'function') {
  String.prototype.trim = function () {
    return this.replace(/^\s+|\s+$/g,'');
  };
}
> " hello ".trim();
"hello"
```

Best practice
If you decide to augment a built-in object, or its prototype with a new
property, do check for the existence of the new property first.

Prototype gotchas

The following are the two important behaviors to consider when dealing with prototypes:

- The prototype chain is live, except for when you completely replace the
  `prototype` object
- The `prototype.constructor` method is not reliable

Let's create a simple constructor function and two objects:

```
> function Dog() {
    this.tail = true;
  }
> var benji = new Dog();
> var rusty = new Dog();
```

Even after you've created the `benji` and `rusty` objects, you can still add properties to the
prototype of `Dog()` and the existing objects will have access to the new properties. Let's
throw in the `say()` method:

```
> Dog.prototype.say = function () {
    return 'Woof!';
  };
```

Both objects have access to the new method:

```
> benji.say();
"Woof!"
  rusty.say();
"Woof!"
```

Up to this point, if you consult your objects, asking which constructor function was used to
create them, they'll report it correctly:

```
> benji.constructor === Dog;
true
> rusty.constructor === Dog;
true
```

Now, let's completely overwrite the `prototype` object with a brand new object:

```
> Dog.prototype = {
    paws: 4,
    hair: true
};
```

It turns out that the old objects do not get access to the new prototype's properties; they still keep the secret link pointing to the old prototype object, as follows:

```
> typeof benji.paws;
"undefined"
> benji.say();
"Woof!"
> typeof benji.__proto__.say;
"function"
> typeof benji.__proto__.paws;
"undefined"
```

Any new objects that you will create from now on will use the updated prototype, which is as follows:

```
> var lucy = new Dog();
> lucy.say();
TypeError: lucy.say is not a function
> lucy.paws;
4
```

The secret __proto__ link points to the new prototype object, as shown in the following lines of code:

```
> typeof lucy.__proto__.say;
"undefined"
> typeof lucy.__proto__.paws;
"number"
```

Now the `constructor` property of the new object no longer reports correctly. You will expect it to point to `Dog()`, but instead it points to `Object()`, as you can see in the following example:

```
> lucy.constructor;
function Object() { [native code] }
> benji.constructor;
function Dog() {
  this.tail = true;
}
```

You can easily prevent this confusion by resetting the `constructor` property after you overwrite the prototype completely, as follows:

```
> function Dog() {}
> Dog.prototype = {};
> new Dog().constructor === Dog;
false
> Dog.prototype.constructor = Dog;
> new Dog().constructor === Dog;
true
```

Best practice

When you overwrite the prototype, remember to reset the `constructor` property.

Exercises

Lets practice the following exercise:

1. Create an object called `shape` that has the type `property` and a `getType()` method.
2. Define a `Triangle()` constructor function whose prototype is `shape`. Objects created with `Triangle()` should have three own properties–a, b, and c, representing the lengths of the sides of a triangle.
3. Add a new method to the prototype called `getPerimeter()`.
4. Test your implementation with the following code:

```
> var t = new Triangle(1, 2, 3);
> t.constructor === Triangle;
    true
> shape.isPrototypeOf(t);
    true
> t.getPerimeter();
    6
> t.getType();
    "triangle"
```

5. Loop over t, showing only your own properties and methods, none of the prototype's.

6. Make the following code work:

```
> [1, 2, 3, 4, 5, 6, 7, 8, 9].shuffle();
  [2, 4, 1, 8, 9, 6, 5, 3, 7]
```

Summary

Let's summarize the most important topics you have learned in this chapter:

- All functions have a property called prototype. Initially, it contains an empty object–an object without any own properties.
- You can add properties and methods to the prototype object. You can even replace it completely with an object of your choice.
- When you create an object using a function as a constructor (with new), the object gets a secret link pointing to the prototype of the constructor and can access the prototype's properties.
- An object's own properties take precedence over a prototype's properties with the same name.
- Use the hasOwnProperty() method to differentiate between an object's own properties and prototype properties.
- There is a prototype chain. When you execute foo.bar, and if your foo object doesn't have a property called bar, the JavaScript interpreter looks for a bar property in the prototype. If none is found, it keeps searching in the prototype's prototype, then the prototype of the prototype's prototype, and it will keep going all the way up to Object.prototype.
- You can augment the prototypes of built-in constructor functions, and all objects will see your additions. Assign a function to Array.prototype.flip and all arrays will immediately get a flip() method, as in [1,2,3].flip(). But, do check whether the method/property you want to add already exists, so you can future-proof your scripts.

7
Inheritance

If you go back to `Chapter 1`, *Object-Oriented JavaScript*, and review the *Object-oriented programming* section, you'll see that you already know how to apply most of them to JavaScript. You know what objects, methods, and properties are. You know that there are no classes in ES5, although you can achieve them using constructor functions. ES6 introduces the notion of classes; we will take a detailed look at how ES6 classes work in the next chapter. Encapsulation? Yes, the objects encapsulate both the data and the means (methods) to do something with the data. Aggregation? Sure, an object can contain other objects. In fact, this is almost always the case since methods are functions and functions are also objects.

Now, let's focus on the inheritance part. This is one of the most interesting features, as it allows you to reuse existing code, thus promoting laziness, which is likely to be what brought human species to computer programming in the first place.

JavaScript is a dynamic language, and there is usually more than one way to achieve any given task. Inheritance is not an exception. In this chapter, you'll see some common patterns for implementing inheritance. Having a good understanding of these patterns will help you pick the right one, or the right mix, depending on your task, project, or style.

Prototype chaining

Let's start with the default way of implementing inheritance – inheritance chaining through the prototype.

As you already know, every function has a `prototype` property, which points to an object. When a function is invoked using the `new` operator, an object is created and returned. This new object has a secret link to the `prototype` object. The secret link (called __proto__ in some environments) allows methods and properties of the `prototype` object to be used as if they belonged to the newly created object.

The `prototype` object is just a regular object and, therefore, it also has the secret link to its prototype. And so, a chain called a prototype chain is created:

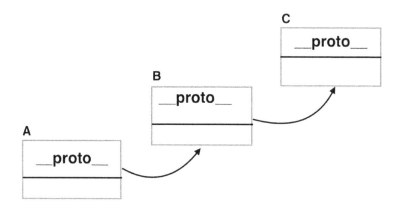

In this illustration, an object **A** contains a number of properties. One of the properties is the hidden __proto__ property, which points to another object, **B**. **B**'s __proto__ property points to **C**. This chain ends with the `Object.prototype` object, the grandparent, and every object inherits from it.

This is all good to know, but how does it help you? The practical side is that when object **A** lacks a property but **B** has it, **A** can still access this property as its own. The same applies if **B** also doesn't have the required property, but **C** does. This is how inheritance takes place – an object can access any property found somewhere down the inheritance chain.

Throughout this chapter, you'll see different examples that use the following hierarchy – a generic `Shape` parent is inherited by a `2D shape`, which in turn is inherited by any number of specific two-dimensional shapes such as a triangle, rectangle, and so on.

Prototype chaining example

Prototype chaining is the default way to implement inheritance. In order to implement the hierarchy, let's define three constructor functions:

```
function Shape(){
this.name = 'Shape';
this.toString = function () {
   return this.name;
  };
}

function TwoDShape(){
  this.name = '2D shape';
}

function Triangle(side, height){
  this.name = 'Triangle';
  this.side = side;
  this.height = height;
  this.getArea = function () {
    return this.side * this.height / 2;
  };
}
```

The code that performs the inheritance magic is as follows:

```
TwoDShape.prototype = new Shape();
Triangle.prototype = new TwoDShape();
```

What's happening here? You take the object contained in the `prototype` property of `TwoDShape`, and instead of augmenting it with individual properties, you completely overwrite it with another object, created by invoking the `Shape()` constructor with `new`. The same process can be followed for `Triangle`–its prototype is replaced by an object created by `new TwoDShape()`. It's important to remember that JavaScript works with objects, not classes. You need to create an instance using the `new Shape()` constructor, and after that, you can inherit its properties; you don't inherit from `Shape()` directly. Additionally, after inheriting, you can modify the `Shape()` constructor, overwrite it, or even delete it, and this will have no effect on `TwoDShape`, because all you needed is one instance to inherit from.

As you know from the previous chapter, overwriting the prototype (as opposed to just adding properties to it), has side effects on the `constructor` property. Therefore, it's a good idea to reset the `constructor` property after inheriting. Consider the following example:

```
TwoDShape.prototype.constructor = TwoDShape;
Triangle.prototype.constructor = Triangle;
```

Now, let's test what has happened so far. Creating a `Triangle` object and calling its own `getArea()` method works as expected:

```
>var my = new Triangle(5, 10);
>my.getArea();
25
```

Although the `my` object doesn't have its own `toString()` method, it inherited one and you can call it. Note how the inherited method `toString()` binds the `this` object to `my`:

```
>my.toString();
"Triangle"
```

It's fascinating to consider what the JavaScript engine does when you call `my.toString()`:

- It loops through all of the properties of `my` and doesn't find a method called `toString()`.
- It looks at the object that `my.__proto__` points to `this` object is the instance `new TwoDShape()` created during the inheritance process.
- Now, the JavaScript engine loops through the instance of `TwoDShape` and doesn't find a `toString()` method. It then checks `__proto__` of that object. This time, `__proto__` points to the instance created by `new Shape()`.
- The instance of `new Shape()` is examined, and `toString()` is finally found.
- This method is invoked in the context of `my`, meaning that `this` points to `my`.

If you ask `my`, Who's your constructor?, it reports it correctly because of the reset of the `constructor` property after the inheritance:

```
>my.constructor === Triangle;
true
```

Using the `instanceof` operator, you can validate that `my` is an instance of all three constructors:

```
> my instanceof Shape;
true
> my instanceofTwoDShape;
true
> my instanceof Triangle;
true
> my instanceof Array;
false
```

The same happens when you call `isPrototypeOf()` on the constructors by passing `my`:

```
>Shape.prototype.isPrototypeOf(my);
true
>TwoDShape.prototype.isPrototypeOf(my);
true
>Triangle.prototype.isPrototypeOf(my);
true
>String.prototype.isPrototypeOf(my);
false
```

You can also create objects using the other two constructors. Objects created with `new TwoDShape()` also get the `toString()` method inherited from `Shape()`:

```
>var td = new TwoDShape();
>td.constructor === TwoDShape;
true
>td.toString();
"2D shape"
>var s = new Shape();
>s.constructor === Shape;
true
```

Moving shared properties to the prototype

When you create objects using a constructor function, own properties are added using `this`. This could be inefficient in cases where properties don't change across instances. In the previous example, `Shape()` was defined as follows:

```
function Shape(){
this.name = 'Shape';
}
```

This means that every time you create a new object using `new Shape()`, a new `name` property is created and stored somewhere in the memory. The other option is to have the `name` property added to the prototype and shared among all the instances:

```
function Shape() {}
Shape.prototype.name = 'Shape';
```

Now, every time you create an object using `new Shape()`, this object doesn't get its own property `name`, but uses the one added to the prototype. This is more efficient, but you should only use it for properties that don't change from one instance to another. Methods are ideal for this type of sharing.

Let's improve the preceding example by adding all methods and suitable properties to `prototype`. In the case of `Shape()` and `TwoDShape()`, everything is meant to be shared:

```
// constructor
function Shape() {}

// augment prototype
Shape.prototype.name = 'Shape';
Shape.prototype.toString = function () {
  return this.name;
};

// another constructor
function TwoDShape() {}

// take care of inheritance
TwoDShape.prototype = new Shape();
TwoDShape.prototype.constructor = TwoDShape;

// augment prototype
TwoDShape.prototype.name = '2D shape';
```

As you can see, you have to take care of inheritance first before augmenting the prototype. Otherwise, anything you add to `TwoDShape.prototype` gets wiped out when you inherit.

The `Triangle` constructor is a little different, because every object it creates is a new triangle, which is likely to have different dimensions. So, it's good to keep `side` and `height` as own properties and share the rest. The `getArea()` method, for example, is the same, regardless of the actual dimensions of each triangle. Again, you do the inheritance bit first and then augment the prototype:

```
function Triangle(side, height) {
this.side = side;
this.height = height;
```

```
}
// take care of inheritance
Triangle.prototype = new TwoDShape();
Triangle.prototype.constructor = Triangle;

// augment prototype
Triangle.prototype.name = 'Triangle';
Triangle.prototype.getArea = function () {
return this.side * this.height / 2;
};
```

All the preceding test code works exactly the same. Here is an example:

```
>var my = new Triangle(5, 10);
>my.getArea();
25
>my.toString();
"Triangle"
```

There is only a slight behind-the-scenes difference when calling `my.toString()`. The difference is that there is one more lookup to be done before the method is found in `Shape.prototype`, as opposed to in the `new Shape()` instance, like it was in the previous example.

You can also play with `hasOwnProperty()` to see the difference between the own property versus a property coming down the prototype chain:

```
>my.hasOwnProperty('side');
true
>my.hasOwnProperty('name');
false
```

The calls to `isPrototypeOf()` and the `instanceof` operator from the previous example work in exactly the same way:

```
>TwoDShape.prototype.isPrototypeOf(my);
true
> my instanceof Shape;
true
```

Inheriting the prototype only

As explained earlier, for reasons of efficiency, you should add the reusable properties and methods to the prototype. If you do so, then it's a good idea to inherit only the prototype, because all the reusable code is there. This means that inheriting the `Shape.prototype` object is better than inheriting the object created with `new Shape()`. After all, `new Shape()` only gives you own shape properties that are not meant to be reused (otherwise, they would be in the prototype). You gain a little more efficiency by:

- Not creating a new object for the sake of inheritance alone
- Having fewer lookups during runtime (when it comes to searching for `toString()`)

For example, here's the updated code; the changes are highlighted:

```
function Shape() {}
// augment prototype
Shape.prototype.name = 'Shape';
Shape.prototype.toString = function () {
  return this.name;
};

function TwoDShape() {}
// take care of inheritance
TwoDShape.prototype = Shape.prototype;
TwoDShape.prototype.constructor = TwoDShape;
// augment prototype
TwoDShape.prototype.name = '2D shape';

function Triangle(side, height) {
  this.side = side;
  this.height = height;
}

// take care of inheritance
Triangle.prototype = TwoDShape.prototype;
Triangle.prototype.constructor = Triangle;
// augment prototype
Triangle.prototype.name = 'Triangle';
Triangle.prototype.getArea = function () {
  return this.side * this.height / 2;
};
```

The test code gives you the same result:

```
>var my = new Triangle(5, 10);
>my.getArea();
25
>my.toString();
"Triangle"
```

What's the difference in the lookups when calling `my.toString()`? First, as usual, the JavaScript engine looks for a `toString()` method of the `my` object itself. The engine doesn't find such a method, so it inspects the prototype. The prototype turns out to be pointing to the same object that the prototype of `TwoDShape` points to and also the same object that `Shape.prototype` points to. Remember that objects are not copied by value, but only by reference. So, the lookup is only a two-step process as opposed to four (in the previous example) or three (in the first example).

Simply copying the prototype is more efficient, but it has a side effect because, all the prototypes of the children and parents point to the same object, when a child modifies the prototype, the parents get the changes and so do the siblings.

Look at the following line:

```
Triangle.prototype.name = 'Triangle';
```

It changes the `name` property, so it effectively changes `Shape.prototype.name` too. If you create an instance using `new Shape()`, its `name` property says `"Triangle"`:

```
>var s = new Shape();
>s.name;
"Triangle"
```

This method is more efficient, but may not suit all your use cases.

A temporary constructor – new F()

A solution to the previously outlined problem, where all prototypes point to the same object and the parents get children's properties, is to use an intermediary to break the chain. The intermediary is in the form of a temporary constructor function. Creating an empty function `F()` and setting its `prototype` to the prototype of the parent constructor allows you to call `new F()` and create objects that have no properties of their own, but inherit everything from the parent's `prototype`.

Let's take a look at the modified code:

```
function Shape() {}
// augment prototype
Shape.prototype.name = 'Shape';
Shape.prototype.toString = function () {
return this.name;
};

function TwoDShape() {}
// take care of inheritance
var F = function () {};
F.prototype = Shape.prototype;
TwoDShape.prototype = new F();
TwoDShape.prototype.constructor = TwoDShape;
// augment prototype
TwoDShape.prototype.name = '2D shape';

function Triangle(side, height) {
this.side = side;
this.height = height;
}

// take care of inheritance
var F = function () {};
F.prototype = TwoDShape.prototype;
Triangle.prototype = new F();
Triangle.prototype.constructor = Triangle;
// augment prototype
Triangle.prototype.name = 'Triangle';
Triangle.prototype.getArea = function () {
return this.side * this.height / 2;
};
```

Creating my triangle and testing the methods:

```
>var my = new Triangle(5, 10);
>my.getArea();
25
>my.toString();
"Triangle"
```

Using this approach, the prototype chain stays in place:

```
>my.__proto__ === Triangle.prototype;
true
>my.__proto__.constructor === Triangle;
true
>my.__proto__.__proto__ === TwoDShape.prototype;
true
>my.__proto__.__proto__.__proto__.constructor === Shape;
true
```

Also, the parents' properties are not overwritten by the children:

```
>var s = new Shape();
>s.name;
"Shape"
>"I am a " + new TwoDShape(); // calling toString()
"I am a 2D shape"
```

At the same time, this approach supports the idea that only properties and methods added to the prototype should be inherited and own properties should not. The rationale behind this is that own properties are likely to be too specific to be reusable.

Uber – access to the parent from a child object

Classical OO languages usually have a special syntax that gives you access to the parent class, also referred to as the superclass. This could be convenient when a child wants to have a method that does everything the parent's method does, plus something in addition to it. In such cases, the child calls the parent's method with the same name and works with the result.

In JavaScript, there is no such special syntax, but it's trivial to achieve the same functionality. Let's rewrite the last example, and while taking care of inheritance, also create an uber property that points to the parent's prototype object:

```
function Shape() {}
// augment prototype
Shape.prototype.name = 'Shape';
Shape.prototype.toString = function () {
var const = this.constructor;
returnconst.uber
    ? this.const.uber.toString() + ', ' + this.name
    : this.name;
```

```
};

function TwoDShape() {}
// take care of inheritance
var F = function () {};
F.prototype = Shape.prototype;
TwoDShape.prototype = new F();
TwoDShape.prototype.constructor = TwoDShape;
TwoDShape.uber = Shape.prototype;
// augment prototype
TwoDShape.prototype.name = '2D shape';

function Triangle(side, height) {
this.side = side;
this.height = height;
}

// take care of inheritance
var F = function () {};
F.prototype = TwoDShape.prototype;
Triangle.prototype = new F();
Triangle.prototype.constructor = Triangle;
Triangle.uber = TwoDShape.prototype;
// augment prototype
Triangle.prototype.name = 'Triangle';
Triangle.prototype.getArea = function () {
return this.side * this.height / 2;
};
```

The new things here are:

- A new `uber` property points to the parent's `prototype`
- The updated `toString()` method

Previously, `toString()` only returned `this.name`. Now, in addition to this, there is a check to see whether `this.constructor.uber` exists and, if it does, call its `toString()` first. The `this.constructor` is the function itself, and `this.constructor.uber` points to the parent's `prototype`. The result is that when you call `toString()` for a `Triangle` instance, all `toString()` methods up the prototype chain are called:

```
>var my = new Triangle(5, 10);
>my.toString();
"Shape, 2D shape, Triangle"
```

The name of the `uber` property could've been superclass, but this would suggest that JavaScript has classes. Ideally, it could've been super (as in Java), but super is a reserved word in JavaScript. The German word uber suggested by Douglas Crockford means more or less the same as super, and you have to admit, it sounds uber cool.

Isolating the inheritance part into a function

Let's move the code that takes care of all the inheritance details from the last example into a reusable `extend()` function:

```
function extend(Child, Parent) {
var F = function () {};
F.prototype = Parent.prototype;
Child.prototype = new F();
Child.prototype.constructor = Child;
Child.uber = Parent.prototype;
}
```

Using this function (or your own custom version of it) helps you keep your code clean with regard to the repetitive inheritance-related tasks. This way, you can inherit by simply using the following two lines of code:

```
extend(TwoDShape, Shape);
extend(Triangle, TwoDShape);
```

Let's see a complete example:

```
// inheritance helper
function extend(Child, Parent) {
  var F = function () {};
  F.prototype = Parent.prototype;
  Child.prototype = new F();
  Child.prototype.constructor = Child;
  Child.uber = Parent.prototype;
}

// define -> augment
function Shape() {}
Shape.prototype.name = 'Shape';
Shape.prototype.toString = function () {
  return this.constructor.uber
    ? this.constructor.uber.toString() + ', ' + this.name
    : this.name;
};
```

```
// define -> inherit -> augment
function TwoDShape() {}
extend(TwoDShape, Shape);
TwoDShape.prototype.name = '2D shape';


// define
function Triangle(side, height) {
  this.side = side;
  this.height = height;
}
// inherit
extend(Triangle, TwoDShape);
// augment
Triangle.prototype.name = 'Triangle';
Triangle.prototype.getArea = function () {
  return this.side * this.height / 2;
};
```

Lets test the following code:

```
> new Triangle().toString();
"Shape, 2D shape, Triangle"
```

Copying properties

Now, let's try a slightly different approach. Since inheritance is all about reusing code, can you simply copy the properties you like from one object to another? Or from a parent to a child? Keeping the same interface as the preceding extend() function, you can create a extend2() function, which takes two constructor functions and copies all the properties from the parent's prototype to the child's prototype. This will, of course, carry over methods too, as methods are just properties that happen to be functions:

```
function extend2(Child, Parent) {
  var p = Parent.prototype;
  var c = Child.prototype;
  for (var i in p) {
    c[i] = p[i];
  }
  c.uber = p;
}
```

As you can see, a simple loop through the properties is all it takes. As with the previous example, you can set an `uber` property if you want to have handy access to parent's methods from the child. Unlike the previous example though, it's not necessary to reset `Child.prototype.constructor` because here, the child `prototype` is augmented, not overwritten completely. So, the `constructor` property points to the initial value.

This method is a little inefficient compared to the previous method because properties of the child `prototype` are being duplicated instead of simply being looked up via the prototype chain during execution. Bear in mind that this is only true for properties containing primitive types. All objects (including functions and arrays) are not duplicated, because these are passed by reference only.

Let's see an example of using two constructor functions, `Shape()` and `TwoDShape()`. The `Shape()` function's `prototype` object contains a primitive property, `name`, and a non-primitive one, the `toString()` method:

```
var Shape = function () {};
var TwoDShape = function () {};
Shape.prototype.name = 'Shape';
Shape.prototype.toString = function () {
  return this.uber
    ? this.uber.toString() + ', ' + this.name
    : this.name;
};
```

If you inherit with `extend()`, neither the objects created with `TwoDShape()` nor its prototype get an own `name` property, but they have access to the one they inherit:

```
> extend(TwoDShape, Shape);
>var td = new TwoDShape();
>td.name;
"Shape"
>TwoDShape.prototype.name;
"Shape"
>td.__proto__.name;
"Shape"
>td.hasOwnProperty('name');
false
> td.__proto__.hasOwnProperty('name');
false
```

However, if you inherit with `extend2()`, the prototype of `TwoDShape()` gets its own copy of the `name` property. It also gets its own copy of `toString()`, but it's a reference only, so the function will not be recreated a second time:

```
>extend2(TwoDShape, Shape);
>var td = new TwoDShape();
> td.__proto__.hasOwnProperty('name');
true
> td.__proto__.hasOwnProperty('toString');
true
> td.__proto__.toString === Shape.prototype.toString;
true
```

As you can see, the two `toString()` methods are the same function object. This is good because it means that no unnecessary duplicates of the methods are created.

So, you can say that `extend2()` is less efficient than `extend()` because it recreates the properties of the prototype. However, this is not so bad because only the primitive data types are duplicated. Additionally, this is beneficial during the prototype chain lookups as there are fewer chain links to follow before finding the property.

Take a look at the `uber` property again. This time, for a change, it's set on the `Parent` object's prototype p, not on the `Parent` constructor. This is why `toString()` uses it as `this.uber` as opposed to `this.constructor.uber`. This is just an illustration that you can shape your favorite inheritance pattern in any way you see fit. Let's test it out:

```
>td.toString();
"Shape, Shape"
```

`TwoDShape` didn't redefine the `name` property, hence the repetition. It can do that at any time, and (the prototype chain being live) all the instances see the update:

```
>TwoDShape.prototype.name = "2D shape";
>td.toString();
"Shape, 2D shape"
```

Heads-up when copying by reference

The fact that objects (including functions and arrays) are copied by reference could sometimes lead to results you don't expect.

Let's create two constructor functions and add properties to the prototype of the first one:

```
> function Papa() {}
>function Wee() {}
>Papa.prototype.name = 'Bear';
>Papa.prototype.owns = ["porridge", "chair", "bed"];
```

Now, let's have `Wee` inherit from `Papa` (either `extend()` or `extend2()` will do):

```
>extend2(Wee, Papa);
```

Using `extend2()`, the `Wee` function's prototype inherited the properties of `Papa.prototype` as its own:

```
>Wee.prototype.hasOwnProperty('name');
true
>Wee.prototype.hasOwnProperty('owns');
true
```

The `name` property is primitive, so a new copy of it is created. The `owns` property is an array object, so it's copied by reference:

```
>Wee.prototype.owns;
["porridge", "chair", "bed"]
>Wee.prototype.owns=== Papa.prototype.owns;
true
```

Changing the `Wee` function's copy of `name` doesn't affect `Papa`:

```
>Wee.prototype.name += ', Little Bear';
"Bear, Little Bear"
>Papa.prototype.name;
"Bear"
```

Changing the `Wee` function's `owns` property, however, affects `Papa`, because both properties point to the same array in memory:

```
>Wee.prototype.owns.pop();
"bed"
>Papa.prototype.owns;
["porridge", "chair"]
```

It's a different story when you completely overwrite the `Wee` function's copy of `owns` with another object (as opposed to modifying the existing one). In this case, `Papa.owns` keeps pointing to the old object, while `Wee.owns` points to a new one:

```
>Wee.prototype.owns= ["empty bowl", "broken chair"];
>Papa.prototype.owns.push('bed');
>Papa.prototype.owns;
["porridge", "chair", "bed"]
```

Think of an object as something that is created and stored in a physical location in memory. Variables and properties merely point to this location, so when you assign a brand new object to `Wee.prototype.owns`, you essentially say–Hey, forget about this other old object, move your pointer to this new one instead.

The following diagram illustrates what happens if you imagine the memory being a heap of objects (like a wall of bricks) and you point to (refer to) some of these objects:

- A new object is created, and **A** points to it.
- A new variable **B** is created and made equal to **A**, meaning it now points to the same place **A** is pointing to.
- A property color is changed using the **B** handle (pointer). The brick is now white. **A** check for `A.color === "white"` would be true.
- A new object is created, and the **B** variable/pointer is recycled to point to that new object. **A** and **B** are now pointing to different parts of the memory pile. They have nothing in common and changes to one of them don't affect the other:

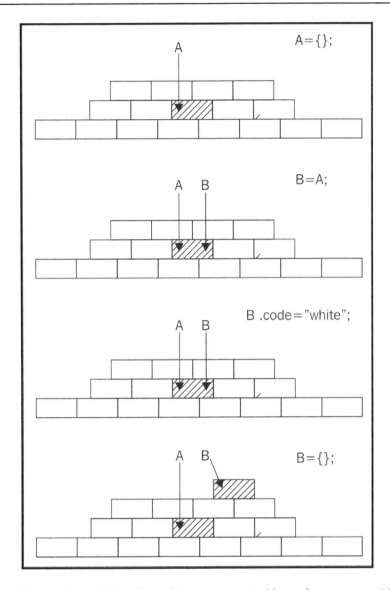

If you want to address the problem that objects are copied by reference, consider a deep copy, described later in the chapter.

Objects inherit from objects

All the examples so far in this chapter assume that you create your objects with constructor functions, and you want objects created with one constructor to inherit properties that come from another constructor. However, you can also create objects without the help of a constructor function, just using the object literal, and this is, in fact, less typing. So, how about inheriting those?

In Java or PHP, you define classes and have them inherit from other classes. That's why you'll see the term classical, because the OO functionality comes from the use of classes. In JavaScript, there are no classes, so programmers that come from a classical background resort to constructor functions, because constructors are the closest to what they are used to. In addition, JavaScript provides the `new` operator, which can further suggest that JavaScript is like Java. The truth is that, in the end, it all comes down to objects. The first example in this chapter used this syntax:

```
Child.prototype = new Parent();
```

Here, the `Child` constructor (or class, if you will) inherits from `Parent`. However, this is done by creating an object using `new Parent()` and inheriting from it. That's why this is also referred to as a **pseudo-classical inheritance pattern**, because it resembles classical inheritance, although it isn't (no classes are involved).

So, why not get rid of the middleman (the constructor/class) and just have objects inherit from objects? In `extend2()`, the properties of the parent `prototype` object were copied as properties of the child `prototype` object. The two prototypes are, in essence, just objects. Forgetting about prototypes and constructor functions, you can simply take an object and copy all of its properties into another object.

You already know that objects can start as a blank canvas without any own properties, using `var o = {};`, and then get properties later. However, instead of starting fresh, you can start by copying all of the properties of an existing object. Here's a function that does exactly this: it takes an object and returns a new copy of it:

```
function extendCopy(p) {
  var c = {};
  for (var i in p) {
    c[i] = p[i];
  }
  c.uber = p;
  return c;
}
```

Simply copying all the properties is a straightforward pattern, and it's widely used. Let's see this function in action. You start by having a base object:

```
var shape = {
name: 'Shape',
toString: function () {
return this.name;
}
};
```

In order to create a new object that builds upon the old one, you can call the extendCopy() function, which returns a new object. Then, you can augment the new object with additional functionality:

```
var twoDee = extendCopy(shape);
twoDee.name = '2D shape';
twoDee.toString = function () {
return this.uber.toString() + ', ' + this.name;
};
```

Here is a triangle object that inherits the 2D shape object:

```
var triangle = extendCopy(twoDee);
triangle.name = 'Triangle';
triangle.getArea = function () {
return this.side * this.height / 2;
};
```

Using the triangle, for example:

```
>triangle.side = 5;
>triangle.height = 10;
>triangle.getArea();
25
>triangle.toString();
"Shape, 2D shape, Triangle"
```

A possible drawback of this method is the somewhat verbose way of initializing the new triangle object, where you manually set values for side and height, as opposed to passing them as values to a constructor. However, this is easily resolved by having a function, for example, called init() (or __construct() if you come from PHP) that acts as a constructor and accepts initialization parameters. Alternatively, have extendCopy() accept two parameters, an object to inherit from and another object literal of properties to add to the copy before it's returned. In other words, just merge two objects.

Deep copy

The `extendCopy()` function discussed previously creates what is called a shallow copy of an object, just like `extend2()` before that. The opposite of a shallow copy would be, naturally, a deep copy. As discussed previously (in the *Heads-up when copying by reference* section of this chapter), when you copy objects, you only copy pointers to the location in memory where the object is stored. This is what happens in a shallow copy. If you modify an object in the copy, you also modify the original. The deep copy avoids this problem.

The deep copy is implemented in the same way as the shallow copy–you loop through the properties and copy them one by one. However, when you encounter a property that points to an object, you call the `deepcopy` function again:

```
function deepCopy(p, c) {
  c = c || {};
  for (var i in p) {
    if (p.hasOwnProperty(i)) {
      if (typeof p[i] === 'object') {
        c[i] = Array.isArray(p[i]) ? [] : {};
deepCopy(p[i], c[i]);
      } else {
        c[i] = p[i];
      }
    }
  }
  return c;
}
```

Let's create an object that has arrays and a subobject as properties:

```
var parent = {
  numbers: [1, 2, 3],
  letters: ['a', 'b', 'c'],
  obj: {
    prop: 1
  },
  bool: true
};
```

Let's test this by creating a deep copy and a shallow copy. Unlike the shallow copy, when you update the `numbers` property of a deep copy, the original is not affected:

```
>var mydeep = deepCopy(parent);
>var myshallow = extendCopy(parent);
>mydeep.numbers.push(4,5,6);
6
```

```
>mydeep.numbers;
[1, 2, 3, 4, 5, 6]
>parent.numbers;
[1, 2, 3]
>myshallow.numbers.push(10);
4
>myshallow.numbers;
[1, 2, 3, 10]
>parent.numbers;
[1, 2, 3, 10]
>mydeep.numbers;
[1, 2, 3, 4, 5, 6]
```

Two side notes about the `deepCopy()` function:

- Filtering out non-own properties with `hasOwnProperty()` is always a good idea to make sure you don't carry over someone's additions to the core prototypes.
- `Array.isArray()` exists since ES5 because it's surprisingly hard otherwise to tell real arrays from objects. The best cross-browser solution (if you need to define `isArray()` in ES3 browsers) looks a little hacky, but it works:

```
if (Array.isArray !== "function") {
Array.isArray = function (candidate) {
    return
Object.prototype.toString.call(candidate) ===
'[object Array]';
};
}
```

Using object() method

Based on the idea that objects inherit from objects, Douglas Crockford advocates the use of an `object()` function that accepts an object and returns a new one that has the parent as a prototype:

```
function object(o) {
function F() {}
F.prototype = o;
return new F();
}
```

If you need access to an `uber` property, you can modify the `object()` function as follows:

```
function object(o) {
var n;
function F() {}
F.prototype = o;
n = new F();
n.uber = o;
return n;
}
```

Using `this` function is the same as using `extendCopy()`, you take an object such as `twoDee`, create a new object from it, and then proceed to augmenting the new object:

```
var triangle = object(twoDee);
triangle.name = 'Triangle';
triangle.getArea = function () {
return this.side * this.height / 2;
};
```

The new triangle still behaves the same way:

```
>triangle.toString();
"Shape, 2D shape, Triangle"
```

This pattern is also referred to as **prototypal inheritance**, because you use a parent object as the prototype of a child object. It's also adopted and built upon in ES5 and called `Object.create()`. Here is an example:

```
>var square = Object.create(triangle);
```

Using a mix of prototypal inheritance and copying properties

When you use inheritance, you will most likely want to take an already existing functionality and then build upon it. This means creating a new object by inheriting from an existing object and then adding additional methods and properties. You can do this with one function call using a combination of the last two approaches just discussed.

You can:

- Use prototypal inheritance to use an existing object as a prototype of a new one
- Copy all the properties of another object into the newly created one:

```
function objectPlus(o, stuff) {
  var n;
  function F() {}
  F.prototype = o;
  n = new F();
  n.uber = o;
  for (var i in stuff) {
    n[i] = stuff[i];
    }
  return n;
}
```

This function takes an object `o` to inherit from and another object `stuff` that has the additional methods and properties that are to be copied. Let's see this in action.

Start with the base `shape` object:

```
var shape = {
name: 'Shape',
toString: function () {
return this.name;
}
};
```

Create a 2D object by inheriting shape and adding more properties. The additional properties are simply created with an object literal:

```
var twoDee = objectPlus(shape, {
  name: '2D shape',
  toString: function () {
    return this.uber.toString() + ', ' + this.name;
  }
});
```

Now, let's create a `triangle` object that inherits from 2D and adds more properties:

```
var triangle = objectPlus(twoDee, {
  name: 'Triangle',
  getArea: function () { return this.side * this.height / 2;
  },
  side: 0,
  height: 0
});
```

You can test how it all works by creating a concrete triangle `my` with defined `side` and `height`:

```
var my = objectPlus(triangle, {
  side: 4, height: 4
});
>my.getArea();
8
>my.toString();
"Shape, 2D shape, Triangle, Triangle"
```

The difference here, when executing `toString()`, is that the `Triangle` name is repeated twice. That's because the concrete instance was created by inheriting `triangle`, so there was one more level of inheritance. You could give the new instance a name:

```
>objectPlus(triangle, {
  side: 4,
  height: 4,
  name: 'My 4x4'
}).toString();
"Shape, 2D shape, Triangle, My 4x4"
```

This `objectPlus()` is even closer to ES5's `Object.create()`; only the ES5 one takes the additional properties (the second argument) using something called property descriptors (discussed in `Appendix C`, *Built-In Objects*).

Multiple inheritance

Multiple inheritance is where a child inherits from more than one parent. Some OO languages support multiple inheritance out of the box and some don't. You can argue both ways, that multiple inheritance is convenient or that it's unnecessary, complicates application design, and it's better to use an inheritance chain instead. Leaving the discussion of multiple inheritance's pros and cons for the long, cold winter nights, let's see how you can do it in practice in JavaScript.

The implementation can be as simple as taking the idea of inheritance by copying properties and expanding it so that it takes an unlimited number of input objects to inherit from.

Let's create a `multi()` function that accepts any number of input objects. You can wrap the loop that copies properties in another loop that goes through all the objects passed as `arguments` to the function:

```
function multi() {
  var n = {}, stuff, j = 0, len = arguments.length;
  for (j = 0; j <len; j++) {
    stuff = arguments[j];
    for (var i in stuff) {
      if (stuff.hasOwnProperty(i)) {
        n[i] = stuff[i];
      }
    }
  }
  return n;
}
```

Let's test this by creating three objects–shape, twoDee, and a third, unnamed object. Then, creating a `triangle` object means calling `multi()` and passing all three objects:

```
var shape = {
  name: 'Shape',
  toString: function () {
    return this.name;
  }
};

var twoDee = {
  name: '2D shape',
  dimensions: 2
};

var triangle = multi(shape, twoDee, {
  name: 'Triangle',
  getArea: function () {
    return this.side * this.height / 2;
  },
  side: 5,
  height: 10
});
```

Does this work? Let's see. The `getArea()` method should be an own property, `dimensions` should come from `twoDee`, and `toString()` should come from `shape`:

```
>triangle.getArea();
25
>triangle.dimensions;
2
>triangle.toString();
"Triangle"
```

Bear in mind that `multi()` loops through the input objects in the order they appear and if it happens that two of them have the same property, the last one wins.

Mixins

You might come across the term mixin. Think of a mixin as an object that provides some useful functionality but is not meant to be inherited and extended by subobjects. The approach to multiple inheritance outlined previously can be considered an implementation of the mixins idea. When you create a new object, you can pick and choose any other objects to mix into your new object. By passing them all to `multi()`, you get all their functionality without making them part of the inheritance tree.

Parasitic inheritance

If you like the fact that you can have all kinds of different ways to implement inheritance in JavaScript and you're hungry for more, here's another one. This pattern, courtesy of Douglas Crockford, is called parasitic inheritance. It's about a function that creates objects by taking all the functionality from another object into a new one, augmenting the new object, and returning it, pretending that it has done all the work.

Here's an ordinary object, defined with an object literal, and unaware of the fact that it's soon going to fall victim to parasitism:

```
var twoD = {
  name: '2D shape',
  dimensions: 2
};
```

A function that creates `triangle` objects could:

- Use the `twoD` object as a prototype of an object called that (similar to this for convenience). This can be done in any way you saw previously, for example, using the `object()` function or copying all the properties.
- Augment that with more properties.
- Return `that`:

```
function triangle(s, h) {
  var that = object(twoD);
  that.name ='Triangle';
  that.getArea = function () {
    return this.side * this.height / 2;
  };
  that.side = s;
  that.height = h;
  return that;
}
```

Because `triangle()` is a normal function, not a constructor, it doesn't require the `new` operator. However, because it returns an object, calling it with `new` by mistake works too:

```
>var t = triangle(5, 10);
>t.dimensions;
 2
>var t2 = new triangle(5,5);
>t2.getArea();
 12.5
```

Note that `that` is just a name, it doesn't have a special meaning, the way `this` does.

Borrowing a constructor

One more way of implementing inheritance (the last one in the chapter, I promise) has to do again with constructor functions and not the objects directly. In this pattern, the constructor of the child calls the constructor of the parent using either the `call()` or `apply()` method. This can be called **stealing a constructor** or **inheritance by borrowing a constructor** if you want to be more subtle about it.

The `call()` and `apply()` methods were discussed in `Chapter 4`, *Objects*, but here's a refresher; they allow you to call a function and pass an object that the function should bind to its `this` value. So for inheritance purposes, the child constructor calls the parent's constructor and binds the child's newly created `this` object as the parent's `this`.

Let's have this parent constructor `Shape()`:

```
function Shape(id) {
  this.id = id;
}
Shape.prototype.name = 'Shape';
Shape.prototype.toString = function () {
  return this.name;
};
```

Now, let's define `Triangle()`, which uses `apply()` to call the `Shape()` constructor, passing `this` (an instance created with `new Triangle()`) and any additional arguments:

```
function Triangle() {
Shape.apply(this, arguments);
}
Triangle.prototype.name = 'Triangle';
```

Note that both `Triangle()` and `Shape()` have added some extra properties to their prototypes.

Now, let's test this by creating a new `triangle` object:

```
>var t = new Triangle(101);
>t.name;
"Triangle"
```

The new `triangle` object inherits the `id` property from the parent, but it doesn't inherit anything added to the parent's `prototype`:

```
>t.id;
101
>t.toString();
"[object Object]"
```

The triangle failed to get the `Shape` function's prototype properties because there was never a `new Shape()` instance created, so the prototype was never used. However, you saw how to do this at the beginning of this chapter. You can redefine `Triangle` as follows:

```
function Triangle() {
   Shape.apply(this, arguments);
}
Triangle.prototype = new Shape();
Triangle.prototype.name = 'Triangle';
```

In this inheritance pattern, the parent's own properties are recreated as the child's own properties. If a child inherits an array or other object, it's a completely new value (not a reference), and modifying it won't affect the parent.

The drawback is that the parent's constructor gets called twice–once with `apply()` to inherit own properties and once with `new` to inherit the prototype. In fact, the own properties of the parent are inherited twice. Let's take this simplified scenario:

```
function Shape(id) {
   this.id = id;
}
function Triangle() {
   Shape.apply(this, arguments);
}
Triangle.prototype = new Shape(101);
```

Here, we will create a new instance:

```
>var t = new Triangle(202);
>t.id;
202
```

There's an own property `id`, but there's also one that comes down the prototype chain, ready to shine through:

```
>t.__proto__.id;
101
> delete t.id;
true
>t.id;
101
```

Borrowing a constructor and copying its prototype

The problem of the double work performed by calling the constructor twice can easily be corrected. You can call apply() on the parent constructor to get all own properties and then copy the prototype's properties using a simple iteration (or extend2() as discussed previously):

```
function Shape(id) {
  this.id = id;
}
Shape.prototype.name = 'Shape';
Shape.prototype.toString = function () {
  return this.name;
};

function Triangle() {
  Shape.apply(this, arguments);
}
extend2(Triangle, Shape);
Triangle.prototype.name = 'Triangle';
```

Lets test the following code:

```
>var t = new Triangle(101);
>t.toString();
"Triangle"
>t.id;
101
```

No double inheritance:

```
>typeoft.__proto__.id;
"undefined"
```

The extend2() method also gives access to uber if needed:

```
>t.uber.name;
"Shape"
```

Case study – drawing shapes

Let's finish off this chapter with a more practical example of using inheritance. The task is to be able to calculate the area and the perimeter of different shapes, as well as to draw them, while reusing as much code as possible.

Analysis

Let's have one `Shape` constructor that contains all the common parts. From there, let's have `Triangle`, `Rectangle`, and `Square` constructors, all inheriting from `Shape`. A square is really a rectangle with the same length sides, so let's reuse `Rectangle` when building `Square`.

In order to define a shape, you'll need points with `x` and `y` coordinates. A generic shape can have any number of points. A triangle is defined with three points, a rectangle (to keep it simpler) with one point and the lengths of the sides. The perimeter of any shape is the sum of its side's lengths. Calculating the area is shape specific and will be implemented by each shape.

The common functionality in `Shape` would be:

- A `draw()` method that can draw any shape given the points
- A `getParameter()` method
- A property that contains an array of `points`
- Other methods and properties as needed

For the drawing part, let's use a `<canvas>` tag. It's not supported in early IEs, but hey, this is just an exercise.

Let's have two other helper constructors–`Point` and `Line`. `Point` will help when defining shapes. `Line` will make calculations easier, as it can give the length of the line connecting any two given points.

You can play with a working example at `http://www.phpied.com/files/canvas/`. Just open your console and start creating new shapes as you'll see in a moment.

Implementation

Let's start by adding a `canvas` tag to a blank HTML page:

```
<canvas height="600" width="800" id="canvas" />
```

Then, put the JavaScript code inside `<script>` tags:

```
<script>
// ... code goes here
</script>
```

Now, let's take a look at what's in the JavaScript part. First is the helper `Point` constructor. It just can't get any simpler than the following:

```
function Point(x, y) {
    this.x = x;
    this.y = y;
}
```

Bear in mind that the coordinates of the points on the `canvas` start from x=0, y=0, which is the top left. The bottom right will be x = 800, y = 600:

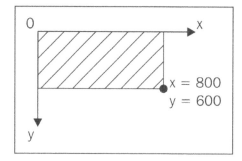

Next comes the `Line` constructor. It takes two points and calculates the length of the line between them, using the Pythagorean theorem $a^2 + b^2 = c^2$ (imagine a right-angled triangle where the hypotenuse connects the two given points):

```
function Line(p1, p2) {
    this.p1 = p1;
    this.p2 = p2;
    this.length = Math.sqrt(
    Math.pow(p1.x - p2.x, 2) +
    Math.pow(p1.y - p2.y, 2)
    );
}
```

Next comes the `Shape` constructor. The shapes will have their points (and the lines that connect them) as own properties. The constructor also invokes an initialization method, `init()`, that will be defined in the prototype:

```
function Shape() {
  this.points = [];
  this.lines= [];
  this.init();
}
```

Now, the big part–the methods of `Shape.prototype`. Let's define all these methods using the object literal notation. Refer to the comments for guidelines as to what each method does:

```
Shape.prototype = {
  // reset pointer to constructor
  constructor: Shape,

  // initialization, sets this.context to point
  // to the context if the canvas object
  init: function () {
    if (this.context === undefined) {
      var canvas = document.getElementById('canvas');
      Shape.prototype.context = canvas.getContext('2d');
    }
  },

  // method that draws a shape by looping through this.points
  draw: function () {
    var i, ctx = this.context;
    ctx.strokeStyle = this.getColor();
    ctx.beginPath();
    ctx.moveTo(this.points[0].x, this.points[0].y);
    for (i = 1; i<this.points.length; i++) {
      ctx.lineTo(this.points[i].x, this.points[i].y);
    }
    ctx.closePath();
    ctx.stroke();
  },

  // method that generates a random color
  getColor: function () {
    var i, rgb = [];
    for (i = 0; i< 3; i++) {
      rgb[i] = Math.round(255 * Math.random());
    }
    return 'rgb(' + rgb.join(',') + ')';
```

```
      },

    // method that loops through the points array,
    // creates Line instances and adds them to this.lines
  getLines: function () {
     if (this.lines.length> 0) {
       return this.lines;
     }
     var i, lines = [];
     for (i = 0; i<this.points.length; i++) {
       lines[i] = new Line(this.points[i],
       this.points[i + 1] || this.points[0]);
     }
     this.lines = lines;
     return lines;
    },

   // shell method, to be implemented by children
   getArea: function () {},
   // sums the lengths of all lines
   getPerimeter: function () {
     var i, perim = 0, lines = this.getLines();
     for (i = 0; i<lines.length; i++) {
       perim += lines[i].length;
     }
     return perim;
   }
 };
```

Now, the children constructor functions. `Triangle` comes first:

```
function Triangle(a, b, c) {
  this.points = [a, b, c];
  this.getArea = function () {
    var p = this.getPerimeter(),
    s = p / 2;
    return Math.sqrt( s * (s - this.lines[0].length) *
      (s - this.lines[1].length) * (s - this.lines[2].length));
  };
}
```

The `Triangle` constructor takes three point objects and assigns them to `this.points` (its own collection of points). Then, it implements the `getArea()` method, using Heron's formula:

```
Area = s(s-a)(s-b)(s-c)
```

`s` is the semi-perimeter (perimeter divided by two).

Next comes the `Rectangle` constructor. It receives one point (the upper-left point) and the lengths of the two sides. Then, it populates its `points` array starting from that one point:

```
function Rectangle(p, side_a, side_b){
this.points = [
p,
new Point(p.x + side_a, p.y),// top right
new Point(p.x + side_a, p.y + side_b), // bottom right
new Point(p.x, p.y + side_b)// bottom left
];
this.getArea = function () {
return side_a * side_b;
};
}
```

The last child constructor is `Square`. A square is a special case of a rectangle, so it makes sense to reuse `Rectangle`. The easiest thing to do here is to borrow the constructor:

```
function Square(p, side){
   Rectangle.call(this, p, side, side);
}
```

Now that all constructors are done, let's take care of inheritance. Any pseudo-classical pattern (one that works with constructors as opposed to objects) will do. Let's try using a modified and simplified version of the prototype-chaining pattern (the first method described in this chapter). This pattern calls for creating a new instance of the parent and setting it as the child's prototype. In this case, it's not necessary to have a new instance for each child–they can all share it:

```
(function () {
var s = new Shape();
Triangle.prototype = s;
Rectangle.prototype = s;
Square.prototype = s;
})();
```

Testing

Let's test this by drawing shapes. First, define three points for a triangle:

```
>var p1 = new Point(100, 100);
>var p2 = new Point(300, 100);
>var p3 = new Point(200, 0);
```

Now you can create a triangle by passing the three points to the `Triangle` constructor:

```
>var t = new Triangle(p1, p2, p3);
```

You can call the methods to draw the triangle on the `canvas` and get its area and perimeter:

```
>t.draw();
>t.getPerimeter();
482.842712474619
>t.getArea();
10000.000000000002
```

Now let's play with a rectangle instance:

```
>var r = new Rectangle(new Point(200, 200), 50, 100);
>r.draw();
>r.getArea();
5000
>r.getPerimeter();
300
```

And finally, let's play with a square:

```
>var s = new Square(new Point(130, 130), 50);
>s.draw();
>s.getArea();
2500
>s.getPerimeter();
200
```

It's fun to draw these shapes. You can also be as lazy as the following example, which draws another square, reusing a triangle's point:

```
> new Square(p1, 200).draw();
```

The result of the tests will be something like the following:

Exercises

Lets do the following exercise:

1. Implement multiple inheritance but with a prototypal inheritance pattern, not property copying. Here is an example:

   ```
   var my = objectMulti(obj, another_obj, a_third, {
   additional: "properties"
   });
   ```

   The `additional` property should be an own property; all the rest should be mixed into the prototype.

2. Use the `canvas` example to practice. Try out different things. Here are some examples:

   - Draw a few triangles, squares, and rectangles.
   - Add constructors for more shapes, such as `Trapezoid`, `Rhombus`, `Kite`, and `Pentagon`. If you want to learn more about the `canvas` tag, create a `Circle` constructor too. It will need to overwrite the `draw()` method of the parent.
   - Can you think of another way to approach the problem and use another type of inheritance?
   - Pick one of the methods that uses `uber` as a way for a child to access its parent. Add functionality where the parents can keep track of who their children are, perhaps using a property that contains a `children` array?

Summary

In this chapter, you learned quite a few ways (patterns) of implementing inheritance, and the following table summarizes them. The different types can roughly be divided into the following:

- Patterns that work with constructors
- Patterns that work with objects

You can also classify the patterns based on whether they:

- Use the prototype
- Copy properties
- Do both (copy properties of the prototype):

#	Name	Example	Classification	Notes
1	Prototype chaining (pseudo-classical)	`Child.prototype = new Parent();`	• Works with constructors • Uses the prototype chain	• The default mechanism • Tip – move all properties/methods that are meant to be reused to the prototype, and add the non-reusable as own properties
2	Inherit only the prototype	`Child.prototype = Parent.prototype;`	• Works with constructors • Copies the prototype (no prototype chain, as all share the same prototype object)	• More efficient; no new instances are created just for the sake of inheritance • Prototype chain lookup during runtime; it is fast, since there's no chain • Drawback: children can modify parents' functionality

#	Name	Example	Classification	Notes
3	Temporary constructor	```function extend(Child, Parent) { var F = function(){}; F.prototype = Parent.prototype; Child.prototype = new F(); Child.prototype.constructor = Child; Child.uber = Parent.prototype; }```	• Works with constructors • Uses the prototype chain	• Unlike #1, it only inherits properties of the prototype; own properties (created with this inside the constructor) are not inherited. • Provides convenient access to the parent (through `uber`)
4	Copying the `prototype` properties	```function extend2(Child, Parent) { var p = Parent.prototype; var c = Child.prototype; for (var i in p) { c[i] = p[i]; } c.uber = p; }```	• Works with constructors • Copies properties • Uses the prototype chain	• All properties of the parent prototype become properties of the child prototype • No need to create a new object only for inheritance purposes • Shorter prototype chains
5	Copy all properties (shallow copy)	```function extendCopy(p) { var c = {}; for (var i in p) { c[i] = p[i]; } c.uber = p; return c; }```	• Works with objects • Copies properties	• Simple • Doesn't use prototypes
6	Deep copy	Same as the previous one, but recurse into objects	• Works with objects • Copies properties	• Same as #5, but clones objects and arrays

[263]

#	Name	Example	Classification	Notes
7	Prototypal inheritance	```function object(o){ function F() {} F.prototype = o; return new F(); }```	• Works with objects • Uses the prototype chain	• No pseudo-classes, objects inherit from objects • Leverages the benefits of the prototype
8	Extend and augment	```function objectPlus(o, stuff) { var n; function F() {} F.prototype = o; n = new F(); n.uber = o; for (var i in stuff) { n[i] = stuff[i]; } return n; }```	• Works with objects • Uses the prototype chain • Copies properties	• Mix of prototypal inheritance (#7) and copying properties (#5) • One function call to inherit and extend at the same time
9	Multiple inheritance	```function multi() { var n = {}, stuff, j = 0, len = arguments.length; for (j = 0; j <len; j++) { stuff = arguments[j]; for (var i in stuff) { n[i] = stuff[i]; } } return n; }```	• Works with objects • Copies properties	• A mixin-style implementation • Copies all the properties of all the parent objects in the order of appearance
10	Parasitic inheritance	```function parasite(victim) { var that = object(victim); that.more = 1; return that; }```	• Works with objects • Uses the prototype chain	• Constructor-like function creates objects • Copies an object, and augments and returns the copy

#	Name	Example	Classification	Notes

11	Borrowing constructors	```function Child() {```
		```Parent.apply(this,```
		```arguments);```
		```}```
			• Works with constructors	• Inherits only own properties
				• Can be combined with #1 to inherit the prototype too
				• Convenient way to deal with the issues when a child inherits a property that is an object (and therefore, passed by reference)

12	Borrow a constructor and copy the prototype	```function Child() {```
		```Parent.apply(this,```
		```arguments);```
		```}```
		```extend2(Child, Parent);```
			• Works with constructors
			• Uses the prototype chain
			• Copies properties
				• Combination of #11 and #4
				• Allows you to inherit both own properties and prototype properties without calling the parent constructor twice

Given so many options, you must be wondering which is the right one. That depends on your style and preferences, your project, task, and team. Are you more comfortable thinking in terms of classes? Then pick one of the methods that work with constructors. Are you going to need just one or a few instances of your class? Then choose an object-based pattern.

Are these the only ways of implementing inheritance? No. You can choose a pattern from the preceding table, you can mix them, or you can think of your own. The important thing is to understand and be comfortable with objects, prototypes, and constructors; the rest is just pure joy.

8
Classes and Modules

In this chapter, we will explore some of the most interesting features introduced in ES6. JavaScript is a prototype-based language and supports prototypical inheritance. In the previous chapter, we discussed the prototype property of an object and how prototypical inheritance works in JavaScript. ES6 brings in classes. If you are coming from traditional object-oriented languages such as Java, you will immediately relate to the well-known concepts of classes. However, they are not the same in JavaScript. Classes in JavaScript are a syntactic sugar over the prototypical inheritance we discussed in the last chapter.

In this chapter, we will take a detailed look at ES6 classes and modules – these are welcome changes to this edition of JavaScript and make **Object Oriented Programming (OOP)** and inheritance significantly easier.

If you are coming from a traditional object-oriented language, prototypical inheritance may feel a bit out of place for you. ES6 classes offer a more traditional syntax for you to get familiarized with prototypical inheritance in JavaScript.

Before we try and delve deeper into classes, let me show you why you should use the ES6 classes syntax over the prototypical inheritance syntax of ES5.

In this snippet, I am creating a class hierarchy of `Person`, `Employee`, and `Engineer`, pretty straightforward. First, we will see the ES5 prototypical inheritance, which is written as follows:

```
var Person = function(firstname) {
    if (!(this instanceof Person)) {
        throw new Error("Person is a constructor");
    }
    this.firstname = firstname;
};

Person.prototype.giveBirth = function() {
```

```
        // ...we give birth to the person
};

var Employee = function(firstname, lastname, job) {
    if (!(this instanceof Employee)) {
        throw new Error("Employee is a constructor");
    }
    Person.call(this, firstname);
    this.job = job;
};
Employee.prototype = Object.create(Person.prototype);
Employee.prototype.constructor = Employee;
Employee.prototype.startJob = function() {
    // ...Employee starts job
};

var Engineer = function(firstname, lastname, job, department) {
    if (!(this instanceof Engineer)) {
        throw new Error("Engineer is a constructor");
    }
    Employee.call(this, firstname, lastname, job);
    this.department = department;
};
Engineer.prototype = Object.create(Employee.prototype);
Engineer.prototype.constructor = Engineer;
Engineer.prototype.startWorking = function() {
    // ...Engineer starts working
};
```

Now let's look at the equivalent code using the ES6 classes syntax:

```
class Person {
    constructor(firstname) {
        this.firsnamet = firstname;
    }
    giveBirth() {
        // ... a person is born
    }
}

class Employee extends Person {
    constructor(firstname, lastname, job) {
        super(firstname);
        this.lastname = lastname;
        this.position = position;
    }

     startJob() {
```

```
        // ...Employee starts job
    }
}

class Engineer extends Employee {
    constructor(firstname, lastname, job, department) {
        super(firstname, lastname, job);
        this.department = department;
    }

    startWorking() {
        // ...Engineer starts working
    }
}
```

If you observe the two preceding code snippets, it will be obvious to you that the second example is pretty neat. If you already know Java or C#, you will feel right at home. However, one important thing to remember is that classes do not introduce any new object-oriented inheritance model to the language, but bring in a much nicer way to create objects and handle inheritance.

Defining classes

Under the hood, classes are special functions. Just like you can define functions using function expressions and declarations, you can define classes as well. One way to define classes is using class declaration.

You can use the `class` keyword and the name of the class. This syntax is very similar to that of Java or C#:

```
class Car {
  constructor(model, year){
    this.model = model;
    this.year = year;
  }
}
console.log(typeof Car); //"function"
```

To establish the fact that classes are a special function, if we get the `typeof` the `Car` class, we will get a function.

There is an important distinction between classes and normal functions. While normal functions are hoisted, classes are not. A normal function is available immediately when you enter a scope in which it is declared; this is called **hoisting**, which means that a normal function can be declared anywhere in the scope, and it will be available. However, classes are not hoisted; they are available only after they are declared. For a normal function, you can say:

```
normalFunction();    //use first
function normalFunction() {}  //declare later
```

However, you cannot use the class before declaring it, for example:

```
var ford = new Car(); //Reference Error
class Car {}
```

The other way to define a class is to use a class expression. A class expression, like a function expression, may or may not have a name.

The following example shows an anonymous class expression:

```
const Car = class {
  constructor(model, year){
    this.model = model;
    this.year = year;
  }
}
```

If you name the class expression, the name is local to the class's body and not available outside:

```
const NamedCar = class Car{
  constructor(model, year){
    this.model = model;
    this.year = year;
  }
  getName() {
      return Car.name;
  }
}
const ford = new NamedCar();
console.log(ford.getName()); // Car
console.log(ford.name); // ReferenceError: name is not defined
```

As you can see, here, we will give a name to the `Car` class. This name is available within the body of the class, but when we try to access it outside the class, we get a reference error.

You cannot use commas while separating members of a class. Semicolons are valid though. This is funny as ES6 ignores semicolons and there is a raging debate about using semicolons in ES6. Consider the following code snippet as an example:

```
class NoCommas {
  method1(){}
  member1;  //This is ignored and can be used to
    separate class members
  member2,  //This is an error
  method2(){}
}
```

Once defined, we can use classes via a `new` keyword and not a function call; here's the example:

```
class Car {
  constructor(model, year){
    this.model = model;
    this.year = year;
  }
}
const fiesta = new Car('Fiesta','2010');
```

Constructor

We have used the `constructor` function in the examples so far. A constructor is a special method used to create and initialize an object created with the class. You can have only one constructor in a class. Constructors are a bit different from the normal constructor functions. Unlike normal constructors, a class constructor can call its parent class constructor via `super()`. We will discuss this in detail when we look at inheritance.

Prototype methods

Prototype methods are prototype properties of the class, and they are inherited by instances of the class.

Prototype methods can also have `getter` and `setter` methods. The syntax of getters and setters is the same as ES5:

```
class Car {
  constructor(model, year){
    this.model = model;
    this.year = year;
```

```
    }
    get model(){
      return this.model
    }
    calculateCurrentValue(){
      return "7000"
    }
}
const fiesta = new Car('Fiesta','2010')
console.log(fiesta.model)
```

Similarly, computed properties are also supported. You can define the name of the method using the expression. The expression needs to be put inside square brackets. We discussed this shorthand syntax in earlier chapters. The following are all equivalent:

```
class CarOne {
    driveCar() {}
}
class CarTwo {
    ['drive'+'Car']() {}
}
const methodName = 'driveCar';
class CarThree {
    [methodName]() {}
}
```

Static methods

Static methods are associated with the class and not with an instance of that class (object). In other words, you can only reach a static method using the name of the class. Static methods are invoked without instantiating the class and they cannot be called on an instance of a class. Static methods are popular in creating utility or helper methods. Consider the following piece of code:

```
class Logger {
  static log(level, message) {
    console.log(`${level} : ${message}`)
  }
}
//Invoke static methods on the Class
Logger.log("ERROR","The end is near") //"ERROR : The end is near"

//Not on instance
const logger = new Logger("ERROR")
logger.log("The end is near")     //logger.log is not a function
```

Static properties

You may ask–well, we have static methods, what about static properties? In the hurry of getting ES6 ready, they did not add static properties. They will be added in future iterations of the language.

Generator methods

We discussed hugely useful generator functions a few chapters back. You can add generator functions as part of class, and they are called generator methods. A generator method is useful because you can define their key as `Symbol.iterator`. The following example shows how generator methods can be defined inside a class:

```
class iterableArg {
    constructor(...args) {
        this.args = args;
    }
    * [Symbol.iterator]() {
        for (const arg of this.args) {
            yield arg;
        }
    }
}

for (const x of new iterableArg('ES6', 'wins')) {
    console.log(x);
}

//ES6
//wins
```

Subclassing

So far, we discussed how to declare classes and the types of members classes can support. A major use of a class is to serve as a template to create other subclasses. When you create a child class from a class, you derive properties of the parent class and extend the parent class by adding more features of its own.

Let's look at the following de facto example of inheritance:

```
class Animal {
    constructor(name) {
        this.name = name;
```

```
    }
    speak() {
      console.log(this.name + ' generic noise');
    }
  }
  class Cat extends Animal {
    speak() {
      console.log(this.name + ' says Meow.');
    }
  }
  var c = new Cat('Grace');
  c.speak();//"Grace says Meow."
```

Here, `Animal` is the base class and the `Cat` class is derived from the class `Animal`. The extend clause allows you to create a subclass of an existing class. This example demonstrates the syntax of subclassing. Let's enhance this example a bit more by writing the following code:

```
  class Animal {
    constructor(name) {
      this.name = name;
    }
    speak() {
      console.log(this.name + ' generic noise');
    }
  }
  class Cat extends Animal {
    speak() {
      console.log(this.name + ' says Meow.');
    }
  }
  class Lion extends Cat {
    speak() {
      super.speak();
      console.log(this.name + ' Roars....');
    }
  }
  var l = new Lion('Lenny');
  l.speak();
  //"Lenny says Meow."
  //"Lenny Roar...."
```

Here, we are using the `super` keyword to call functions from the parent class. The following are the three ways in which the `super` keyword can be used:

- You can use `super (<params>)` as a function call to invoke the constructor of the parent class
- You can use `super.<parentClassMethod>` to access the parent class methods
- You can use `super.<parentClassProp>` to access the parent class properties

In the derive class constructor, you must call the `super()` method before you can use, `this` keyword; for example, the following piece of code will fail:

```
class Base {}
class Derive extends Base {
  constructor(name){
    this.name = name; //'this' is not allowed before super()
  }
}
```

You can't implicitly leave a derived constructor with a `super()` method as an error:

```
class Base {}
class Derive extends Base {
  constructor(){  //missing super() call in constructor
  }
}
```

If you don't provide a constructor for the base class, the following constructor is used:

```
constructor() {}
```

For the derived classes, the default constructor is as follows:

```
constructor(...args){
  super(...args);
}
```

Mixins

JavaScript supports only single inheritance. At most, a class can have one superclass. This is limiting when you want to create class hierarchies but also want to inherit tool methods from different sources.

Let's say we have a scenario where we have a `Person` class, and we create a subclass, `Employee`:

```
class Person {}
class Employee extends Person{}
```

We also want to inherit functions from two utility classes, `BackgroundCheck`–this class does employee background checks–and `Onboard`–this class handles employee onboarding processes, such as printing badges and so on:

```
class BackgroundCheck {
  check() {}
}
class Onboard {
  printBadge() { }
}
```

Both `BackgroundCheck` and `Onboard` classes are templates, and their functionality will be used multiple times. Such templates (abstract subclasses) are called mixins.

As multiple inheritance is not possible in JavaScript, we will employ a different technique to achieve this. A popular way of implementing mixins in ES6 is to write a function with a superclass as an input and a subclass extending that superclass as the output, for example:

```
class Person {}
const BackgroundCheck = Tools => class extends Tools {
  check() {}
};
const Onboard = Tools => class extends Tools {
  printBadge() {}
};
class Employee extends BackgroundCheck(Onboard(Person)){
}
```

This essentially means that `Employee` is a subclass of `BackgroundCheck`, which in turn is a subclass of `Onboard`, which in turn is a subclass of `Person`.

Modules

JavaScript modules are not new. In fact, there were have been libraries that support modules for some time now. ES6, however, offers built-in modules. Traditionally, JavaScript's major use was on browsers, where most of the JavaScript code was either embedded or small enough to manage without much trouble. Things have changed. JavaScript projects are now on a massive scale. Without an efficient system of spreading the code into files and directories, managing code becomes a nightmare.

ES6 modules are files. One module per file and one file per module. There is no module keyword. Whatever code you write in the module file is local to the module unless you export it. You may have a bunch of functions in a module, and you want to export only a few of them. You can export module functionality in a couple of ways.

The first way is to use the `export` keyword. You can export any top-level `function`, `class`, `var`, `let`, or `const`.

The following example shows a module inside `server.js` where we export a `function`, a `class`, and a `const`. We don't export the `processConfig()` function, and any file importing this module won't be able to access the unexported function:

```
//----------------server.js--------------------
export const port = 8080;
export function startServer() {
  //...start server
}
export class Config {
  //...
}
function processConfig() {
  //...
}
```

Any code that has access to `server.js` can import the exported functionality:

```
//-------------app.js------------------------
import {Config, startServer} from 'server'
startServer(port);
```

In this case, another JavaScript file is importing `Config` and `startServer` from the `server` module (with the corresponding JavaScript file `server.js`, we drop the file extension).

You can also import everything that was exported from the module:

```
import * from 'server'
```

If you have only one thing to export, you can use the default export syntax. Consider the following piece of code as an example:

```
//---------------server.js--------------------
export default class {
  //...
}
//------------app.js-------------------------
import Server from 'server';
const s = new Server();
```

In this example, we will keep the class anonymous as we can use the module name itself as the reference outside.

Before ES6 modules, external libraries supported several approaches to modules. They established fairly good guidelines/styles for ES6 to follow. The following style is followed by ES6:

- Modules are singletons. A module is imported only once, even if you try to import it several times in your code.
- Variable, functions, and other type of declarations are local to the module. Only declarations marked with `export` are available outside the module for `import`.
- Modules can import from other modules. The following are the three options for referring to other modules:
    - You can use relative paths (`"../lib/server"`); these paths are resolved relatively to the file importing the module. For example, if you are importing the module from `<project_path>/src/app.js`, and the module file is located at `<project_path>/lib/server.js`, you will need to provide a path relative to the `app.js` – `../lib/server` in this case.
    - Absolute paths can also point to the module file directly.
    - You can drop the file `.js` extension while importing the module.

Before we go into more details of the ES6 module system, we need to understand how ES5 supported them via external libraries. ES5 has two non-compatible module systems, which are as follows:

- **CommonJS**: This is the dominant standard as Node.js adopted it
- **AMD** (**Asynchronous Module Definition**): This is slightly more complicated than CommonJS and designed for asynchronous module loading, and targeted toward browsers

ES6 modules were aimed to be easy to use for engineers coming from any of these systems.

Export lists

Instead of tagging each exported function or class from your module with the `export` keyword, you can write a single list of all the things you want to export from the module, which are as follows:

```
export {port, startServer, Config};
const port = 8080;
function startServer() {
  //...start server
}
class Config {
  //...
}
function processConfig() {
  //...
}
```

The first line of the module is the list of exports. You can have multiple `export` lists in the module file and the list can appear anywhere in the file. You can also have a mix of `export` list and `export` declarations in the same module file, but you can `export` one name only once.

In a large project, there are cases when you encounter name conflicts. Suppose you import two modules, and both of them export a function with the same name. In such cases, you can rename the imports as follows:

```
import {trunc as StringLib} from "../lib/string.js"
import {trunc as MathLib} from "../lib/math.js"
```

Here, both the imported modules exported a name, `trunc`, and hence created a conflict of names. We can alias them to resolve this conflict.

You can do the renaming while exporting as well, which is as follows:

```
function v() {}
function v2() {}
export {
  v as functionV(),
  v2 as functionV2(),
  v2 as functionLatest()
}
```

If you are already using ES5 module systems, ES6 modules may look redundant. However, it was very important for the language to have support for such an important feature. ES6 module syntax is also standardized and more compact than the other alternatives.

Summary

In this chapter, we focused on understanding ES6 classes. ES6 classes give formal support to the common JavaScript pattern of simulating class-like inheritance hierarchies using functions and prototypes. They are syntactic sugaring over prototype-based OO, offering a convenient declarative form for class patterns which encourage interoperability. ES6 classes offer a much nicer, cleaner, and clearer syntax for creating these objects and dealing with inheritance. ES6 classes provide support for constructors, instance and static methods, (prototype-based) inheritance, and super calls.

So far, JavaScript lacked one of the most basic features – modules. Before ES6, we wrote modules using either CommonJS or AMD. ES6 brings modules into JavaScript officially. In this chapter, we took a detailed look at how modules are used in ES6.

The next chapter focuses on another interesting addition to ES6 – proxies and promises.

9
Promises and Proxies

This chapter introduces the important concept of **asynchronous programming** and how JavaScript is an ideal language to utilize it. The other topic that we will cover in this chapter is meta programming with proxies. These two concepts are introduced in ES6.

In this chapter, our primary focus is to understand asynchronous programming, before we jump into the language – specific constructs, let's spend time in understanding the concept first.

The first model–the **synchronous model–**is where it all began. This is the simplest model of programming. Each task is executed one at a time, and only after the first task completes execution can, the next task start. When you program in this model, we expect that all tasks before the current task are complete and there is no error. Take a look at the following figure:

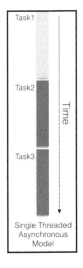

The **single threaded asynchronous model** is a familiar model we all know. However, this model can be wasteful and optimized. For any nontrivial programs composed of several different tasks, this model can be slow. Consider the following hypothetical scenario as an example:

```
var result = database.query("SELECT * FROM table");
console.log("After reading from the database");
```

With the synchronous model in mind, two tasks are executed one after the other. This means that the second statement will only be executed once the first has completed execution. Assuming the first statement is a costly one and takes 10 seconds (it is normal to take even more time to read from a remote database), the second statement will be blocked.

This is a serious problem when you need to write high – performance and scalable systems. There is another problem that manifests when you are writing programs where you need to write interfaces for human interactions like we do on websites that run on a browser. While you are performing a task that may take some time, you cannot block the user. They may be entering something in an input field while the costly task is running; it would be a terrible experience if we block user input while we are busy doing a costly operation. In such scenarios, the costly tasks need to be run in the background while we can happily take input from the user.

To solve this, one solution is to split each task into its own thread of control. This is called the **multi-threaded** or **threaded model**. Consider the following figure:

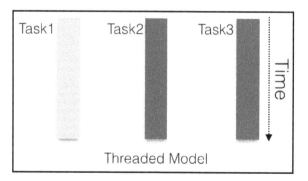

Threaded Model

The difference is how the tasks are split. In the threaded model, each task is performed in its own thread of control. Usually, threads are managed by the operating system and can be run in parallel on different CPU cores or on a single core with appropriate thread scheduling done by the CPU. With modern CPUs, the threaded model can be extremely optimal in performance. Several languages support this popular model. Although a popular model, the threaded model can be complex to implement in practice. The threads need to communicate and coordinate with each other. Inter-thread communication can get tricky very quickly. There are variations of the threaded model where the state is immutable. In such cases, the model becomes simpler as each thread is responsible for immutable state and there is no need to manage state between threads.

Asynchronous programming model

The third model is what interests us the most. In this model, tasks are interleaved in a single thread of control. Consider the following figure:

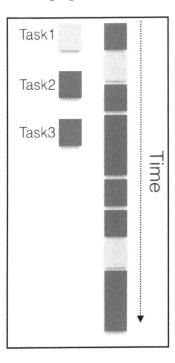

The **asynchronous model** is simpler because you have only one thread. When you are executing one task, you are sure that only that task is being executed. This model doesn't require complex mechanism for inter-thread coordination and, hence, is more predictable. There is one more difference between the threaded and the asynchronous models; in the threaded model, you don't have a way to control the thread execution as the thread scheduling is mostly done by the operating system. However, in the asynchronous model, there is no such challenge.

In which scenarios can the asynchronous model outperform the synchronous model? If we are simply splitting tasks into smaller chunks, intuitively, even the smaller chunks will take quite an amount of time when you add them up in the end.

There is a significant factor we have not yet considered. When you execute a task, you will end up waiting on something–a disk read, a database query, or a network call; these are blocking operations. When you enter a blocked mode, your task simply waits in the synchronous model. Take a look at the following figure:

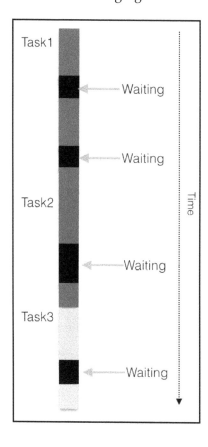

In the preceding diagram, the black blocks are where a task is waiting on something. What are the typical operations that can cause such a block? A task is performed in a CPU and RAM. A typical CPU and RAM can handle data transfer orders of magnitude faster than a typical disc read or a network call.

> Please refer to a comparison (`https://gist.github.com/jboner/2841832`) of latencies between CPU, internal memory, and discs.

When your tasks wait on an **I/O** (**Input/Output**) from such sources, the latency is unpredictable. For a synchronous program that does a lot of I/O, this is a recipe for bad performance.

The most important difference between the synchronous and asynchronous models is the way they handle blocking operations. In the asynchronous model, a program, when faced with a task that encounters a block, executes another task without waiting for the blocking operation to finish. In a program where there are potential blocks, an asynchronous program outperforms an equivalent synchronous program because less time is spent on waiting. A slightly inaccurate visualization of such a model would be as seen in the following figure:

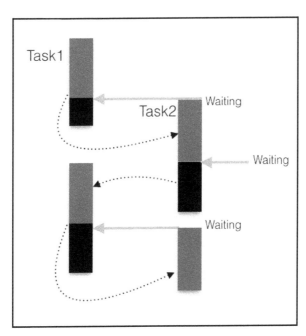

With this conceptual background of the asynchronous model with us, we can look at language – specific constructs to support this model.

JavaScript call stack

In JavaScript, function calls form a stack of frames. Consider the following example:

```
function c(z2) {
    console.log(new Error().stack);
}
function b(z1) {
    c(z1+ 1);
}
function a(z) {
    b(z + 1);
}
a(1);

//at c (eval at <anonymous>)
//at b (eval at <anonymous>)
//at a (eval at <anonymous>)
```

When we call function `a()`, the first frame in the stack is created with arguments to the function and all local variables in the `a()` function. When function `a()` calls function `b()`, a second frame is created and pushed to the top of the stack. This goes on for all function calls. When the `c()` function returns, the top frame from the stack is popped out, leaving functions `b()` and `a()`; this goes on until the entire stack is empty. This is necessary to maintain because once the function finishes execution, JavaScript will need to know where to return.

Message queue

The JavaScript runtime contains a message queue. This queue contains the list of messages to be processed. These messages are queued in response to events such as `click` or an HTTP response received. Each message is associated with a callback function.

Event loop

A browser tab runs in a single thread–an event loop. This loop continuously picks messages from the message queue and executes the callbacks associated with them. The event loop simply keeps picking tasks from the message queues while other processes add tasks to the message queue. Other processes such as timers and event handlers run in parallel and keep adding tasks to the queue.

Timers

The `setTimeout()` method creates a timer and waits until it fires. When the timer is executed, a task is added to the message queue. The `setTimeOut()` method takes two arguments: a callback, and the duration in milliseconds. After the duration, the callback is added to the message queue. Once the callback is added to the message queue, the event loop will eventually pick it up and execute it. There is, however, no guarantee when the callback will be picked up by the event loop.

Run to completion

When the event loop picks up a message from the queue, the associated callback is run to completion. This means that a message is processed completely before the next message from the queue is processed. This property gives the asynchronous model a sense of predictability. As there is no intervention to preempt any of the messages in between execution, this model is much simpler than other models, where any unit of execution can be halted in between. However, once the message is picked up, even if the execution takes too long, any other interaction on the browser is blocked.

Events

You can register event handlers for an object and receive results of a method asynchronously. The following example shows how we can set up event handlers for the XMLHttpRequest API:

```
var xhr = new XMLHttpRequest();
xhr.open('GET', 'http://babeljs.io', true);
xhr.onload = function(e) {
  if (this.status == 200) {
    console.log("Works");
  }
};
xhr.send();
```

In the preceding snippet, we are creating the object of the XMLHttpRequest class. Once the request object is created, we will register event handlers for it. Event handlers, such as onload(), are triggered asynchronously when the response is received from the open() method.

The send() method doesn't actually initiate the request, it adds the request to the message queue for the event loop to pick it up and execute necessary callbacks associated with it.

Callbacks

The Node.js application popularized this style of receiving asynchronous data. A callback is a function passed as the last argument to the asynchronous function call.

To illustrate the usage, let's use the following example of reading a file in Node.js:

```
fs.readFile('/etc/passwd', (err, data) => {
  if (err) throw err;
 console.log(data);
});
```

Don't worry about a few details here. We are using the filesystem module as an fs alias. This module has a readFile method to read a file asynchronously. We will pass the file path and filename as the first argument and a callback function as the last argument of the function. We are using an anonymous function as the callback in the example.

The callback function has two arguments–error and data. When the `readFile()` method is successful, the callback function receives `data`, and if it fails, the `error` argument will have the error details.

We can also use a slightly functional style to write the same callback. Consider the following example:

```
fs.readFile('/etc/passwd',
  //success
  function(data) {
    console.log(data)
  },
  //error
  function(error) {
    console.log(error)
  }
);
```

This style of passing callbacks is also called **continuous-passing style** (**CPS**); the next step of execution or continuation is passed as a parameter. The following example further illustrates the CPS style of callbacks:

```
console.log("1");
cps("2", function cps_step2(val2){
  console.log(val2);
  cps("3", function cos_step3(val3){
    console.log(val3);
  })
  console.log("4");
});
console.log("5");
//1 5 2 4 3

function cps(val, callback) {
  setTimeout(function () {
      callback(val);
  }, 0);
}
```

We will provide the continuation (the next callback) to each step. This nested callback style also causes a problem sometimes referred to as callback hell.

Callbacks and the CPS introduce a radically different style of programming. Although it is easier to understand callbacks compared to other constructs, callbacks can create slightly difficult to understand code.

Promises

ES6 introduces promises as an alternate to callbacks. Like callbacks, promises are used to retrieve the results of an asynchronous function call. Using promises is easier than callbacks and produces more readable code. However, to implement promises for your asynchronous functions requires more work.

A promise object represents a value that may be available now or in the future, or possibly never. As the name suggests, a promise may be fulfilled or rejected. A promise acts as a placeholder for the eventual result.

A promise has three mutually exclusive states, which are as follows:

1. A promise is **pending** before the result is ready; this is the initial state.
2. A promise is **fulfilled** when the result is ready.
3. On an error, a promise is **rejected**.

When a pending promise is either fulfilled or rejected, associated callbacks/handlers that are queued up by the then() method of the promise are executed.

The purpose of promises is to provide a better syntax for the CPS callbacks. The typical CPS style asynchronous functions like the following one:

```
asyncFunction(arg, result => {
  //...
})
```

The preceding code can be written a bit differently with promises, as shown in the following lines of code:

```
asyncFunction(arg).
then(result=>{
  //...
});
```

The asynchronous function now returns a promise, which is the placeholder for an eventual result. Callbacks registered with the then() method are notified when the result is ready.

You can chain the `then()` method. When the `then()` method sees that the callback triggered another asynchronous action that returns a promise, it returns that promise. Take a look at the following example:

```
asyncFunction(arg)
.then(resultA=>{
  //...
  return asyncFunctionB(argB);
})
.then(resultB=>{
  //...
})
```

Let's see a real example of how we can use promises. We saw a typical example of asynchronous file reads in Node.js; now let's see what that example will look like when used with promises. To jog our memories, we wrote something like the following:

```
fs.readFile('text.json',
  function (error, text) {
      if (error) {
          console.error('Error while reading text file');
      } else {
          try {
              //...
          } catch (e) {
              console.error('Invalid content');
          }
      }
  });
```

We see callbacks as continuation here; now let's see how the same function can be written using promises:

```
readFileWithPromises('text.json')
.then(text=>{
  //...process text
})
.catch(error=>{
  console.error('Error while reading text file');
})
```

Now the callbacks are invoked via the result and methods `then()` and `catch()`. The error handling is much cleaner because we are not writing the `if...else` and `try...catch` constructs anymore.

Creating promises

We saw how we can consume promises. Now, let's look at how we can produce them.

As a producer, you can create a `Promise` object and send a result via the `Promise`. The construct looks like the following code snippet:

```
const p = new Promise(
  function (resolve, reject) { // (1)
      if (   ) {
          resolve(value); // success
      } else {
          reject(reason); // failure
      }
  });
```

The parameter to `Promise` is an executor function. The executor handles two states of the promise, which are as follows:

- **Resolving**: If the result was generated successfully, the executor sends the results back via the `resolve()` method. This method usually fulfills the `Promise` object.
- **Rejecting**: If an error happened, the executor notifies the consumer via the `reject()` method. If an exception occurs, it is notified via the `reject()` method as well.

As a consumer, you are notified of either fulfillment of promise or rejection of promise via the `then()` and `catch()` methods. Consider the following piece of code as an example:

```
promise
.then(result => { /* promise fulfilled */ })
.catch(error => { /* promise rejected */ });
```

Now that we have some background on how to produce promises, let's rewrite our earlier example of the asynchronous file's `read` method to produce promises. We will use Node.js's filesystem module and the `readFile()` method as we did last time. If you don't understand any Node.js specific construct in the following snippet, please don't worry. Consider the following code:

```
import {readFile} from 'fs';
function readFileWithPromises(filename) {
    return new Promise(
        function (resolve, reject) {
            readFile(filename,
                (error, data) => {
                    if (error) {
                        reject(error);
                    } else {
                        resolve(data);
                    }
                });
        });
}
```

In the preceding snippet, we are creating a new `Promise` object and returning it to the consumer. As we saw earlier, the parameter to the `Promise` object is the executor function and the executor function takes care of two states of `Promise`–fulfilled and rejected. The executor function takes in two arguments, `resolve` and `reject`. These are the functions that notify the state of the `Promise` object to the consumer.

Inside the executor function, we will call the actual function–the `readFile()` method; if this function is successful, we will return the result using the `resolve()` method and if there is an error, we will notify the consumer using the `reject()` method.

If an error happens in one of the `then()` reactions, they are caught in the subsequent `catch()` block. Take a look at the following code:

```
readFileWithPromises('file.txt')
.then(result=> { 'something causes an exception'})
.catch(error=> {'Something went wrong'});
```

In this case, the `then()` reaction causes an exception or error, and the subsequent `catch()` block can handle this.

Similarly, an exception thrown inside a `then()` or `catch()` handler is passed to the next error handler. Consider the following code snippet:

```
readFileWithPromises('file.txt')
.then(throw new Error())
.catch(error=> {'Something went wrong'});
```

Promise.all()

One interesting use case is to create an iterable over promises. Let's assume that you have a list of URLs you want to visit and parse the results. You can create promises for each of the fetch URL calls and use them individually, or you can create an iterator with all the URLs and use the promise in one go. The `Promise.all()` method takes the iterable of promises as an argument. When all of the promises are fulfilled, an array is filled with their results. Consider the following code as an example:

```
Promise.all([
    f1(),
    f2()
])
.then(([r1,r2]) => {
    //
})
.catch(err => {
    //..
});
```

Metaprogramming and proxies

Metaprogramming refers to a method of programming where the program is aware of its structure and can manipulate itself. Many languages have support for metaprogramming in the form of macros. Macros are important constructs in functional languages such as **LISP (Locator/ID Separation Protocol)**. In languages such as Java and C#, reflection is a form of metaprogramming because a program can examine information about itself using reflection.

In JavaScript, you can say that methods of object allow you to examine the structure and hence, they offer metaprogramming. There are three types of metaprogramming paradigms (*The Art of the Metaobject Protocol,* Kiczales et al, `https://mitpress.mit.edu/books/art-metaobject-protocol`):

- **Introspection**: This gives a read-only access to the internals of a program
- **Self-modification**: This makes structural changes possible to the program
- **Intercession**: This changes language semantics

The `Object.keys()` method is an example of introspection. In the following example, the program is examining its own structure:

```
const introspection = {
  intro() {
    console.log("I think therefore I am");
  }
}
for (const key of Object.keys(introspection)){
  console.log(key);   //intro
}
```

Self-modification is also possible in JavaScript by mutating the properties of an object.

However, intercession, or the ability to change language semantics, is something not available in JavaScript till ES6. Proxies are introduced to open up this possibility.

Proxy

You can use a proxy to determine the behavior of an object, which is called the target, whenever its properties are accessed. A proxy is used to define custom behavior for basic operations on an object, such as looking up a property, function invocation, and assignment.

A proxy needs two parameters, which are as follows:

- **Handler**: For each operation you want to customize, you need a `handler` method. This method intercepts the operations and is sometimes called a trap.
- **Target**: When the `handler` does not intercept the operation, the `target` is used as a fallback.

Let's take a look at the following example to understand this concept better:

```
var handler = {
  get: function(target, name){
    return name in target ? target[name] :42;
  }
}
var p = new Proxy({}, handler);
p.a = 100;
p.b = undefined;
console.log(p.a, p.b); // 100, undefined
console.log('c' in p, p.c); // false, 42
```

In this example, we are trapping the operation of getting a property from the object. We return 42 as a default property value if the property does not exist. We are using the get handler to trap this operation.

You can use proxies to validate values before setting them on an object. For this, we can trap the set handler as follows:

```
let ageValidator = {
  set: function(obj, prop, value) {
    if (prop === 'age') {
      if (!Number.isInteger(value)) {
        throw new TypeError('The age is not an number');
      }
      if (value > 100) {
        throw new RangeError('You cant be older than 100');
      }
    }
    // If no error - just store the value in the property
    obj[prop] = value;
  }
};
let p = new Proxy({}, ageValidator);
p.age = 100;
console.log(p.age); // 100
p.age = 'Two'; // Exception
p.age = 300; // Exception
```

In the preceding example, we are trapping the set handler. When we set a property of the object, we are trapping that operation and introducing validation of values. If the value is valid, we will set the property.

Function traps

There are two operations that can be trapped if the target is a function: `apply` and `construct`.

To intercept function calls, you will need to trap the `get` and `apply` operations. First get the function and then apply to call the function. So, you `get` the function and return the function.

Let's consider the following example to understand how method interception works:

```
var car = {
  name: "Ford",
  method_1: function(text){
    console.log("Method_1 called with "+ text);
  }
}
var methodInterceptorProxy = new Proxy(car, {
 //target is the object being proxied, receiver is the proxy
 get: function(target, propKey, receiver){
  //I only want to intercept method calls, not property access
  var propValue = target[propKey];
  if (typeof propValue != "function"){
   return propValue;
  }
  else{
   return function(){
    console.log("intercepting call to " + propKey
      + " in car " + target.name);
    //target is the object being proxied
    return propValue.apply(target, arguments);
   }
  }
 }
});
methodInterceptorProxy.method_1("Mercedes");
//"intercepting call to method_1 in car Ford"
//"Method_1 called with Mercedes"
```

In the preceding example, we are trapping the `get` operation. If the type of the property being `get` is a function, we will use `apply` to invoke that function. If you see the output, we are getting two `console.logs`; the first is from the proxy where we trapped the `get` operation and the second is from the actual method call.

Metaprogramming is an interesting construct to use. However, any kind of introspection or reflection comes at the cost of performance. Care should be taken while using proxies as they can be slow.

Summary

In this chapter, we looked at two important concepts. ES6 proxies are useful meta programming constructs used to define custom behavior for fundamental operations (for example, property lookup, assignment, enumeration, function invocation, and so on). We looked at how to use handlers, traps, and proxy targets to intercept and modify the default behavior of operations. This gives us very powerful meta programming capabilities earlier lacking in JavaScript.

The other important construct we discussed in this chapter was ES6 promises. Promises are important because they make asynchronous programming constructs easier to work with. A promise acts as a proxy for a value not necessarily known when the promise is created. This lets asynchronous methods return values like synchronous methods – instead of the final value, the asynchronous method returns a promise for the value at some point in the future.

These are two very powerful constructs in ES6 that greatly enhance the language's core capabilities.

In the next chapter, we will look at the fascinating possibilities around browsers and DOM manipulation using JavaScript.

10
The Browser Environment

You know that JavaScript programs need a host environment. Most of what you learned so far in this book was related to core ECMAScript/JavaScript and can be used in many different host environments. Now, let's shift the focus to the browser as this is the most popular and natural host environment for JavaScript programs. In this chapter, you will learn the following topics:

- The **Browser Object Model (BOM)**
- The **Document Object Model (DOM)**
- Browser events
- The XMLHttpRequest object

Including JavaScript in an HTML page

To include JavaScript in an HTML page, you will need to use the `<script>` tag as follows:

```
<!DOCTYPE>
<html>
  <head>
    <title>JS test</title>
    <script src="somefile.js"></script>
  </head>
  <body>
    <script>
      var a = 1;
      a++;
    </script>
  </body>
</html>
```

In this example, the first `<script>` tag includes an external file, `somefile.js`, which contains JavaScript code. The second `<script>` tag includes the JavaScript code directly in the HTML code of the page. The browser executes the JavaScript code in the sequence it finds it on the page and all the code in all tags share the same global namespace. This means that when you define a variable in `somefile.js`, it also exists in the second `<script>` block.

BOM and DOM – an overview

The JavaScript code in a page has access to a number of objects. These objects can be divided into the following types:

- **Core ECMAScript objects**: This consists of all the objects mentioned in the previous chapters
- **DOM**: This consists of objects that have to do with the currently loaded page, which is also called the document
- **BOM**: This consists of objects that deal with everything outside the page-the browser window and the desktop screen

DOM stands for Document Object Model and BOM for Browser Object Model.

The DOM is a standard governed by the **World Wide Web Consortium** (**W3C**) and has different versions, called levels, such as DOM Level 1, DOM Level 2, and so on. Browsers in use today have different degrees of compliance with the standard, but in general, they almost all completely implement DOM Level 1. The DOM was standardized post factum after the browser vendors had each implemented their own ways to access the document. The legacy part from before the W3C took over is still around and is referred to as DOM 0, although, no real DOM Level 0 standard exists. Some parts of DOM 0 have become de facto standards as all major browsers support them; some of these were added to the DOM Level 1 standard. The rest of DOM 0 that didn't find its way to DOM 1 is too browser specific and won't be discussed here.

Historically, BOM was not a part of any standard. Similar to DOM 0, it has a subset of objects that is supported by all major browsers, and another subset that is browser-specific. The HTML5 standard codifies common behavior among browsers, and it includes common BOM objects. Additionally, mobile devices come with their specific objects (and HTML5 aims to standardize those as well), which traditionally were not necessary for desktop computers, but make sense in a mobile world, for example, geolocation, camera access, vibration, touch events, telephony, and SMS.

This chapter discusses only cross-browser subsets of BOM and DOM Level 1, unless noted otherwise in the text. Even these safe subsets constitute a large topic, and a full reference is beyond the scope of this book. You can also consult the following references:

- Mozilla DOM reference
  (`http://developer.mozilla.org/en/docs/Gecko_DOM_Reference`)
- Mozilla's HTML5 wiki
  (`https://developer.mozilla.org/en-US/docs/HTML/HTML5`)
- Microsoft's documentation for Internet Explorer
  (`http://msdn2.microsoft.com/en-us/library/ms533050(vs.85).aspx`)
- W3C's DOM specifications (`http://www.w3.org/DOM/DOMTR`)

BOM

The BOM is a collection of objects that give you access to the browser and the computer screen. These objects are accessible through the global object `window`.

The window object revisited

As you already know, in JavaScript, there's a global object provided by the host environment. In the browser environment, this global object is accessible using `window`. All global variables are also accessible as properties of the `window` object. For example, take a look at the following code:

```
> window.somevar = 1;
      1
> somevar;
      1
```

Additionally, all the core JavaScript functions, discussed in Chapter 2, *Primitive Data Types, Arrays, Loops, and Conditions*, are methods of the global object. Consider the following piece of code:

```
> parseInt('123a456');
      123
> window.parseInt('123a456');
      123
```

In addition to being a reference to the global object, the `window` object also serves a second purpose-providing information about the browser environment. There's a `window` object for every frame, iframe, pop up, or browser tab.

Let's see some of the browser-related properties of the `window` object. Again, these can vary from one browser to another, so let's only consider the properties that are implemented consistently and reliably across all major browsers.

Using window.navigator property

The `navigator` is an object that has some information about the browser and its capabilities. One property is `navigator.userAgent`, which is a long string of browser identification. In Firefox, you'll get the following output:

```
> window.navigator.userAgent;
  "Mozilla/5.0 (Macintosh; Intel Mac OS X 10_8_3)
    AppleWebKit/536.28.10
    (KHTML, like Gecko) Version/6.0.3 Safari/536.28.10"
```

The `userAgent` string in Microsoft Internet Explorer is something as follows:

```
  "Mozilla/5.0 (compatible; MSIE 10.0; Windows NT 6.1; Trident/6.0)"
```

As the browsers have different capabilities, developers are using the `userAgent` string to identify the browser and provide different versions of the code. For example, the following code snippet searches for the presence of the `MSIE` string to identify Internet Explorer:

```
if (navigator.userAgent.indexOf('MSIE') !== -1) {
  // this is IE
} else {
  // not IE
}
```

It's better not to rely on the `userAgent` string, but to use feature sniffing (also called capability detection) instead. The reason for this is that it's hard to keep track of all browsers and their different versions. It's much easier to simply check if the feature you intend to use is indeed available in the user's browser. For example, take a look at the following code snippet:

```
if (typeof window.addEventListener === 'function') {
  // feature is supported, let's use it
} else {
  // hmm, this feature is not supported, will have to
  // think of another way
}
```

Another reason to avoid `userAgent` sniffing is that some browsers allow users to modify the string and pretend they are using a different browser.

Your console is a cheat sheet

The console lets you inspect what's in an object and this includes all the BOM and DOM properties. Just type the following code:

```
> navigator;
```

Then click on the result. The result is a list of properties and their values, as shown in the following screenshot:

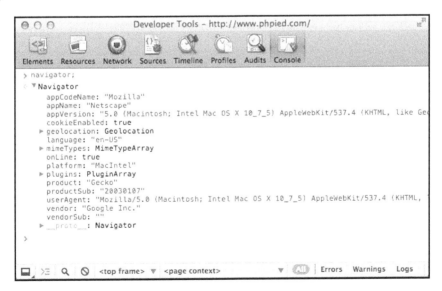

Using window.location property

The `location` property points to an object that contains information about the URL of the currently loaded page. For example, `location.href` is the full URL and `location.hostname` is only the domain. With a simple loop, you can see the full list of properties of the `location` object.

Imagine you're on a page with the following URL:

`http://search.phpied.com:8080/search?q=java&what=script#results.`

Consider the following code:

```
for (var i in location) {
  if (typeof location[i] === "string") {
    console.log(i + ' = "' + location[i] + '"');
  }
}
      href = "http://search.phpied.com:8080/search?
        q=java&what=script#results"
      hash = "#results"
      host = "search.phpied.com:8080"
      hostname = "search.phpied.com"
      pathname = "/search"
      port = <<8080>>
      protocol = <<http:>>
      search = "?q=java&what=script"
```

There are also three methods that `location` property provides, namely `reload()`, `assign()`, and `replace()`.

It's interesting how many different ways exist for you to navigate to another page. The following are a few ways:

```
> window.location.href = 'http://www.packtpub.com';
> location.href = 'http://www.packtpub.com';
> location = 'http://www.packtpub.com';
> location.assign('http://www.packtpub.com');
```

The `replace()` method is almost the same as `assign()`. The difference is that it doesn't create an entry in the browser's history list as follows:

```
> location.replace('http://www.yahoo.com');
```

To reload a page, you can use the following code:

```
> location.reload();
```

Alternatively, you can use `location.href` to point it to itself, as follows:

```
> window.location.href = window.location.href;
```

Or, simply use the following code:

```
> location = location;
```

Using window.history property

The `window.history` property allows limited access to the previously visited pages in the same browser session. For example, you can see how many pages the user has visited before coming to your page, as follows:

```
> window.history.length;
    5
```

You cannot see the actual URLs though. For privacy reasons, this doesn't work. See the following code:

```
> window.history[0];
```

You can, however, navigate back and forth through the user's session as if the user had clicked on the back/forward browser buttons, as follows:

```
> history.forward();
> history.back();
```

You can also skip pages back and forth with `history.go()`. This is the same as calling `history.back()`. The code for `history.go()` is as follows:

```
> history.go(-1);
```

To go two pages back, use the following code:

```
> history.go(-2);
```

Reload the current page using the following code:

```
> history.go(0);
```

More recent browsers also support HTML5 history API, which lets you change the URL without reloading the page. This is perfect for dynamic pages because they can allow users to bookmark a specific URL, which represents the state of the application, and when they come back, or share with their friends, the page can restore the application state based on the URL. To get a sense of the history API, go to any page and write the following lines of code in the console:

```
> history.pushState({a: 1}, "", "hello");
> history.pushState({b: 2}, "", "hello-you-too");
> history.state;
```

Notice how the URL changes, but the page is the same. Now, experiment with back and forward buttons in the browser and inspect the `history.state` object again.

using window.frames property

The `window.frames` property is a collection of all of the frames in the current page. It doesn't distinguish between frames and iframes (inline frames). Regardless of whether there are frames on the page or not, `window.frames` always exists and points to `window`, as follows:

```
> window.frames === window;
    true
```

Let's consider an example where you have a page with one iframe, as follows:

```
<iframe name="myframe" src="hello.html" />
```

In order to tell if there are any frames on the page, you can check the `length` property. In case of one iframe, you'll see the following output:

```
> frames.length
    1
```

Each frame contains another page, which has its own global `window` object.

To get access to the iframe's `window`, you can execute any of the following:

```
> window.frames[0];
> window.frames[0].window;
> window.frames[0].window.frames;
> frames[0].window;
> frames[0];
```

From the parent page, you can access properties of the child frame as well. For example, you can reload the frame as follows:

```
> frames[0].window.location.reload();
```

From inside the child, you can access the parent as follows:

```
> frames[0].parent === window;
      true
```

Using a property called `top`, you can access the top-most page-the one that contains all the other frames-from within any frame, as follows:

```
> window.frames[0].window.top === window;
      true
> window.frames[0].window.top === window.top;
      true
> window.frames[0].window.top === top;
      true
```

In addition, `self` is the same as `window`, as you can see in the following code snippet:

```
> self === window;
      true
> frames[0].self == frames[0].window;
      true
```

If a frame has a `name` attribute, you cannot only access the frame by name, but also by index, as shown in the following piece of code:

```
> window.frames['myframe'] === window.frames[0];
      true
```

Or, alternatively, you can use the following code:

```
> frames.myframe === window.frames[0];
      true
```

Using window.screen property

The `screen` property provides information about the environment outside the browser. For example, the `screen.colorDepth` property contains the color bit depth (the color quality) of the monitor. This is mostly used for statistical purposes. Take a look at the following line of code:

```
> window.screen.colorDepth;
     32
```

You can also check the available screen real estate (the resolution), as follows:

```
> screen.width;
     1440
> screen.availWidth;
     1440
> screen.height;
     900
> screen.availHeight;
     847
```

The difference between `height` and `availHeight` is that `height` is the whole screen, while `availHeight` subtracts any operating system menus, such as the Windows task bar. The same is the case for `width` and `availWidth`.

Somewhat related is the property mentioned in the following code:

```
> window.devicePixelRatio;
     1
```

It tells you the difference (ratio) between physical pixels and device pixels in the retina displays in mobile devices, for example, value 2 in iPhone.

window.open()/close() method

Having explored some of the most common cross-browser properties of the `window` object, let's move to some of the methods. One such method is `open()`, which allows you to open new browser windows (pop ups). Various browser policies and user settings may prevent you from opening a pop up (due to abuse of the technique for marketing purposes), but generally, you should be able to open a new window if it was initiated by the user. Otherwise, if you try to open a pop up as the page loads, it will most likely be blocked, because the user didn't initiate it explicitly.

The `window.open()` method accepts the following parameters:

- URL to load in the new window
- Name of the new window that can be used as the value of a form's `target` attribute
- Comma-separated list of features, which is as follows:
    - `resizable`: Should the user be able to resize the new window
    - `width`, `height`: Width and height of the pop up
    - `status`: Should the status bar be visible

The `window.open()` method returns a reference to the `window` object of the newly created browser instance. The following is an example:

```
var win = window.open('http://www.packtpub.com', 'packt',
   'width=300,height=300,resizable=yes');
```

The `win` variable points to the `window` object of the pop up. You can check if `win` has a falsy value, which means that the pop up was blocked.

The `win.close()` method closes the new window.

It's best to stay away from opening new windows for accessibility and usability reasons. If you don't like sites popping up windows to you, why do it to your users? There are legitimate purposes, such as providing help information while filling out a form, but often, the same can be achieved with alternative solutions, such as using a floating `<div>` inside the page.

window.moveTo() and window.resizeTo() methods

Continuing with the shady practices from the past, the following are more methods to irritate your users, provided their browser and personal settings allow you to do so:

- `window.moveTo(100, 100)`: This moves the browser window to screen location `x = 100` and `y = 100`, which is counted from the top-left corner
- `window.moveBy(10, -10)`: This moves the window 10 pixels to the right and 10 pixels up from its current location
- `window.resizeTo(x, y)` and `window.resizeBy(x, y)`: These accept the same parameters as the move methods, but they resize the window as opposed to moving it

Again, try to solve the problem you're facing without resorting to these methods.

window.alert(), window.prompt(), and window.confirm() methods

In Chapter 2, *Primitive Data Types, Arrays, Loops, and Conditions*, we talked about the alert() function. Now you know that global functions are accessible as methods of the global object, so alert('Watchout!') and window.alert('Watchout!') are exactly the same.

The alert() function is not an ECMAScript function but a BOM method. In addition to it, two other BOM methods allow you to interact with the user through system messages. The following are the methods:

- confirm(): This gives the user two options, **OK** and **Cancel**
- prompt(): This collects textual input

This is how it works:

```
> var answer = confirm('Are you cool?');
> answer;
```

It presents you with a window similar to the following screenshot (the exact look depends on the browser and the operating system):

You'll notice the following things:

- Nothing gets written to the console until you close this message, which means that any JavaScript code execution freezes, waiting for the user's answer
- Clicking on **OK** returns `true`, clicking on **Cancel** or closing the message using the **X** icon, or the ESC key, returns `false`

This is handy to confirm user actions, as shown in the following piece of code:

```
if (confirm('Sure you want to delete this?')) {
  // delete
} else {
  // abort
}
```

Make sure you provide an alternative way to confirm user actions for people who have disabled JavaScript, or for search engine spiders.

The `window.prompt()` method presents the user with a dialog to enter text, as follows:

```
> var answer = prompt('And your name was?');
> answer;
```

This results in the following dialog box (Chrome, MacOS):

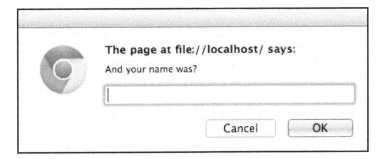

The value of `answer` is one of the following:

- `null`: This happens if you click on **Cancel**, the **X** icon, or press ESC key
- `""` (empty string): This happens if you click on OK or press Enter without typing anything
- A text string: This is if you type something and then click on **OK** or press Enter

The function also takes a string as a second parameter and displays it as a default value prefilled into the input field.

Using window.setTimeout() and window.setInterval() methods

The setTimeout() and setInterval() methods allow scheduling the execution of a piece of code. The setTimeout() method attempts to execute the given code once, after a specified number of milliseconds. The setInterval() method attempts to execute it repeatedly after a specified number of milliseconds has passed.

This shows an alert after approximately 2 seconds (2000 milliseconds). Consider the following code:

```
> function boo() { alert('Boo!'); }
> setTimeout(boo, 2000);
      4
```

As you can see, the function returned an integer (in this case, 4) representing the ID of the timeout. You can use this ID to cancel the timeout using clearTimeout(). In the following example, if you're quick enough, and clear the timeout before 2 seconds have passed, the alert will never be shown, as you can see in the following code:

```
> var id = setTimeout(boo, 2000);
> clearTimeout(id);
```

Let's change boo() to something less intrusive, as follows:

```
> function boo() { console.log('boo'); }
```

Now, using setInterval(), you can schedule boo() to execute every 2 seconds, until you cancel the scheduled execution with clearInterval(). Consider the following code:

```
> var id = setInterval(boo, 2000);
        boo
        boo
        boo
        boo
        boo
        boo
> clearInterval(id);
```

Note that both functions accept a pointer to a callback function as a first parameter. They can also accept a string, which is evaluated with eval(); however, as you know, eval() is evil, so it should be avoided. Moreover, what if you want to pass arguments to the function? In such cases, you can just wrap the function call inside another function.

The following code is valid, but not recommended:

```
// bad idea
var id = setInterval("alert('boo, boo')", 2000);
```

This alternative is preferred:

```
var id = setInterval(
  function () {
    alert('boo, boo');
  },
  2000
);
```

Be aware that scheduling a function in some amount of milliseconds is not a guarantee that it will execute exactly at that time. One reason is that most browsers don't have millisecond resolution time. If you schedule something in 3 milliseconds, it will execute after a minimum of 15 in older IEs and sooner in more modern browsers, but most likely, not in 1 millisecond. The other reason is that the browsers maintain a queue of what you request them to do. 100 milliseconds timeout means add to the queue after 100 milliseconds. However, if the queue is delayed by something slow happening, your function will have to wait and execute after, say, 120 milliseconds.

More recent browsers implement the `requestAnimationFrame()` function. It's preferable to the timeout functions because you're asking the browser to call your function whenever it has available resources, not after a predefined time in milliseconds. Try executing the following code snippet in your console:

```
function animateMe() {
  webkitRequestAnimationFrame(function(){
    console.log(new Date());
    animateMe();
  });
}

animateMe();
```

window.document property

The `window.document` property is a BOM object that refers to the currently loaded document (page). Its methods and properties fall into the DOM category of objects. Take a deep breath (and maybe first look at the BOM exercises at the end of the chapter) and let's dive into the DOM.

DOM

The DOM represents an XML or an HTML document as a tree of nodes. Using DOM methods and properties, you can access any element on the page, modify or remove elements, or add new ones. The DOM is a language-independent API and can be implemented not only in JavaScript, but also in any other language. For example, you can generate pages on the server-side with PHP's DOM implementation (http://php.net/dom).

Take a look at this example HTML page:

```
<!DOCTYPE html>
<html>
  <head>
    <title>My page</title>
  </head>
  <body>
    <p class="opener">first paragraph</p>
    <p><em>second</em> paragraph</p>
    <p id="closer">final</p>
    <!-- and that's about it -->
  </body>
</html>
```

Consider the second paragraph (`<p><em>second</em> paragraph</p>`). You will see that it's a `<p>` tag, and it's contained in the `<body>` tag. If you think in terms of family relationships, you can say that `<body>` is the parent of `<p>` and `<p>` is the child. The first and the third paragraphs would also be children of the `<body>` tag, and at the same time, siblings of the second paragraph. The `<em>` tag is a child of the second `<p>`, so `<p>` is its parent. The parent-child relationships can be represented graphically in an ancestry tree, called the DOM tree:

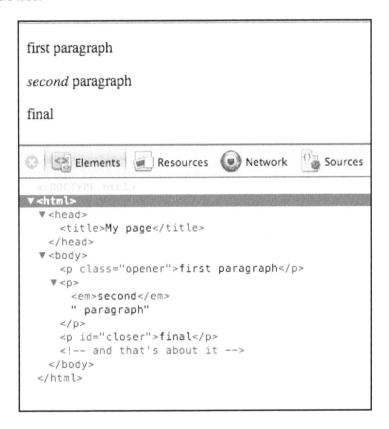

The previous screenshot shows what you'll see in the WebKit console's **Elements** tab after you expand each node.

You can see how all of the tags are shown as expandable nodes on the tree. Although not shown, there exists the so-called text nodes, for example, the text inside the <em> tag (the word second) is a text node. Whitespace is also considered a text node. Comments inside the HTML code are also nodes in the tree, the <!-- and that's about it --> comment in the HTML source is a comment node in the tree.

Every node in the DOM tree is an object and the **Properties** section on the right lists all of the properties and methods you can use to work with these objects, following the inheritance chain of how this object was created:

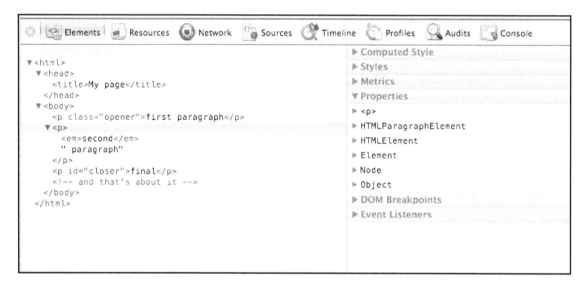

You can also see the constructor function that was used behind the scenes to create each of these objects. Although, this is not too practical for day-to-day tasks, it may be interesting to know that, for example, <p> is created by the HTMLParagraphElement() constructor, the object that represents the head tag is created by HTMLHeadElement(), and so on. You cannot create objects using these constructors directly, though.

Core DOM and HTML DOM

One last diversion before moving on to more practical examples. As you now know, the DOM represents both XML documents and HTML documents. In fact, HTML documents are XML documents, but a little more specific. Therefore, as part of DOM Level 1, there is a Core DOM specification that is applicable to all XML documents, and there is also an HTML DOM specification, which extends and builds upon the core DOM. Of course, the HTML DOM doesn't apply to all XML documents, but only to HTML documents. Let's see some examples of Core DOM and HTML DOM constructors:

Constructor	Inherits from	Core or HTML	Comment
Node		**Core**	**Any node on the tree**
Document	Node	Core	The document object, the main entry point to any XML document
HTMLDocument	Document	HTML	This is window.document or simply document, the HTML-specific version of the previous object, which you'll use extensively
Element	Node	Core	Every tag in the source is represented by an element. That's why you say-the P element meaning the <p></p> tag
HTMLElement	Element	HTML	General-purpose constructor, all constructors for HTML elements inherit from it
HTMLBodyElement	HTMLElement	HTML	Element representing the <body> tag
HTMLLinkElement	HTMLElement	HTML	An A element: an <a href="..."></a> tag
And other such constructors	HTMLElement	HTML	All the rest of the HTML elements
CharacterData	Node	Core	General-purpose constructor for dealing with texts
Text	CharacterData	Core	Text node inside a tag; in <em>second</em>, you have the element node EM and the text node with value second

Constructor	Inherits from	Core or HTML	Comment
`Comment`	`CharacterData`	Core	`<!-- any comment -->`
`Attr`	`Node`	Core	Represents an attribute of a tag; in `<p id="closer">`, the `id` attribute is a DOM object created by the `Attr()` constructor
`NodeList`		Core	A list of nodes, an array-like object that has a `length` property
`NamedNodeMap`		Core	Same as `NodeList`, but the nodes can be accessed by name, not only by numeric index.
`HTMLCollection`		HTML	Similar to `NamedNodeMap` but specific for HTML.

These are, by no means, all of the Core DOM and HTML DOM objects. For the full list, consult `http://www.w3.org/TR/DOM-Level-1/`.

Now that this bit of the DOM theory is behind you, let's focus on the practical side of working with the DOM. In the following sections, you'll learn how to do the following topics:

- Access DOM nodes
- Modify nodes
- Create new nodes
- Remove nodes

Accessing DOM nodes

Before you can validate the user input in a form on a page or swap an image, you need to get access to the element you want to inspect or modify. Luckily, there are many ways to get to any element, either by navigating around traversing the DOM tree or by using a shortcut.

It's best if you start experimenting with all of the new objects and methods. The examples you'll see use the same simple document that you saw at the beginning of the DOM section, and which you can access at `http://www.phpied.com/files/jsoop/ch7.html`. Open your console, and let's get started.

The document node

The `document` node gives you access to the current document. To explore this object, you can use your console as a cheat sheet. Type `console.dir(document)` and click on the result:

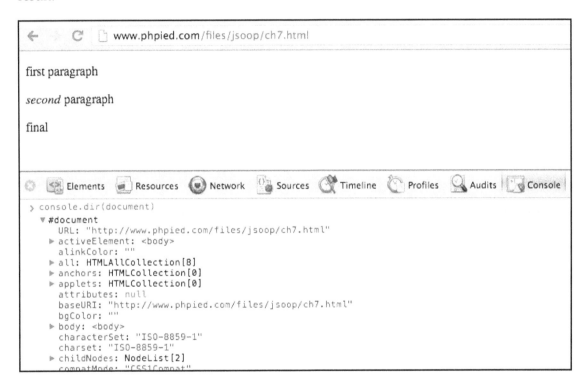

Alternatively, you can browse all of the properties and methods of the `document` object DOM properties in the **Elements** panel:

All nodes, including the document node, text nodes, element nodes, and attribute nodes have `nodeType`, `nodeName` and `nodeValue` properties:

```
> document.nodeType;
    9
```

There are 12 node types, represented by integers. As you can see, the document node type is 9. The most commonly used are 1 (element), 2 (attribute), and 3 (text).

Nodes also have names. For HTML tags, the node name is the tag name (`tagName` property). For text nodes, it's `#text`, and for document nodes, the name is as follows:

```
> document.nodeName;
      "#document"
```

Nodes can also have node values. For example, for text nodes, the value is the actual text. The document node doesn't have a value, which can be seen as follows:

```
> document.nodeValue;
      null
```

documentElement

Now, let's move around the tree. XML documents always have one root node that wraps the rest of the document. For HTML documents, the root is the `<html>` tag. To access the root, you will use the `documentElement` property of the `document` object.

```
> document.documentElement;
      <html>...</html>
```

`nodeType` is `1` (an element node) which can be seen as follows:

```
> document.documentElement.nodeType;
      1
```

For element nodes, both `nodeName` and `tagName` properties contain the name of the tag, as seen in the following output:

```
> document.documentElement.nodeName;
      "HTML"
> document.documentElement.tagName;
      "HTML"
```

Child nodes

In order to tell if a node has any children, you will use `hasChildNodes()`, as follows:

```
> document.documentElement.hasChildNodes();
    true
```

The HTML element has three children, the `head` and the `body` elements and the whitespace between them (whitespace is counted in most, but not all browsers). You can access them using the `childNodes` array-like collection, as follows:

```
> document.documentElement.childNodes.length;
    3
> document.documentElement.childNodes[0];
    <head>...</head>
> document.documentElement.childNodes[1];
    #text
> document.documentElement.childNodes[2];
    <body>...</body>
```

Any child has access to its parent through the `parentNode` property, as seen in the following code:

```
> document.documentElement.childNodes[1].parentNode;
    <html>...</html>
```

Let's assign a reference to body to a variable, as follows:

```
> var bd = document.documentElement.childNodes[2];
```

How many children does the `body` element have? Consider the following piece of code

```
> bd.childNodes.length;
    9
```

As a refresher, here, again, is the body of the document:

```
<body>
  <p class="opener">first paragraph</p>
  <p><em>second</em> paragraph</p>
  <p id="closer">final</p>
  <!-- and that's about it -->
</body>
```

How come body has 9 children? Well, three paragraphs plus one comment makes four nodes. The whitespace between these four nodes makes three more text nodes. This makes a total of seven so far. The whitespace between <body> and the first <p> is the eighth node. The whitespace between the comment and the closing </body> is another text node. This makes a total of nine child nodes. Just type bd.childNodes in the console to inspect them all.

Attributes

As the first child of the body is a whitespace, the second child (index 1) is the first paragraph. Refer to the following piece of code:

```
> bd.childNodes[1];
    <p class="opener">first paragraph</p>
```

You can check whether an element has attributes using hasAttributes(), as follows:

```
> bd.childNodes[1].hasAttributes();
    true
```

How many attributes? In this example, one is the class attribute, which can be seen as follows:

```
> bd.childNodes[1].attributes.length;
    1
```

You can access the attributes by index and name. You can also get the value using the getAttribute() method, which is as follows:

```
> bd.childNodes[1].attributes[0].nodeName;
    "class"
> bd.childNodes[1].attributes[0].nodeValue;
    "opener"
> bd.childNodes[1].attributes['class'].nodeValue;
    "opener"
> bd.childNodes[1].getAttribute('class');
    "opener"
```

Accessing the content inside a tag

Let's take a look at the first paragraph:

```
> bd.childNodes[1].nodeName;
    "P"
```

You can get the text contained in the paragraph using the `textContent` property. It doesn't exist in older IEs, but another property called `innerText` returns the same value, as seen in the following output:

```
> bd.childNodes[1].textContent;
    "first paragraph"
```

There is also the `innerHTML` property. It's a relatively new addition to the DOM standard, despite the fact that it previously existed in all major browsers. It returns (or sets) HTML code contained in a node. You can see how this is a little inconsistent as DOM treats the document as a tree of nodes, not as a string of tags. However, `innerHTML` is so convenient to use that you'll see it everywhere. Refer to the following code:

```
> bd.childNodes[1].innerHTML;
    "first paragraph"
```

The first paragraph contains only text, so `innerHTML` is the same as `textContent` (or `innerText` in IE). However, the second paragraph does contain an em node, so you can see the difference as follows:

```
> bd.childNodes[3].innerHTML;
    "<em>second</em> paragraph"
> bd.childNodes[3].textContent;
    "second paragraph"
```

Another way to get the text contained in the first paragraph is by using the `nodeValue` method of the text node contained inside the p node, as follows:

```
> bd.childNodes[1].childNodes.length;
    1
> bd.childNodes[1].childNodes[0].nodeName;
    "#text"
> bd.childNodes[1].childNodes[0].nodeValue;
    "first paragraph"
```

DOM access shortcuts

Using `childNodes`, `parentNode`, `nodeName`, `nodeValue`, and `attributes`, you can navigate up and down the tree and do anything with the document. However, the fact that whitespace is a text node makes this a fragile way of working with the DOM. If the page changes, your script may no longer work correctly. Also, if you want to get to a node deeper in the tree, it could take a bit of code before you get there. That's why you have shortcut methods, namely, `getElementsByTagName()`, `getElementsByName()`, and `getElementById()`.

The `getElementsByTagName()` method takes a tag name (the name of an element node) and returns an HTML collection (array-like object) of nodes with the matching tag name. For example, the following example asks-give me a count of all paragraphs, which is given as follows:

```
> document.getElementsByTagName('p').length;
    3
```

You can access an item in the list using the brackets notation, or the `item()` method, and passing the index (0 for the first element). Using `item()` is discouraged, as array brackets are more consistent and also shorter to type. Refer to the following piece of code:

```
> document.getElementsByTagName('p')[0];
        <p class="opener">first paragraph</p>
> document.getElementsByTagName('p').item(0);
        <p class="opener">first paragraph</p>
```

Getting the contents of the first p can be done as follows:

```
> document.getElementsByTagName('p')[0].innerHTML;
    "first paragraph"
```

Accessing the last p can be done as follows:

```
> document.getElementsByTagName('p')[2];
        <p id="closer">final</p>
```

To access the attributes of an element, you can use the `attributes` collection or `getAttribute()`, as shown previously. However, a shorter way is to use the attribute name as a property of the element you're working with. So, to get the value of the `id` attribute, you will just use `id` as a property, which is as follows:

```
> document.getElementsByTagName('p')[2].id;
    "closer"
```

Getting the `class` attribute of the first paragraph won't work though. It's an exception because it just happens so that class is a reserved word in ECMAScript. You can use `className` instead, as follows:

```
> document.getElementsByTagName('p')[0].className;
    "opener"
```

Using `getElementsByTagName()`, you can get all of the elements on the page, as follows:

```
> document.getElementsByTagName('*').length;
    8
```

In earlier versions of IE before IE7, `*` is not acceptable as a tag name. To get all elements, you can use IE's proprietary `document.all` collection, although, selecting every element is rarely needed.

The other shortcut mentioned is `getElementById()`. This is probably the most common way of accessing an element. You just assign IDs to the elements you plan to play with and they'll be easy to access later on, as seen in the following code:

```
> document.getElementById('closer');
<p id="closer">final</p>
```

Additional shortcut methods in more recent browsers include the following:

- `getElementByClassName()`:This method finds elements using their class attribute
- `querySelector()`: This method finds an element using a CSS selector string
- `querySelectorAll()`: This method is the same as the previous one but returns all matching elements, not just the first

Siblings, body, first, and last child

The `nextSibling` and `previousSibling` are two other convenient properties to navigate the DOM tree once you have a reference to one element. Consider the following code:

```
> var para = document.getElementById('closer');
> para.nextSibling;
     #text
> para.previousSibling;
     #text
> para.previousSibling.previousSibling;
     <p>...</p>
> para.previousSibling.previousSibling.previousSibling;
     #text
> para.previousSibling.previousSibling.nextSibling.nextSibling;
     <p id="closer">final</p>
```

The `body` element is used so often that it has its own shortcut, which is as follows:

```
> document.body;
     <body>...</body>
> document.body.nextSibling;
     null
> document.body.previousSibling.previousSibling;
     <head>...</head>
```

The `firstChild` and `lastChild` properties are also convenient. The `firstChild` property is the same as `childNodes[0]` and `lastChild` is the same as `childNodes[childNodes.length - 1]` properties:

```
> document.body.firstChild;
     #text
> document.body.lastChild;
     #text
> document.body.lastChild.previousSibling;
     <!-- and that's about it -->
> document.body.lastChild.previousSibling.nodeValue;
     " and that's about it "
```

The following screenshot shows the family relationships between the body and the three paragraphs in it. For simplicity, all the whitespace text nodes are removed from the screenshot:

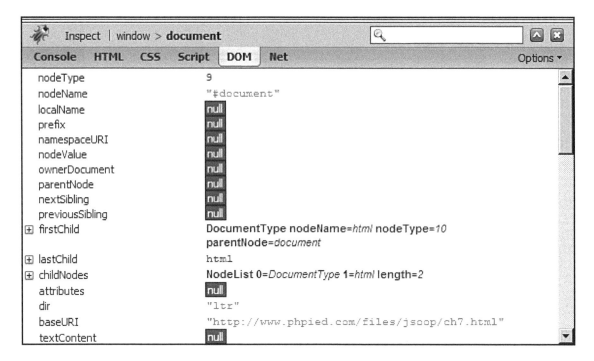

Walk the DOM

To wrap up, here's a function that takes any node and walks through the DOM tree recursively, starting from the given node, as follows:

```
function walkDOM(n) {
    do {
      console.log(n);
      it (n.hasChildNodes()) {
        walkDOM(n.firstChild);
      }
    } while (n = n.nextSibling);
}
```

You can test the function as follows:

```
> walkDOM(document.documentElement);
> walkDOM(document.body);
```

Modifying DOM nodes

Now that you know a whole lot of methods to access any node of the DOM tree and its properties, let's see how you can modify these nodes:

Let's assign a pointer to the last paragraph to the variable `my`, as follows:

```
> var my = document.getElementById('closer');
```

Now, changing the text of the paragraph can be as easy as changing the `innerHTML` value, which is as follows:

```
> my.innerHTML = 'final!!!';
      "final!!!"
```

As `innerHTML` accepts a string of HTML source code, you can also create a new `em` node in the DOM tree as follows:

```
> my.innerHTML = '<em>my</em> final';
      "<em>my</em> final"
```

The new `em` node becomes a part of the tree. Lets take a look at the following code:

```
> my.firstChild;
      <em>my</em>
> my.firstChild.firstChild;
      "my"
```

Another way to change text is to get the actual text node and change its `nodeValue`, as shown in the following piece of code:

```
> my.firstChild.firstChild.nodeValue = 'your';
      "your"
```

Modifying styles

Often you don't change the content of a node, but its presentation. The elements have a `style` property, which in turn has a property mapped to each CSS property. For example, changing the style of the paragraph to add a red border, as follows:

```
> my.style.border = "1px solid red";
      "1px solid red"
```

CSS properties often have dashes, but dashes are not acceptable in JavaScript identifiers. In such cases, you skip the dash and uppercase the next letter. So, `padding-top` becomes `paddingTop`, `margin-left` becomes `marginLeft`, and so on. Take a look at the following code:

```
> my.style.fontWeight = 'bold';
    "bold"
```

You also have access to the `cssText` property of `style`, which lets you work with styles as strings, as you can see in the following code snippet:

```
> my.style.cssText;
    "border: 1px solid red; font-weight: bold;"
```

Moreover, modifying styles is a string manipulation:

```
> my.style.cssText += " border-style: dashed;"
"border: 1px dashed red; font-weight: bold; border-style: dashed;"
```

Fun with forms

As mentioned earlier, JavaScript is great for client-side input validation and can save a few round-trip to the server. Let's practice form manipulations and play a little bit with a form located on a popular page, `www.google.com`:

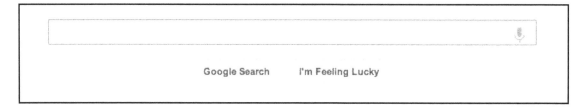

Finding the first text input using the `querySelector()` method and a CSS selector string is as follows:

```
> var input = document.querySelector('input[type=text]');
```

Accessing the search box. Consider the following code:

```
> input.name;
    "q"
```

Changing the search query by setting the text contained in the `value` attribute is done as follows:

```
> input.value = 'my query';
  "my query"
```

Now, let's have some fun and change the word **Lucky** with **Tricky** in the button:

```
> var feeling = document.querySelectorAll("button")[2];
> feeling.textContent = feelingtextContent.replace(/Lu/, 'Tri');
  "I'm Feeling Tricky"
```

Now, let's implement the tricky part and make that button show and hide for one second. You can do this with a simple function. Let's call it `toggle()`. Every time you call the function, it checks the value of the CSS property `visibility`, and sets it to visible if it's hidden and vice versa using the following code snippet:

```
function toggle() {
  var st = document.querySelectorAll('button')[2].style;
  st.visibility = (st.visibility === 'hidden')
    ? 'visible'
    : 'hidden';
}
```

Instead of calling the function manually, let's set an interval and call it every second:

```
> var myint = setInterval(toggle, 1000);
```

The result? The button starts blinking, making it trickier to click. When you're tired of chasing it, just remove the timeout interval by writing the following line of code:

```
> clearInterval(myint);
```

[331]

Creating new nodes

To create new nodes, you can use the `createElement()` and `createTextNode()` methods. Once you have the new nodes, you can add them to the DOM tree using `appendChild()`, `insertBefore()`, or `replaceChild()`.

Reload `http://www.phpied.com/files/jsoop/ch7.html` and let's play.

Create a new p element and set its `innerHTML`, as shown in the following code:

```
> var myp = document.createElement('p');
> myp.innerHTML = 'yet another';
      "yet another"
```

The new element automatically gets all the default properties, such as `style`, which you can modify as follows:

```
> myp.style;
      CSSStyleDeclaration
> myp.style.border = '2px dotted blue';
      "2px dotted blue"
```

Using `appendChild()`, you can add the new node to the DOM tree. Calling this method on the `document.body` node means creating one more child node right after the last child, as follows:

```
> document.body.appendChild(myp);
      <p style="border: 2px dotted blue;">yet another</p>
```

Here's an illustration of how the page looks like after the new node is appended:

first paragraph

second paragraph

final

yet another

DOM-only method

The `innerHTML` property gets things done a little more quickly than using pure DOM. In pure DOM, you will need to perform the following steps:

1. Create a new text node containing yet another text.
2. Create a new paragraph node.
3. Append the text node as a child to the paragraph.
4. Append the paragraph as a child to the body.

This way, you can create any number of text nodes and elements and nest them, however you like. Let's say, you want to add the following HTML to the end of the body:

```
<p>one more paragraph<strong>bold</strong></p>
```

Presenting the preceding code as a hierarchy would be something like the following code snippet:

```
P element
    text node with value "one more paragraph"
    STRONG element
        text node with value "bold"
```

The code that accomplishes this is as follows:

```
// create P
var myp = document.createElement('p');
// create text node and append to P
var myt = document.createTextNode('one more paragraph');
myp.appendChild(myt);
// create STRONG and append another text node to it
var str = document.createElement('strong');
str.appendChild(document.createTextNode('bold'));
// append STRONG to P
myp.appendChild(str);
// append P to BODY
document.body.appendChild(myp);
```

Using cloneNode() method

Another way to create nodes is by copying or cloning existing ones. The `cloneNode()` method does this and accepts a Boolean parameter (`true` = deep copy with all the children, `false` = shallow copy, only this node). Let's test the method.

Getting a reference to the element you want to clone can be done as follows:

```
> var el = document.getElementsByTagName('p')[1];
```

Now, `el` refers to the second paragraph on the page that looks like the following code:

```
<p><em>second</em> paragraph</p>
```

Let's create a shallow clone of `el` and append it to the `body` as follows:

```
> document.body.appendChild(el.cloneNode(false));
```

You won't see a difference on the page because the shallow copy only copied the P node without any children. This means that the text inside the paragraph, which is a text node child, was not cloned. The preceding line will be equivalent to the following code line:

```
> document.body.appendChild(document.createElement('p'));
```

However, if you create a deep copy, the whole DOM subtree starting from P is copied, and this includes text nodes and the EM element. This line copies (visually too) the second paragraph to the end of the document. Consider the following line of code:

```
> document.body.appendChild(el.cloneNode(true));
```

You can also copy only the EM if you want, as shown in the following lines of code:

```
> document.body.appendChild(el.firstChild.cloneNode(true));
    <em>second</em>
```

Or, you can copy only the text node with value second, as follows:

```
> document.body.appendChild(
    el.firstChild.firstChild.cloneNode(false));
    "second"
```

Using insertBefore() method

Using `appendChild()`, you can only add new children at the end of the selected element. For more control over the exact location, there is `insertBefore()`. This is the same as `appendChild()`, but accepts an extra parameter specifying where (before which element) to insert the new node. For example, the following code inserts a text node at the end of the `body` element:

```
> document.body.appendChild(document.createTextNode('boo!'));
```

Moreover, this creates another text node and adds it as the first child of the `body` element:

```
document.body.insertBefore(
  document.createTextNode('first boo!'),
  document.body.firstChild
);
```

Removing nodes

To remove nodes from the DOM tree, you can use the `removeChild()` method. Again, let's start fresh with the same page with the body:

```
<body>
  <p class="opener">first paragraph</p>
  <p><em>second</em> paragraph</p>
  <p id="closer">final</p>
  <!-- and that's about it -->
</body>
```

Here's how you can remove the second paragraph:

```
> var myp = document.getElementsByTagName('p')[1];
> var removed = document.body.removeChild(myp);
```

The method returns the removed node if you want to use it later. You can still use all the DOM methods even though the element is no longer in the tree. Lets take a look on the following code:

```
> removed;
      <p>...</p>
> removed.firstChild;
      <em>second</em>
```

There's also the `replaceChild()` method that removes a node and puts another one in its place.

After removing the node, the tree looks as follows:

```
<body>
  <p class="opener">first paragraph</p>
  <p id="closer">final</p>
  <!-- and that's about it -->
</body>
```

Now, the second paragraph is the one with the ID `"closer"`, which is as follows:

```
> var p = document.getElementsByTagName('p')[1];
> p;
      <p id="closer">final</p>
```

Let's replace this paragraph with the one in the `removed` variable. Consider the following code:

```
> var replaced = document.body.replaceChild(removed, p);
```

Just like `removeChild()`, `replaceChild()` returns a reference to the node that is now out of the tree:

```
> replaced;
      <p id="closer">final</p>
```

Now, the body looks like the following piece of code:

```
<body>
  <p class="opener">first paragraph</p>
  <p><em>second</em> paragraph</p>
  <!-- and that's about it -->
</body>
```

A quick way to wipe out all of the content of a subtree is to set `innerHTML` to a blank string. This removes all the children of the `body` element:

```
> document.body.innerHTML = '';
      ""
```

Testing is done as follows:

```
> document.body.firstChild;
      null
```

Removing with `innerHTML` is fast and easy. The DOM-only way will be to go over all of the child nodes and remove each one individually. Here's a little function that removes all nodes from a given start node:

```
function removeAll(n) {
  while (n.firstChild) {
    n.removeChild(n.firstChild);
  }
}
```

If you want to delete all the children from the `body` element and leave the page with an empty `<body></body>`, use the following code:

```
> removeAll(document.body);
```

HTML – only DOM objects

As you already know, the DOM applies to both XML and HTML documents. What you've learned earlier about traversing the tree and then adding, removing, or modifying nodes, applies to any XML document. There are, however, some HTML-only objects and properties.

The `document.body` is one such HTML-only object. It's so common to have a `<body>` tag in HTML documents, and it's accessed so often, that it makes sense to have an object that's shorter and friendlier than the equivalent `document.getElementsByTagName('body')[0]`.

The `document.body` element is one example of a `legacy` object inherited from the prehistoric DOM Level 0 and moved to the HTML extension of the DOM specification. There are other objects similar to `document.body` element. For some of them, there is no core DOM equivalent, for others, there is an equivalent; however, the DOM 0 original was anyway ported for simplicity and legacy purposes. Let's see some of those objects.

Primitive ways to access the document

to the elements of an HTML document. This was done mainly through a number of collections, which are as follows:

Unlike the DOM, which gives you access to any element, and even comments and whitespace, initially, JavaScript had only limited access to the elements of an HTML document. This was done mainly through a number of collections, which are as follows:

- `document.images`: This is a collection of all of the images on the page. The Core DOM equivalent is `document.getElementsByTagName('img')`.
- `document.applets`: This is the same as `document.getElementsByTagName('applet')`.
- `document.links`: The document.links collection contains a list of all `<a href="...">` `</a>` tags on the page, meaning the `<a>` tags that have an `href` attribute.
- `document.anchors`: The document.anchors collection contains all links with a name attribute (`<a name="...">` `</a>`).
- `document.forms`: One of the most widely used collections is `document.forms`, which contains a list of `<form>` elements.

Let's play with a page that contains a form and an input (`http://www.phpied.com/files/jsoop/ch7-form.html`). The following line of code gives you access to the first form on the page:

```
> document.forms[0];
```

It's the same as the following line of code:

```
> document.getElementsByTagName('forms')[0];
```

The `document.forms` collection contains collections of input fields and buttons, accessible through the `elements` property. Here's how to access the first input of the first form on the page:

```
> document.forms[0].elements[0];
```

Once you have access to an element, you can access its attributes as object properties. The first field of the first form in the test page is as follows:

```
<input name="search" id="search" type="text" size="50"
    maxlength="255" value="Enter email..." />
```

[338]

You can change the text in the field (the value of the `value` attribute) using the following code:

```
> document.forms[0].elements[0].value = 'me@example.org';
   "me@example.org"
```

If you want to disable the field dynamically, use the following code:

```
> document.forms[0].elements[0].disabled = true;
```

When forms or `form` elements have a `name` attribute, you can access them by name too, as shown in the following code:

```
> document.forms[0].elements['search']; // array notation
> document.forms[0].elements.search;    // object property
```

Using document.write() method

The `document.write()` method allows you to insert HTML into the page while the page is being loaded. You can have something like the following code:

```
<p>It is now
  <script>
    document.write("<em>" + new Date() + "</em>");
  </script>
</p>
```

This is the same as if you had the date directly in the source of the HTML document, as follows:

```
<p>It is now
  <em>Fri Apr 26 2013 16:55:16 GMT-0700 (PDT)</em>
</p>
```

Note that you can only use `document.write()` method while the page is being loaded. If you try it after page load, it will replace the content of the whole page.

It's rare that you would need `document.write()` method, and if you think you do, try an alternative approach. The ways to modify the contents of the page provided by DOM Level 1 are preferred and are much more flexible.

Cookies, title, referrer, and domain

The four additional properties of document you'll see in this section are also ported from DOM Level 0 to the HTML extension of DOM Level 1. Unlike the previous ones, for these properties, there are no core DOM equivalents.

The document.cookie is a property that contains a string. This string is the content of the cookies exchanged between the server and the client. When the server sends a page to the browser, it may include the Set-Cookie HTTP header. When the client sends a request to the server, it sends the cookie information back with the Cookie header. Using document.cookie, you can alter the cookies the browser sends to the server. For example, visiting cnn.com and typing document.cookie in the console gives you the following output:

```
> document.cookie;
"mbox=check#true#1356053765|session#1356053704195-121286#1356055565;...
```

The document.title property allows you to change the title of the page displayed in the browser window. For example, see the following code:

```
> document.title = 'My title';
  "My title"
```

Note that this doesn't change the value of the <title> element, but only the display in the browser window, so it's not equivalent to document.querySelector('title').

The document.referrer property tells you the URL of the previously visited page. This is the same value the browser sends in the Referer HTTP header when requesting the page. (Note that Referer is misspelled in the HTTP headers, but is correct in JavaScript's document.referrer). If you've visited the CNN page by searching on Yahoo first, you can see something like the following:

```
> document.referrer;
  "http://search.yahoo.com/search?p=cnn&ei=UTF-8&fr=moz2"
```

The document.domain property gives you access to the domain name of the currently loaded page. This is commonly used when you need to perform so-called domain relaxation. Imagine your page is www.yahoo.com, and inside it, you have an iframe hosted on music.yahoo.com subdomain. These are two separate domains, so the browser's security restrictions won't allow the page and the iframe to communicate. To resolve this, you can set document.domain property on both pages to yahoo.com and they'll be able to talk to each other.

Note that you can only set the domain to a less specific one, for example, you can change `www.yahoo.com` to `yahoo.com`, but you cannot change `yahoo.com` to `www.yahoo.com`, or any other non-yahoo domain. Consider the following code:

```
> document.domain;
  "www.yahoo.com"
> document.domain = 'yahoo.com';
  "yahoo.com"
> document.domain = 'www.yahoo.com';
  Error: SecurityError: DOM Exception 18
> document.domain = 'www.example.org';
  Error: SecurityError: DOM Exception 18
```

Previously, in this chapter, you saw the `window.location` object. Well, the same functionality is also available as `document.location` object:

```
> window.location === document.location;
  true
```

Events

Imagine you are listening to a radio program and they announce, "Big event! Huge! Aliens have landed on Earth!" You might think, "Yeah, whatever"; some other listeners might think "They come in peace"; and some might think, "We're all gonna die!". Similarly, the browser broadcasts events, and your code can be notified should it decide to tune in and listen to the events as they happen. Some example events are as follows:

- The user clicks a button
- The user types a character in a form field
- The page finishes loading

You can attach a JavaScript function called event listener or event handler to a specific event and the browser will invoke your function as soon as the event occurs. Let's see how this is done.

Inline HTML attributes

Adding specific attributes to a tag is the laziest but the least maintainable way; take the following line of code as an example:

```
<div onclick="alert('Ouch!')">click</div>
```

In this case, when the user clicks on `<div>`, the click event fires and the string of JavaScript code contained in the `onclick` attribute is executed. There's no explicit function that listens to the click event; however, behind the scenes, a function is still created, and it contains the code you specified as a value of the `onclick` attribute.

Element Properties

Another way to have some code executed when a click event fires is to assign a function to the `onclick` property of a DOM node element. For example, take a look at the following piece of code:

```
<div id="my-div">click</div>
<script>
  var myelement = document.getElementById('my-div');
  myelement.onclick = function () {
    alert('Ouch!');
    alert('And double ouch!');
  };
</script>
```

This way is better because it helps you keep your `<div>` tag clean of any JavaScript code. Always keep in mind that HTML is for content, JavaScript for behavior, and CSS for formatting, and you should keep these three separate as much as possible.

This method has the drawback that you can attach only one function to the event, as if the radio program has only one listener. It's true that you can have a lot happening inside the same function, but this is not always convenient, as if all the radio listeners are in the same room.

DOM event listeners

The best way to work with browser events is to use the event listener approach outlined in DOM Level 2, where you can have many functions listening to an event. When an event fires, all the functions are executed. All of the listeners don't need to know about each other and can work independently. They can tune in and out at any time, without affecting the other listeners.

Let's use the same simple markup from the previous section, which is available for you to play with at `http://www.phpied.com/files/jsoop/ch7.html`. It has this piece of markup, which is as follows:

```
<p id="closer">final</p>
```

Your JavaScript code can assign listeners to the click event using the `addEventListener()` method. Let's attach two listeners as follows:

```
var mypara = document.getElementById('closer');
mypara.addEventListener('click', function () {
  alert('Boo!');
}, false);
mypara.addEventListener(
  'click', console.log.bind(console), false);
```

As you can see, `addEventListeners`

Capturing and bubbling

In the calls to `addEventListener()`, there was a third parameter-`false`. Let's see what it is for.

Let's say you have a link inside an unordered list, which is as follows:

```
<body>
  <ul>
    <li><a href="http://phpied.com">my blog</a></li>
  </ul>
</body>
```

When you click on the link, you're actually also clicking on the list item, `<li>`, the `<ul>` list, the `<body>` tag, and eventually, the document as a whole. This is called event propagation. A click on a link can also be seen as a click on the document. The process of propagating an event can be implemented in the two following ways:

- **Event capturing**: This click happens in the document first, then it propagates down to the body, the list, the list item, and finally, to the link
- **Event bubbling**: This click happens on the link and then bubbles up to the document

DOM level 2 events specification suggests that the events propagate in three phases, namely, capturing, at target, and bubbling. This means that the event propagates from the document to the link (target) and then bubbles back up to the document. The event objects have an `eventPhase` property, which reflects the current phase:

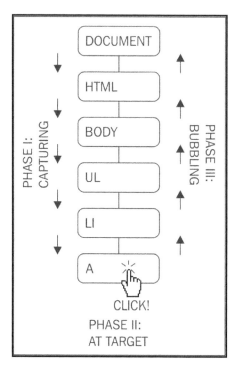

Historically, IE and Netscape (working on their own and without a standard to follow) implemented the exact opposites. IE implemented only bubbling and Netscape only capturing. Today, long after the DOM specification, modern browsers implement all three phases.

The practical implications related to the event propagation are as follows:

- The third parameter to `addEventListener()` specifies whether or not capturing should be used. In order to have your code more portable across browsers, it's better to always set this parameter to `false` and use bubbling only.
- You can stop the propagation of the event in your listeners so that it stops bubbling up and never reaches the document. To do this, you can call the `stopPropagation()` method of the event object; there is an example in the next section.
- You can also use event delegation. If you have ten buttons inside `<div>`, you can always attach ten event listeners, one for each button. However, a smarter thing to do is to attach only one listener to the wrapping `<div>` and once the event happens, check which button was the target of the click.

As a side note, there is a way to use event capturing in old IEs too (using `setCapture()` and `releaseCapture()` methods) but only for mouse events. Capturing any other events (keystroke events for example) is not supported.

Stop propagation

Let's see an example of how you can stop the event from bubbling up. Going back to the test document, there is this piece of code:

```
<p id="closer">final</p>
```

Let's define a function that handles clicks on the paragraph, as follows:

```
function paraHandler() {
  alert('clicked paragraph');
}
```

Now, let's attach this function as a listener to the click event:

```
var para = document.getElementById('closer');
para.addEventListener('click', paraHandler, false);
```

Let's also attach listeners to the click event on the body, the document, and the browser window:

```
document.body.addEventListener('click', function () {
  alert('clicked body');
}, false);
document.addEventListener('click', function () {
  alert('clicked doc');
}, false);
window.addEventListener('click', function () {
  alert('clicked window');
}, false);
```

Note that the DOM specifications don't say anything about events on the window. And why would they, as DOM deals with the document and not the browser. So browsers implement window events inconsistently.

Now, if you click on the paragraph, you'll see four alerts saying:

- clicked paragraph
- clicked body
- clicked doc
- clicked window

This illustrates how the same single click event propagates (bubbles up) from the target all the way up to the window.

The opposite of `addEventLister()` is `removeEventListener()`, and it accepts exactly the same parameters. Let's remove the listener attached to the paragraph by writing the following line of code:

```
> para.removeEventListener('click', paraHandler, false);
```

If you try now, you'll see alerts only for the click event on the body, document, and window, but not on the paragraph.

Now, let's stop the propagation of the event. The function you add as a listener receives the event object as a parameter, and you can call the `stopPropagation()` method of that event object as follows:

```
function paraHandler(e) {
  alert('clicked paragraph');
  e.stopPropagation();
}
```

Adding the modified listener is done as follows:

```
para.addEventListener('click', paraHandler, false);
```

Now, when you click on the paragraph, you will see only one alert because the event doesn't bubble up to the body, the document, or the window.

Note that when you remove a listener, you have to pass a pointer to the same function you previously attached. Otherwise, doing the following does not work because the second argument is a new function, not the same you passed when adding the event listener, even if the body is exactly the same. Consider the following code:

```
document.body.removeEventListener('click',
  function () {
    alert('clicked body');
  },
false); //  does NOT remove the handler
```

Prevent default behavior

Some browser events have a predefined behavior. For example, clicking a link causes the browser to navigate to another page. You can attach listeners to clicks on a link, and you can also disable the default behavior by calling the `preventDefault()` method on the event object.

Let's see how you can annoy your visitors by asking "Are you sure you want to follow this link?" every time they click a link? If the user clicks on **Cancel** (causing `confirm()` to return `false`), the `preventDefault()` method is called, which is shown as follows:

```
// all links
var all_links = document.getElementsByTagName('a');
for (var i = 0; i < all_links.length; i++) { // loop all links
  all_links[i].addEventListener(
    'click',        // event type
    function (e) { // handler
      if (!confirm('Sure you want to follow this link?')) {
        e.preventDefault();
      }
    },
    false // don't use capturing
  );
}
```

Note that not all events allow you to prevent the default behavior. Most do, but if you want to be sure, you can check the `cancellable` property of the event object.

Cross-browser event listeners

As you already know, most modern browsers almost fully implement the DOM Level 1 specification. However, the events were not standardized until DOM 2. As a result, there are quite a few differences in how IE, before version 9, implements this functionality compared to modern browsers.

Check out an example that causes `nodeName` of a clicked element (the target element) to be written to the console:

```
document.addEventListener('click', function (e) {
  console.log(e.target.nodeName);
}, false);
```

Now, let's take a look at how IE is different:

- In IE, there's no `addEventListener()` method; although, since IE Version 5, there is an equivalent `attachEvent()` method. For earlier versions, your only choice is accessing the property directly, such as `onclick`.
- The `click` event becomes `onclick` when using `attachEvent()`.
- If you listen to events the old fashioned way (for example, by setting a function value to the `onclick` property), when the callback function is invoked, it doesn't get an event object passed as a parameter. However, regardless of how you attach the listener in IE, there is always a global object `window.event` that points to the latest event.
- In IE, the event object doesn't get a target attribute telling you the element on which the event fired, but it does have an equivalent property called `srcElement`.
- As mentioned earlier, event capturing doesn't apply to all events, so only bubbling should be used.
- There's no `stopPropagation()` method, but you can set the IE-only `cancelBubble` property to `true`.
- There's no `preventDefault()` method, but you can set the IE-only `returnValue` property to `false`.
- To stop listening to an event, instead of `removeEventListener()` in IE, you'll need `detachEvent()`.

So, here's the revised version of the previous code that works across browsers:

```
function callback(evt) {
  // prep work
  evt = evt || window.event;
  var target = evt.target || evt.srcElement;

  // actual callback work
  console.log(target.nodeName);
}

//  start listening for click events
if (document.addEventListener) { // Modern browsers
  document.addEventListener('click', callback, false);
} else if (document.attachEvent) { // old IE
  document.attachEvent('onclick', callback);
} else {
  document.onclick = callback; // ancient
}
```

Types of events

Now you know how to handle cross-browser events. However, all of the preceding examples used only click events. What other events are happening out there? As you can probably guess, different browsers provide different events. There is a subset of cross-browser events, and some browser-specific ones. For a full list of events, you should consult the browser's documentation, but here's a selection of cross-browser events:

- Mouse events
    - `mouseup`, `mousedown`, `click` (the sequence is mousedown-up-click), `dblclick`
    - `mouseover` (mouse is over an element), `mouseout` (mouse was over an element but left it), `mousemove`
- Keyboard events
    - `keydown`, `keypress`, `keyup` (occur in this sequence)

- Loading/window events
    - `load` (an image or a page and all of its components are done loading), `unload` (user leaves the page), `beforeunload` (the script can provide the user with an option to stop the unload)
    - `abort` (user stops loading the page or an image in IE), `error` (a JavaScript error, also when an image cannot be loaded in IE)
    - `resize` (the browser window is resized), `scroll` (the page is scrolled), `contextmenu` (the right-click menu appears)
- Form events
    - `focus` (enter a form field), `blur` (leave the form field)
    - `change` (leave a field after the value has changed), `select` (select text in a text field)
    - `reset` (wipe out all user input), `submit` (send the form)

Additionally, modern browsers provide drag events (`dragstart`, `dragend`, `drop`, and among others) and touch devices provide `touchstart`, `touchmove`, and `touchend`.

This concludes the discussion of events. Refer to the exercise section at the end of this chapter for a little challenge of creating your own event utility to handle cross-browser events.

XMLHttpRequest

`XMLHttpRequest()` is an object (a constructor function) that allows you to send HTTP requests from JavaScript. Historically, XHR (`XMLHttpRequest`) was introduced in IE and was implemented as an ActiveX object. Starting with IE7, it's a native browser object, the same way as it's in the other browsers. The common implementation of this object across browsers gave birth to the so-called Ajax applications, where it's no longer necessary to refresh the whole page every time you need new content. With JavaScript, you can make an HTTP request to the server, get the response, and update only a part of the page. This way, you can build much more responsive and desktop-like web pages.

Ajax stands for **Asynchronous JavaScript and XML**:

- Asynchronous because, after sending an HTTP request, your code doesn't need to wait for the response; however, it can do other stuff and be notified, through an event, when the response arrives.
- JavaScript because it's obvious that XHR objects are created with JavaScript.
- XML because initially developers were making HTTP requests for XML documents and were using the data contained in them to update the page. This is no longer a common practice, though, as you can request data in plain text, in the much more convenient JSON format, or simply as HTML ready to be inserted into the page.

There are two steps to using the `XMLHttpRequest` object, which are as follows:

- **Send the request**: This includes creating an `XMLHttpRequest` object and attaching an event listener
- **Process the response**: This happens when your event listener gets notified that the response has arrived, and your code gets busy doing something amazing with the response

Sending the request

In order to create an object, you will simply use the following code (let's deal with browser inconsistencies in just a bit):

```
var xhr = new XMLHttpRequest();
```

The next thing is to attach an event listener to the `readystatechange` event fired by the object:

```
xhr.onreadystatechange = myCallback;
```

Then, you will need to call the `open()` method, as follows:

```
xhr.open('GET', 'somefile.txt', true);
```

The first parameter specifies the type of HTTP request, such as `GET`, `POST`, `HEAD`, and so on. `GET` and `POST` are the most common ones. Use `GET` when you don't need to send much data with the request and your request doesn't modify (write) data on the server, otherwise, use `POST`. The second parameter is the URL you are requesting. In this example, it's the text file `somefile.txt` located in the same directory as the page. The last parameter is a Boolean specifying whether the request is asynchronous (`true`, always prefer this) or not (`false`, blocks all the JavaScript execution and waits until the response arrives).

The last step is to fire off the request, which is done as follows:

```
xhr.send('');
```

The `send()` method accepts any data you want to send with the request. For `GET` requests, this is an empty string because the data is in the URL. For `POST` request, it's a query string in the `key=value&key2=value2` form.

At this point, the request is sent and your code and the user can move on to other tasks. The callback function, `myCallback`, will be invoked when the response comes back from the server.

Processing the response

A listener is attached to the `readystatechange` event. So, what exactly is the ready state and how does it change?

There is a property of the XHR object called `readyState`. Every time it changes, the `readystatechange` event fires. The possible values of the `readyState` property are as follows:

- 0-uninitialized
- 1-loading
- 2-loaded
- 3-interactive
- 4-complete

When `readyState` gets the value of `4`, it means the response is back and ready to be processed. In `myCallback`, after you make sure `readyState` is `4`, the other thing to check is the status code of the HTTP request. You might have requested a non-existing URL, for example, and got a `404` (File not found) status code. The interesting code is the `200` (`OK`) code, so `myCallback` should check for this value. The status code is available in the `status` property of the XHR object.

Once `xhr.readyState` is `4` and `xhr.status` is `200`, you can access the contents of the requested URL using the `xhr.responseText` property. Let's see how `myCallback` can be implemented to simply `alert()` the contents of the requested URL:

```
function myCallback() {

  if (xhr.readyState < 4) {
    return; // not ready yet
  }
  if (xhr.status !== 200) {
    alert('Error!'); // the HTTP status code is not OK
    return;
  }

  //  all is fine, do the work
  alert(xhr.responseText);
}
```

Once you've received the new content you requested, you can add it to the page, use it for some calculations, or for any other purpose you find suitable.

Overall, this two-step process (send request and process response) is the core of the whole XHR/Ajax functionality. Now that you know the basics, you can move on to building the next Gmail. Oh yes, let's take a look at some minor browser inconsistencies.

Creating XMLHttpRequest objects in IE prior to Version 7

In Internet Explorer, prior to version 7, the `XMLHttpRequest` object was an ActiveX object, so creating an XHR instance is a little different. It goes as follows:

```
var xhr = new ActiveXObject('MSXML2.XMLHTTP.3.0');
```

`MSXML2.XMLHTTP.3.0` is the identifier of the object you want to create. There are several versions of the `XMLHttpRequest` object, and if your page visitor doesn't have the latest one installed, you can try two older ones before you give up.

For a fully-cross-browser solution, you should first test to see if the user's browser supports `XMLHttpRequest` as a native object, and if not, try the IE way. Therefore, the whole process of creating an XHR instance could be like the following:

```
var ids = ['MSXML2.XMLHTTP.3.0',
        'MSXML2.XMLHTTP',
        'Microsoft.XMLHTTP'];
var xhr;
if (XMLHttpRequest) {
  xhr = new XMLHttpRequest();
} else {
  // IE: try to find an ActiveX object to use
  for (var i = 0; i < ids.length; i++) {
    try {
      xhr = new ActiveXObject(ids[i]);
      break;
    } catch (e) {}
  }
}
```

What is this doing? The `ids` array contains a list of ActiveX program IDs to try. The `xhr` variable points to the new XHR object. The code first checks to see if `XMLHttpRequest` exists. If so, this means that the browser supports `XMLHttpRequest()` natively, so the browser is relatively modern. If it is not, the code loops through ids trying to create an object. The `catch(e)` block quietly ignores failures and the loop continues. As soon as an `xhr` object is created, you break out of the loop.

As you can see, this is quite a bit of code, so it's best to abstract it into a function. Actually, one of the exercises at the end of the chapter prompts you to create your own Ajax utility.

A is for Asynchronous

Now you know how to create an XHR object, give it a URL and handle the response to the request. What happens when you send two requests asynchronously? What if the response to the second request comes before the first?

In the preceding example, the XHR object was global and `myCallback` was relying on the presence of this global object in order to access its `readyState`, `status`, and `responseText` properties. Another way, which prevents you from relying on global variables, is to wrap the callback in a closure. Let's see how:

```
var xhr = new XMLHttpRequest();

xhr.onreadystatechange = (function (myxhr) {
  return function () {
    myCallback(myxhr);
  };
}(xhr));

xhr.open('GET', 'somefile.txt', true);
xhr.send('');
```

In this case, `myCallback()` receives the XHR object as a parameter and will not go looking for it in the global space. This also means that at the time the response is received, the original `xhr` might be reused for a second request. The closure keeps pointing to the original object.

X is for XML

Although these days JSON (discussed in the next chapter) is preferred over XML as a data transfer format, XML is still an option. In addition to the `responseText` property, the XHR objects also have another property called `responseXML`. When you send an HTTP request for an XML document, `responseXML` points to an XML DOM document object. To work with this document, you can use all of the core DOM methods discussed previously in this chapter, such as `getElementsByTagName()`, `getElementById()`, and so on.

An example

Let's wrap up the different XHR topics with an example. You can visit the page located at `http://www.phpied.com/files/jsoop/xhr.html` to work on the example yourself.

The main page, `xhr.html`, is a simple static page that contains nothing but three `<div>` tags, which are as follows:

```
<div id="text">Text will be here</div>
<div id="html">HTML will be here</div>
<div id="xml">XML will be here</div>
```

Using the console, you can write code that requests three files and loads their respective contents into each `<div>`.

The three files to load are as follows:

- `content.txt`: This is a simple text file containing the text `I am a text file`
- `content.html`: This is a file containing HTML code `I am <strong>formatted</strong> <em>HTML</em>`
- `content.xml`: This is an XML file containing the following code:

```
<?xml version="1.0" ?>
<root>
    I'm XML data.
</root>
```

All of the files are stored in the same directory as `xhr.html`.

 For security reasons, you can only use the original `XMLHttpRequest` to request files that are on the same domain. However, modern browsers support XHR2, which lets you make cross-domain requests, provided that the appropriate Access-Control-Allow-Origin HTTP header is in place.

First, let's create a function to abstract the request/response part:

```
function request(url, callback) {
  var xhr = new XMLHttpRequest();
  xhr.onreadystatechange = (function (myxhr) {
    return function () {
      if (myxhr.readyState === 4 && myxhr.status === 200) {
        callback(myxhr);
      }
    };
  }(xhr));
  xhr.open('GET', url, true);
  xhr.send('');
}
```

This function accepts a URL to request and a callback function to call once the response arrives. Let's call the function three times, once for each file, as follows:

```
request(
  'http://www.phpied.com/files/jsoop/content.txt',
  function (o) {
    document.getElementById('text').innerHTML =
      o.responseText;
  }
);
request(
  'http://www.phpied.com/files/jsoop/content.html',
  function (o) {
    document.getElementById('html').innerHTML =
      o.responseText;
  }
);
request(
  'http://www.phpied.com/files/jsoop/content.xml',
  function (o) {
    document.getElementById('xml').innerHTML =
      o.responseXML
        .getElementsByTagName('root')[0]
        .firstChild
        .nodeValue;
  }
);
```

The callback functions are defined inline. The first two are identical. They just replace the HTML of the corresponding <div> with the contents of the requested file. The third one is a little different as it deals with the XML document. First, you will access the XML DOM object as o.responseXML. Then, using getElementsByTagName(), you will get a list of all the <root> tags (there is only one). The firstChild of <root> is a text node and nodeValue is the text contained in it (I'm XML data). Then, just replace the HTML of <div id="xml"> with the new content. The result is shown in the following screenshot:

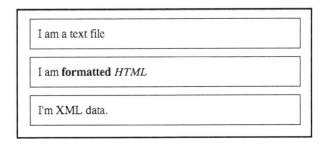

When working with the XML document, you can also use
`o.responseXML.documentElement` to get to the `<root>` element instead of
`o.responseXML.getElementsByTagName('root')[0]`. Remember that
`documentElement` gives you the root node of an XML document. The root in HTML
documents is always the `<html>` tag.

Exercises

In the previous chapters, the solutions to the exercises could be found in the text of the
chapter. This time, some of the exercises require you to do some more reading, or
experimentation, outside this book.

1. BOM: As a BOM exercise, try coding something wrong, obtrusive, user-
   unfriendly, and all in all, very Web 1.0, the shaking browser window. Try
   implementing code that opens a 200 x 200 pop up window and then resizes it
   slowly and gradually to 400 x 400. Next, move the window around as if there's an
   earthquake. All you'll need is one of the `move*()` functions, one or more calls to
   `setInterval()`, and maybe one to `setTimeout()`/`clearInterval()` to stop
   the whole thing. Or, here's an easier one-print the current date/time in
   `document.title` and update it every second, like a clock.

2. DOM:

   - Implement `walkDOM()` differently. Also, make it accept a callback function
     instead of hard coding `console.log()`.

   - Removing content with `innerHTML` is easy (`document.body.innerHTML = ''`),
     but not always best. The problem will be when there are event listeners attached
     to the removed elements; they won't be removed in IE, causing the browser to
     leak memory because it stores references to something that doesn't exist.
     Implement a general-purpose function that deletes DOM nodes, but removes any
     event listeners first. You can loop through the attributes of a node and check if
     the value is a function. If it is, it's most likely an attribute like `onclick`. You need
     to set it to `null` before removing the element from the tree.

   - Create a function called `include()` that includes external scripts on demand.
     This means you need to create a new `<script>` tag dynamically, set its `src`
     attribute, and append to the document's `<head>`. Test it by using the following
     code:

     ```
     > include('somescript.js');
     ```

3. Events:

- Create an event utility (object) called `myevent`, which has the following methods working cross-browser:
  - The `addListener(element, event_name, callback)`, where `element` can also be an array of elements
  - `removeListener(element, event_name, callback)`
  - `getEvent(event)` just to check for a `window.event` for older versions of IE
  - getTarget(event)
  - stopPropagation(event)
  - preventDefault(event)
- Usage example is as follows:

```
function myCallback(e) {
  e = myevent.getEvent(e);
  alert(myevent.getTarget(e).href);
  myevent.stopPropagation(e);
  myevent.preventDefault(e);
}
myevent.addListener(document.links, 'click', myCallback);
```

- The result of the example code should be that all of the links in the document lead nowhere, but only alert the `href` attribute.
- Create an absolutely positioned `<div>`, say at x = 100px, y = 100px. Write the code to be able to move div around the page using the arrow keys or the *J* (left), *K* (right), *M* (down), and *I* (up) keys. Reuse your own event utility from 3.1.

4. XMLHttpRequest:

- Create your own XHR utility (object) called `ajax`. For example, take a look at the following code:

```
function myCallback(xhr) {
  alert(xhr.responseText);
}
ajax.request('somefile.txt', 'get', myCallback);
ajax.request('script.php', 'post', myCallback,
'first=John&last=Smith');
```

Summary

You learned quite a bit in this chapter. You learned the following cross-browser BOM objects:

- Properties of the global `window` object, such as `navigator`, `location`, `history`, `frames`, `screen`
- Methods such as `setInterval()` and `setTimeout()`; `alert()`, `confirm()` and `prompt()`; `moveTo/By()` and `resizeTo/By()`

Then, you learned about the DOM, an API to represent an HTML or XML document as a tree structure, where each tag or text is a node on the tree. You also learned how to perform the following actions:

- Accessing nodes:
  - Using parent/child relationship properties, such as `parentNode`, `childNodes`, `firstChild`, `lastChild`, `nextSibling`, and `previousSibling`
  - Using `getElementsById()`, `getElementsByTagName()`, `getElementsByName()`, and `querySelectorAll()`
- Modifying nodes:
  - Using `innerHTML` or `innerText/textContent`
  - Using `nodeValue` or `setAttribute()`, or just using attributes as object properties
- Removing nodes with `removeChild()` or `replaceChild()`
- Adding new ones with `appendChild()`, `cloneNode()`, and `insertBefore()`

You also learned the following DOM 0 (pre-standardization) properties, ported to DOM Level 1:

- Collections, such as `document.forms`, `images`, `links`, `anchors`, `applets`. Using these are discouraged as DOM1 has the much more flexible `getElementsByTagName()` method.
- The `document.body` element, which gives you convenient access to `<body>`.
- The `document.title`, `cookie`, `referrer`, and `domain`.

Next, you learned how the browser broadcasts events that you can listen to. It's not straightforward to do this in a cross-browser manner, but it's possible. Events bubble up, so you can use event delegation to listen to events more globally. You can also stop the propagation of events and interfere with the default browser behavior.

Finally, you learned about the XMLHttpRequest object that allows you to build responsive web pages that do the following tasks:

- Make HTTP requests to the server to get pieces of data
- Process the response to update portions of the page

11
Coding and Design Patterns

Now that you know all about the objects in JavaScript, mastered prototypes and inheritance, and seen some practical examples of using browser-specific objects, let's move forward, or rather, move a level up. Let's take a look at some common JavaScript patterns.

But first, what's a pattern? In short, a pattern is a good solution to a common problem. Codifying the solution into a pattern makes it repeatable as well.

Sometimes, when you're facing a new programming problem, you may recognize right away that you've previously solved another, suspiciously similar problem. In such cases, it's worth isolating this class of problems and searching for a common solution. A pattern is a proven and reusable solution (or an approach to a solution) to a class of problems.

There are cases where a pattern is nothing more than an idea or a name. Sometimes, just using a name helps you think more clearly about a problem. Also, when working with other developers in a team, it's much easier to communicate when everybody uses the same terminology to discuss a problem or a solution.

Other times, you may come across a unique problem that doesn't look like anything you've seen before and doesn't readily fit into a known pattern. Blindly applying a pattern just for the sake of using a pattern, is not a good idea. It's preferable to not use any known pattern than to try to tweak your problem so that it fits an existing solution.

This chapter talks about two types of patterns, which are as follows:

- **Coding patterns**: These are mostly JavaScript-specific best practices
- **Design patterns**: These are language-independent patterns, popularized by the famous *Gang of Four* book

Coding patterns

Let's start with some patterns that reflect JavaScript's unique features. Some patterns aim to help you organize your code, for example, namespacing; others are related to improving performance, such as lazy definitions and init-time branching; and some make up for missing features, such as private properties. The patterns discussed in this section include the following topics:

- Separating behavior
- Namespaces
- Init-time branching
- Lazy definition
- Configuration objects
- Private variables and methods
- Privileged methods
- Private functions as public methods
- Immediate functions
- Chaining
- JSON

Separating behavior

As discussed previously, the three building blocks of a web page are as follows:

- Content (HTML)
- Presentation (CSS)
- Behavior (JavaScript)

Content

HTML is the content of the web page, the actual text. Ideally, the content should be marked-up using the least amount of HTML tags that sufficiently describe the semantic meaning of that content. For example, if you're working on a navigation menu, it's a good idea to use the `<ul>` and `<li>` tags as a navigation menu is in essence, just a list of links.

Your content (HTML) should be free from any formatting elements. Visual formatting belongs to the presentation layer and should be achieved through the use of **CSS** (**Cascading Style Sheets**). This means the following:

- The style attribute of HTML tags should not be used, if possible.
- Presentational HTML tags such as `<font>` should not be used at all.
- Tags should be used for their semantic meaning, not because of how browsers render them by default. For instance, developers sometimes use a `<div>` tag where a `<p>` would be more appropriate. It's also favorable to use `<strong>` and `<em>` instead of `<b>` and `<i>` as the latter describe the visual presentation rather than the meaning.

Presentation

A good approach to keep presentation out of the content is to reset or nullify all browser defaults, for example, using `reset.css` from the Yahoo! UI library. This way, the browser's default rendering won't distract you from consciously thinking about the proper semantic tags to use.

Behavior

The third component of a web page is the behavior. Behavior should be kept separate from both the content and the presentation. It is usually added by using JavaScript that is isolated to `<script>` tags, and preferably contained in external files. This means not using any inline attributes, such as `onclick`, `onmouseover`, and so on. Instead, you can use the `addEventListener/attachEvent` methods from the previous chapter.

The best strategy to separate behavior from content is as follows:

- Minimize the number of `<script>` tags
- Avoid inline event handlers
- Do not use CSS expressions
- Toward the end of your content, when you are ready to close the `<body>` tag, insert a single `external.js` file

Example of separating behavior

Let's say you have a search form on a page, and you want to validate the form with JavaScript. So, you go ahead and keep the `form` tags free from any JavaScript, and then immediately before closing the `</body>` tag, you insert a `<script>` tag that links to an external file, as follows:

```
<body>
  <form id="myform" method="post" action="server.php">
  <fieldset>
    <legend>Search</legend>
    <input
      name="search"
      id="search"
      type="text"
    />
    <input type="submit" />
    </fieldset>
  </form>
  <script src="behaviors.js"></script>
</body>
```

In `behaviors.js` you attach an event listener to the submit event. In your listener, you can check to see if the text input field was left blank and, if so, stop the form from being submitted. This way, you will save a roundtrip between the server and the client and make the application immediately responsive.

The content of `behaviors.js` is given in the following code. It assumes that you've created your `myevent` utility from the exercise at the end of the previous chapter:

```
// init
myevent.addListener('myform', 'submit', function (e) {
  // no need to propagate further
  e = myevent.getEvent(e);
  myevent.stopPropagation(e);
  // validate
  var el = document.getElementById('search');
  if (!el.value) { // too bad, field is empty
    myevent.preventDefault(e); // prevent the form submission
    alert('Please enter a search string');
  }
});
```

Asynchronous JavaScript loading

You noticed how the script was loaded at the end of the HTML, right before closing the body. The reason is that JavaScript blocks the DOM construction of the page, and in some browsers, even downloads of the other components that follow. By moving the scripts to the bottom of the page, you ensure that the script is out of the way, and when it arrives, it simply enhances the already usable page.

Another way to prevent external JavaScript files from blocking the page is to load them asynchronously. This way you can start loading them earlier. HTML5 has the `defer` attribute for this purpose. Consider the following line of code:

```
<script defer src="behaviors.js"></script>
```

Unfortunately, the `defer` attribute is not supported by older browsers, but luckily, there is a solution that works across browsers, old and new. The solution is to create a `script` node dynamically and append it to the DOM. In other words, you can use a bit of inline JavaScript to load the external JavaScript file. You can have this script loader snippet at the top of your document so that the download has an early start. Take a look at the following code example:

```
...
<head>
<script>
(function () {
  var s = document.createElement('script');
  s.src = 'behaviors.js';
  document.getElementsByTagName('head')[0].appendChild(s);
}());
</script>
</head>
...
```

Namespaces

Global variables should be avoided in order to reduce the possibility of variable naming collisions. You can minimize the number of globals by namespacing your variables and functions. The idea is simple, you will create only one global object, and all your other variables and functions become properties of that object.

An Object as a namespace

Let's create a global object called `MYAPP`:

```
// global namespace
var MYAPP = MYAPP || {};
```

Now, instead of having a global `myevent` utility (from the previous chapter), you can have it as an `event` property of the `MYAPP` object, as follows:

```
// sub-object
MYAPP.event = {};
```

Adding the methods to the `event` utility is still the same. Consider the following example:

```
// object together with the method declarations
MYAPP.event = {
  addListener: function (el, type, fn) {
    // .. do the thing
  },
  removeListener: function (el, type, fn) {
    // ...
  },
  getEvent: function (e) {
    // ...
  }
  // ... other methods or properties
};
```

Namespaced constructors

Using a namespace doesn't prevent you from creating constructor functions. Here is how you can have a DOM utility that has an `Element` constructor, which allows you to create DOM elements easily:

```
MYAPP.dom = {};
MYAPP.dom.Element = function (type, properties) {
  var tmp = document.createElement(type);
  for (var i in properties) {
    if (properties.hasOwnProperty(i)) {
      tmp.setAttribute(i, properties[i]);
    }
  }
  return tmp;
};
```

Chapter 11

Similarly, you can have a `Text` constructor to create text nodes. Consider the following code example:

```
MYAPP.dom.Text = function (txt) {
  return document.createTextNode(txt);
};
```

Using the constructors to create a link at the bottom of a page can be done as follows:

```
var link = new MYAPP.dom.Element('a',
  {href: 'http://phpied.com', target: '_blank'});
var text = new MYAPP.dom.Text('click me');
link.appendChild(text);
document.body.appendChild(link);
```

A namespace() method

You can create a namespace utility that makes your life easier so that you can use more convenient syntax as follows:

```
MYAPP.namespace('dom.style');
```

Instead of the more verbose syntax as follows:

```
MYAPP.dom = {};
MYAPP.dom.style = {};
```

Here's how you can create such a `namespace()` method. First, you will create an array by splitting the input string using the period (.) as a separator. Then, for every element in the new array, you will add a property to your global object, if one doesn't already exist, as follows:

```
var MYAPP = {};
MYAPP.namespace = function (name) {
  var parts = name.split('.');
  var current = MYAPP;
  for (var i = 0; i < parts.length; i++) {
    if (!current[parts[i]]) {
      current[parts[i]] = {};
    }
    current = current[parts[i]];
  }
};
```

[369]

Testing the new method is done as follows:

```
MYAPP.namespace('event');
MYAPP.namespace('dom.style');
```

The result of the preceding code is the same as if you did the following:

```
var MYAPP = {
  event: {},
  dom: {
    style: {}
  }
};
```

Init-time branching

In the previous chapter, you noticed that sometimes, different browsers have different implementations for the same or similar functionalities. In such cases, you will need to branch your code, depending on what's supported by the browser currently executing your script. Depending on your program, this branching can happen far too often and, as a result, may slow down the script execution.

You can mitigate this problem by branching some parts of the code during initialization, when the script loads, rather than during runtime. Building upon the ability to define functions dynamically, you can branch and define the same function with a different body, depending on the browser. Let's see how.

First, let's define a namespace and placeholder method for the event utility:

```
var MYAPP = {};
MYAPP.event = {
  addListener: null,
  removeListener: null
};
```

At this point, the methods to add or remove a listener are not implemented. Based on the results from feature sniffing, these methods can be defined differently, as follows:

```
if (window.addEventListener) {
  MYAPP.event.addListener = function (el, type, fn) {
    el.addEventListener(type, fn, false);
  };
  MYAPP.event.removeListener = function (el, type, fn) {
    el.removeEventListener(type, fn, false);
  };
```

```
    } else if (document.attachEvent) { // IE
      MYAPP.event.addListener = function (el, type, fn) {
        el.attachEvent('on' + type, fn);
      };
      MYAPP.event.removeListener = function (el, type, fn) {
        el.detachEvent('on' + type, fn);
      };
    } else { // older browsers
      MYAPP.event.addListener = function (el, type, fn) {
        el['on' + type] = fn;
      };
      MYAPP.event.removeListener = function (el, type) {
        el['on' + type] = null;
      };
    }
```

After this script executes, you have the `addListener()` and `removeListener()` methods defined in a browser-dependent way. Now, every time you invoke one of these methods, there's no more feature-sniffing, and it results in less work and faster execution.

One thing to watch out for when sniffing features is not to assume too much after checking for one feature. In the previous example, this rule is broken because the code only checks for `addEventListener` support, but then defines both `addListener()` and `removeListener()`. In this case, it's probably safe to assume that if a browser implements `addEventListener()`, it also implements `removeEventListener()`. However, imagine what happens if a browser implements `stopPropagation()` but not `preventDefault()`, and you haven't checked for these individually. You have assumed that because `addEventListener()` is not defined, the browser must be an old IE and write your code using your knowledge and assumptions of how IE works. Remember that all of your knowledge is based on the way a certain browser works today, but not necessarily the way it will work tomorrow. So, to avoid many rewrites of your code as new browser versions are shipped, it's best to individually check for features you intend to use and don't generalize on what a certain browser supports.

Lazy definition

The lazy definition pattern is similar to the previous init-time branching pattern. The difference is that the branching happens only when the function is called for the first time. When the function is called, it redefines itself with the best implementation. Unlike the init-time branching, where the if happens once, during loading, here it may not happen at all, in cases when the function is never called. The lazy definition also makes the initialization process lighter as there's no init-time branching work to be done.

Let's see an example that illustrates this via the definition of an `addListener()` function. The function is first defined with a generic body. It checks which functionality is supported by the browser when it's called for the first time and then redefines itself using the most suitable implementation. At the end of the first call, the function calls itself, so that the actual event attaching is performed. The next time you call the same function, it will be defined with its new body and be ready for use, so no further branching is necessary. The following is the code snippet:

```
var MYAPP = {};
MYAPP.myevent = {
  addListener: function (el, type, fn) {
      if (el.addEventListener) {
        MYAPP.myevent.addListener = function (el, type, fn) {
          el.addEventListener(type, fn, false);
        };
      } else if (el.attachEvent) {
        MYAPP.myevent.addListener = function (el, type, fn) {
          el.attachEvent('on' + type, fn);
        };
      } else {
        MYAPP.myevent.addListener = function (el, type, fn) {
          el['on' + type] = fn;
        };
      }
      MYAPP.myevent.addListener(el, type, fn);
  }
};
```

Configuration object

This pattern is convenient when you have a function or method that accepts a lot of optional parameters. It's up to you to decide how many constitutes a lot. But generally, a function with more than three parameters is not convenient to call, because you have to remember the order of the parameters, and it is even more inconvenient when some of the parameters are optional.

Instead of having many parameters, you can use one parameter and make it an object. The properties of the object are the actual parameters. This is suitable to pass configuration options because these tend to be numerous and optional (with smart defaults). The beauty of using a single object as opposed to multiple parameters is described as follows:

- The order doesn't matter
- You can easily skip parameters that you don't want to set
- It's easy to add more optional configuration attributes
- It makes the code more readable because the configuration object's properties are present in the calling code along with their names

Imagine you have some sort of UI widget constructor you use to create fancy buttons. It accepts the text to put inside the button (the `value` attribute of the `<input>` tag) and an optional parameter of the `type` of button. For simplicity, let's say the fancy button takes the same configuration as a regular button. Take a look at the following code:

```
// a constructor that creates buttons
MYAPP.dom.FancyButton = function (text, type) {
  var b = document.createElement('input');
  b.type = type || 'submit';
  b.value = text;
  return b;
};
```

Using the constructor is simple; you just give it a string. Then, you can add the new button to the body of the document as follows:

```
document.body.appendChild(
  new MYAPP.dom.FancyButton('puuush')
);
```

This is all well and works fine, but then you decide you also want to be able to set some of the style properties of the button, such as colors and fonts. You can end up with a definition like the following:

```
MYAPP.dom.FancyButton =
  function (text, type, color, border, font) {
  // ...
};
```

Now, using the constructor can become a little inconvenient, especially when you want to set the third and fifth parameter, but not the second or the fourth. Consider the following example:

```
new MYAPP.dom.FancyButton(
    'puuush', null, 'white', null, 'Arial');
```

A better approach is to use one `config` object parameter for all the settings. The function definition can become something like the following code snippet:

```
MYAPP.dom.FancyButton = function (text, conf) {
    var type = conf.type || 'submit';
    var font = conf.font || 'Verdana';
    // ...
};
```

Using the constructor is shown as follows:

```
var config = {
    font: 'Arial, Verdana, sans-serif',
    color: 'white'
};
new MYAPP.dom.FancyButton('puuush', config);
```

Another usage example is as follows:

```
document.body.appendChild(
    new MYAPP.dom.FancyButton('dude', {color: 'red'})
);
```

As you can see, it's easy to set only some of the parameters and to switch around their order. In addition, the code is friendlier and easier to understand when you see the names of the parameters at the same place where you call the method.

A drawback of this pattern is the same as its strength. It's trivial to keep adding more parameters, which means trivial to abuse the technique. Once you have an excuse to add to this free-for-all bag of properties, you will find it tempting to keep adding some that are not entirely optional, or some that are dependent on other properties.

As a rule of thumb, all these properties should be independent and optional. If you have to check all possible combinations inside your function ("oh, A is set, but A is only used if B is also set"), this is a recipe for a large function body, which quickly becomes confusing and difficult, if not impossible, to test, because of all the combinations.

Private properties and methods

JavaScript doesn't have the notion of access modifiers, which set the privileges of the properties in an object. Other languages often have access modifiers, as follows:

- Public: All users of an object can access these properties or methods
- Private: Only the object itself can access these properties
- Protected: Only objects inheriting the object in question can access these properties

JavaScript doesn't have a special syntax to denote private properties or methods, but as discussed in Chapter 3, *Functions*, you can use local variables and methods inside a function and achieve the same level of protection.

Continuing with the example of the FancyButton constructor, you can have local variable styles that contains all the defaults, and a local setStyle() function. These are invisible to the code outside of the constructor. Here's how FancyButton can make use of the local private properties:

```
var MYAPP = {};
MYAPP.dom = {};
MYAPP.dom.FancyButton = function (text, conf) {
  var styles = {
    font: 'Verdana',
    border: '1px solid black',
    color: 'black',
    background: 'grey'
  };
  function setStyles(b) {
    var i;
    for (i in styles) {
      if (styles.hasOwnProperty(i)) {
        b.style[i] = conf[i] || styles[i];
      }
    }
  }
  conf = conf || {};
  var b = document.createElement('input');
  b.type = conf.type || 'submit';
  b.value = text;
  setStyles(b);
  return b;
};
```

In this implementation, `styles` is a private property and `setStyle()` is a private method. The constructor uses them internally (and they can access anything inside the constructor), but they are not available to code outside of the function.

Privileged methods

Privileged methods (this term was coined by Douglas Crockford) are normal public methods that can access private methods or properties. They can act like a bridge in making some of the private functionality accessible, but in a controlled manner, wrapped in a privileged method.

Private functions as public methods

Let's say you've defined a function that you absolutely need to keep intact, so you make it private. However, you also want to provide access to the same function, so that outside code can also benefit from it. In this case, you can assign the private function to a publicly available property.

Let's define `_setStyle()` and `_getStyle()` as private functions, but then assign them to the public `setStyle()` and `getStyle()`, consider the following example:

```
var MYAPP = {};
MYAPP.dom = (function () {
  var _setStyle = function (el, prop, value) {
    console.log('setStyle');
  };
  var _getStyle = function (el, prop) {
    console.log('getStyle');
  };
  return {
    setStyle: _setStyle,
    getStyle: _getStyle,
    yetAnother: _setStyle
  };
}());
```

Now, when you call `MYAPP.dom.setStyle()`, it invokes the private `_setStyle()` function. You can also overwrite `setStyle()` from the outside as follows:

```
MYAPP.dom.setStyle = function () {alert('b');};
```

Now, the result is as follows:

- `MYAPP.dom.setStyle` points to the new function
- `MYAPP.dom.yetAnother` still points to `_setStyle()`
- `_setStyle()` is always available when any other internal code relies on it to be working as intended, regardless of the outside code

When you expose something private, keep in mind that objects (functions and arrays are objects too) are passed by reference and, therefore, can be modified from the outside.

Immediate functions

Another pattern that helps you keep the global namespace clean is to wrap your code in an anonymous function and execute that function immediately. This way, any variables inside the function are local, as long as you use the `var` statement, and are destroyed when the function returns, if they aren't part of a closure. This pattern was discussed in more detail in `Chapter 3`, *Functions*. Take a look at the following code:

```
(function () {
  // code goes here...
}());
```

This pattern is especially suitable for on-off initialization task, performed when the script loads.

The immediate self-executing function pattern can be extended to create and return objects. If the creation of these objects is more complicated and involves some initialization work, then you can do this in the first part of the self-executable function and return a single object that can access and benefit from any private properties at the top portion, as follows:

```
var MYAPP = {};
MYAPP.dom = (function () {
  // initialization code...
  function _private() {
    // ...
  }
  return {
    getStyle: function (el, prop) {
```

```
      console.log('getStyle');
      _private();
    },
    setStyle: function (el, prop, value) {
      console.log('setStyle');
    }
  };
}());
```

Modules

Combining several of the previous patterns gives you a new pattern, commonly referred to as a module pattern. The concept of modules in programming is convenient as it allows you to code separate pieces or libraries and combine them as needed, just like pieces of a puzzle.

The module pattern includes the following:

- Namespaces to reduce naming conflicts among modules
- An immediate function to provide a private scope and initialization
- Private properties and methods

 ES5 doesn't have a built-in concept of modules. There is the module specification from http://www.commonjs.org, which defines a require() function and an exports object.
ES6, however, supports modules. Chapter 8, Classes and Modules has covered modules in detail.

- Returning an object that has the public API of the module as follows:

```
namespace('MYAPP.module.amazing');

MYAPP.module.amazing = (function () {

  // short names for dependencies
  var another = MYAPP.module.another;

  // local/private variables
  var i, j;

  // private functions
  function hidden() {}
```

```
      // public API
      return {
        hi: function () {
          return "hello";
        }
      };
    }());
```

And, you can use the module in the following way:

```
MYAPP.module.amazing.hi(); // "hello"
```

Chaining

Chaining is a pattern that allows you to invoke multiple methods on one line as if the methods are the links in a chain. This is convenient when calling several related methods. You invoke the next method on the result of the previous without the use of an intermediate variable.

Say you've created a constructor that helps you work with DOM elements. The code to create a new <span> tag that is added to the <body> tag can look something like the following:

```
var obj = new MYAPP.dom.Element('span');
obj.setText('hello');
obj.setStyle('color', 'red');
obj.setStyle('font', 'Verdana');
document.body.appendChild(obj);
```

As you know, constructors return the object referred to as this keyword that they create. You can make your methods, such as setText() and setStyle(), also return this keyword, which allows you to call the next method on the instance returned by the previous one. This way, you can chain method calls, as follows:

```
var obj = new MYAPP.dom.Element('span');
obj.setText('hello')
    .setStyle('color', 'red')
    .setStyle('font', 'Verdana');
document.body.appendChild(obj);
```

You don't even need the `obj` variable if you don't plan on using it after the new element has been added to the tree, so the code looks like the following:

```
document.body.appendChild(
    new MYAPP.dom.Element('span')
        .setText('hello')
        .setStyle('color', 'red')
        .setStyle('font', 'Verdana')
);
```

A drawback of this pattern is that it makes it a little harder to debug when an error occurs somewhere in a long chain, and you don't know which link is to blame because they are all on the same line.

JSON

Let's wrap up the coding patterns section of this chapter with a few words about JSON. JSON is not technically a coding pattern, but you can say that using it is a good pattern.

JSON is a popular lightweight format to exchange data. It's often preferred over XML when using `XMLHttpRequest()` to retrieve data from the server. There's nothing specifically interesting about **JSON** other than the fact that it's extremely convenient. The JSON format consists of data defined using object and array literals. Here is an example of a JSON string that your server can respond with after an XHR request:

```
{
    'name':   'Stoyan',
    'family': 'Stefanov',
    'books':  ['OOJS', 'JSPatterns', 'JS4PHP']
}
```

An XML equivalent of this will be something like the following piece of code:

```
<?xml version="1.1" encoding="iso-8859-1"?>
<response>
    <name>Stoyan</name>
    <family>Stefanov</family>
    <books>
        <book>OOJS</book>
        <book>JSPatterns</book>
        <book>JS4PHP</book>
    </books>
</response>
```

First, you can see how JSON is lighter in terms of the number of bytes. However, the main benefit is not the smaller byte size, but the fact that it's trivial to work with JSON in JavaScript. Let's say, you've made an `XHR` request and have received a JSON string in the `responseText` property of the `XHR` object. You can convert this string of data into a working JavaScript object by simply using `eval()`. Consider the following example:

```
// warning: counter-example
var response = eval('(' + xhr.responseText + ')');
```

Now, you can access the data in `obj` as object properties as follows:

```
console.log(response.name); // "Stoyan"
console.log(response.books[2]); // "JS4PHP"
```

The problem is that `eval()` is insecure, so it's best if you use the JSON object to parse the JSON data (a fallback for older browsers is available at `http://json.org/`). Creating an object from a JSON string is still trivial as follows:

```
var response = JSON.parse(xhr.responseText);
```

To do the opposite, that is, to convert an object to a JSON string, you can use the `stringify()` method, as follows:

```
var str = JSON.stringify({hello: "you"});
```

Due to its simplicity, JSON has quickly become popular as a language-independent format to exchange data, and you can easily produce JSON on the server side using your preferred language. In PHP, for example, there are the `json_encode()` and `json_decode()` functions that let you serialize a PHP array or object into a JSON string, and vice versa.

Higher order functions

Functional programming was confined to a limited set of languages so far. With more languages adding features to support functional programming, interest in the area is gaining momentum. JavaScript is evolving to support common features of functional programming. You will gradually see a lot of code written in this style. It is important to understand the functional programming style, even if you don't feel inclined just yet to use it in your code.

Higher order functions are one of the important mainstays of functional programing. Higher order function is a function that does at least one of the following:

- Takes one or more functions as arguments
- Returns a function as a result

As functions are first class objects in JavaScript, passing and returning functions to and from a function is a pretty routine affair. Callbacks are higher order functions. Let's take a look at how we can take these two principles together and write a higher order function.

Let's write a `filter` function; this function filters out values from an array based on a criteria determined by a function. This function takes two arguments–a function, which returns a Boolean value, `true` for keeping this element.

For example, with this function, we are filtering all odd values from an array. Consider the following lines of code:

```
console.log([1, 2, 3, 4, 5].filter(function(ele){
  return ele % 2 == 0; }));
//[2,4]
```

We are passing an anonymous function to the `filter` function as the first argument. This function returns a Boolean based on a condition that checks if the element is odd or even.

This is an example of one of the several higher order functions added to ECMAScript 5. The point we are trying to make here is that you will increasingly see similar patterns of usage in JavaScript. You must first understand how higher order functions work and later, once you are comfortable with the concept, try to incorporate them in your code as well.

With ES6 function syntax changes, it is even more elegant to write higher order functions. Let's take a small example in ES5 and see how that translates into its ES6 equivalent:

```
function add(x){
  return function(y){
    return y + x;
  };
}
 var add3 = add(3);
console.log(add3(3));          // => 6
console.log(add(9)(10));       // => 19
```

The `add` function takes `x` and returns a function that takes `y` as an argument and then returns value of expression `y+x`.

When we looked at arrow functions, we discussed that arrow functions return results of a single expression implicitly. So, the preceding function can be turned into an arrow function by making the body of the arrow function another arrow function. Take a look at the following example:

```
const add = x => y => y + x;
```

Here, we have an outer function, x => [inner function with x as argument], and we have an inner function, y => y+x.

This introduction will help you get familiar with the increasing usage of higher order functions, and their increased importance in JavaScript.

Design patterns

The second part of this chapter presents a JavaScript approach to a subset of the design patterns introduced by *Design Patterns: Elements of Reusable Object-Oriented Software*, an influential book most commonly referred to as the *Book of Four*, the *Gang of Four*, or *GoF* (after its four authors). The patterns discussed in the *GoF* book are divided into the three following groups:

- Creational patterns that deal with how objects are created (instantiated)
- Structural patterns that describe how different objects can be composed in order to provide new functionality
- Behavioral patterns that describe ways for objects to communicate with each other

There are 23 patterns in the *Book of Four*, and more patterns have been identified since the book's publication. It's way beyond the scope of this book to discuss all of them, so the remainder of the chapter demonstrates only four, along with examples of their implementation in JavaScript. Remember that the patterns are more about interfaces and relationships rather than implementation. Once you have an understanding of a design pattern, it's often not difficult to implement it, especially in a dynamic language such as JavaScript.

The patterns discussed through the rest of the chapter are as follows:

- Singleton
- Factory
- Decorator
- Observer

Singleton pattern

Singleton is a creational design pattern, meaning that its focus is on creating objects. It helps you when you want to make sure there is only one object of a given kind or class. In a classical language, this would mean that an instance of a class is only created once, and any subsequent attempts to create new objects of the same class would return the original instance.

In JavaScript, because there are no classes, a singleton is the default and most natural pattern. Every object is a singleton object.

The most basic implementation of the singleton in JavaScript is the object literal. Take a look at the following line of code:

```
var single = {};
```

That was easy, right?

Singleton 2 pattern

If you want to use a class-like syntax and still implement the singleton pattern, things become a bit more interesting. Let's say, you have a constructor called `Logger()`, and you want to be able to do something like the following:

```
var my_log = new Logger();
my_log.log('some event');

// ... 1000 lines of code later in a different scope ...

var other_log = new Logger();
other_log.log('some new event');
console.log(other_log === my_log); // true
```

The idea is that, although you use `new`, only one instance needs to be created, and this instance is then returned in consecutive calls.

Global variable

One approach is to use a global variable to store the single instance. Your constructor could look like the following code snippet:

```
function Logger() {
   if (typeof global_log === "undefined") {
```

```
    global_log = this;
  }
  return global_log;
}
```

Using this constructor gives the expected result, which is as follows:

```
var a = new Logger();
var b = new Logger();
console.log(a === b); // true
```

The drawback is, obviously, the use of a global variable. It can be overwritten at any time, even accidentally, and you can lose the instance. The opposite, your global variable overwriting someone else's is also possible.

Property of the constructor

As you know, functions are objects and they have properties. You can assign the single instance to a property of the constructor function, as follows:

```
function Logger() {
  if (!Logger.single_instance) {
    Logger.single_instance = this;
  }
  return Logger.single_instance;
}
```

If you write `var a = new Logger()`, a points to the newly created `Logger.single_instance` property. A subsequent `var b = new Logger()` call results in b pointing to the same `Logger.single_instance` property, which is exactly what you want.

This approach certainly solves the global namespace issue because no global variables are created. The only drawback is that the property of the `Logger` constructor is publicly visible, so it can be overwritten at any time. In such cases, the single instance can be lost or modified. Of course, you can only provide so much protection against fellow programmers shooting themselves in the foot. After all, if someone can mess with the single-instance property, they can mess up the `Logger` constructor directly as well.

In a private property

The solution to the problem of overwriting the publicly visible property is not to use a public property, but a private one. You already know how to protect variables with a closure, so as an exercise, you can implement this approach to the singleton pattern.

Factory pattern

The factory is another creational design pattern, as it deals with creating objects. The factory can help you when you have similar types of objects and you don't know in advance which one you want to use. Based on user input or other criteria, your code determines the type of object it needs on the fly.

Let's say you have three different constructors that implement similar functionality. All the objects they create take a URL but do different things with it. One creates a text DOM node; the second creates a link; and the third, an image, as follows:

```
var MYAPP = {};
MYAPP.dom = {};
MYAPP.dom.Text = function (url) {
  this.url = url;
  this.insert = function (where) {
    var txt = document.createTextNode(this.url);
    where.appendChild(txt);
  };
};
MYAPP.dom.Link = function (url) {
  this.url = url;
  this.insert = function (where) {
    var link = document.createElement('a');
    link.href = this.url;
    link.appendChild(document.createTextNode(this.url));
    where.appendChild(link);
  };
};
MYAPP.dom.Image = function (url) {
  this.url = url;
  this.insert = function (where) {
    var im = document.createElement('img');
    im.src = this.url;
    where.appendChild(im);
  };
};
```

Using the three different constructors is exactly the same–pass the `url` variable and call the `insert()` method, as follows:

```
var url = 'http://www.phpied.com/images/covers/oojs.jpg';

var o = new MYAPP.dom.Image(url);
o.insert(document.body);

var o = new MYAPP.dom.Text(url);
o.insert(document.body);

var o = new MYAPP.dom.Link(url);
o.insert(document.body);
```

Imagine your program doesn't know in advance which type of object is required. The user decides, during runtime, by clicking on a button for example. If `type` contains the required type of object, you'll need to use an `if` or a `switch` statement, and write something like the following piece of code:

```
var o;
if (type === 'Image') {
  o = new MYAPP.dom.Image(url);
}
if (type === 'Link') {
  o = new MYAPP.dom.Link(url);
}
if (type === 'Text') {
  o = new MYAPP.dom.Text(url);
}
o.url = 'http://...';
o.insert();
```

This works fine; however, if you have a lot of constructors, the code becomes too lengthy and hard to maintain. Also, if you are creating a library or a framework that allows extensions or plugins, you don't even know the exact names of all the constructor functions in advance. In such cases, it's convenient to have a factory function that takes care of creating an object of the dynamically determined type.

Let's add a factory method to the `MYAPP.dom` utility:

```
MYAPP.dom.factory = function (type, url) {
  return new MYAPP.dom[type](url);
};
```

Now, you can replace the three `if` functions with the simpler code, as follows:

```
var image = MYAPP.dom.factory("Image", url);
image.insert(document.body);
```

The example `factory()` method in the previous code was simple; however, in a real-life scenario, you'd want to do some validation against the type value (for example, check if `MYAPP.dom[type]` exists) and optionally do some set up work common to all object types (for example, set up the URL all constructors use).

Decorator pattern

The decorator design pattern is a structural pattern; it doesn't have much to do with how objects are created, but rather how their functionality is extended. Instead of using inheritance, where you extend in a linear way (parent-child-grandchild), you can have one base object and a pool of different decorator objects that provide extra functionality. Your program can pick and choose which decorators it wants, and in which order. For a different program or code path, you may have a different set of requirements and pick different decorators out of the same pool. Take a look at the following code snippet to see how the usage part of the decorator pattern can be implemented:

```
var obj = {
  doSomething: function () {
    console.log('sure, asap');
  }
  //  ...
};
obj = obj.getDecorator('deco1');
obj = obj.getDecorator('deco13');
obj = obj.getDecorator('deco5');
obj.doSomething();
```

You can see how you can start with a simple object that has a `doSomething()` method. Then, you can pick one of the decorator objects you have lying around and which can be identified by name. All decorators provide a `doSomething()` method that first calls the same method of the previous decorator and then proceeds with its own code. Every time you add a decorator, you overwrite the base `obj` with an improved version of it. In the end, when you are finished adding decorators, you call `doSomething()`. As a result, all of the `doSomething()` methods of all the decorators are executed in sequence. Let's see an example.

Decorating a christmas tree

Let's illustrate the decorator pattern with an example of decorating a Christmas tree. You can start with the `decorate()` method as follows:

```
var tree = {};
tree.decorate = function () {
  alert('Make sure the tree won't fall');
};
```

Now, let's implement a `getDecorator()` method that adds extra decorators. The decorators will be implemented as constructor functions, and they'll all inherit from the base `tree` object as follows:

```
tree.getDecorator = function (deco) {
  tree[deco].prototype = this;
  return new tree[deco];
};
```

Now, let's create the first decorator, `RedBalls()`, as a property of `tree`, in order to keep the global namespace cleaner. The red ball objects also provide a `decorate()` method, but they make sure they call their parent's `decorate()` first. For example, take a look at the following code:

```
tree.RedBalls = function () {
  this.decorate = function () {
    this.RedBalls.prototype.decorate();
    alert('Put on some red balls');
  };
};
```

Similarly, implement `BlueBalls()` and `Angel()` decorators as follows:

```
tree.BlueBalls = function () {
  this.decorate = function () {
    this.BlueBalls.prototype.decorate();
    alert('Add blue balls');
  };
};
tree.Angel = function () {
  this.decorate = function () {
    this.Angel.prototype.decorate();
    alert('An angel on the top');
  };
};
```

Now, let's add all of the decorators to the base object, as shown in the following code snippet:

```
tree = tree.getDecorator('BlueBalls');
tree = tree.getDecorator('Angel');
tree = tree.getDecorator('RedBalls');
```

Finally, run the `decorate()` method as follows:

```
tree.decorate();
```

This single call results in the following alerts, specifically in this order:

1. Make sure the tree won't fall.
2. Add the blue balls.
3. Add an angel at the top.
4. Add some red balls.

As you see, this functionality allows you to have as many decorators as you like, and to choose and combine them in any way you like.

Observer pattern

The observer pattern, also known as the **subscriber-publisher** pattern, is a behavioral pattern, which means that it deals with how different objects interact and communicate with each other. When implementing the observer pattern, you have the following objects:

- One or more publisher objects that announce when they do something important.
- One or more subscribers tuned in to one or more publishers. They listen to what the publishers announce and then act appropriately.

The observer pattern may look familiar to you. It sounds similar to the browser events discussed in the previous chapter, and rightly so, because the browser events are one example application of this pattern. The browser is the publisher; it announces the fact that an event, such as a `click`, has happened. Your event listener functions that are subscribed to listen to this type of event will be notified when it happens. The browser-publisher sends an event object to all of the subscribers. In your custom implementations, you can send any type of data you find appropriate.

There are two subtypes of the observer pattern: push and pull. Push is where the publishers are responsible to notify each subscriber, and pull is where the subscribers monitor for changes in a publisher's state.

Let's take a look at an example implementation of the push model. Let's keep the observer-related code in a separate object and then use this object as a mix-in, adding its functionality to any other object that decides to be a publisher. In this way, any object can become a publisher and any function can become a subscriber. The observer object will have the following properties and methods:

- An array of `subscribers` that are just callback functions
- The `addSubscriber()` and `removeSubscriber()` methods that add to, and remove from, the `subscribers` collection
- A `publish()` method that takes data and calls all subscribers, passing the data to them
- A `make()` method that takes any object and turns it into a publisher by adding all of the methods mentioned previously to it

Here's the observer mix-in object that contains all the subscription-related methods and can be used to turn any object into a publisher:

```
var observer = {
  addSubscriber: function (callback) {
    if (typeof callback === "function") {
      this.subscribers[this.subscribers.length] = callback;
    }
  },
  removeSubscriber: function (callback) {
    for (var i = 0; i < this.subscribers.length; i++) {
      if (this.subscribers[i] === callback) {
        delete this.subscribers[i];
      }
    }
  },
  publish: function (what) {
    for (var i = 0; i < this.subscribers.length; i++) {
      if (typeof this.subscribers[i] === 'function') {
        this.subscribers[i](what);
      }
    }
  },
  make: function (o) { // turns an object into a publisher
    for (var i in this) {
      if (this.hasOwnProperty(i)) {
        o[i] = this[i];
```

```
                 o.subscribers = [];
            }
        }
    }
};
```

Now, let's create some publishers. A publisher can be any object and its only duty is to call the `publish()` method whenever something important occurs. Here's a `blogger` object that calls `publish()` every time a new blog posting is ready:

```
var blogger = {
    writeBlogPost: function() {
        var content = 'Today is ' + new Date();
        this.publish(content);
    }
};
```

Another object can be the LA Times newspaper that calls `publish()` when a new newspaper issue is out. Consider the following lines of code:

```
var la_times = {
    newIssue: function() {
        var paper = 'Martians have landed on Earth!';
        this.publish(paper);
    }
};
```

You can turn these objects into publishers as follows:

```
observer.make(blogger);
observer.make(la_times);
```

Now, let's have the following two simple objects, `jack` and `jill`:

```
var jack = {
    read: function(what) {
        console.log("I just read that " + what)
    }
};
var jill = {
    gossip: function(what) {
        console.log("You didn't hear it from me, but " + what)
    }
};
```

The `jack` and `jill` objects can subscribe to the `blogger` object by providing the callback methods they want to call when something is published, as follows:

```
blogger.addSubscriber(jack.read);
blogger.addSubscriber(jill.gossip);
```

What happens now, when the `blogger` object writes a new post? The result is that `jack` and `jill` will get notified:

```
> blogger.writeBlogPost();
    I just read that Today is Fri Jan 04 2013 19:02:12 GMT-0800 (PST)
    You didn't hear it from me, but Today is Fri Jan 04 2013 19:02:12
GMT-0800
        (PST)
```

At any time, `jill` may decide to cancel her subscription. Then, when writing another blog post, the unsubscribed object is no longer notified. Consider the following code snippet:

```
> blogger.removeSubscriber(jill.gossip);
> blogger.writeBlogPost();
I just read that Today is Fri Jan 04 2013 19:03:29 GMT-0800 (PST)
```

The `jill` object may decide to subscribe to LA Times, as an object can be a subscriber to many publishers, as follows:

```
> la_times.addSubscriber(jill.gossip);
```

Then, when LA Times publishes a new issue, `jill` gets notified and `jill.gossip()` is executed, as follows:

```
> la_times.newIssue();
You didn't hear it from me, but Martians have landed on Earth!
```

Summary

In this chapter, you learned about common JavaScript coding patterns and learned how to make your programs cleaner, faster, and better at working with other programs and libraries. Then, you saw a discussion and sample implementations of a handful of the design patterns from the *Book of Four*. You can see how JavaScript is a fully featured dynamic programming language, and that implementing classical patterns in a dynamic loosely typed language is pretty easy. The patterns are, in general, a large topic, and you can join the author of this book in a further discussion of the JavaScript patterns at `JSPatterns.com`, or take a look at the *JavaScript Patterns* book. The next chapter focuses on testing and debugging methodologies.

12
Testing and Debugging

As you write JavaScript applications, you will soon realize that having a sound testing strategy is indispensable. In fact, not writing enough tests is almost always a bad idea. It is essential to cover all nontrivial functionality of your code to make sure of the following points:

- Existing code behaves as per the specifications
- Any new code does not break the behavior defined by the specifications

Both these points are very important. Many engineers consider only the first point as the sole reason to cover your code with enough tests. The most obvious advantage of test coverage is to really make sure that the code being pushed to production system is mostly error free. Writing test cases to smartly cover maximum functional areas of the code, generally gives good indication around the overall quality of the code. There should be no arguments or compromises around this point. Although, it is unfortunate that many production systems are still bereft of adequate code coverage. It is very important to build an engineering culture where developers think about writing tests as much as they think about writing code.

The second point is even more important. Legacy systems are usually very difficult to manage. When you are working on code, either written by someone else or written by a large distributed team, it is fairly easy to introduce bugs and break things. Even the best engineers make mistakes. When you are working on a large code base you are unfamiliar with, if there is no sound test coverage to help you, you will introduce bugs. As you won't have the confidence in the changes you are making, because there are no test cases to confirm your changes, your code releases will be shaky, slow, and obviously full of hidden bugs.

You will refrain from refactoring or optimizing your code, because you won't be really sure what changes to the code base would potentially break something (again, because there are no test case to confirm your changes); all this is a vicious circle. It's like a civil engineer saying–although I have constructed this bridge, I have no confidence on the quality of the construction. It may collapse immediately or never. Although this may sound like an exaggeration, I have seen a lot of high impact production code being pushed with no test coverage. This is risky and should be avoided. When you are writing enough test cases to cover majority of your functional code, when you make change to those pieces, you will immediately realize if there is a problem with this new change. If your changes make the test case fail, you will realize the problem. If your refactor breaks the test scenario, you will realize the problem; all of this happens much before the code is pushed to production.

In recent years, ideas like test-driven development and self-testing code are gaining prominence, especially in agile methodology. These are fundamentally sound ideas and will help you write robust code – the code you are confident of. We will discuss all these ideas in this chapter. We will understand how to write good test cases in modern JavaScript. We will also look at several tools and methods to debug your code. JavaScript was traditionally a bit difficult to test and debug, primarily due to lack of tools, but modern tools make both of these easy and natural.

Unit testing

When we talk about test cases, we mostly mean unit tests. It is incorrect to assume that the unit we want to test is always a function. The unit, or unit of work, is a logical unit that constitutes single behavior. This unit should be able to be invoked via a public interface and should be testable independently.

Thus, a unit test can perform the following functions:

- It tests a single logical function
- It can run without a specific order of execution
- It takes care of its own dependencies and mock data
- It always returns the same result for the same input
- It should be self-explanatory, maintainable, and readable

Martin Fowler advocates the *Test Pyramid* (`http://martinfowler.com/bliki/TestPyramid.html`) strategy to make sure we have a high number of unit tests to ensure maximum code coverage. There are two important testing strategies that we will discuss in this chapter.

Test Driven Development

Test driven development (**TDD**) has gained a lot of prominence in the last few years. The concept was first proposed as part of the extreme programming methodology. The idea is to have short repetitive development cycles where the focus is on writing the test cases first. The cycle looks like the following:

1. Add a test case as per the specifications for the specific unit of code.
2. Run existing suite of test cases to see if the new test case you wrote fails; it should, because there is no code for that unit yet. This step ensures that the current test harness works well.
3. Write the code that mainly serves to confirm to the test case. This code is not optimized, refactored, or even entirely correct. However, this is fine at this moment.
4. Rerun tests and see if all the test cases pass. After this step, you are confident that the new code is not breaking anything.
5. Refactor code to make sure you are optimizing the unit and handling all corner cases

These steps are repeated for any new code you add. This is an elegant strategy that works really well for agile methodology. TDD will be successful only if the testable units of code are small and confirms only to the test case.

Behavior Driven Development

A very common problem while trying to follow TDD is vocabulary and the definition of correctness. BDD tries to introduce a ubiquitous language while writing the test cases when you are following TDD. This language makes sure that both the business and the engineering are talking about the same thing.

We will use Jasmine as the primary BDD framework and explore various testing strategies.

 You can install Jasmine by downloading the standalone package from `https://github.com/jasmine/jasmine/releases/download/v2.3.4/jasm ine-standalone-2.3.4.zip`.

When you unzip this package, you will see the following directory structure:

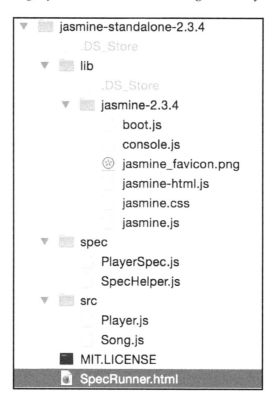

The `lib` directory contains the JavaScript files that you need in your project to start writing Jasmine test cases. If you open `SpecRunner.html`, you will find the following JavaScript files included in it:

```
<script src="lib/jasmine-2.3.4/jasmine.js"></script>
<script src="lib/jasmine-2.3.4/jasmine-html.js"></script>
<script src="lib/jasmine-2.3.4/boot.js"></script>

<!-- include source files here... -->
<script src="src/Player.js"></script>
<script src="src/Song.js"></script>
<!-- include spec files here... -->
<script src="spec/SpecHelper.js"></script>
<script src="spec/PlayerSpec.js"></script>
```

The first three are Jasmine's own framework files. The next section includes the source files we want to test and the actual test specifications.

Let's experiment with Jasmine via a very ordinary example. Create a `bigfatjavascriptcode.js` file and place it in the `src/` directory. The function we will test is as follows:

```
function capitalizeName(name){
   return name.toUpperCase();
}
```

This is a simple function that does one single thing. It receives a string and returns a capitalized string. We will test various scenarios around this function. This is the unit of code, which we discussed earlier.

Next, create the test specifications. Create one JavaScript file, `test.spec.js`, and place it in the `spec/` directory. You will need to add the following two lines into your `SpecRunner.html`: The file should contain the following:

```
<script src="src/bigfatjavascriptcode.js"></script>
<script src="spec/test.spec.js"></script>
```

The order of this inclusion does not matter. When we run `SpecRunner.html`, you will see something like the following image:

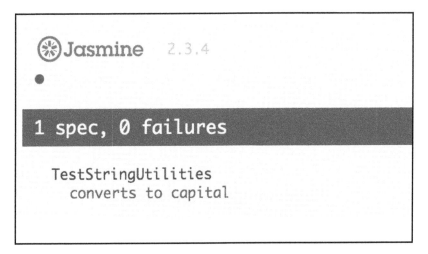

This is the Jasmine report that shows details about the number of tests that were executed and the count of failures and successes. Now, let's make the test case fail. We want to test a case where an `undefined` variable is passed to the function. Let's add one more test case, as follows:

```
it("can handle undefined", function() {
    var str= undefined;
    expect(capitalizeName(str)).toEqual(undefined);
});
```

Now, when you run `SpecRunner`, you will see the following result:

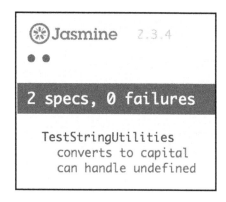

As you can see, the failure is displayed for this test case in a detailed error stack. Now, we will go about fixing this. In your original JS code, handle undefined as follows:

```
function capitalizeName(name){
   if(name){
      return name.toUpperCase();
   }
}
```

With this change, your test case will pass, and you will see the following result in the Jasmine report:

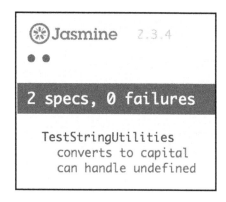

This is very similar to what a test-driven development would look like. You write test cases and then fill the necessary code to confirm to the specifications and rerun the test suite. Let's understand the structure of the Jasmine tests.

Our test specification looks like the following piece of code:

```
describe("TestStringUtilities", function() {
    it("converts to capital", function() {
        var str = "albert";
        expect(capitalizeName(str)).toEqual("ALBERT");
    });
    it("can handle undefined", function() {
        var str= undefined;
        expect(capitalizeName(str)).toEqual(undefined);
    });
});
```

The `describe("TestStringUtilities"` is what a test suite is. The name of the test suite should describe the unit-of-code we are testing; this can be a function or a group of related functionality. Inside the specs, you will call the global Jasmine function, `it`, to which you will pass the title of the spec and the function that validates the condition of the testcase This function is the actual test case. You can catch one or more assertions or the general expectations using the `expect` function. When all expectations are `true`, your spec is passed. You can write any valid JavaScript code inside `describe` and `it` functions. The values you verify as part of the expectations are matched using a matcher. In our example, `toEqual` is the matcher that matches two values for equality. Jasmine contains a rich set of matches to suit most of the common use cases. Some common matchers supported by Jasmine are as follows:

- `toBe`: This matcher checks if two objects being compared are equal. This is same as the `===` comparison. For example, check out the following code snippet:

```
var a = { value: 1};
var b = { value: 1 };

expect(a).toEqual(b);   // success, same as == comparison
expect(b).toBe(b);      // failure, same as === comparison
expect(a).toBe(a);      // success, same as === comparison
```

- `not`: You can negate a matcher with a not prefix. For example,
  `expect(1).not.toEqual(2);` will negate the match made by `toEqual()`.

- `toContain`: This checks if an element is part of an array. It is not an exact object match as `toBe`. For example, take a look at the following lines of code:

```
expect([1, 2, 3]).toContain(3);
expect("astronomy is a science").toContain("science");
```

- `toBeDefined` and `toBeUndefined`: These two matches are handy to check whether a variable is `undefined` or not.
- `toBeNull`: This checks if a variable's value is `null`.
- `toBeGreaterThan` and `toBeLessThan`: These matcher performs numeric comparison (works on strings too). For example, consider the following piece of code:

```
expect(2).toBeGreaterThan(1);
expect(1).toBeLessThan(2);
expect("a").toBeLessThan("b");
```

An interesting feature of Jasmine is the spies. When you are writing a large system, it is not possible to make sure that all systems are always available and correct. At the same time, you don't want your unit tests to fail due to a dependency that may be broken or unavailable. To simulate a situation where all dependencies are available for a unit of code we want to test, we will mock this dependency to always give the response we expect. Mocking is an important aspect of testing, and most testing frameworks provide support for mocking. Jasmine allows mocking using a feature called a **Spy**. Jasmine spies essentially stubs the functions we may not have ready at the time of writing the test case, but as part of the functionality, we will need to track that we are executing those dependencies and not ignoring them. Consider the following example:

```
describe("mocking configurator", function() {
  var cofigurator = null;
  var responseJSON = {};

  beforeEach(function() {
    configurator = {
      submitPOSTRequest: function(payload) {
        //This is a mock service that will eventually be replaced
        //by a real service
        console.log(payload);
        return {"status": "200"};
      }
    };
    spyOn(configurator, 'submitPOSTRequest').and.returnValue
      ({"status": "200"});
    configurator.submitPOSTRequest({
      "port":"8000",
```

```
        "client-encoding":"UTF-8"
      });
    });

    it("the spy was called", function() {
      expect(configurator.submitPOSTRequest).toHaveBeenCalled();
    });

    it("the arguments of the spy's call are tracked", function() {
      expect(configurator.submitPOSTRequest).toHaveBeenCalledWith(
        {"port":"8000", "client-encoding":"UTF-8"});
    });
  });
```

In this example, while we are writing this test case, we either don't have the real implementation of the dependency, `configurator.submitPOSTRequest()`, or someone is fixing this particular dependency; in any case, we don't have it available. For our test to work, we will need to mock it. Jasmine spies allow us to replace a function with its mock and allows us to track its execution.

In this case, we will need to ensure that we called the dependency. When the actual dependency is ready, we will revisit this test case to make sure it fits the specifications; however, at this time, all we need to ensure that the dependency is called. Jasmine function `tohaveBeenCalled()` lets us track the execution of a function that may be a mock. We can use `toHaveBeenCalledWith()`, which allows us to determine if the stub function was called with correct parameters. There are several other interesting scenarios you can create using Jasmine spies. The scope of this chapter won't permit us to cover them all, but I would encourage you to discover those areas on your own.

Mocha, Chai and Sinon

Though Jasmine is the most prominent JavaScript testing framework, mocha and chai are gaining prominence in the `Node.js` environment:

- Mocha is the testing framework used to describe and run test cases
- Chai is the assertion library supported by Mocha
- Sinon comes in handy while creating mocks and stubs for your tests

We won't discuss these frameworks in this book; however, experience on Jasmine will be handy if you want to experiment with these frameworks.

JavaScript debugging

If you are not a completely new programmer, I am sure you must have spent some amount of time debugging your or someone else's code. Debugging is almost like an art form. Every language has different methods and challenges around the debugging. JavaScript is traditionally a difficult language to debug. I have spent days and nights in misery, trying to debug badly written JavaScript code using `alert()` functions. Fortunately, modern browsers, such as Mozilla, Firefox, and Google Chrome, have excellent **Developer Tools** to help debug JavaScript in the browser. There are IDEs like IntelliJ IDEA and WebStorm with great debugging support for JavaScript and Node.js. In this chapter, we will focus primarily on Google Chrome's built-in developer tool. Firefox also supports Firebug extension and has excellent built-in developer tools, but as they behave more or less the same as Google Chrome's **Developer Tools**, we will discuss common debugging approaches that work in both of these tools.

Before we talk about the specific debugging techniques, let's understand the type of errors we would be interested in while we try to debug our code.

Syntax errors

When your code has something that does not confirm to the JavaScript language grammar, the interpreter rejects that piece of code. These are easy to catch if your IDE is helping you with syntax checking. Most modern IDEs help with these errors. Earlier, we discussed the usefulness of tools, such as JSLint and JSHint, around catching syntax issues with your code. They analyze the code and flag errors in the syntax. The JSHint output can be very illuminating. For example, the following output shows up so many things we can change in the code. The following code snippet is from one of my existing projects:

```
temp git:(dev_branch) X jshint test.js
test.js: line 1, col 1, Use the function form of "use strict".
test.js: line 4, col 1, 'destructuring expression'
  is available in ES6 (use esnext option) or
  Mozilla JS extensions (use moz).
test.js: line 44, col 70, 'arrow function syntax (=>)'
  is only available in ES6 (use esnext option).
test.js: line 61, col 33, 'arrow function syntax (=>)'
  is only available in ES6 (use esnext option).
test.js: line 200, col 29, Expected ')' to match '(' from
  line 200 and instead saw ':'.
test.js: line 200, col 29, 'function closure expressions'
  is only available in Mozilla JavaScript extensions (use moz option).
test.js: line 200, col 37, Expected '}' to match '{' from
  line 36 and instead saw ')'.
```

```
test.js: line 200, col 39, Expected ')' and instead saw '{'.
test.js: line 200, col 40, Missing semicolon.
```

Using strict

We briefly discussed the strict mode in earlier chapters. When you enable strict mode, JavaScript stops being accepting of syntactical errors in your code. Rather than silently failing, strict mode makes these failure throw errors instead. It also helps you convert mistakes into actual errors. There are two ways of enforcing strict mode. If you want the strict mode for the entire script, you can just add the use strict statement (with the quotes) as the first line of your JavaScript program. If you want a specific function to confirm to strict mode, you can add the directive as the first line of a function. For example, take a look at the following code snippet:

```
function strictFn(){
  // This line makes EVERYTHING under this scrict mode
  'use strict';
  ...
  function nestedStrictFn() {
    //Everything in this function is also nested
    ...
  }
}
```

Runtime exceptions

These errors appear when you execute the code, try to refer to an undefined variable, or try to process a null. When a runtime exception occurs, any code after that particular line, which caused the exception, does not get executed. It is essential to correctly handle such exceptional scenarios in the code. While exception handling can help prevent crashes, they also aid in debugging. You can wrap the code that may encounter a runtime exception into a try{ } block. When any code inside this block generates a runtime exception, a corresponding handler captures it. The handler is defined by a catch(exception){} block. Let's clarify this using the following example:

```
try {
  var a = doesnotexist; // throws a runtime exception
} catch(e) {
  console.log(e.message);  //handle the exception
  //prints - "doesnotexist is not defined"
}
```

In this example, the `var a = doesnotexist` line tries to assign an `undefined` variable, `doesnotexist`, to another variable a. This causes a runtime exception. When we wrap this problematic code into `try{}catch(){}` block or when the exception occurs (or is thrown), the execution stops in the `try{}` block and goes directly to the `catch() {}` handler. The catch handler is responsible for handling the exceptional scenario. In this case, we are displaying the error message on the console for debugging purposes. You can explicitly throw an exception to trigger an unhandled scenario in the code. Consider the following example:

```
function engageGear(gear){
  if(gear==="R"){ console.log ("Reversing");}
  if(gear==="D"){ console.log ("Driving");}
  if(gear==="N"){ console.log ("Neutral/Parking");}
  throw new Error("Invalid Gear State");
}
try
{
  engageGear("R");   //Reversing
  engageGear("P");   //Invalid Gear State
}
catch(e){
  console.log(e.message);
}
```

In this example, we are handling valid states of a gear shift: R, N, and D; however, when we receive an invalid state, we are explicitly throwing an exception clearly stating the reason. When we call the function which we think may throw an exception, we will wrap the code in the `try{}` block and attach a `catch(){}` handler with it. When the exception is caught by the `catch()` block, we will handle the exceptional condition appropriately.

Console.log and asserts

Displaying the state of execution on console can be very useful while debugging. Although, modern developer tools allow you to put breakpoints and halt execution to inspect a particular value during runtime. You can quickly detect small issues by logging some variable state on the console.

With these concepts with us, let's see how we can use Chrome **Developer Tools** to debug JavaScript code.

Chrome Developer Tools

You can start Chrome **Developer Tools** by clicking **menu** | **More tools** | **Developer Tools**. Take a look at the following screenshot:

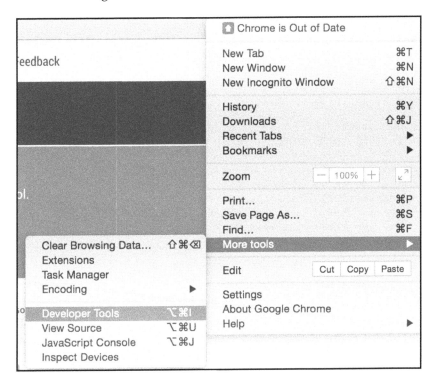

Chrome developer tool opens up on the lower pane of your browser and has a bunch of very useful sections. Consider the following screenshot:

The **Elements** panel helps you inspect and monitor the DOM tree and associated style sheet for each of these components.

The **Network** panel is useful to understand network activity. For example, you can monitor the resources being downloaded over the network in real time.

The most important pane for us is the **Sources** pane. This pane is where the JavaScript and the debugger are displayed. Let's create a sample HTML with the following content:

```html
<!DOCTYPE html>
<html>
<head>
  <meta charset="utf-8">
  <title>This test</title>
  <script type="text/javascript">
  function engageGear(gear){
    if(gear==="R"){ console.log ("Reversing");}
    if(gear==="D"){ console.log ("Driving");}
    if(gear==="N"){ console.log ("Neutral/Parking");}
    throw new Error("Invalid Gear State");
  }
  try
  {
    engageGear("R");   //Reversing
    engageGear("P");   //Invalid Gear State
  }
  catch(e){
    console.log(e.message);
  }
  </script>
</head>
<body>
</body>
</html>
```

Save this HTML file and open it in Google Chrome. Open **Developer Tools** in the browser, and you will see the following screen:

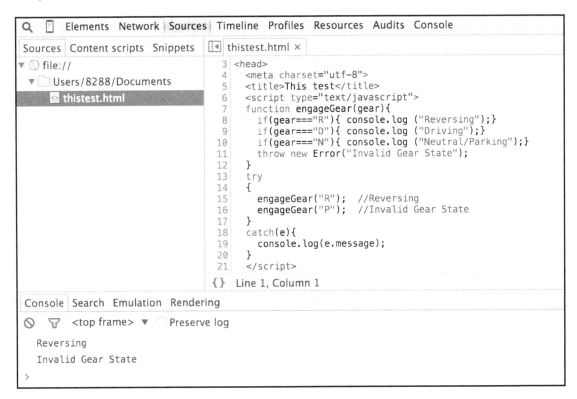

This is the view of the **Sources** panel. You can see the HTML and embedded JavaScript source in this panel. You can see the **Console** window as well, and you can see that the file is executed and the output is displayed on console.

On the right side, you will see the debugger window, as shown in the following screenshot:

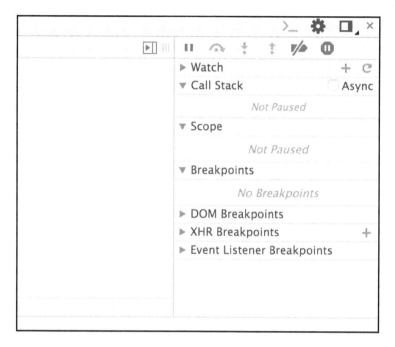

In the **Sources** panel, click on the line numbers **8** and **15** to add a breakpoint. The breakpoints allow you to stop execution of the script at the specified point. Consider the following screenshot:

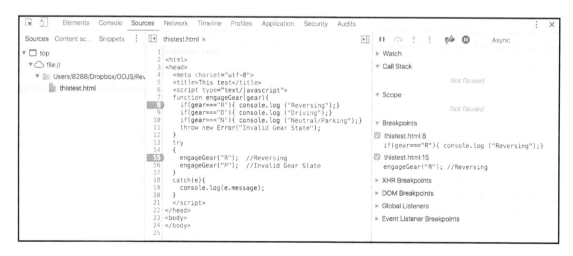

In the debug pane, you can see all existing breakpoints. Take a look at the following screenshot:

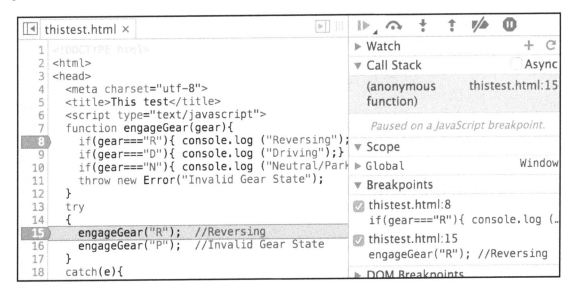

Now, when you rerun the same page, you will see that the execution stops at the debug point. Consider the following screenshot:

This window now has all the action. You can see that the execution is paused on line **15**. In the debug window, you can see which breakpoint is being triggered. You can also see the **Call Stack** and resume execution in several ways. The debug command window has a bunch of actions. Take a look at the following screenshot:

You can resume execution, which will execute until the next breakpoint, by clicking on the following button:

When you do that, the execution continues until the next breakpoint is encountered. In our case, we will halt at line **8**. Consider the following screenshot:

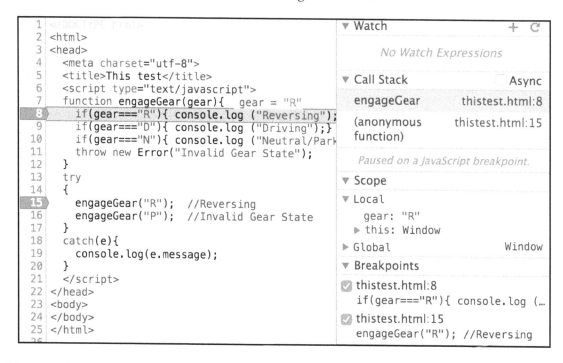

You can observe that the **Call Stack** window shows how we arrived at line **8**. The **Scope** panel shows the **Local** scope where you can see the variables in the scope when the breakpoint was arrived at. You can also Step-Into or Step-over the next function.

There are other very useful mechanisms to debug and profile your code using Chrome **Developer Tools**. I would suggest you to experiment with the tool and make it a part of your regular development flow.

Summary

Both testing and debugging phases are essential to developing robust JavaScript code. TDD and BDD are approaches closely associated with the agile methodology and is widely embraced by the JavaScript developer community. In this chapter, we reviewed best practices around TDD and the usage of Jasmine as the testing framework. Additionally, we saw various methods of debugging JavaScript using Chrome **Developer Tools**.

In the next chapter, we will explore the new and exciting world of ES6, DOM Manipulation and cross-browser strategies.

13
Reactive Programming and React

Along with ES6, several new ideas are emerging. These are powerful ideas and can help you build powerful systems with more streamlined code and design. In this chapter, we will introduce you to two such ideas–reactive programming and react. Although they sound similar, they are very different. This chapter does not go into practical details of these ideas but gives you necessary information to become aware of what these ideas are capable of. With that information, you can start incorporating these ideas and frameworks into your projects. We will discuss the basic idea of reactive programming and take a bit more detailed look at react.

Reactive programming

Reactive programming is getting a lot of focus lately. This idea is relatively new and, like many new ideas, has lots of confusing, and sometimes contradictory information floating around. We discussed asynchronous programming earlier in this book. JavaScript takes asynchronous programming to new heights by providing first class language constructs that support it.

Reactive programming is essentially programming with asynchronous event streams. An event stream is a sequence of events happening over time. Consider the following diagram:

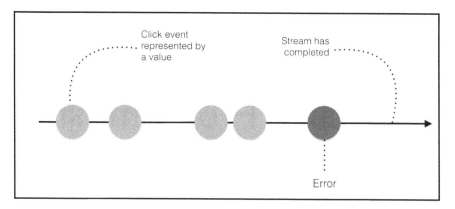

In the preceding diagram, time passes from left to right and different events occur over time. As the event happens over time, we can add an event listener to this whole sequence. Whenever an event happens, we can react to it by doing something.

Another type of sequence in JavaScript is an array. For example, consider the following lines of code:

```
var arr = [1,1,13,'Rx',0,0];
console.log(arr);
>>> [1, 1, 13, "Rx", 0, 0]
```

In this case, the entire sequence lives in memory at the same time. However, in case of event stream, events happen over time and there is no state at this point of time. Consider the following lines of code:

```
var arr = Rx.Observable.interval(500).take(9).map(
  a=>[1,1,13,'Rx',0,0][a]);
var result = arr;
result.subscribe(x=>console.log(x));
```

Don't worry too much about what is going on in this example just yet. Here, events are happening over time. Instead of having a fixed bunch of elements in an array, here they are happening over time, after 500 ms.

We will add an event listener to the `arr` event stream, and when an event happens, we will print the element on console. You can see a similarity between the methods in arrays and the event streams. Now, to expand on this similarity, let's say, you want to filter all non-numbers from this list. You can use the `map` function to this event stream, just like you would use it on an array, and then you would want to filter the results to show only integers. Consider the following lines of code:

```
var arr = [1,1,13,'Rx',0,0];
var result = arr.map(x => parseInt(x)).filter(x => !isNan(x));
console.log(result);
```

Interestingly, the same methods work for event streams as well. Take a look at the following code example:

```
var arr = Rx.Observable.interval(500).take(9).map(
  a=>[1,1,13,'Rx',0,0][a]);
var result = arr.map(x => parseInt(x)).filter(x => !isNaN(x));
result.subscribe(x=>console.log(x));
```

These are simpler examples just to make sure you start seeing how event streams flow over time. Please don't bother about the syntax and construct just yet. Before we can look at them, we will need to make sure we understand how to think in reactive programming. Event streams are fundamental to reactive programming; they allow you to define the dynamic behavior of a value at declaration time (definition taken from Andre Staltz's blog).

Let's say you have an `a` variable, which has initially the value 3. Then, you have a `b` variable, which is `10 * a`. If we console log out `b`, we will see 30. Consider the following lines of code:

```
let a = 3;
let b = a * 10;
console.log(b); //30
a = 4;
console.log(b); // Still 30
```

We know the result is very straightforward. When we change the value of `a` to 4, the value of `b` will not change. This is how static declaration works. When we talk about reactive programming and event streams, this is the area where people find difficulty in understanding how events flow. Ideally, we want to create a formula, *b=a*10*, and over time, whenever the value of `a` changes, the changed value is reflected in the formula.

That is what we can accomplish with event streams. Let's say a is an event stream of just the value 3. Then, we have `streamB`, which is `streamA` mapped. Each of these a values will be mapped to `10 * a`.

If we add an event listener to that `streamB`, and we console log, we will see b being 30. Take a look at the following example:

```
var streamA = Rx.Observable.of(3, 4);
var streamB = streamA.map(a => 10 * a);
streamB.subscribe(b => console.log(b));
```

If we do this, we have an event stream that simply has just two events. It has event 3, and then it has event 4, and b will change accordingly whenever a changes. If we run this, we see b being 30 and 40.

Now that we have spent some time in getting the basics of reactive programming sorted, you may ask the following question.

Why should you consider reactive programming?

As we write highly responsive and interactive UI applications on modern web and mobile, there is a strong need to find a way to deal with real-time events without stopping the user interactions on the UI. When you are dealing with multiple UI and server events being fired, you will be spending most of your time writing code to deal with these events. This is tedious. Reactive programming gives you a structured framework to deal with asynchronous events with minimal code while you focus on the business logic for your application.

Reactive programming is not limited to JavaScript. Reactive extensions are available in many platforms and languages, such as Java, Scala, Clojure, Ruby, Python, and Object C/Cocoa. `Rx.js` and `Bacon.js` are popular JavaScript libraries that provide reactive programming support.

A deep dive into `Rx.js` is not the intention of this chapter. The idea was to introduce you to the idea of reactive programming. If you are keen on adopting reactive programming for your projects, you should take look at Andre Staltz's excellent introduction (`https://gist.github.com/staltz/868e7e9bc2a7b8c1f754`).

React

React is taking the JavaScript world by storm. Facebook created the react framework to solve an age-old problem–how to deal efficiently with the view part of the traditional **Model-View-Controller** applications.

React provides a declarative and flexible way to build user interfaces. The most important thing to remember about react is that it deals with only one thing–the view, or the UI. React does not deal with data, data bindings, or anything else. There are complete frameworks, such as Angular, that deal with data, bindings, and UI; React is not that.

React gives a template language and a small set of functions to render HTML. React components can store their own state in memory. To build a full-fledged application, you will need other pieces as well; React is just to handle the view part of that application.

A big challenge when writing complex UI is to manage state of the UI elements when the model changes. React provides a declarative API so that you don't have to worry about exactly what changes on every update. This makes writing applications a lot easier. React uses **Virtual DOM** and **diffing** algorithm, so that component updates are predictable while being fast enough for high-performance apps.

Virtual DOM

Let's take a moment to understand what is a Virtual DOM. We discussed **DOM** (**document object model**), a tree structure of HTML element on a web page. DOM is de facto, and the primary rendering mechanism of the web. The DOM APIs, such as `getElementById()`, allow traversing and modification of the elements in the DOM tree. DOM is a tree and this structure works pretty well with traversal and updating of elements. However, both the traversing and updating of DOM is not very quick. For a large page, the DOM tree can be pretty big. When you want a complex UI that has bunch of user interactions, updating DOM elements can be tedious and slow. We have tried jQuery and other libraries to reduce the tedious syntax for frequent DOM modifications, but DOM as a structure itself is quite limited.

What if we don't have to traverse the DOM over and over again to modify elements? What if you just declare how a component should look like and let someone handle the logic of how to render that component? react does exactly that. React lets you declare how you want your UI element to look like and abstracts out low-level DOM manipulation APIs. Apart from this very useful abstraction, react does something pretty smart to solve the performance problem as well.

React uses something called a Virtual DOM. A virtual DOM is a lightweight abstraction of the HTML DOM. You can think of it as a local in-memory copy of the HTML DOM. React uses it to do all computations necessary to render the state of a UI component.

You can find more details of this optimization at
`https://facebook.github.io/react/docs/reconciliation.html`.

React's primary strength, however, is not just Virtual DOM. React is a fantastic abstraction that makes composition, unidirectional dataflow, and static modeling easier while developing large applications.

Installing and running react

First, let's install react. Earlier, installing and getting react set up on your machine needed a bunch of dependencies to be taken care of. However, we will use a relatively faster way to get react up and running. We will use `create-react-app` to which we can install react without any build configuration. Installation is done via `npm` which is as follows:

```
npm install -g create-react-app
```

Here, we are installing the `create-react-app` node module globally. Once `create-react-app` is installed, you can set up the directory for your application. Consider the following commands:

```
create-react-app react-app
cd react-app/
npm start
```

Then, open `http://localhost:3000/` to see your app. You should see something like the following screenshot:

If you open the directory in an editor, you will see several files created for you, as you can see in the following screenshot:

In this project, `node_modules` are the dependencies required to run this project and dependencies of react itself. The important directory is `src`, where the source code is kept. For this example, let's keep only two files–`App.js` and `index.js`. The `/public/index.html` file should contain just the root `div`, which will be used as a target for our react components. Consider the following code snippet:

```html
<!doctype html>
<html lang="en">
  <head>
    <title>React App</title>
  </head>
  <body>
    <div id="root"></div>
  </body>
</html>
```

The moment you make this change, you will see the following error:

```
@ ./src/App.js 14:12-33

Error in ./src/App.js
Module not found: ./App.css in /Users/8288/source_code/react-app/src
```

Beauty of developing with react is that the code changes are live-reloaded, and you can get immediate feedback.

Next, clear off all content of `App.js`, and replace it with the following lines of code:

```javascript
import React from 'react';
const App = () => <h1>Hello React</h1>
export default App
```

Now, go to `index.js` and remove the `import ./index.css;` line. Without you doing anything, such as restarting server and refreshing browser, you will see the modified page on the browser. Consider the following screenshot:

Before we create a `HelloWorld` react component, a couple of important things to notice so far.

In `App.js` and `index.js`, we are importing two libraries necessary to create react components. Consider the following lines of code:

```
import React from 'react';
import ReactDOM from 'react-dom';
```

Here, we're importing `React`, which is the library that allows us to build react components. We're also importing `ReactDOM`, which is the library that allows us to place our components and work with them in the context of the DOM. Then, we're importing the component that we just worked on–the App component.

We also created our first component in `App.js`. Consider the following line of code:

```
const App = () => <h1>Hello React</h1>
```

This is a stateless function component. The other way to create a component is to create a class component. We can replace the preceding component with the following class component:

```
class App extends React.Component {
  render(){
    return <h1>Hello World</h1>
  }
}
```

There are a bunch of interesting things going on here. First, we are creating a class component with the `class` keyword that extends from the superclass `React.Component`.

Our component `App` is a react component class or react component type. A component takes in parameters, also called `props`, and returns a hierarchy of views to display via the `render` function.

The `render` method returns a description of what you want to render, and then react takes that description and renders it to the screen. In particular, `render` returns a react element, which is a lightweight description of what to render. Most react developers use a special syntax called JSX, which makes it easier to write these structures. The `<div />` syntax is transformed at build time to `React.createElement('div')`. The JSX expression, `<h1>Hello World</h1>`, is transformed at build time into the following:

```
return React.createElement('h1', null, 'Hello World');
```

The difference between the class component and stateless function component is that the class component can contain a state while the stateless (hence the name) function component cannot.

The `render` method of the react component is allowed to return only a single node. If you do something like the following:

```
return <h1>Hello World</h1><p>React Rocks</p>
```

You will get the following error:

```
Error in ./src/App.js
Syntax error: Adjacent JSX elements must be wrapped in
  an enclosing tag (4:31)
```

This is because you are essentially returning two `React.createElement` functions, and that is not valid JavaScript. While this may seem like a deal breaker, this is easy to solve. We can wrap our nodes into a parent node and return that parent node from the `render` function. We can create a parent `div` and wrap other nodes under it. Consider the following example:

```
render(){
    return (
      <div>
        <h1>Hello World</h1>
        <p>React Rocks</p>
      </div>
      )
}
```

Components and props

Components can be conceptually considered as JavaScript functions. They take arbitrary number of inputs like normal functions. These inputs are called props. To illustrate this, let's consider the following function:

```
function Greet(props) {
  return <h1>Hello, {props.name}</h1>;
}
```

This is a normal function and also a valid react component. It takes an input called `props` and returns a valid JSX. We can use the `props` inside JSX using curly braces and properties such as `name` using a standard object notation. Now that `Greet` is a first class react component, let's use it in the `render()` function as follows:

```
render(){
  return (
    return <Greet name="Joe"/>
  )
}
```

We are calling `Greet()` as a normal component and passing `this.props` to it. It is required to capitalize your own components. React considers component names starting with a lowercase as standard HTML tags and expects custom component names to start with a capital letter. As we saw earlier, we can create a class component using ES6 class. This component is a subclass of `React.component`. An equivalent component to our `Greet` function is as follows:

```
class Greet extends React.Component {
  render(){
      return <h1>Hello, {this.props.name}</h1>
  }
}
```

For all practical purposes, we will use this method of creating components. We will soon know why.

One important point to note is that a component cannot modify its own props. This may seem like a limitation because, in almost all non-trivial applications, you will want user interactions where the UI component state is changed in react, for example, update date of birth in a form, `props` are read-only but there is a much robust mechanism to handle UI updates.

State

State is similar to props, but it is private and fully controlled by the component. As we saw earlier that both functional and class components are equivalent in react, one important distinction is that the state is available only in class components. Hence, for all practical purposes, we will use class components.

We can change our existing greeting example to use state, and whenever the state changes, we will update our `Greet` component to reflect the changed value.

First, we will set up the state inside our `App.js`, as follows:

```
class Greet extends React.Component {
    constructor(props) {    super(props);
    this.state = { greeting: "this is default greeting text" }
    }
  render(){
      return <h1>{this.state.greeting}, {this.props.name} </h1>
  }
}
```

There are a few important things to notice in this example. First, we are calling class `constructor` to initialize `this.state`. We also call the base class constructor, `super()`, and pass `props` to it. After calling `super()`, we initialize our default state by setting `this.state` to an object. For example, we assign a `greeting` property with a value here. In the `render` method, we will use this property using `{this.state.greeting}`. Having setup our initial state, we can add UI elements to update this state. Let's add an input box, and on change of that input box, we will update our state and the `greeting` element. Consider the following lines of code:

```
class Greet extends React.Component {
  constructor(props) {
    super(props);
    this.state = {
      greeting: "this is default greeting text"
    }
  }
  updateGreeting(event){ this.setState({ greeting:
    event.target.value,     })   }
  render(){
      return (
      <div>
        <input type="text" onChange={this.updateGreeting.bind(this)}/>
        <h1>{this.state.greeting}, {this.props.name} </h1>
      </div>
      )
  }
}
```

Here, we add an input box and update the state of the component when the `onChange` method of the input box is invoked. We use a custom `updateGreeting()` method to update the state by calling `this.setState` and updating the property. When you run this example, you will notice that as you type something on the text box, only the `greeting` element is updated and not the `name`. Take a look at the following screenshot:

An important feature of react is the fact that a react component can output or render other react components. We've got a very simple component here. It has a state with a value of text. It's got an `update` method which will update that value of text from an event. What we'll do is create a new component. This will be a stateless function component. We'll call it widget. It will take in `props`. We'll return this JSX input right here. Consider the following code snippet:

```
render(){
    return (
        <div>
        <Widget update={this.updateGreeting.bind(this)} />
        <Widget update={this.updateGreeting.bind(this)} />
        <Widget update={this.updateGreeting.bind(this)} />
        <h1>{this.state.greeting}, {this.props.name} </h1>
        </div>
    )
  }
}
const Widget = (props) => <input type="text"
  onChange={props.update}/>
```

First, we extract our input element into a stateless function component and call it a `Widget`. We pass `props` to this component. Then, we change `onChange` to use `props.update`. Now, inside our `render` method, we use the `Widget` component and pass a prop `update` that binds the `updateGreeting()` method. Now that `Widget` is a component, we can reuse it anywhere in the `Greet` component. We are creating three instances of the `Widget`, and when any of the `Widget` is updated, the greeting text is updated, as shown in the following screenshot:

Life cycle events

When you have a bunch of components with several state changes and events, the housekeeping becomes important. React provides you with several component life cycle hooks to handle life cycle events of components. Understanding the component life cycle will enable you to perform certain actions when a component is created or destroyed. Furthermore, it gives you the opportunity to decide if a component should be updated in the first place, and to react to `props` or state changes accordingly.

There are three phases that the component goes through–mounting, updating, and unmouting. For each of these stages, we have hooks. Take a look at the following diagram:

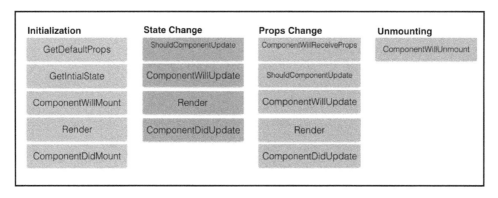

Two methods are called when a component is initially rendered, `getDefaultProps` and `getInitialState`, and, as their names suggest, we can set default `props` and initial state of a component in these methods.

The `componentWillMount` is called before the `render` method is executed. We already know `render` to be the place where we return the component to be rendered. As soon as the `render` method finishes, the `componentDidMount` method is invoked. You can access DOM in this method, and it is recommended to perform any DOM interactions in this method.

State changes invoke a few methods. The `shouldComponentUpdate` method is invoked before the `render` method, and it lets us decide if we should allow rerendering or skip it. This method is never called on the initial rendering. The `componentWillUpdate` method gets called immediately once the `shouldComponentUpdate` method returns `true`. The `componentDidUpdate` method is rendered after `render` finishes.

Any change to the `props` object triggers similar methods as a state change. One additional method called is `componentWillReceiveProps`; it is called only when the `props` have changed, and it is not initial rendering. You can update state based on new and old props in this method.

When a component is removed from DOM, `componentWillUnmount` is called. This is a useful method to perform cleanups.

Great thing about react is that when you start using it, the framework feels very natural to you. There are very few moving parts you will need to learn, and the abstraction is just right.

Summary

This chapter was aimed at some of the important new ideas that are gaining a lot of prominence lately. Both reactive programming and react can significantly boost programmer productivity. React is definitely one of the most important emerging technologies backed by the likes of Facebook and Netflix.

This chapter was intended to give you an introduction to both these technologies and help you start exploring them in more detail.

Reserved Words

This appendix provides two lists of reserved keywords as defined in ECMAScript 5 (ES5). The first one is the current list of words, and the second is the list of words reserved for future implementations.

There's also a list of words that are no longer reserved, although they used to be in ES3.

You cannot use reserved words as variable names:

```
var break = 1; // syntax error
```

If you use these words as object properties, you have to quote them:

```
var o = {break: 1};    // OK in many browsers, error in IE
var o = {"break": 1}; // Always OK
alert(o.break);        // error in IE
alert(o["break"]);     // OK
```

Keywords

The list of words currently reserved in ES5 is as follows:

- break
- case
- catch
- continue

- debugger
- default
- delete
- do
- else
- finally
- for
- function
- if
- in
- instanceof
- new
- return
- switch
- this
- throw
- try
- typeof
- var
- void
- while
- with

ES6 reserved words

The following keywords are reserved in ES6:

- class
- const
- enum
- export
- extends

- implements
- import
- interface
- let
- package
- private
- protected
- public
- static
- super
- yield

Future reserved words

These keywords are not used currently but they are reserved for the future versions:

- enum
- await

Previously reserved words

The following words are no longer reserved starting with ES5, but it's best to stay away from them for the sake of older browsers:

- abstract
- boolean
- byte
- char
- double
- final
- float
- goto

- int
- long
- native
- short
- synchronized
- throws
- transient
- volatile

B
Built-in Functions

This appendix contains a list of the built-in functions (methods of the global object), discussed in `Chapter 3`, *Functions*:

Function	Description
`parseInt()`	Takes two parameters: an input object and radix; then tries to return an integer representation of the input. Doesn't handle exponents in the input. The default radix is `10` (a decimal number). Returns `NaN` on failure. Omitting the radix may lead to unexpected results (for example for inputs such as `08`), so it's best to always specify it: ```\n> parseInt('10e+3');\n10\n> parseInt('FF');\nNaN\n> parseInt('FF', 16);\n255\n```
`parseFloat()`	Takes a parameter and tries to return a floating-point number representation of it. Understands exponents in the input: ```\n> parseFloat('10e+3');\n10000\n> parseFloat('123.456test');\n123.456\n```

isNaN()	Abbreviated from "Is Not a Number". Accepts a parameter and returns `true` if the parameter is not a valid number, `false` otherwise. Attempts to convert the input to a number first: ``` > isNaN(NaN); true > isNaN(123); false > isNaN(parseInt('FF')); true > isNaN(parseInt('FF', 16)); false ```
isFinite()	Returns `true` if the input is a number (or can be converted to a number), but if it is not a number `Infinity` or `-Infinity`. Returns `false` for infinity or non-numeric values: ``` > isFinite(1e+1000); false > isFinite(-Infinity); false > isFinite("123"); true ```
encodeURIComponent()	Converts the input into a URL-encoded string. For more details on how URL encoding works, refer to the Wikipedia article at `http://en.wikipedia.org/wiki/Url_encode`: ``` > encodeURIComponent ('http://phpied.com/'); "http%3A%2F%2Fphpied.com%2F" > encodeURIComponent ('some script?key=v@lue'); "some%20script%3Fkey%3Dv%40lue" ```
decodeURIComponent()	Takes an URL-encoded string and decodes it: ``` > decodeURIComponent('%20%40%20'); " @ " ```
encodeURI()	URL-encodes the input, but assumes a full URL is given, so returns a valid URL by not encoding the protocol (for example, `http://`) and hostname (for example, `www.phpied.com`): ``` > encodeURI('http://phpied.com/'); "http://phpied.com/" > encodeURI('some script?key=v@lue'); "some%20script?key=v@lue" ```
decodeURI()	Opposite of `encodeURI()`: ``` > decodeURI("some%20script?key=v@lue"); "some script?key=v@lue" ```

eval()	Accepts a string of JavaScript code and executes it. Returns the result of the last expression in the input string. To be avoided where possible:
| | ```
> eval('1 + 2');
3
> eval('parseInt("123")');
123
> eval('new Array(1, 2, 3)');
[1, 2, 3]
> eval('new Array(1, 2, 3); 1 +   2;');
3
``` |
```

Built-in Objects

This appendix lists the built-in constructor functions outlined in the **ECMAScript** (**ES**) standard, together with the properties and methods of the objects created by these constructors. ES5-specific APIs are listed separately.

Object

`Object()` is a constructor that creates objects, for example:

```
> var o = new Object();
```

This is the same as using the object literal:

```
> var o = {}; // recommended
```

You can pass anything to the constructor and it will try to guess what it is and use a more appropriate constructor. For example, passing a string to `new Object()` will be the same as using the `new String()` constructor. This is not a recommended practice (it's better to be explicit than let guesses creep in), but still possible:

```
> var o = new Object('something');
> o.constructor;
function String() { [native code] }
> var o = new Object(123);
> o.constructor;
function Number() { [native code] }
```

All other objects, built-in or custom, inherit from `Object`. So the properties and methods listed in the following sections apply to all types of objects.

Members of the Object constructor

Following are the members of the Object constructor:

Property/method	Description
Object.prototype	The prototype of all objects (also an object itself). Anything you add to this prototype will be inherited by all other objects, so be careful: ``` > var s = new String('noodles'); > Object.prototype.custom = 1; 1 > s.custom; 1 ```

The Object.prototype members

Instead of saying "members of the Objects created by the Object constructor", let's say headings "Object.prototype members". It is the same for Array.prototype and so on further in this appendix:

Property/method	Description
constructor	Points back to the constructor function used to create the object, in this case, Object: ``` > Object.prototype.constructor === Object; true > var o = new Object(); > o.constructor === Object; true ```
toString(radix)	Returns a string representation of the object. If the object happens to be a Number object, the radix parameter defines the base of the returned number. The default radix is 10: ``` > var o = {prop: 1}; > o.toString(); "[object Object]" > var n = new Number(255); > n.toString(); "255" > n.toString(16); "ff" ```

`toLocaleString()`	Same as `toString()`, but matching the current locale. Meant to be customized by objects, such as `Date()`, `Number()`, and `Array()` and provide locale-specific values, such as different date formatting. In the case of `Object()` instances as with most other cases, it just calls `toString()`. In browsers, you can figure out the language using the property `language` (or `userLanguage` in IE) of the navigator BOM object: ``` > navigator.language; "en-US" ```
`valueOf()`	Returns a primitive representation of `this`, if applicable. For example, `Number` objects return a primitive number and `Date` objects return a timestamp. If no suitable primitive makes sense, it simply returns `this`: ``` > var o = {}; > typeof o.valueOf(); "object" > o.valueOf() === o; true > var n = new Number(101); > typeof n.valueOf(); "number" > n.valueOf() === n; false > var d = new Date(); > typeof d.valueOf(); "number" > d.valueOf(); 1357840170137 ```
`hasOwnProperty(prop)`	Returns `true` if a property is an own property of the object, or `false` if it was inherited from the prototype chain. Also returns `false` if the property doesn't exist: ``` > var o = {prop: 1}; > o.hasOwnProperty('prop'); true > o.hasOwnProperty('toString'); false > o.hasOwnProperty('fromString'); false ```

`isPrototypeOf(obj)`	Returns `true` if an object is used as a prototype of another object. Any object from the prototype chain can be tested, not only the direct creator: ```\n> var s = new String('');\n> Object.prototype.isPrototypeOf(s);\ntrue\n> String.prototype.isPrototypeOf(s);\ntrue\n> Array.prototype.isPrototypeOf(s);\nfalse\n```
`propertyIsEnumerable(prop)`	Returns `true` if a property shows up in a `for...in` loop: ```\n> var a = [1, 2, 3];\n> a.propertyIsEnumerable('length');\nfalse\n> a.propertyIsEnumerable(0);\ntrue\n```

ECMAScript 5 additions to objects

In ECMAScript 3 all object properties can be changed, added, or deleted at any time, except for a few built-in properties (for example, `Math.PI`). In ES5 you have the ability to define properties that cannot be changed or deleted, a privilege previously reserved for built-ins. ES5 introduces the concept of **property descriptors** that give you tighter control over the properties you define.

Think of a property descriptor as an object that specifies the features of a property. The syntax to describe these features is a regular object literal, so property descriptors have properties and methods of their own, but let's call them **attributes** to avoid confusion. The attributes are:

- `value` – what you get when you access the property
- `writable` – can you change this property
- `enumerable` – should it appear in `for...in` loops
- `configurable` – can you delete it
- `set()` – a function called any time you update the value
- `get()` – called when you access the value of the property

Further there's a distinction between **data descriptors** (you define the properties enumerable, configurable, value, and writable) and **accessor descriptors** (you define enumerable, configurable, set(), and get()). If you define set() or get(), the descriptor is considered an accessor and attempting to define value or writable will raise an error.

Defining a regular old school ES3-style property:

```
var person = {};
person.legs = 2;
```

Same using an ES5 data descriptor:

```
var person = {};
Object.defineProperty(person, "legs", {
  value: 2,
  writable: true,
  configurable: true,
  enumerable: true
});
```

The value of value if set to undefined by default, all others are false. So you need to set them to true explicitly if you want to be able to change this property later.

Or the same property using an ES5 accessor descriptor:

```
var person = {};
Object.defineProperty(person, "legs", {
  set: function (v) {this.value = v;},
  get: function (v) {return this.value;},
  configurable: true,
  enumerable: true
});
person.legs = 2;
```

As you can see property descriptors are a lot more code, so you only use them if you really want to prevent someone from mangling your property, and also you forget about backwards compatibility with ES3 browsers because, unlike additions to Array.prototype for example, you cannot "shim" this feature in old browsers.

And the power of the descriptors in action (defining a nonmalleable property):

```
> var person = {};
> Object.defineProperty(person, 'heads', {value: 1});
> person.heads = 0;
0
> person.heads;
1
> delete person.heads;
false
> person.heads;
1
```

The following is a list of all ES5 additions to `Object`:

Property/method	Description

`Object.getPrototypeOf(obj)`	While in ES3 you have to guess what is the prototype of a given object is using the method `Object.prototype.isPrototypeOf()`, in ES5 you can directly ask "Who is your prototype?"
	
	`> Object.getPrototypeOf([]) ===`
	`    Array.prototype;`
	`true`

`Object.create(obj, descr)`	Discussed in Chapter 7, *Inheritance*. Creates a new object, sets its prototype and defines properties of that object using property descriptors (discussed earlier):
	
	`> var parent = {hi: 'Hello'};`
	`> var o = Object.create(parent,`
	`{ prop: {value: 1 }});`
	`> o.hi;`
	`"Hello"`
	
	It even lets you create a completely blank object, something you cannot do in ES3:
	
	`> var o = Object.create(null);`
	`> typeof o.toString;`
	`"undefined"`

`Object.getOwnPropertyDescriptor(obj, property)`	Allows you to inspect how a property was defined. You can even peek into the built-ins and see all these previously hidden attributes:
	`> Object.getOwnProperty`
	`  Descriptor (Object.prototype,`
	`  'toString');`
	`Object`
	`configurable: true`
	`enumerable: false`
	`value: function toString() {`
	`  [native code] }`
	`writable: true`

`Object.getOwnPropertyNames(obj)`	Returns an array of all own property names (as strings), enumerable or not. Use `Object.keys()` to get only enumerable ones:
	`> Object.getOwnPropertyNames(`
	`  Object.prototype);`
	`["constructor", "toString",`
	`"toLocaleString", "valueOf",`
	`...`

`Object.defineProperty(obj, descriptor)`	Defines a property of an object using a property descriptor. See the discussion preceding this table.

`Object.defineProperties(obj, descriptors)`	Same as `defineProperty()`, but lets you define multiple properties at once:
	`> var glass =`
	`  Object.defineProperties({}, {`
	`    "color": {`
	`      value: "transparent",`
	`      writable: true`
	`    },`
	`    "fullness": {`
	`      value: "half",`
	`      writable: false`
	`    }`
	`  });`
	`> glass.fullness;`
	`"half"`

`Object.preventExtensions(obj)`
`Object.isExtensible(obj)`
	`preventExtensions()` disallows adding further properties to an object and `isExtensible()` checks whether you can add properties:
	```> var deadline = {};\n> Object.isExtensible(deadline);\ntrue\n> deadline.date = "yesterday";\n"yesterday"\n> Object.preventExtensions(\n deadline);\n> Object.isExtensible(deadline);\nfalse\n> deadline.date = "today";\n"today"\n> deadline.date;\n"today"```
	Attempting to add properties to a non-extensible object is not an error, but simply doesn't work:
	```> deadline.report = true;\n> deadline.report;\nundefined```

`Object.seal(obj)` `Object.isSealed(obj)`	`seal()` does the same as `preventExtensions()` and additionally makes all existing properties non-configurable. This means you can change the value of an existing property, but you cannot delete it or reconfigure it (using `defineProperty()` won't work). So you cannot, for example, make an enumerable property non-enumerable.
`Object.freeze(obj)` `Object.isFrozen(obj)`	Everything that `seal()` does plus prevents changing the values of properties: ```> var deadline = Object.freeze(\n {date: "yesterday"});\n> deadline.date = "tomorrow";\n> deadline.excuse = "lame";\n> deadline.date; "yesterday">\ndeadline.excuse; undefined>\nObject.isSealed(deadline); true```

`Object.keys(obj)`	An alternative to a `for...in` loop. Returns only own properties (unlike `for...in`). The properties need to be enumerable in order to show up (unlike `Object.getOwnPropertyNames()`). The return value is an array of strings.
	`>Object.prototype.customProto =`
	`  101;`
	`> Object.getOwnPropertyNames(`
	`  Object.prototype);`
	`["constructor", "toString", ...,`
	`  "customProto"]`
	`> Object.keys(Object.prototype);`
	`["customProto"]`
	`> var o = {own: 202};`
	`> o.customProto;`
	`  101`
	`> Object.keys(o);`
	`  "own"]`

ES6 addition to objects

ES6 has a few interesting object definition and property syntax. This new syntax is to make working with objects easier and concise.

Property shorthand

ES6 provides a shorter syntax for common object definition.

ES5: `obj = { x: x, y: y };`

ES6: `obj = {x,y};`

Computed property names

It is possible to compute property names in the new ES6 object definition syntax:

```
let obj = {
  foo: "bar",
  [ "baz" + q() ]: 42
}
```

Here the property name is computed where `"baz"` is concatenated with the result of the function call.

Object.assign

The `Object.assign()` method is used to copy the values of all enumerable own properties from one or more source objects to a target object:

```
var dest  = { quux: 0 }
var src1 = { foo: 1, bar: 2 }
var src2 = { foo: 3, baz: 4 }
Object.assign(dst, src1, src2)
```

Array

The `Array` constructor creates array objects:

```
> var a = new Array(1, 2, 3);
```

This is the same as the array literal:

```
> var a = [1, 2, 3]; //recommended
```

When you pass only one numeric value to the `Array` constructor, it's assumed to be the array length:

```
> var un = new Array(3);
> un.length;
3
```

You get an array with the desired length and if you ask for the value of each of the array elements, you get `undefined`:

```
> un;
[undefined, undefined, undefined]
```

There is a subtle difference between an array full of elements and array with no elements, but just length:

```
> '0' in a;
true
> '0' in un;
false
```

This difference in the `Array()` constructor's behavior when you specify one versus more parameters can lead to unexpected behavior. For example, the following use of the array literal is valid:

```
> var a = [3.14];
> a;
[3.14]
```

However, passing the floating-point number to the `Array` constructor is an error:

```
> var a = new Array(3.14);
Range Error: invalid array length
```

The Array.prototype members

The following are the list of all the elements of an `Array`:

Property/method	Description

`length`	The number of elements in the array:
	```> [1, 2, 3, 4].length;```
	```4```

`concat(i1, i2, i3,...)`	Merges arrays together:
	```> [1, 2].concat([3, 5], [7, 11]);```
	```[1, 2, 3, 5, 7, 11]```

`join(separator)`	Turns an array into a string. The separator parameter is a string with comma as the default value:
	```> [1, 2, 3].join();```
	```"1,2,3"```
	```> [1, 2, 3].join('|');```
	```"1|2|3"```
	```> [1, 2, 3].join(' is less than ');```
	```"1 is less than 2 is less than 3"```

`pop()`	Removes the last element of the array and returns it:
	```> var a = ['une', 'deux', 'trois'];```
	```> a.pop();```
	```"trois"```
	```> a;```
	```["une", "deux"]```

`push(i1, i2, i3,...)`	Appends elements to the end of the array and returns the length of the modified array: ``` > var a = []; > a.push('zig', 'zag', 'zebra','zoo'); 4 ```
`reverse()`	Reverses the elements of the array and returns the modified array: ``` > var a = [1, 2, 3]; > a.reverse(); [3, 2, 1] > a; [3, 2, 1] ```
`shift()`	Like `pop()` but removes the first element, not the last: ``` > var a = [1, 2, 3]; > a.shift(); 1 > a; [2, 3] ```
`slice(start_index, end_index)`	Extracts a piece of the array and returns it as a new array, without modifying the source array: ``` > var a = ['apple', 'banana', 'js', 'css', 'orange']; > a.slice(2,4); ["js", "css"] > a; ["apple", "banana", "js", "css", "orange"] ```

sort(callback)	Sorts an array. Optionally accepts a callback function for custom sorting. The callback function receives two array elements as arguments and should return 0 if they are equal, a positive number if the first is greater, and a negative number if the second is greater. An example of a custom sorting function that does a proper numeric sort (since the default is character sorting): ```\nfunction customSort(a, b) {\n if (a > b) return 1;\n if (a < b) return -1;\n return 0;\n}\nExample use of sort():\n> var a = [101, 99, 1, 5];\n> a.sort();\n [1, 101, 5, 99]\n> a.sort(customSort);\n [1, 5, 99, 101]\n> [7, 6, 5, 9].sort(customSort);\n [5, 6, 7, 9]\n```
splice(start, delete_count, i1, i2, i3,...)	Removes and adds elements at the same time. The first parameter is where to start removing, the second is how many items to remove and the rest of the parameters are new elements to be inserted in the place of the removed ones: ```\n> var a = ['apple', 'banana',\n 'js', 'css', 'orange'];\n> a.splice(2, 2, 'pear', 'pineapple');\n["js", "css"]\n> a;\n["apple", "banana", "pear",\n "pineapple", "orange"]\n```
unshift(i1, i2, i3,...)	Like push() but adds the elements at the beginning of the array as opposed to the end. Returns the length of the modified array: ```\n> var a = [1, 2, 3];\n> a.unshift('one', 'two');\n5\n> a;\n["one", "two", 1, 2, 3]\n```

ECMAScript 5 additions to Array

Following are the ECMAScript 5 additions to `Array`:

Property/method	Description

`Array.isArray(obj)`	Tells if an object is an array because `typeof` is not good enough:
	
	```\n> var arraylike = {0: 101,\nlength: 1};\n> typeof arraylike;\n"object"\n> typeof [];\n"object"\n```
	Neither is duck-typing (if it walks like a duck and quacks like a duck, it must be a duck):
	
	```\ntypeof arraylike.length;\n"number"\n```
	In ES3 you need the verbose:
	
	```\n> Object.prototype.toString\n.call\n([]) === "[object Array]";\ntrue\n>\nObject.prototype.toString.call\n(arraylike) ===\n"[object Array]";\nfalse\n```
	In ES5 you get the shorter:
	
	```\nArray.isArray([]);\ntrue\nArray.isArray(arraylike);\nfalse\n```

`Array.prototype.indexOf(needle, idx)`	Searches the array and returns the index of the first match. Returns −1 if there's no match. Optionally can search starting from a specified index:
	`> var ar = ['one', 'two',`
	`  'one',   'two'];`
	`> ar.indexOf('two');`
	`1`
	`> ar.indexOf('two', 2);`
	`3`
	`> ar.indexOf('toot');`
	`−1`

`Array.prototype.lastIndexOf(needle, idx)`	Like `indexOf()` only searches from the end:
	`> var ar = ['one', 'two',`
	`'one', 'two'];`
	`> ar.lastIndexOf('two');`
	`3`
	`> ar.lastIndexOf('two', 2);`
	`1`
	`> ar.indexOf('toot');`
	`−1`

`Array.prototype.forEach(callback, this_obj)`	An alternative to a `for` loop. You specify a callback function that will be called for each element of the array. The callback function gets the arguments: the element, its index and the whole array:
	`> var log =`
	`console.log.bind(console);`
	`> var ar = ['itsy', 'bitsy',`
	`  'spider'];`
	`> ar.forEach(log);`
	`itsy       0    ["itsy",`
	`"bitsy", "spider"]`
	`bitsy      1    ["itsy",`
	`"bitsy", "spider"]`
	`spider  2    ["itsy",`
	`"bitsy", "spider"]`
	Optionally, you can specify a second parameter: the object to be bound to this inside the callback function. So this works too:
	`> ar.forEach(console.log,`
	`  console);`

`Array.prototype.every(callback, this_obj)`	You provide a callback function that tests each element of the array. Your callback is given the same arguments as `forEach()` and it must return `true` or `false` depending on whether the given element satisfies your test. If all elements satisfy your test, `every()` returns `true`. If at least one doesn't, `every()` returns `false`:
	
	```\n> function hasEye(el, idx,\n ar) {\n return el.indexOf('i') !==\n -1;\n }\n> ['itsy', 'bitsy',\n 'spider'].\n every(hasEye);\ntrue\n> ['eency', 'weency',\n 'spider'].every(hasEye);\nfalse\n```
	
	If at some point during the loop it becomes clear that the result will be `false`, the loop stops and returns `false`:
	
	```\n> [1,2,3].every(function (e)\n {\n console.log(e);\n return false;\n });\n1\n false\n```

`Array.prototype.some(callback, this_obj)`	Like `every()`, only it returns `true` if at least one element satisfies your test: ```\n> ['itsy', 'bitsy',\n 'spider'].some(hasEye);\n true\n> ['eency', 'weency',\n 'spider'].some(hasEye);\n true\n```

`Array.prototype.filter(callback, this_obj)`	Similar to `some()` and `every()` but it returns a new array of all elements that satisfy your test: ```\n> ['itsy', 'bitsy',\n 'spider'].filter(hasEye);\n["itsy", "bitsy",\n "spider"]\n> ['eency', 'weency',\n 'spider'].filter(hasEye);\n["spider"]\n```
`Array.prototype.map(callback, this_obj)`	Similar to `forEach()` because it executes a callback for each element, but additionally it constructs a new array with the returned values of your callback and returns it. Let's capitalize all strings in an array: ```\n> function uc(element, index,\n array) {\n return\nelement.toUpperCase();\n }\n> ['eency', 'weency',\n 'spider'].map(uc);\n["EENCY", "WEENCY", "SPIDER"]\n```

`Array.prototype.reduce(callback, start)`	Executes your callback for each element of the array. Your callback returns a value. This value is passed back to your callback with the next iteration. The whole array is eventually reduced to a single value:
	
	```\n> function sum(res, element,\n idx, arr) {\n return res + element;\n }\n> [1, 2, 3].reduce(sum);\n6\n```
	
	Optionally you can pass a start value which will be used by the first callback call:
	
	```\n> [1, 2, 3].reduce(sum, 100);\n106\n```

`Array.prototype.reduceRight(callback, start)`	Like `reduce()` but loops from the end of the array:
	 ``
	> function concat(
	result_so_far, el) {
	return "" + result_so_far
	+ el;
	}
	> [1, 2, 3].reduce(concat);
	"123"
	> [1, 2, 3].reduceRight
	(concat);
	"321"
	``

ES6 addition to arrays

Following are the addition to arrays:

`Array.from(arrayLike, mapFunc?, thisArg?)`	The `Array.from()` **method's basic functionality is to convert two kinds of values to arrays**–`arrayLike` **values and** `Iterable` **values:**
	 ``
	const arrayLike = { length:
	 2, 0: 'a', 1: 'b' };
	const arr =
	Array.from(arrayLike);
	for (const x of arr) {
	 // OK, iterable
	console.log(x);
	}
	// Output:
	// a
	// b
	``

`Array.of(...items)`	Creates an array out of the items passed to the method
	 ``
	let a = Array.of(
	 1,2,3,'foo');
	console.log(a); //[1, 2,
	 3, "foo"]
	``

`Array.prototype.entries()`
`Array.prototype.keys()`
`Array.prototype.values()`
	The result of these methods is a sequence of values. These methods returns an iterator of keys, values and entries respectively.
	<pre>let a = Array.of(1,2,
	3,'foo');
	let k,v,e;
	for (k of a.keys()) {
	console.log(k); //0 1 2 3
	}
	for (v of a.values()) {
	console.log(v); //1 2
	3 foo
	}
	for (e of a.entries()){
	console.log(e);
	}
	//[[0,1],[1,2],[2,3]
	[3,'foo']]</pre>

`Array.prototype.find(predicate,`
`thisArg?)`
	Returns the first array element for which the callback function returns `true`. If there is no such element, it returns `undefined`:
	<pre>[1, -2, 3].find(x => x < 0)
	//-2</pre>

`Array.prototype.findIndex(predicate,`
`thisArg?)`
	Returns the index of the first element for which the callback function returns true. If there is no such element, it returns -1:
	<pre>[1, -2, 3].find(x => x < 0)
	//1</pre>

`Array.prototype.fill(value : any,`
`start=0, end=this.length) : This`
	It fills an array with the given value:
	<pre>const arr = ['a', 'b', 'c'];
	arr.fill(7)
	[7, 7, 7]</pre>You can specify start and end ranges.
	<pre>['a', 'b', 'c'].fill(7, 1, 2)
	['a', 7, 'c']</pre>

Function

JavaScript functions are objects. They can be defined using the `Function` constructor, like so:

```
var sum = new Function('a', 'b', 'return a + b;');
```

This is a (generally not recommended) alternative to the function literal (also known as function expression):

```
var sum = function (a, b) {
   return a + b;
};
```

Or, the more common function definition:

```
function sum(a, b) {
   return a + b;
}
```

The Function.prototype members

Following are the list of members of the `Function` constructor:

Property/Method	Description

`apply(this_obj, params_array)`	Allows you to call another function while overwriting the other function's `this` value. The first parameter that `apply()` accepts is the object to be bound to this inside the function and the second is an array of arguments to be sent to the function being called:
	`function whatIsIt(){`
	  `return this.toString();`
	`}`
	`> var myObj = {};`
	`> whatIsIt.apply(myObj);`
	`"[object Object]"`
	`> whatIsIt.apply(window);`
	`"[object Window]"`

`call(this_obj, p1, p2, p3, ...)`	Same as `apply()` but accepts arguments one by one, as opposed to as one array.

length	The number of parameters the function expects:
	```\n> parseInt.length;\n2\n```
	If you forget the difference between `call()` and `apply()`:
	```\n> Function.prototype.call.length;\n1\n> Function.prototype.apply.length;\n2\n```
	The `call()` property's length is `1` because all arguments except the first one are optional.

ECMAScript 5 additions to a Function

Following are the ECMAScript 5 addition to a `Function` constructor:

Property/method	Description
`Function.prototype.bind()`	When you want to call a function that uses this internally and you want to define what this is. The methods `call()` and `apply()` invoke the function while `bind()` returns a new function. Useful when you provide a method as a callback to a method of another object and and you want this to be an object of your choice: ```\n> whatIsIt.apply(window);\n"[object Window]"\n```

ECMAScript 6 additions to a Function

Following are the ECMAScript 6 addition to a `Function` constructor:

Arrow Functions
An arrow function expression has a shorter syntax compared to function expressions and does not bind its own this, arguments, super, or `new.target`. Arrow functions are always anonymous.
	```() => { ... }```
	`// no parameter`
	`x => { ... }`
	`// one`
	`parameter, an`
	`identifier`
	`(x, y) =>`
	`{ ... }`
	`// several`
	`parameters`
	`const squares =`
	`[1, 2, 3].map(`
	`x => x * x);`

Statement Bodies are more expressive and concise closure syntax	`arr.forEach(v =>`
	`{ if (v % 5`
	`===0)`
	`filtered:ist.push(v)`
	`})`

Boolean

The `Boolean` constructor creates Boolean objects (not to be confused with Boolean primitives). The Boolean objects are not that useful and are listed here for the sake of completeness.

```
> var b = new Boolean();
> b.valueOf();
false
> b.toString();
"false"
```

A Boolean object is not the same as a Boolean primitive value. As you know, all objects are truthy:

```
> b === false;
false
> typeof b;
"object"
```

Boolean objects don't have any properties other than the ones inherited from `Object`.

Number

This creates number objects:

```
> var n = new Number(101);
> typeof n;
"object"
> n.valueOf();
101
```

The `Number` objects are not primitive objects, but if you use any `Number.prototype` method on a primitive number, the primitive will be converted to a `Number` object behind the scenes and the code will work.

```
> var n = 123;
> typeof n;
"number"
> n.toString();
"123"
```

Used without `new`, the `Number` constructor returns a primitive number.

```
> Number("101");
101
> typeof Number("101");
"number"
> typeof new Number("101");
"object"
```

Members of the Number constructor

Consider the following members of the `Number` constructor:

Property/method	Description

`Number.MAX_VALUE`	A constant property (cannot be changed) that contains the maximum allowed number:
	`> Number.MAX_VALUE;`
	`1.7976931348623157e+308`

`Number.MIN_VALUE`	The smallest number you can work with in JavaScript:
	`> Number.MIN_VALUE;`
	`5e-324`

`Number.NaN`	Contains the Not A Number number. Same as the global NaN:
	`> Number.NaN;`
	`NaN`
	NaN is not equal to anything including itself:
	`> Number.NaN === Number.NaN;`
	`false`

`Number.POSITIVE_INFINITY`	Same as the global `Infinity` number.
`Number.NEGATIVE_INFINITY`	Same as `-Infinity`.

The Number.prototype members

Following are the members of the `Number` constructor:

Property/method	Description

`toFixed(fractionDigits)`	Returns a string with the fixed-point representation of the number. Rounds the returned value:
	`> var n = new Number(Math.PI);`
	`> n.valueOf();`
	`3.141592653589793`
	`> n.toFixed(3);`
	`"3.142"`

toExponential(fractionDigits)	Returns a string with exponential notation representation of the number object. Rounds the returned value:
	<pre>> var n = new Number(56789);
	> n.toExponential(2);
	"5.68e+4"</pre>

toPrecision(precision)	String representation of a number object, either exponential or fixed-point, depending on the number object:
	<pre>> var n = new Number(56789);
	> n.toPrecision(2);
	"5.7e+4"
	> n.toPrecision(5);
	"56789"
	> n.toPrecision(4);
	"5.679e+4"
	> var n = new Number(Math.PI);
	> n.toPrecision(4);
	"3.142"</pre>

String

The `String()` constructor creates string objects. Primitive strings are turned into objects behind the scenes if you call a method on them as if they were objects. Omitting `new` gives you primitive strings.

Creating a string object and a string primitive:

```
> var s_obj = new String('potatoes');
> var s_prim = 'potatoes';
> typeof s_obj;
"object"
> typeof s_prim;
"string"
```

[463]

The object and the primitive are not equal when compared by type with ===, but they are when compared with == which does type coercion:

```
> s_obj === s_prim;
false
> s_obj == s_prim;
true
```

length is a property of the string objects:

```
> s_obj.length;
8
```

If you access length on a primitive string, the primitive is converted to an object behind the scenes and the operation is successful:

```
> s_prim.length;
8
```

String literals work fine too:

```
> "giraffe".length;
7
```

Members of the String constructor

Following are the members of the String constructor:

Property/method	Description
String.fromCharCode (code1, code2, code3, ...)	Returns a string created using the Unicode values of the input: ```> String.fromCharCode(115, 99, 114, 105, 112, 116); "script"```

The String.prototype members

Consider the following `String.prototype` members:

Property/method	Description

`length`	The number of characters in the string:
	`> new String('four').length;`
	`4`

`charAt(position)`	Returns the character at the specified position. Positions start at 0:
	`> "script".charAt(0);`
	`"s"`
	Since ES5, it's also possible to use array notation for the same purpose. (This feature has been long supported in many browsers before ES5, but not IE):
	`> "script"[0];`
	`"s"`

`charCodeAt(position)`	Returns the numeric code (Unicode) of the character at the specified position:
	`> "script".charCodeAt(0);`
	`115`

`concat(str1, str2, ....)`	Returns a new string glued from the input pieces:
	`> "".concat('zig', '-',    'zag');`
	`"zig-zag"`

`indexOf(needle, start)`	If the needle matches a part of the string, the position of the match is returned. The optional second parameter defines where the search should start from. Returns −1 if no match is found:
	`> "javascript".indexOf('scr');`
	`4`
	`> "javascript".indexOf('scr',   5);`
	`−1`

`lastIndexOf(needle, start)`	Same as `indexOf()` but starts the search from the end of the string. The last occurrence of `a`:
	`> "javascript".lastIndexOf('a');`
	`3`

`localeCompare(needle)`	Compares two strings in the current locale. Returns `0` if the two strings are equal, `1` if the needle gets sorted before the string object, `-1` otherwise:
	
	`> "script".localeCompare('crypt');`
	`1`
	`> "script".localeCompare('sscript');`
	`-1`
	`> "script".localeCompare('script');`
	`0`

`match(regexp)`	Accepts a regular expression object and returns an array of matches:
	
	`> "R2-D2 and C-3PO".match(/[0-9]/g);`
	`["2", "2", "3"]`

`replace(needle, replacement)`	Allows you to replace the matching results of a regexp pattern. The replacement can also be a callback function. Capturing groups are available as `$1, $2,...$9`:
	
	`> "R2-D2".replace(/2/g, '-two');`
	`"R-two-D-two"`
	`> "R2-D2".replace(/(2)/g,'$1$1');`
	`"R22-D22"`

`search(regexp)`	Returns the position of the first regular expression match:
	
	`> "C-3PO".search(/[0-9]/);`
	`2`

`slice(start, end)`	Returns the part of a string identified by the start and end positions. If `start` is negative, the start position is `length + start`, similarly if the `end` parameter is negative, the end position is `length + end`:
	
	`> "R2-D2 and C-3PO".slice(4,    13);`
	`"2 and C-3"`
	`> "R2-D2 and C-3PO".slice(4,    -1);`
	`"2 and C-3P"`

`split(separator, limit)`	Turns a string into an array. The second parameter, limit, is optional. As with `replace()`, `search()`, and `match()`, the separator is a regular expression but can also be a string:
	
	`> "1,2,3,4".split(/,/);`
	`["1", "2", "3",    "4"]`
	`> "1,2,3,4".split(',',    2);`
	`["1", "2"]`

`substring(start, end)`	Similar to `slice()`. When start or end are negative or invalid, they are considered 0. If they are greater than the string length, they are considered to be the length. If `end` is greater than `start`, their values are swapped.
	`> "R2-D2 and C-3PO".substring(4, 13);`
	`"2 and C-3"`
	`> "R2-D2 and C-3PO".substring(13, 4);`
	`"2 and C-3"`

`toLowerCase()`
`toLocaleLowerCase()`
	Transforms the string to lowercase:
	`> "Java".toLowerCase();`
	`"java"`

`toUpperCase()`
`toLocaleUpperCase()`
	Transforms the string to uppercase:
	`> "Script".toUpperCase();`
	`"SCRIPT"`

ECMAScript 5 additions to String

Following are the ECMAScript 5 additions to String:

Property/method	Description

`String.prototype.trim()`	Instead of using a regular expression to remove whitespace before and after a string (as in ES3), you have a `trim()` method in ES5.
	`> " \t beard \n".trim();`
	`"beard"`
	`Or in ES3:`
	`> " \t beard \n".replace(/\s/g, "");`
	`"beard"`

ECMAScript 6 additions to String

Following are the list of all the ECMAScript 6 additions to String:

Template Literals are used to interpolate single or multi-line strings. Template literals are enclosed by the back-tick (` `` `) (grave accent) character instead of double or single quotes. Template literals can contain place holders. These are indicated by the Dollar sign and curly braces (`${expression}`). The expressions in the place holders and the text between them get passed to a function. The default function just concatenates the parts into a single string.	```var a = 5;``` ``` var b = 10;``` ```console.log(`Fifteen``` ``` is ${a + b}`);```

`String.prototype.repeat` – this method allows you to repeat a string n number of times	```" ".repeat(4 *```
	``` depth)```
	``` "foo".repeat(3)```

`String.prototype.startsWith`
`String.prototype.endsWith`
`String.prototype.includes`
These are new string searching methods
	```"hello".startsWith(```
	``` "ello", 1) // true```
	``` "hello".endsWith(```
	``` "hell",4) // true```
	```"hello".includes(```
	``` "ell")```
	``` // true```
	```"hello".includes(```
	``` "ell", 1) // true```
	```"hello".includes(```
	``` "ell", 2) // false```

Date

The `Date` constructor can be used with several types of input:

- You can pass values for year, month, date of the month, hour, minute, second, and millisecond, like so:

  ```
  > new Date(2015, 0, 1, 13, 30, 35, 505);
  Thu Jan 01 2015 13:30:35 GMT-0800 (PST)
  ```

- You can skip any of the input parameters, in which case they are assumed to be 0. Note that month values are from 0 (January) to 11 (December), hours are from 0 to 23, minutes and seconds 0 to 59, and milliseconds 0 to 999.

- You can pass a timestamp:

```
> new Date(1420147835505);
Thu Jan 01 2015 13:30:35 GMT-0800 (PST)
```

- If you don't pass anything, the current date/time is assumed:

```
> new Date();
Fri Jan 11 2013 12:20:45 GMT-0800 (PST)
```

- If you pass a string, it's parsed in an attempt to extract a possible date value:

```
> new Date('May 4, 2015');
Mon May 04 2015 00:00:00 GMT-0700 (PDT)
```

Omitting `new` gives you a string version of the current date:

```
> Date() === new Date().toString();
true
```

Members of the Date constructor

Following are the members of the Date constructor:

Property/method	Description

`Date.parse(string)`	Similar to passing a string to new `Date()` constructor, this method parses the input string in attempt to extract a valid date value. Returns a timestamp on success, NaN on failure:
	
	`> Date.parse('May 5, 2015');`
	`1430809200000`
	`> Date.parse('4th');`
	`NaN`

`Date.UTC(year, month, date, hours, minutes, seconds, ms)`	Returns a timestamp but in UTC (Coordinated Universal Time), not in local time.
	
	`> Date.UTC`
	`(2015, 0, 1, 13, 30, 35, 505);`
	`1420119035505`

The Date.prototype members

Following are the list of `Date.prototype` members:

Property/method	Description/example

`toUTCString()`	Same as `toString()` but in universal time. Here's how Pacific Standard (PST) local time differs from UTC:
	`> var d = new Date(2015, 0, 1);`
	`> d.toString();`
	`"Thu Jan 01 2015 00:00:00 GMT-0800 (PST)"`
	`> d.toUTCString();`
	`"Thu, 01 Jan 2015 08:00:00   GMT"`

`toDateString()`	Returns only the date portion of `toString()`:
	`> new Date(2015, 0,   1).toDateString();`
	`"Thu Jan 01 2010"`

`toTimeString()`	Returns only the time portion of `toString()`:
	`> new Date(2015, 0,   1).toTimeString();`
	`"00:00:00 GMT-0800 (PST)"`

`toLocaleString()`
`toLocaleDateString()`
`toLocaleTimeString()`
	Equivalent to `toString()`, `toDateString()`, and `toTimeString()` respectively, but in a friendlier format, according to the current user's locale:
	`> new Date(2015, 0,   1).toString();`
	`"Thu Jan 01 2015 00:00:00 GMT-0800 (PST)"`
	`> new Date(2015, 0,   1).toLocaleString();`
	`"1/1/2015 12:00:00 AM"`

`getTime()`
`setTime(time)`
	Get or set the time (using a timestamp) of a date object. The following example creates a date and moves it one day forward:
	`> var d = new Date(2015, 0, 1);`
	`> d.getTime();`
	`1420099200000`
	`> d.setTime(d.getTime() +`
	`  1000 * 60 * 60 *   24);`
	`1420185600000`
	`> d.toLocaleString();`
	`"Fri Jan 02 2015 00:00:00`
	`  GMT-0800 (PST)"`

`getFullYear()`
`getUTCFullYear()`
`setFullYear(year, month, date)`
`setUTCFullYear(year, month, date)`
	Get or set a full year using local or UTC time. There is also `getYear()` but it is not Y2K compliant, so use `getFullYear()` instead:
	`> var d = new Date(2015, 0, 1);`
	`> d.getYear();`
	`115`
	`> d.getFullYear();`
	`2015`
	`> d.setFullYear(2020);`
	`1577865600000`
	`> d;`
	`Wed Jan 01 2020 00:00:00 GMT-0800`
	`  (PST)`

`getMonth()`
`getUTCMonth()`
`setMonth(month, date)`
`setUTCMonth(month, date)`
	Get or set month, starting from 0 (January):
	`> var d = new Date(2015, 0, 1);`
	`> d.getMonth();`
	`0`
	`> d.setMonth(11);`
	`1448956800000`
	`> d.toLocaleDateString();`
	`"12/1/2015"`

`getDate()`
`getUTCDate()`
`setDate(date)`
`setUTCDate(date)`
	Get or set date of the month.
	`> var d = new Date(2015, 0, 1);`
	`> d.toLocaleDateString();`
	`"1/1/2015"`
	`> d.getDate();`
	`1`
	`> d.setDate(31);`
	`1422691200000`
	`> d.toLocaleDateString();`
	`"1/31/2015"`

`getHours()`
`getUTCHours()`
`setHours(hour, min, sec,`
`ms)`
`setUTCHours(hour, min, sec,`
`ms)`
`getMinutes()`
`getUTCMinutes()`
`setMinutes(min, sec, ms)`
`setUTCMinutes(min, sec, ms)`
`getSeconds()`
`getUTCSeconds()`
`setSeconds(sec, ms)`
`setUTCSeconds(sec, ms)`
`getMilliseconds()`
`getUTCMilliseconds()`
`setMilliseconds(ms)`
`setUTCMilliseconds(ms)`
	Get/Set hour, minutes, seconds, milliseconds, all starting from 0:
	
	``
	> var d = new Date(2015, 0, 1);
	> d.getHours() + ':' + d.getMinutes();
	"0:0"
	> d.setMinutes(59);
	1420102740000
	> d.getHours() + ':' + d.getMinutes();
	"0:59"
	``

`getTimezoneOffset()`	Returns the difference between local and universal (UTC) time, measured in minutes. For example the difference between PST (Pacific Standard Time) and UTC:
	
	``
	> new Date().getTimezoneOffset();
	480
	> 420 / 60; // hours
	8
	``

`getDay()` `getUTCDay()`	Returns the day of the week, starting from 0 (Sunday): ``` > var d = new Date(2015, 0, 1); > d.toDateString(); "Thu Jan 01 2015" > d.getDay(); 4 > var d = new Date(2015, 0, 4); > d.toDateString(); "Sat Jan 04 2015" > d.getDay(); 0 ```

[472]

ECMAScript 5 additions to Date

Following are the additions to the `Date` constructor:

Property/method	Description

`Date.now()`	A convenient way to get the current timestamp:
	`> Date.now() === new   Date().getTime();`
	`true`

`Date.prototype.toISOString()`	Yet another `toString()`:
	`> var d = new Date(2015, 0, 1);`
	`> d.toString();`
	`"Thu Jan 01 2015 00:00:00 GMT-0800`
	`  (PST)"`
	`> d.toUTCString();`
	`"Thu, 01 Jan 2015 08:00:00   GMT"`
	`> d.toISOString();`
	`"2015-01-01T00:00:00.000Z"`

`Date.prototype.toJSON()`	Used by `JSON.stringify()` (refer to the end of this appendix) and returns the same as `toISOString()`:
	`> var d = new Date();`
	`> d.toJSON() === d.toISOString();`
	`true`

Math

`Math` is a different from the other built-in objects because it cannot be used as a constructor to create objects. It's just a collection of static functions and constants. Some examples to illustrate the difference are as follows:

```
> typeof Date.prototype;
"object"
> typeof Math.prototype;
"undefined"
> typeof String;
"function"
> typeof Math;
"object"
```

Members of the Math object

Following are the members of the `Math` object:

Property/method	Description
Math.E Math.LN10 Math.LN2 Math.LOG2E Math.LOG10E Math.PI Math.SQRT1_2 Math.SQRT2	These are some useful math constants, all read-only. Here are their values: > Math.E; 2.718281828459045 > Math.LN10; 2.302585092994046 > Math.LN2; 0.6931471805599453 > Math.LOG2E; 1.4426950408889634 > Math.LOG10E; 0.4342944819032518 > Math.PI; 3.141592653589793 > Math.SQRT1_2; 0.7071067811865476 > Math.SQRT2; 1.4142135623730951
Math.acos(x) Math.asin(x) Math.atan(x) Math.atan2(y, x) Math.cos(x) Math.sin(x) Math.tan(x)	Trigonometric functions
Math.round(x) Math.floor(x) Math.ceil(x)	round() gives you the nearest integer, ceil() rounds up, and floor() rounds down: > Math.round(5.5); 6 > Math.floor(5.5); 5 > Math.ceil(5.1); 6

`Math.max(num1, num2, num3, ...)`
`Math.min(num1, num2, num3, ...)`
	`max()` returns the largest and `min()` returns the smallest of the numbers passed to them as arguments. If at least one of the input parameters is NaN, the result is also NaN:
	`> Math.max(4.5, 101, Math.PI);`
	`101`
	`> Math.min(4.5, 101, Math.PI);`
	`3.141592653589793`

`Math.abs(x)`	Absolute value:
	`> Math.abs(-101);`
	`101`
	`> Math.abs(101);`
	`101`

`Math.exp(x)`	Exponential function: `Math.E` to the power of x:
	`> Math.exp(1) === Math.E;`
	`true`

`Math.log(x)`	Natural logarithm of x: `> Math.log(10) === Math.LN10;` **`true`**

`Math.sqrt(x)`	Square root of x:
	`> Math.sqrt(9);`
	`3`
	`> Math.sqrt(2) === Math.SQRT2;`
	`true`

`Math.pow(x, y)`	x to the power of y:
	`> Math.pow(3, 2);`
	`9`

`Math.random()`	Random number between 0 and 1 (including 0).
	`> Math.random();`
	`0.8279076443185321`
	`For an random integer in a range,`
	` say between 10 and 100:`
	`> Math.round(Math.random() * 90  + 10);`
	`79`

RegExp

You can create a regular expression object using the `RegExp()` constructor. You pass the expression pattern as the first parameter and the pattern modifiers as the second:

```
> var re = new RegExp('[dn]o+dle', 'gmi');
```

This matches "noodle", "doodle", "doooodle", and so on. It's equivalent to using the regular expression literal:

```
> var re = ('/[dn]o+dle/gmi'); // recommended
```

`Chapter 4`, *Objects* and `Appendix D`, *Regular Expressions* contain more information on regular expressions and patterns.

The RegExp.prototype members

Following are the `RegExp.prototype` members:

Property/method	Description
global	Read-only `true` if the g modifier was set when creating the `regexp` object.
ignoreCase	Read-only. `true` if the i modifier was set when creating the `regexp` object.
multiline	Read-only. `true` if the m modifier was set when creating the `regexp` object

lastIndex	Contains the position in the string where the next match should start. `test()` and `exec()` set this position after a successful match. Only relevant when the g (global) modifier was used:
	```> var re = /[dn]o+dle/g;```
	```> re.lastIndex;```
	```0```
	```> re.exec("noodle doodle");```
	```["noodle"]```
	```> re.lastIndex;```
	```6```
	```> re.exec("noodle doodle");```
	```["doodle"]```
	```> re.lastIndex;```
	```13```
	```> re.exec("noodle doodle");```
	```null```
	```> re.lastIndex;```
	```0```

source	Read-only. Returns the regular expression pattern (without the modifiers):
	```> var re = /[nd]o+dle/gmi;```
	```> re.source;```
	```"[nd]o+dle"```

exec(string)	Matches the input string with the regular expression. On a successful match returns an array containing the match and any capturing groups. With the g modifier, it matches the first occurrence and sets the lastIndex property. Returns null when there's no match:
	```\n> var re = /([dn])(o+)dle/g;\n> re.exec("noodle doodle");\n["noodle", "n", "oo"]\n> re.exec("noodle doodle");\n["doodle", "d", "oo"]\n```
	The arrays returned by exec() have two additional properties: index (of the match) and input (the input string being searched).
test(string)	Same as exec() but only returns true or false:
	```\n> /noo/.test('Noodle');\nfalse\n> /noo/i.test('Noodle');\ntrue\n```

Error objects

Error objects are created either by the environment (the browser) or by your code:

```
> var e = new Error('jaavcsritp is _not_ how you spell it');
> typeof e;
"object"
```

Other than the Error constructor, six additional ones exist and they all inherit Error:

- EvalError
- RangeError
- ReferenceError
- SyntaxError
- TypeError
- URIError

The Error.prototype members

Following are the `Error.prototype` members:

Property	Description

name	The name of the error constructor used to create the object:
	`> var e = new EvalError('Oops');`
	`> e.name;`
	`"EvalError"`

message	Additional error information:
	`> var e = new Error('Oops...    again');`
	`> e.message;`
	`"Oops... again"`

JSON

The JSON object is new to ES5. It's not a constructor (similarly to `Math`) and has only two methods: `parse()` and `stringify()`. For ES3 browsers that don't support JSON natively, you can use the "shim" from `http://json.org`.

JSON stands for **JavaScript Object Notation**. It's a lightweight data interchange format. It's a subset of JavaScript that only supports primitives, object literals, and array literals.

Members of the JSON object

Following are the members of the JSON object:

Method	Description

`parse(text,`
`callback)`
	Takes a JSON-encoded string and returns an object:
	```> var data = '{"hello": 1, "hi": [1, 2, 3]}';```
	```> var o = JSON.parse(data);```
	```> o.hello;```
	```1```
	```> o.hi;```
	```[1, 2, 3]```
	
	The optional callback lets you provide your own function that can inspect and modify the result. The callback takes `key` and `value` arguments and can modify the `value` or delete it (by returning `undefined`).
	```> function callback(key, value) {```
	``` console.log(key, value);```
	``` if (key === 'hello') {```
	``` return 'bonjour';```
	``` }```
	``` if (key === 'hi') {```
	``` return undefined;```
	``` }```
	``` return value;```
	``` }```
	```> var o = JSON.parse(data, callback);```
	```hello 1```
	```0 1```
	```1 2```
	```2 3```
	```hi [1, 2, 3]```
	```Object {hello: "bonjour"}```
	```> o.hello;```
	```"bonjour"```
	```> 'hi' in o;```
	```false```

`stringify(value, callback, white)`	Takes any value (most commonly an object or an array) and encodes it to a JSON string.
	
	```\n> var o = {\nhello: 1,\nhi: 2,\nwhen: new Date(2015, 0, 1)\n};\n> JSON.stringify(o);\n"{"hello":1,"hi":2,"when":\n"2015-01-01T08:00:00.000Z"}"\n```
	
	The second parameter lets you provide a callback (or a whitelist array) to customize the return value. The whitelist contains the keys you're interested in:
	
	```\nJSON.stringify(o, ['hello', 'hi']);\n"{"hello":1,"hi":2}"\n```
	
	The last parameter helps you get a human-readable version. You specify the number of spaces as a string or a number:
	
	```\n> JSON.stringify(o, null, 4);\n"{\n"hello": 1,\n"hi": 2,\n"when": "2015-01-01T08:00:00.000Z"\n}"\n```

D
Regular Expressions

When you use regular expressions (discussed in `Chapter 4`, *Objects*), you can match literal strings, for example:

```
> "some text".match(/me/);
["me"]
```

However, the true power of regular expressions comes from matching patterns, not literal strings. The following table describes the different syntax you can use in your patterns, and provides some examples of their use:

Pattern	Description

`[abc]`	**Matches a class of characters:**
	```> "some text".match(/[otx]/g);```
	```["o", "t", "x", "t"]```

`[a-z]`	A class of characters defined as a range. For example, [a-d] is the same as [abcd], [a-z] matches all lowercase characters, [a-zA-Z0-9_] matches all characters, numbers, and the underscore character:
	```> "Some Text".match(/[a-z]/g);```
	```["o", "m", "e", "e", "x", "t"]```
	```> "Some Text".match(/[a-zA-Z]/g);```
	```["S", "o", "m", "e", "T", "e", "x", "t"]```

`[^abc]`	Matches everything that is not matched by the class of characters:
	```> "Some Text".match(/[^a-z]/g);```
	```["S", " ", "T"]```

Pattern	Description

a|b	Matches a or b. The pipe character means OR, and it can be used more than once:
	`> "Some Text".match(/t|T/g);`
	`["T", "t"]`
	`> "Some Text".match(/t|T|Some/g);`
	`["Some", "T",    "t"]`

a(?=b)	Matches a only if followed by b:
	`> "Some Text".match(/Some(?=Tex)/g);`
	`null`
	`> "Some Text".match(/Some(?=Tex)/g);`
	`["Some"]`

a(?!b)	Matches a only when not followed by b:
	`> "Some Text".match(/Some(?!Tex)/g);`
	`null`
	`> "Some Text".match(/Some(?!Tex)/g);`
	`["Some"]`

\	Escape character used to help you match the special characters used in patterns as literals:
	`> "R2-D2".match(/[2-3]/g);`
	`["2", "2"]`
	`> "R2-D2".match(/[2\-3]/g);`
	`["2", "-", "2"]`

\n \r \f \t \v	New line Carriage return Form feed Tab Vertical tab

\s	White space, or any of the previous five escape sequences:
	`> "R2\n D2".match(/\s/g);`
	`["\n", " "]`

\S	Opposite of the above; matches everything but white space. Same as [^\s]:
	`> "R2\n D2".match(/\S/g);`
	`["R", "2", "D",    "2"]`

\w	Any letter, number, or underscore. Same as [A-Za-z0-9_]:
	`> "S0m3 text!".match(/\w/g);`
	`["S", "0", "m",    "3", "t", "e", "x", "t"]`

\W	Opposite of \w:
	`> "S0m3 text!".match(/\W/g);`
	`[" ", "!"]`

Pattern	Description

\d	Matches a number, same as [0-9]:
	`> "R2-D2 and C-3PO".match(/\d/g);`
	`["2", "2", "3"]`

\D	Opposite of \d; matches non-numbers, same as [^0-9] or [^\d]:
	`> "R2-D2 and C-3PO".match(/\D/g);`
	`["R", "-", "D", " ", "a", "n", "d",`
	`" ", "C", "-", "P", "O"]`

\b	Matches a word boundary such as space or punctuation.
	Matching R or D followed by 2:
	`> "R2D2 and C-3PO".match(/[RD]2/g);`
	`["R2", "D2"]`
	Same as above but only at the end of a word:
	`> "R2D2 and C-3PO".match(/[RD]2\b/g);`
	`["D2"]`
	Same pattern but the input has a dash, which is also an end of a word:
	`> "R2-D2 and C-3PO".match(/[RD]2\b/g);`
	`["R2", "D2"]`

\B	The opposite of \b:
	`> "R2-D2 and C-3PO".match(/[RD]2\B/g);`
	`null`
	`> "R2D2 and C-3PO".match(/[RD]2\B/g);`
	`["R2"]`

[\b]	Matches the backspace character.
\0	The null character.

\u0000	Matches a Unicode character, represented by a four-digit hexadecimal number:
	`> "стоян".match(/\u0441\u0442\u043E/);`
	`["сто"]`

\x00	Matches a character code represented by a two-digit hexadecimal number:
	`> "\x64";`
	`"d"`
	`> "dude".match(/\x64/g);`
	`["d", "d"]`

[483]

Pattern	Description
^	The beginning of the string to be matched. If you set the `m` modifier (multi-line), it matches the beginning of each line: ``` > "regular\nregular\nexpression".match(/r/g); ["r", "r", "r", "r", "r"] > "regular\nregular\nexpression".match(/^r/g); ["r"] > "regular\nregular\nexpression".match(/^r/mg); ["r", "r"] ```
$	Matches the end of the input or, when using the multiline modifier, the end of each line: ``` > "regular\nregular\nexpression".match(/r$/g); null > "regular\nregular\nexpression".match(/r$/mg); ["r", "r"] ```
.	Matches any single character except for the new line and the line feed: ``` > "regular".match(/r./g); ["re"] > "regular".match(/r.../g); ["regu"] ```
*	Matches the preceding pattern if it occurs zero or more times. For example, `/.*/` will match anything including nothing (an empty input): ``` > "".match(/.*/); [""] > "anything".match(/.*/); ["anything"] > "anything".match(/n.*h/); ["nyth"] ``` Keep in mind that the pattern is "greedy", meaning it will match as much as possible: ``` > "anything within".match(/n.*h/g); ["nything with"] ```
?	Matches the preceding pattern if it occurs zero or one times: ``` > "anything".match(/ny?/g); ["ny", "n"] ```
+	Matches the preceding pattern if it occurs at least once (or more times): ``` > "anything".match(/ny+/g); ["ny"] > "R2-D2 and C-3PO".match(/[a-z]/gi); ["R", "D", "a", "n", "d", "C", "P", "O"] > "R2-D2 and C-3PO".match(/[a-z]+/gi); ["R", "D", "and", "C", "PO"] ```

Pattern	Description

`{n}`	Matches the preceding pattern if it occurs exactly n times:
	<pre>> "regular expression".match(/s/g);
	["s", "s"]
	> "regular expression".match(/s{2}/g);
	["ss"]
	> "regular expression".match(/\b\w{3}/g);
	["reg", "exp"]</pre>

`{min,max}`	Matches the preceding pattern if it occurs between min and max number of times. You can omit max, which will mean no maximum, but only a minimum. You cannot omit min.
	An example where the input is "doodle" with the "o" repeated 10 times:
	<pre>> "dooooooooooodle".match(/o/g);
	["o", "o", "o", "o", "o",
	"o", "o", "o", "o", "o"]
	> "dooooooooooodle".match(/o/g).length;
	10
	> "dooooooooooodle".match(/o{2}/g);
	["oo", "oo", "oo", "oo", "oo"]
	> "dooooooooooodle".match(/o{2,}/g);
	["oooooooooo"]
	> "dooooooooooodle".match(/o{2,6}/g);
	["oooooo", "oooo"]</pre>

`(pattern)`	When the pattern is in parentheses, it is remembered so that it can be used for replacements. These are also known as capturing patterns.
	The captured matches are available as $1, $2,… $9
	Matching all "r" occurrences and repeating them:
	<pre>> "regular expression".replace(/(r)/g, '$1$1');
	"rregularr exprression"</pre>Matching "re" and turning it to "er":
	<pre>> "regular expression".replace(/(r)(e)/g, '$2$1');
	"ergular experssion"</pre>

`(?:pattern)`	Non-capturing pattern, not remembered and not available in $1, $2…
	Here's an example of how "re" is matched, but the "r" is not remembered and the second pattern becomes $1:
	<pre>> "regular expression".replace(/(?:r)(e)/g, '$1$1');
	"eegular expeession"</pre>

Make sure you pay attention when a special character can have two meanings, as is the case with ^, ?, and \b.

Answers to Exercise Questions

This appendix lists possible answers to the exercises at the end of the chapters. Possible answers meaning they are not the only ones, so don't worry if your solution is different.

As with the rest of the book, you should try them in your console and play around a bit.

The first and the last chapters don't have the *Exercises* section, so let's start with Chapter 2, *Primitive Data Types, Arrays, Loops, and Conditions*.

Chapter 2, Primitive Data Types, Arrays, Loops, and Conditions

Lets try and solve the following exercises:

Exercises

1. The result will be as follows:

    ```
    > var a; typeof a;
    "undefined"
    ```

    When you declare a variable but do not initialize it with a value, it automatically gets the undefined value. You can also check:

    ```
    > a === undefined;
    true
    ```

The value of v will be:

```
> var s = '1s'; s++;
NaN
```

Adding 1 to the string '1s' returns the string '1s1', which is *Not A Number*, but the ++ operator should return a number; so it returns the special NaN number.

The program is as follows:

```
> !!"false";
true
```

The tricky part of the question is that "false" is a string and all strings are true when cast to Booleans (except the empty string ""). If the question wasn't about the string "false" but the Boolean false instead, the double negation !! returns the same Boolean:

```
> !!false;
false
```

As you'd expect, single negation returns the opposite:

```
> !false;
true
> !true;
false
```

You can test with any string and it will cast to a Boolean true, except the empty string:

```
> !!"hello";
true
> !!"0";
true
> !!"";
false
```

The output after executing undefined is as follows:

```
> !!undefined;
false
```

Here `undefined` is one of the falsy values and it casts to `false`. You can try with any of the other falsy values, such the empty string `""` in the previous example, NaN, or 0.

```
> typeof -Infinity;
"number"
```

The number type includes all numbers, `NaN`, positive and negative `Infinity`.

The output after executing the following is:

```
> 10 % "0";
NaN
```

The string `"0"` is cast to the number 0. Division by 0 is `Infinity`, which has no remainder.

The output after executing the following is:

```
> undefined == null;
true
```

Comparison with == operator doesn't check the types, but converts the operands; in this case both are falsy values. Strict comparison checks the types too:

```
> undefined === null;
false
```

The following is the code line and its output:

```
> false === "";
false
```

Strict comparison between different types (in this case Boolean and string) is doomed to fail, no matter what the values are.

The following is the code line and its output:

```
> typeof "2E+2";
"string"
```

Anything in quotes is a string, even though:

```
> 2E+2;
200
> typeof 2E+2;
"number"
```

The following is the code line and its output:

```
> a = 3e+3; a++;
3000
```

3e+3 is 3 with three zeroes, meaning 3000. Then ++ is a post-increment, meaning it returns the old value and then it increments it and assigns it to a. That's why you get the return value 3000 in the console, although a is now 3001:

```
> a;
3001
```

2. The value of v after executing the following is:

```
> var v = v || 10;
> v;
10
```

If v has never been declared, it's undefined so this is the same as:

```
> var v = undefined || 10;
> v;
10
```

However, if v has already been defined and initialized with a non-falsy value, you'll get the previous value.

```
> var v = 100;
> var v = v || 10;
> v;
100
```

The second use of var doesn't "reset" the variable.

If v was already a falsy value (not a 100), the check v || 10 will return 10.

```
> var v = 0;
> var v = v || 10;
> v;
10
```

3. For printing multiplication tables, perform the following:

```
for (var i = 1; i <= 12; i++) {
  for (var j = 1; j <= 12; j++) {
    console.log(i + ' * ' + j + ' = ' + i * j);
  }
}
```

Or:

```
var i = 1, j = 1;
while (i <= 12) {
  while (j <= 12) {
    console.log(i + ' * ' + j + ' = ' + i * j);
    j++;
  }
  i++;
  j = 1;
}
```

Chapter 3, Functions

Lets do the following exercises:

Exercises

1. To convert Hex colors to RGB, perform the following:

```
function getRGB(hex) {
  return "rgb(" +
    parseInt(hex[1] + hex[2], 16) + ", " +
    parseInt(hex[3] + hex[4], 16) + ", " +
    parseInt(hex[5] + hex[6], 16) + ")";
}
Testing:
> getRGB("#00ff00");
      "rgb(0, 255, 0)"
> getRGB("#badfad");
      "rgb(186, 223, 173)"
```

One problem with this solution is that array access to strings like `hex[0]` is not in ECMAScript 3, although many browsers have supported it for a long time and is now described in ES5.

However, But at this point in the book, there was as yet no discussion of objects and methods. Otherwise an ES3-compatible solution would be to use one of the string methods, such as `charAt()`, `substring()`, or `slice()`. You can also use an array to avoid too much string concatenation:

```
function getRGB2(hex) {
  var result = [];
  result.push(parseInt(hex.slice(1, 3), 16));
  result.push(parseInt(hex.slice(3, 5), 16));
  result.push(parseInt(hex.slice(5), 16));
  return "rgb(" + result.join(", ") + ")";
}
```

Bonus exercise: Rewrite the preceding function using a loop so you don't have to type `parseInt()` three times, but just once.

2. The result is as follows:

```
> parseInt(1e1);
10
Here, you're parsing something that is already an integer:
> parseInt(10);
10
> 1e1;
10
```

Here, the parsing of a string gives up on the first non-integer value. `parseInt()` doesn't understand exponential literals, it expects integer notation:

```
> parseInt('1e1');
1
```

This is parsing the string `'1e1'` while expecting it to be in decimal notation, including exponential:

```
> parseFloat('1e1');
10
```

The following is the code line and its output:

```
> isFinite(0 / 10);
true
```

Because `0/10` is `0` and `0` is finite.

The following is the code line and its output:

```
> isFinite(20 / 0);
false
```

Because division by 0 is `Infinity`:

```
> 20 / 0;
Infinity
```

The following is the code line and its output:

```
> isNaN(parseInt(NaN));
true
```

Parsing the special NaN value is NaN.

3. What is the result of:

```
var a = 1;
function f() {
  function n() {
    alert(a);
  }
  var a = 2;
  n();
}
f();
```

This snippet alerts 2 even though `n()` was defined before the assignment, `a = 2`. Inside the function `n()` you see the variable `a` that is in the same scope, and you access its most recent value at the time invocation of `f()` (and hence `n()`). Due to hoisting `f()` acts as if it was:

```
function f() {
  var a;
  function n() {
    alert(a);
  }
  a = 2;
  n();
}
```

More interestingly, consider this code:

```
var a = 1;
function f() {
  function n() {
    alert(a);
  }
  n();
  var a = 2;
  n();
}
f();
```

It alerts `undefined` and then `2`. You might expect the first alert to say `1`, but again due to variable hoisting, the declaration (not initialization) of `a` is moved to the top of the function. As if `f()` was:

```
var a = 1;
function f() {
  var a; // a is now undefined
  function n() {
    alert(a);
  }
  n(); // alert undefined
  a = 2;
  n(); // alert 2
}
f();
```

The local `a` "shadows" the global `a`, even if it's at the bottom.

4. Why all these alert "Boo!"

The following is the result of Example 1:

```
var f = alert;
eval('f("Boo!")');
```

The following is the result of Example 2. You can assign a function to a different variable. So `f()` points to `alert()`. Evaluating this string is like doing:

```
> f("Boo");
```

The following is the output after we execute `eval()`:

```
var e;
var f = alert;
eval('e=f')('Boo!');
```

The following is the output of Example 3. `eval()` returns the result on the evaluation. In this case it's an assignment `e = f` that also returns the new value of e. Like the following:

```
> var a = 1;
> var b;
> var c = (b = a);
> c;
1
```

So `eval('e=f')` gives you a pointer to `alert()` that is executed immediately with `"Boo!"`.

The immediate (self-invoking) anonymous function returns a pointer to the function `alert()`, which is also immediately invoked with a parameter `"Boo!"`:

```
(function(){
  return alert;
})()('Boo!');
```

Chapter 4, Objects

Lets solve the following exercises:

Exercises

1. What happens here? What is `this` and what's `o`?

```
function F() {
  function C() {
    return this;
  }
  return C();
}
var o = new F();
```

Here, `this` `===` `window` because `C()` was called without `new`.

Also `o` `===` `window` because `new F()` returns the object returned by `C()`, which is `this`, and `this` is `window`.

You can make the call to `C()` a constructor call:

```
function F() {
    function C() {
        return this;
    }
    return new C();
}
var o = new F();
```

Here, `this` is the object created by the `C()` constructor. So is `o`:

```
> o.constructor.name;
"C"
```

It becomes more interesting with ES5's strict mode. In the strict mode, non-constructor invocations result in `this` being `undefined`, not the global object. With `"use strict"` inside `F()` or `C()` constructor's body, `this` would be `undefined` in `C()`. Therefore, `return C()` cannot return the non-object `undefined` (because all constructor invocations return some sort of object) and returns `F` instances' `this` (which is in the closure scope). Try it:

```
function F() {
    "use strict";
    this.name = "I am F()";
    function C() {
        console.log(this); // undefined
        return this;
    }
    return C();
}
```

Testing:

```
> var o = new F();
> o.name;
"I am F()"
```

2. What happens when invoking this constructor with `new`?

```
function C() {
   this.a = 1;
   return false;
}
And testing:
> typeof new C();
"object"
> new C().a;
 1
```

`new C()` is an object, not Boolean, because constructor invocations always produce an object. It's the `this` object you get unless you return some other object in your constructor. Returning non-objects doesn't work and you still get `this`.

3. What does this do?

```
> var c = [1, 2, [1, 2]];
> c.sort();
> c;
 [1, Array[2], 2]
```

This is because `sort()` compares strings. `[1, 2].toString()` is `"1,2"`, so it comes after `"1"` and before `"2"`.

The same thing with `join()`:

```
> c.join('--');
> c;
"1--1,2--2"
```

4. Pretend `String()` doesn't exist and create `MyString()` mimicking `String()`. Treat the input primitive strings as arrays (array access officially supported in ES5).

Here's a sample implementation with just the methods the exercise asked for. Feel free to continue with the rest of the methods. Refer to `Appendix C`, *Built-in Objects* for the full list.

```
function MyString(input) {
   var index = 0;

   // cast to string
   this._value = '' + input;
```

```
    // set all numeric properties for array access
    while (input[index] !== undefined) {
      this[index] = input[index];
      index++;
    }

    // remember the length
    this.length = index;
  }

MyString.prototype = {
  constructor: MyString,
  valueOf: function valueOf() {
    return this._value;
  },
  toString: function toString() {
    return this.valueOf();
  },
  charAt: function charAt(index) {
    return this[parseInt(index, 10) || 0];
  },
  concat: function concat() {
    var prim = this.valueOf();
    for (var i = 0, len = arguments.length; i < len; i++) {
      prim += arguments[i];
    }
    return prim;
  },
  slice: function slice(from, to) {
    var result = '',
        original = this.valueOf();
    if (from === undefined) {
      return original;
    }
    if (from > this.length) {
      return result;
    }
    if (from < 0) {
      from = this.length - from;
    }
    if (to === undefined || to > this.length) {
      to = this.length;
    }
    if (to < 0) {
      to = this.length + to;
    }
    // end of validation, actual slicing loop now
    for (var i = from; i < to; i++) {
```

```
      result += original[i];
    }
    return result;
  },
  split: function split(re) {
    var index = 0,
        result = [],
        original = this.valueOf(),
        match,
        pattern = '',
        modifiers = 'g';

    if (re instanceof RegExp) {
      // split with regexp but always set "g"
      pattern = re.source;
      modifiers += re.multiline  ? 'm' : '';
      modifiers += re.ignoreCase ? 'i' : '';
    } else {
      // not a regexp, probably a string, we'll convert it
      pattern = re;
    }
    re = RegExp(pattern, modifiers);

    while (match = re.exec(original)) {
      result.push(this.slice(index, match.index));
      index = match.index + new MyString(match[0]).length;
    }
    result.push(this.slice(index));
    return result;
  }
};
```

Testing:

```
 > var s = new MyString('hello');
> s.length;
 5
> s[0];
"h"
 > s.toString();
 "hello"
> s.valueOf();
 "hello"
> s.charAt(1);
 "e"
> s.charAt('2');
"l"
> s.charAt('e');
```

```
"h"
> s.concat(' world!');
"hello world!"
> s.slice(1, 3);
"el"
> s.slice(0, -1);
"hell"
> s.split('e');
 ["h", "llo"]
> s.split('l');
 ["he", "", "o"]
```

Feel free to play splitting with a regular expression.

5. Update `MyString()` with a `reverse()` method:

```
> MyString.prototype.reverse = function reverse() {
    return this.valueOf().split("").reverse().join("");
};
> new MyString("pudding").reverse();
 "gniddup"
```

6. Imagine `Array()` is gone and the world needs you to implement `MyArray()`.
   Here are a handful of methods to get you started:

```
function MyArray(length) {
  // single numeric argument means length
  if (typeof length === 'number' &&
      arguments[1] === undefined) {
    this.length = length;
    return this;
  }
  // usual case
   this.length = arguments.length;
  for (var i = 0, len = arguments.length; i < len; i++) {
    this[i] = arguments[i];
  }
  return this;
  // later in the book you'll learn how to support
  // a non-constructor invocation too
}

MyArray.prototype = {
  constructor: MyArray,
  join: function join(glue) {
    var result = '';
    if (glue === undefined) {
      glue = ',';
```

```
    }
    for (var i = 0; i < this.length - 1; i++) {
      result += this[i] === undefined ? '' : this[i];
      result += glue;
    }
    result += this[i] === undefined ? '' : this[i];
    return result;
  },
  toString: function toString() {
    return this.join();
  },
  push: function push() {
    for (var i = 0, len = arguments.length; i < len; i++) {
      this[this.length + i] = arguments[i];
    }
    this.length += arguments.length;
    return this.length;
  },
  pop: function pop() {
    var poppd = this[this.length - 1];
    delete this[this.length - 1];
    this.length--;
    return poppd;
  }
};
```

Testing:

```
> var a = new MyArray(1, 2, 3, "test");
> a.toString();
"1,2,3,test"
> a.length;
 4
> a[a.length - 1];
"test"
> a.push('boo');
 5
> a.toString();
"1,2,3,test,boo"
> a.pop();
"boo"
> a.toString();
"1,2,3,test"
> a.join(',');
"1,2,3,test"
> a.join(' isn't ');
"1 isn't 2 isn't 3 isn't test"
```

If you found this exercise amusing, don't stop with `join()`; go on with as many methods as possible.

7. Create `MyMath` object that also has `rand()`, `min([])`, `max([])`.

The point here is that `Math` is not a constructor, but an object that has some "static" properties and methods. Below are some methods to get you started.

Let's also use an immediate function to keep some private utility functions. You can also take this approach with `MyString` above, where `this._value` could be really private.

```
var MyMath = (function () {

  function isArray(ar) {
      return
        Object.prototype.toString.call(ar) ===
          '[object Array]';
  }

   function sort(numbers) {
      // not using numbers.sort() directly because
      // `arguments` is not an array and doesn't have sort()
      return Array.prototype.sort.call(numbers, function (a, b) {
        if (a === b) {
          return 0;
        }
        return  1 * (a > b) - 0.5; // returns 0.5 or -0.5
     });
   }

   return {
      PI:   3.141592653589793,
      E:    2.718281828459045,
      LN10: 2.302585092994046,
      LN2:  0.6931471805599453,
      // ... more constants
      max: function max() {
        // allow unlimited number of arguments
        // or an array of numbers as first argument
        var numbers = arguments;
        if (isArray(numbers[0])) {
          numbers = numbers[0];
        }
        // we can be lazy:
        // let Array sort the numbers and pick the last
        return sort(numbers)[numbers.length - 1];
```

```
      },
    min: function min() {
      // different approach to handling arguments:
      // call the same function again
      if (isArray(numbers)) {
        return this.min.apply(this, numbers[0]);
      }

      // Different approach to picking the min:
      // sorting the array is an overkill, it's too much
      // work since we don't worry about sorting but only
      // about the smallest number.
      // So let's loop:
      var min = numbers[0];
      for (var i = 1; i < numbers.length; i++) {
        if (min > numbers[i]) {
          min = numbers[i];
        }
      }
      return min;
    },
    rand: function rand(min, max, inclusive) {
      if (inclusive) {
        return Math.round(Math.random() * (max - min) + min);
        // test boundaries for random number
        // between 10 and 100 *inclusive*:
        // Math.round(0.000000 * 90 + 10); // 10
        // Math.round(0.000001 * 90 + 10); // 10
        // Math.round(0.999999 * 90 + 10); // 100

      }
      return Math.floor(Math.random() * (max - min - 1) + min + 1);
      // test boundaries for random number
      // between 10 and 100 *non-inclusive*:
      // Math.floor(0.000000 * (89) + (11)); // 11
      // Math.floor(0.000001 * (89) + (11)); // 11
      // Math.floor(0.999999 * (89) + (11)); // 99
    }
  };
})();
```

After you have finished the book and know about ES5 you can try using
`defineProperty()` for tighter control and closer replication of the built-ins.

Chapter 5, Prototype

Lets try and solve the following exercise:

Exercises

1. Create an object called `shape` that has a `type` property and a `getType()` method:

```
var shape = {
  type: 'shape',
  getType: function () {
    return this.type;
  }
};
```

2. The following is the program for a `Triangle ()` constructor:

```
function Triangle(a, b, c) {
  this.a = a;
  this.b = b;
  this.c = c;
}

Triangle.prototype = shape;
Triangle.prototype.constructor = Triangle;
Triangle.prototype.type = 'triangle';
```

3. To add the `getPerimeter()` method, use the following code:

```
Triangle.prototype.getPerimeter = function () {
  return this.a + this.b + this.c;
};
```

4. Test the following code:

```
> var t = new Triangle(1, 2, 3);
> t.constructor === Triangle;
true
> shape.isPrototypeOf(t);
true
> t.getPerimeter();
6
> t.getType();
"triangle"
```

5. Loop over `t` showing only own properties and methods:

```
for (var i in t) {
  if (t.hasOwnProperty(i)) {
     console.log(i, '=', t[i]);
  }
}
```

6. Randomize array elements using the following code snippet:

```
Array.prototype.shuffle = function () {
  return this.sort(function () {
    return Math.random() - 0.5;
  });
};
```

Testing:

```
> [1, 2, 3, 4, 5, 6, 7, 8, 9].shuffle();
[4, 2, 3, 1, 5, 6, 8, 9, 7]
> [1, 2, 3, 4, 5, 6, 7, 8, 9].shuffle();
[2, 7, 1, 3, 4, 5, 8, 9, 6]
> [1, 2, 3, 4, 5, 6, 7, 8, 9].shuffle();
[4, 2, 1, 3, 5, 6, 8, 9, 7]
```

Chapter 6, Inheritance

Lets solve the following exercise:

Exercises

1. Multiple inheritance by mixing into the prototype, for example:

```
var my = objectMulti(obj, another_obj, a_third, {
  additional: "properties"
});
A possible solution:
function objectMulti() {
  var Constr, i, prop, mixme;

// constructor that sets own properties
var Constr = function (props) {
  for (var prop in props) {
```

```
          this[prop] = props[prop];
        }
      };

    // mix into the prototype
    for (var i = 0; i < arguments.length - 1; i++) {
      var mixme = arguments[i];
      for (var prop in mixme) {
        Constr.prototype[prop] = mixme[prop];
      }
    }

  return new Constr(arguments[arguments.length - 1]);
}
```

Testing:

```
> var obj_a = {a: 1};
> var obj_b = {a: 2, b: 2};
> var obj_c = {c: 3};
> var my = objectMulti(obj_a, obj_b, obj_c, {hello: "world"});
> my.a;
  2
```

Property a is 2 because obj_b overwrote the property with the same name from obj_a (last one wins):

```
> my.b;
2
> my.c;
3
> my.hello;
"world"
> my.hasOwnProperty('a');
false
> my.hasOwnProperty('hello');
true
```

2. Practice with the canvas example at http://www.phpied.com/files/canvas/.

Draw a few triangles using the following code snippet:

```
new Triangle(
  new Point(100, 155),
  new Point(30, 50),
  new Point(220, 00)).draw();

new Triangle(
```

```
      new Point(10, 15),
      new Point(300, 50),
      new Point(20, 400)).draw();
```

Draw a few squares using the following code snippet:

```
new Square(new Point(150, 150), 300).draw();
new Square(new Point(222, 222), 222).draw();
```

Draw a few rectangles using the following code snippet:

```
new Rectangle(new Point(100, 10), 200, 400).draw();
new Rectangle(new Point(400, 200), 200, 100).draw();
```

3. To add Rhombus, Kite, Pentagon, Trapezoid, and Circle (reimplements `draw()`), use the following code:

```
function Kite(center, diag_a, diag_b, height) {
  this.points = [
    new Point(center.x - diag_a / 2, center.y),
    new Point(center.x, center.y + (diag_b - height)),
    new Point(center.x + diag_a / 2, center.y),
    new Point(center.x, center.y - height)
  ];
  this.getArea = function () {
    return diag_a * diag_b / 2;
  };
}

function Rhombus(center, diag_a, diag_b) {
  Kite.call(this, center, diag_a, diag_b, diag_b / 2);
}

function Trapezoid(p1, side_a, p2, side_b) {
  this.points = [p1, p2, new Point(p2.x + side_b, p2.y),
  new Point(p1.x + side_a, p1.y)
  ];

  this.getArea = function () {
    var height = p2.y - p1.y;
    return height * (side_a + side_b) / 2;
  };
}
// regular pentagon, all edges have the same length
function Pentagon(center, edge) {
  var r = edge / (2 * Math.sin(Math.PI / 5)),
      x = center.x,
      y = center.y;
```

```
      this.points = [new Point(x + r, y),
  new Point(x + r * Math.cos(2 * Math.PI / 5), y - r *
   Math.sin(2 * Math.PI / 5)),
  new Point(x - r * Math.cos(    Math.PI / 5), y - r *
   Math.sin(    Math.PI / 5)),
  new Point(x - r * Math.cos(    Math.PI / 5), y + r *
   Math.sin(    Math.PI / 5)),
  new Point(x + r * Math.cos(2 * Math.PI / 5), y + r *
   Math.sin(2 * Math.PI / 5))
    ];

    this.getArea = function () {
      return 1.72 * edge * edge;
    };
  }

  function Circle(center, radius) {
    this.getArea = function () {
      return Math.pow(radius, 2) * Math.PI;
    };
    this.getPerimeter = function () {
      return 2 * radius * Math.PI;
    };
    this.draw = function () {
      var ctx = this.context;
      ctx.beginPath();
      ctx.arc(center.x, center.y, radius, 0, 2 * Math.PI);
      ctx.stroke();
    };
  }

  (function () {
    var s = new Shape();
    Kite.prototype = s;
    Rhombus.prototype = s;
    Trapezoid.prototype = s;
    Pentagon.prototype = s;
    Circle.prototype = s;
  }());
```

Testing:

```
  new Kite(new Point(300, 300), 200, 300, 100).draw();
  new Rhombus(new Point(200, 200), 350, 200).draw();
  new Trapezoid(
    new Point(100, 100), 100,
    new Point(50, 250), 400).draw();
  new Pentagon(new Point(400, 400), 100).draw();
```

```
new Circle(new Point(500, 300), 270).draw();
```

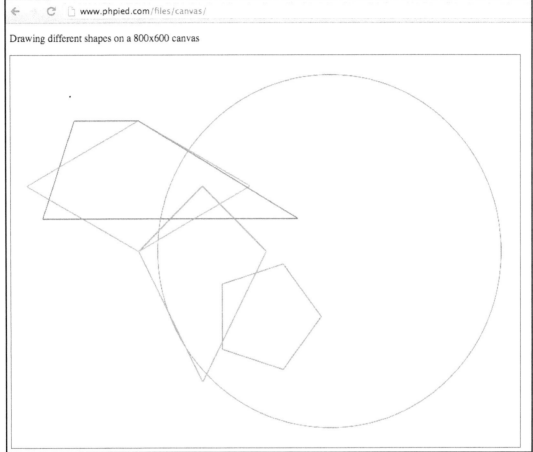

The result of testing new shapes

4. Think of another way to do the inheritance part. Use `uber` so kids can have access to their parents. Also, get parents to be aware of their children.

Keep in mind that not all children inherit `Shape`; for example, `Rhombus` inherits `Kite` and `Square` inherits `Rectangle`. You end up with something like this:

```
// inherit(Child, Parent)
inherit(Rectangle, Shape);
inherit(Square, Rectangle);
```

In the inheritance pattern from the chapter and the previous exercise, all children were sharing the same prototype, for example:

```
var s = new Shape();
Kite.prototype = s;
Rhombus.prototype = s;
```

While this is convenient, it also means no one can touch the prototype because it will affect everyone else's prototype. The drawback is that all custom methods need to own properties, for example `this.getArea`.

It's a good idea to have methods shared among instances and defined in the prototype, instead of recreating them for every object. The following example moves the custom `getArea()` methods to the prototype.

In the inheritance function, you'll see the children only inherit the parent's prototype. So own properties such as `this.lines` will not be set. Therefore, you need to have each child constructor call its `uber` in order to get the own properties, for example:

```
Child.prototype.uber.call(this, args...)
```

Another nice-to-have feature is carrying over the prototype properties already added to the child. This allows the child to inherit first and then add more customizations or the other way around as well, which is just a little more convenient.

```
function inherit(Child, Parent) {
  // remember prototype
  var extensions = Child.prototype;

  // inheritance with an intermediate F()
  var F = function () {};
   F.prototype = Parent.prototype;
  Child.prototype = new F();
  // reset constructor
  Child.prototype.constructor = Child;
  // remember parent
  Child.prototype.uber = Parent;

  // keep track of who inherits the Parent
  if (!Parent.children) {
    Parent.children = [];
  }
  Parent.children.push(Child);
```

```
    // carry over stuff previsouly added to the prototype
    // because the prototype is now overwritten completely
    for (var i in extensions) {
      if (extensions.hasOwnProperty(i)) {
        Child.prototype[i] = extensions[i];
      }
    }
  }
}
```

Everything about `Shape()`, `Line()`, and `Point()` stays the same. The changes are in the children only:

```
function Triangle(a, b, c) {
  Triangle.prototype.uber.call(this);
  this.points = [a, b, c];
}

Triangle.prototype.getArea = function () {
  var p = this.getPerimeter(), s = p / 2;
  return Math.sqrt(s * (s - this.lines[0].length) *
(s - this.lines[1].length) * (s - this.lines[2].length));
};


function Rectangle(p, side_a, side_b) {
  // calling parent Shape()
  Rectangle.prototype.uber.call(this);

  this.points = [ p,
    new Point(p.x + side_a, p.y),
    new Point(p.x + side_a, p.y + side_b),
    new Point(p.x, p.y + side_b)
  ];
}

Rectangle.prototype.getArea = function () {
    // Previsouly we had access to side_a and side_b
    // inside the constructor closure. No more.
    // option 1: add own properties this.side_a and this.side_b
    // option 2: use what we already have:
    var lines = this.getLines();
    return lines[0].length * lines[1].length;
};


function Square(p, side) {
  this.uber.call(this, p, side, side);
  // this call is shorter than Square.prototype.uber.call()
```

```
        // but may backfire in case you inherit
        // from Square and call uber
        // try it :-)
    }
```

Inheritance:

```
inherit(Triangle, Shape);
inherit(Rectangle, Shape);
inherit(Square, Rectangle);
```

Testing:

```
> var sq = new Square(new Point(0, 0), 100);
> sq.draw();
> sq.getArea();
10000
```

Testing that `instanceof` is correct:

```
> sq.constructor === Square;
true
> sq instanceof Square;
true
> sq instanceof Rectangle;
true
> sq instanceof Shape;
true
```

The `children` arrays:

```
> Shape.children[1] === Rectangle;
true
> Rectangle.children[0] === Triangle;
false
> Rectangle.children[0] === Square;
true
> Square.children;
undefined
```

And uber looks ok too:

```
> sq.uber === Rectangle;
true
```

Calling `isPrototypeOf()` also returns expected results:

```
Shape.prototype.isPrototypeOf(sq);
true
Rectangle.prototype.isPrototypeOf(sq);
true
Triangle.prototype.isPrototypeOf(sq);
false
```

The full code is available at `http://www.phpied.com/files/canvas/index2.html`, together with the additional `Kite()`, `Circle()`, and so on from the previous exercise.

Chapter 7, The Browser Environment

Lets practice the following exercise:

Exercises

1. The title clock program is as follows:

```
setInterval(function () {
  document.title = new Date().toTimeString();
}, 1000);
```

2. To animate resizing of a 200 x 200 pop up to 400 x 400, use the following code:

```
var w = window.open(
    'http://phpied.com', 'my',
    'width = 200, height = 200');

var i = setInterval((function () {
  var size = 200;
  return function () {
    size += 5;
    w.resizeTo(size, size);
    if (size === 400) {
      clearInterval(i);
    }
  };
}()), 100);
```

Every 100 ms (1/10th of a second) the pop-up size increases by five pixels. You keep a reference to the interval `i` so you can clear it once done. The variable `size` tracks the pop-up size (and why not keep it private inside a closure).

3. The earthquake program is as follows:

```
var i = setInterval((function () {
   var start = +new Date(); // Date.now() in ES5
   return function () {
     w.moveTo(
       Math.round(Math.random() * 100),
       Math.round(Math.random() * 100));
     if (new Date() - start > 5000) {
       clearInterval(i);
     }
   };
}()), 20);
```

Try all of them, but using `requestAnimationFrame()` instead of `setInterval()`.

4. A different `walkDOM()` with a callback is as follows:

```
function walkDOM(n, cb) {
   cb(n);
   var i,
       children = n.childNodes,
       len = children.length,
       child;
   for (i = 0; i < len; i++) {
   child = n.childNodes[i];
     if (child.hasChildNodes()) {
       walkDOM(child, cb);
     }
   }
}
```

Testing:

```
> walkDOM(document.documentElement,
  console.dir.bind(console));
html
head
title
body
h1
...
```

5. To remove content and clean up functions, use the following code:

```
// helper
function isFunction(f) {
  return Object.prototype.toString.call(f) ===
    "[object Function]";
}

function removeDom(node) {
  var i, len, attr;

  // first drill down inspecting the children
  // and only after that remove the current node
  while (node.firstChild) {
    removeDom(node.firstChild);
  }

  // not all nodes have attributes, e.g. text nodes don't
  len = node.attributes ? node.attributes.length : 0;

  // cleanup loop
  // e.g. node === <body>,
  // node.attributes[0].name === "onload"
  // node.onload === function()...
  // node.onload is not enumerable so we can't use
  // a for-in loop and have to go the attributes route
  for (i = 0; i < len; i++) {
    attr = node[node.attributes[i].name];
    if (isFunction(attr)) {
      // console.log(node, attr);
      attr = null;
    }
  }

  node.parentNode.removeChild(node);
}
```

Testing:

```
> removeDom(document.body);
```

6. To include scripts dynamically, use the following code:

```
function include(url) {
  var s = document.createElement('script');
  s.src = url;
  document.getElementsByTagName('head')[0].
  appendChild(s);
}
```

Testing:

```
> include("http://www.phpied.com/files/jinc/1.js");
> include("http://www.phpied.com/files/jinc/2.js");
```

7. **Events**: The event utility program is as follows:

```
var myevent = (function () {

  // wrap some private stuff in a closure
  var add, remove, toStr = Object.prototype.toString;

  // helper
  function toArray(a) {
    // already an array
    if (toStr.call(a) === '[object Array]') {
      return a;
    }
    // duck-typing HTML collections, arguments etc
    var result, i, len;
    if ('length' in a) {
      for (result = [], i = 0, len = a.length; i < len; i++)
      {
        result[i] = a[i];
      }
      return result;
    }

    // primitives and non-array-like objects
    // become the first and single array element
    return [a];
  }

  // define add() and remove() depending
  // on the browser's capabilities
  if (document.addEventListener) {
    add = function (node, ev, cb) {
      node.addEventListener(ev, cb, false);
    };
```

```
      remove = function (node, ev, cb) {
        node.removeEventListener(ev, cb, false);
      };
    } else if (document.attachEvent) {
      add = function (node, ev, cb) {
        node.attachEvent('on' + ev, cb);
      };
      remove = function (node, ev, cb) {
        node.detachEvent('on' + ev, cb);
      };
    } else {
      add = function (node, ev, cb) {
        node['on' + ev] = cb;
      };
      remove = function (node, ev) {
        node['on' + ev] = null;
      };
    }

    // public API
    return {

      addListener: function (element, event_name, callback) {
        // element could also be an array of elements
        element = toArray(element);
        for (var i = 0; i < element.length; i++) {
          add(element[i], event_name, callback);
        }
      },

      removeListener: function (element, event_name, callback) {
        // same as add(), only practicing a different loop
        var i = 0, els = toArray(element), len = els.length;
        for (; i < len; i++) {
          remove(els[i], event_name, callback);
        }
      },

      getEvent: function (event) {
        return event || window.event;
      },
      getTarget: function (event) {
        var e = this.getEvent(event);
        return e.target || e.srcElement;
      },

      stopPropagation: function (event) {
        var e = this.getEvent(event);
```

```
      if (e.stopPropagation) {
        e.stopPropagation();
      } else {
        e.cancelBubble = true;
      }
    },

    preventDefault: function (event) {
      var e = this.getEvent(event);
      if (e.preventDefault) {
        e.preventDefault();
      } else {
        e.returnValue = false;
      }
    }

  };
}());
```

Testing: Go to any page with links, execute the following, and then click any link:

```
function myCallback(e) {
  e = myevent.getEvent(e);
  alert(myevent.getTarget(e).href);
  myevent.stopPropagation(e);
  myevent.preventDefault(e);
}
myevent.addListener(document.links, 'click', myCallback);
```

8. Move a `div` around with the keyboard using the following code:

```
// add a div to the bottom of the page
var div = document.createElement('div');
div.style.cssText = 'width: 100px; height:
 100px; background: red; position: absolute;';
document.body.appendChild(div);

// remember coordinates
var x = div.offsetLeft;
var y = div.offsetTop;

myevent.addListener(document.body,
 'keydown', function (e) {
 // prevent scrolling
  myevent.preventDefault(e);

  switch (e.keyCode) {
    case 37: // left
```

[518]

```
        x--;
        break;
      case 38: // up
        y--;
        break;
      case 39: // right
        x++;
        break;
      case 40: // down
        y++;
        break;
      default:
        // not interested
    }

    // move
    div.style.left = x + 'px';
    div.style.top  = y + 'px';

  });
```

9. Your own Ajax utility:

```
    var ajax = {
      getXHR: function () {
        var ids = ['MSXML2.XMLHTTP.3.0',
          'MSXML2.XMLHTTP', 'Microsoft.XMLHTTP'];
        var xhr;
        if (typeof XMLHttpRequest === 'function') {
          xhr = new XMLHttpRequest();
        } else {
          // IE: try to find an ActiveX object to use
          for (var i = 0; i < ids.length; i++) {
            try {
              xhr = new ActiveXObject(ids[i]);
              break;
            } catch (e) {}
          }
        }
        return xhr;

      },
      request: function (url, method, cb, post_body) {
        var xhr = this.getXHR();
        xhr.onreadystatechange = (function (myxhr) {
          return function () {
            if (myxhr.readyState === 4 && myxhr.status === 200) {
              cb(myxhr);
```

```
        }
      };
    }(xhr));
    xhr.open(method.toUpperCase(), url, true);
    xhr.send(post_body || '');
  }
};
```

When testing, remember that same origin restrictions apply, so you have to be on the same domain. You can go to http://www.phpied.com/files/jinc/, which is a directory listing and then test in the console:

```
function myCallback(xhr) {
  alert(xhr.responseText);
}
ajax.request('1.css', 'get', myCallback);
ajax.request('1.css', 'post', myCallback,
  'first=John&last=Smith');
```

The result of the two is the same, but if you look into the **Network** tab of the Web Inspector, you can see that the second is indeed a POST request with a body.

Index

Lightning Source UK Ltd.
Milton Keynes UK
UKHW031534070319
338675UK00004B/145/P